D1539193

THOMAS HARDY
A BIBLIOGRAPHICAL STUDY

THOMAS HARDY
A BIBLIOGRAPHICAL STUDY

RICHARD LITTLE PURDY

GEOFFREY CUMBERLEGE
OXFORD UNIVERSITY PRESS
LONDON   NEW YORK   TORONTO
1954

ST. PAUL
PUBLIC LIBRARY

REFERENCE ROOM

Z
8386.5
P98T

COPY 1

Oxford University Press, Amen House, London E.C.4

GLASGOW NEW YORK TORONTO MELBOURNE WELLINGTON

BOMBAY CALCUTTA MADRAS KARACHI CAPE TOWN IBADAN

Geoffrey Cumberlege, Publisher to the University

———————

PRINTED IN GREAT BRITAIN

ST. PAUL
PUBLIC LIBRARY

To

F. E. H.

in affectionate remembrance

PREFACE

WHEN I began this study I thought of it as a bibliography of Hardy along familiar lines, a detailed description of first editions and an attempt to record every printing of his works. I had done something of this kind on a very small scale in the catalogue I prepared for a memorial exhibition of Hardy's books and manuscripts in the Yale University Library in 1928. Even at that time the bibliographies by A. P. Webb and Henry Danielson, both published in 1916, were inadequate and obviously incomplete. The same was true of John Lane's, made for Lionel Johnson's *The Art of Thomas Hardy* in 1894 and revised in 1923, and since then there has been nothing beyond the catalogues of several private collections. With the publication by Mrs. Hardy of *The Early Life of Thomas Hardy* in 1928 and *The Later Years of Thomas Hardy* in 1930 Hardy's biography took on a definitive form, but those volumes, by their nature, offered relatively little bibliographical information. The details of printing and publishing have no place in a biography, and neither Hardy nor his wife was equipped to provide them. It was, then, to supply the bibliographical materials for Hardy's life (and the criticism of his prose and verse), to supplement the *Early Life* and the *Later Years*, that I began my work.

It has taken a rather different course from the one I anticipated. I have given a full and detailed description of the first edition of every one of Hardy's books and I have recorded the original appearance in print of everything that he wrote, so far as I have been able to discover it. But I have also located and described manuscripts where they survive, I have collected what can be known about composition and publication, and I have traced the development of texts through subsequent editions. Where the poems are concerned I have often added notes that are unexpected in a work of this sort, drawing freely on unpublished papers and private sources. Here I had in mind the peculiar nature of the *Early Life* and the *Later Years* and the statement (Hardy's own) that 'Speaking generally, there is more autobiography in a hundred lines of Mr. Hardy's poetry than in all the novels.' These notes may easily prove the most useful thing I have done. On the other hand I have made no attempt to record every printing of Hardy's works. I have singled out those of textual significance, for the most part. The many reprintings in authorized and pirated editions and in eclectic magazines make long lists of no special value. They enforce the outlines of Hardy's reputation and its growth, but those outlines are already familiar. I have made no attempt, either, to record translations of Hardy's

vii

works. Their author had no part in these and no sufficient command of any foreign language to judge the result. His own copies of most of them remained unopened. My constant concern, in short, has been to show how Hardy's novels and poems got written and how they got published and by what stages they came to the form in which we now know them. Some of this Hardy himself could not have shown, a little of it he was unwilling to reveal. I cannot hope to have gathered every fact that belongs in this book nor to have escaped every inaccuracy that can creep into such a mass of detail. 'Let me only observe, as a specimen of my trouble,' Boswell wrote in a preface of his own, 'that I have sometimes been obliged to run half over London, in order to fix a date correctly; which, when I had accomplished, I well knew would obtain me no praise, though a failure would have been to my discredit.' The book has become, one might almost say, a biography of Hardy in bibliographical form. No form, certainly, can better reveal 'His whole sincere symmetric history'.

From the first my work had the approval and the generous support of Mrs. Hardy and Sir Sydney Cockerell, Hardy's literary executors. Both of them gave me access to the materials in their possession without restriction, and for their long-continued help and friendship I am deeply grateful. The books and papers at Max Gate proved to be limited in their bibliographical value. It was probably not to be expected that Hardy should have kept any detailed records of this sort over so long and varied a literary life, though at one time he did start 'A Chronological List of Thomas Hardy's Works in verse and prose—Giving date of writing, where known, and date of publication' and at another made some desultory notes in a copy of Webb's *Bibliography* (at Sir Sydney's suggestion), but his own collection of his works was by no means complete and he had destroyed many diaries and letters during the writing of his biography. These Max Gate books and papers, further reduced by Mrs. Hardy near the end of her life (carrying out her husband's instructions) and by the sale of a portion of the library after her death, are now with a few exceptions deposited in the Dorset County Museum in Dorchester under the provisions of her will. They still represent an incomparable mine for the student of Hardy.

No bibliographer in the field of Victorian literature can fail to acknowledge a debt to Mr. John Carter, Mr. Percy H. Muir, and Mr. Michael Sadleir. Mr. Sadleir's *Trollope: A Bibliography* suggested a form for my own work, and his studies and Mr. Carter's in Victorian binding and publishing practices helped to solve a number of my problems. Mr. Muir has done a great deal to bring the standards of McKerrow to the bibliography of nineteenth-century and modern books, beset as it was in the 30's—and Hardy's bibliography with the rest—by foolish 'points' and imaginary 'issues'. To each, for many personal favours, I express my thanks.

Work of this kind owes much to the private collector, and I have been fortunate in the friendship of four men who have assembled Hardy collections of remarkable extent and quality—Mr. Howard Bliss, Mr. Frederick B. Adams, Jr., the late Morris L. Parrish (whose collection is now in the Princeton University Library), and the late Carroll A. Wilson. All four of them shared with me their libraries and their knowledge on the most generous terms, but I owe most, perhaps, to Mr. Bliss. His unrivalled collection and his unrivalled knowledge of Hardy have been at my disposal since I began this study. His name appears here very frequently, but not by his choice.

It only remains to thank Hardy's various printers and publishers, English and American, who almost without exception gave me help, and the directors and assistants of the libraries where I have worked, in particular the British Museum, the Bodleian Library, the Fitzwilliam Museum and the University Library, Cambridge, the Brotherton Library at Leeds, the Yale University Library, the Houghton Library at Harvard, the Library of Congress, and the Berg Collection in the New York Public Library; and to record my gratitude to Mrs. Allhusen, Professor Bertrand H. Bronson, Sir Arthur Comyns Carr, Mr. Philip Comyns Carr, the late Marquess of Crewe, the late W. S. Douglas, Miss Eva Dugdale, Miss Constance T. Dugdale, the late Lady Grogan, Professor Gordon S. Haight, Mrs. St. John Hornby, the Countess of Ilchester, Major H. O. Lock, Dr. E. W. Mann, Sir Owen Morshead, Mr. Henry Reed, Mrs. Richardson, Mr. Carl P. Rollins, Professor William Ruff, the late Mrs. Reginald J. Smith, Mrs. Soundy, Professor Chauncey B. Tinker, Mr. Gilbert McC. Troxell, and in special measure to Lieut.-Col. Charles D. Drew, Curator of the Dorset County Museum, and Miss Irene Cooper Willis, co-executor of Mrs. Hardy's will. Other debts I have acknowledged as they occur in the text.

R. L. P.

ALL references to Hardy's works, unless otherwise given, are to the definitive Wessex Edition (24 vols., London, 1912–31). *Early Lfie* and *Later Years* are abbreviations for Florence Emily Hardy, *The Early Life of Thomas Hardy 1840–1891* (London, 1928) and *The Later Years of Thomas Hardy 1892–1928* (London, 1930). Where no place of publication is indicated, London may be understood.

CONTENTS

ILLUSTRATIONS

PART I

EDITIONES PRINCIPES

DESPERATE REMEDIES. / 𝔄 𝔑𝔬𝔳𝔢𝔩. / [*rule*] / "Though a course of adventures which are only connected with each other by / having happened to the same individual is what most frequently occurs in / nature, yet the province of the romance-writer being artificial, there is more / required from him than a mere compliance with the simplicity of reality." / Sir W. Scott. / [*rule*] / IN THREE VOLUMES. / VOL. I. [*II.*] [*III.*] / LONDON: / TINSLEY BROTHERS, 18, CATHERINE ST., STRAND. / 1871. / [*The Right of Translation is Reserved.*]

Collation. VOL. I. π^1, [A]^2, B–U^8; pp. vi+304; [i] half-title; [ii] blank; [iii] title-page; [iv] printers' imprint: London: / Bradbury, Evans, and Co., Printers, Whitefriars. / ; [v]–vi Contents; [1]–304 text, printers' imprint at foot of p. 304: Bradbury, Evans, and Co., Printers, Whitefriars.

VOL. II. π^1, [A]^2, B–T^8, U^2; pp. [vi]+292; [i]–[iv] as in VOL. 1; [v] Contents; [vi] blank; [1]–291 text, printers' imprint at foot of p. 291: Bradbury, Evans, and Co., Printers, Whitefriars. / ; [292] blank.

VOL. III. π^1, [A]^2, B–S^8, T^1; pp. vi+274; preliminary pages as in VOL. 1; [1]–274 text, printers' imprint at foot of p. 274: Bradbury, Evans, and Co., Printers, Whitefriars.

Binding. Red sand-grain cloth; blocked in blind on front and back with 3-rule border and scroll frame; gold-lettered on spine with ornamental bands at top and bottom: Desperate / Remedies / [*rule*] / A Novel / [*rule*] / Vol. I. [*II.*] [*III.*] / [*designs blocked in gold and blind*] / Tinsley Brothers / .

Cream-white end-papers; top uncut, fore-edge and tail trimmed; leaves measure $5'' \times 7\frac{1}{2}''$.

Binding Variants. A single copy is known (Dorset County Museum) bound in green cloth, conforming in all other respects to the description above. It would seem to be a trial binding and was given by Hardy to his first wife, with an inscription on the fly-leaf of each volume, 'The Author to E. L. Gifford.' Hardy has also corrected the quotation from Scott's Introduction to *The Monastery* on the title-page of Vol. I, a correction followed in subsequent editions.

Some copies bound in red cloth are blocked in blind on front and back with an advertisement of *Tinsleys' Magazine*, a decorative border incorporating the words TINSLEY'S [*sic*] MAGAZINE—ONE SHILLING—MONTHLY—ILLUSTRATED and headed ADVERTISEMENT. There is no evidence to show this style is not part of the original binding order, though it is much less common and the cloth might be shown to differ very slightly in quality. It usually appears in combination with the normal binding, on one or two volumes only of a set.

Remainder Binding. The novel was remaindered, 3 volumes bound in one, in green and maroon sand-grain cloth; blocked in blind on front and back with a conventional design of panels and flowers; gold-lettered on spine with bands at top and bottom: Desperate / Remedies. / [*ornament*] / .

Manuscript. No MS. of *Desperate Remedies* has survived. The original (and possibly Miss Gifford's fair copy) was destroyed by Hardy himself, soon after it was written and while he was still in lodgings.

Notes on Composition and Publication. Desperate Remedies was begun in the autumn of 1869 at Weymouth, which forms one of the scenes of the story. It was written there and at Higher Bockhampton and finished (save for the last 3 or 4 chapters) by March 1870. *The Poor Man and the Lady* had been abandoned (see below, pp. 275–6), and Hardy had set himself to write the novel with a 'plot' that Meredith advised. The MS., 'representing about seven-eighths of the whole', was submitted to Alexander Macmillan on 5 March but rejected a month later as 'of far too sensational an order for us to think of publishing'.[1] It was next submitted to Tinsley Brothers, and though their reader found 'rather strong reasons why the book should not be published without some alteration', William Tinsley wrote on 5 May offering the possibility of publication if Hardy would share the expense—'£75 to be paid when the book is put into the printer's hands.'[2] During the autumn of 1870 the novel was altered and finished and early in December returned to Tinsley, in a fair copy made by Miss Gifford, Hardy's future wife. Tinsley wrote on 19 December, 'My Reader has looked through your M.S. again and he thinks with the alterations you have made the book

---

[1] For John Morley's report as reader, see Charles Morgan, *The House of Macmillan* (London, 1943), pp. 93–94.

[2] For a calendar of Hardy's correspondence with Tinsley, see Appendix, pp. 329 ff.

Tinsley Brothers' account for the publishing of *Desperate Remedies*, as submitted to Hardy 22 February 1872. The note after 'Author' is in Hardy's hand

ought to sell. He (the Reader) considers the woman who is Mrs. Man-
ston's *substitute* need not be put forward quite so prominently as his
mistress. I suppose the reader thinks the word mistress does not sound
well, and I agree with him. However I have no doubt the book is clever
and believing so I am quite willing to publish it upon the terms mentioned in my former letter.'[1] And with Hardy's payment of the stipulated £75 the novel was sent to press in January.

Desperate Remedies was published anonymously at 31s. 6d. in an edition
of 500 copies on 25 March 1871.[2] Hardy kept four notices of the novel
in a scrap-book of reviews: the *Athenaeum* (1 April), the *Morning Post*
(13 April), the *Spectator* (22 April), and the *Saturday Review* (30
September). The *Spectator* was so savage that Hardy never forgot his
bitterness and discouragement on first reading it, and, whether or not
it had snuffed out the book as he imagined, by June *Desperate Remedies*
was being offered in Smith and Son's and Mudie's reduced lists at 2s. 6d.
and 3s. The favourable notice in the *Saturday Review* (almost certainly
by H. M. Moule, Hardy's friend and patron) came too late to do
any good; and though a quotation from it was used in the advertisements as Hardy suggested, Tinsley wrote to him that it 'caused the
book to be asked for but the librarians would not buy copies only at
a cheap rate', and in the final accounting on 19 March 1872 he returned Hardy only £59. 12s. 7d. of the £75 he had contributed to the
expenses of publication.

Subsequent Editions (*see also* COLLECTED EDITIONS). *Desperate Remedies*
was never reprinted in its original three-volume form. It was first
published in America by Henry Holt & Co. in their Leisure Hour
Series in March 1874, and Hardy was permitted to make certain revisions in the text for this edition. A 'New Edition' was published in
1889 by Ward and Downey, with a frontispiece by F. Barnard and a
Prefatory Note by Hardy dated January 1889; and a 'Popular Edition'
in 1892 by Heinemann. Additions were made to the Prefatory Note in
February 1896 (for Osgood, McIlvaine's edition of the Wessex Novels)
and in August 1912 (for Macmillan's definitive Wessex Edition).

---

[1] In what sense these terms 'were worse now than they had been in the first place'
(*Early Life*, p. 109) is not apparent. But see Appendix, p. 329 (letter of 14 September 1869).

[2] *Early Life*, p. 110. It seems to have been advertised as ready, though, as early as
11 March.

1872: UNDER THE GREENWOOD TREE (2 Vols.)

UNDER THE / GREENWOOD TREE / A / 𝕽ural 𝕻ainting of the 𝔇utch 𝔖chool. / BY THE / AUTHOR OF 'DESPERATE REME-DIES.' / IN TWO VOLUMES. / VOL. I. [*II*.] / LONDON: / TINS-LEY BROTHERS, 18 CATHERINE ST. STRAND. /1872. / [*All rights reserved.*]

Collation. VOL. I. π^1, [A]², B–O⁸, P⁴; pp. [vi]+216; [i] half-title; [ii] blank; [iii] title-page; [iv] printers' imprint: London: / Robson and Sons, Printers, Pancras Road, N.W. / ; [v] Contents; [vi] blank; [1]–215 text, printers' imprint (as above) at foot of p. 215; [216] blank.

VOL. II. π^1, [A]², B–O⁸, P⁴; pp. [vi]+216; preliminary pages as in VOL. 1; [1]–216 text, printers' imprint (as above) at foot of p. 216.

Binding. Green sand-grain cloth, bevelled edges; blocked in black on front and back with Oxford frame; gold-lettered on spine with bands blocked in black and gold at top and bottom: Under / The / Greenwood / Tree / [*rule*] / Vol. I. [*II*.] / By / the Author of / Desperate / Remedies / Tinsley Brothers / .

Cream-white end-papers; top uncut, fore-edge and tail trimmed; leaves measure 5″×7½″.

Binding Variants. Single copies are known bound in brown and plum sand-grain cloth but conforming in all other respects to the description above. They would seem to be trial bindings. The former (Dorset County Museum) belonged to Hardy's first wife and has her signature on the fly-leaf of Vol. I, 'E. L. Gifford June 1872' (Hardy's signatures in the 2 volumes are much later).

Remainder Binding. The novel was remaindered after the success of *Far from the Madding Crowd* in 1874, 2 volumes bound in one, in green, blue, and red sand-grain cloth; blocked in black on front and blind on back with conventional design; gold-lettered on spine, with designs blocked in gold and black: Under the / Greenwood / Tree. / By the Author of / 'Far from the / Madding Crowd' / Tinsley Bros.

Manuscript. The MS. of *Under the Greenwood Tree* is written on 194 leaves, measuring 6½″× 8⅜″. The leaves have been numbered 1–203 by Hardy, but though the MS. is complete as printed, many leaves are fragmentary

6

and 9 are wanting altogether (5 of these are at the end of Part I, Chap. III), suggesting extensive cancellations. The last page was missing and was rewritten at a later date to complete the MS. The title originally stood *The Mellstock Quire or Under the Greenwood Tree*, and a majority of the chapters have been retitled. The clean condition of many pages (and perhaps the fact that the first 28 leaves—running about two-thirds through Chap. IV—and several others are a different paper) may be some indication of passages the novel incorporates from the rejected MS. of *The Poor Man and the Lady*.

The MS. is bound in three-quarters green morocco and bears an inscription from Hardy to his second wife. At her death it was deposited in the Dorset County Museum under the provisions of her will. The first page is reproduced in facsimile in *Early Life*, facing p. 116.

Notes on Composition and Publication. Under the Greenwood Tree was written at Weymouth and Higher Bockhampton in the early summer of 1871. Some of its pages, however, must date from the autumn of 1867, since it incorporates material from the discarded novel, *The Poor Man and the Lady*. The MS., like *Desperate Remedies*, was first sent to Macmillan (whose reader, John Morley, had praised the country scenes in *The Poor Man and the Lady*) 7 August 1871, and Hardy wrote to the publishers at the same time, 'The accessories of one scene in it may possibly be recognised by you as appearing originally in a tale submitted a long time ago (which never saw the light). They were introduced advisedly, as giving a good background to the love portion.'[1] The comparatively brief time in which the novel was written is significant, and there is reason to believe that it preserves more of *The Poor Man and the Lady* than Hardy indicated (see also *Early Life*, p. 113). Alexander Macmillan returned it 18 October, offering to reconsider it in the spring if it were still available but adding he was afraid 'the public will find the tale very slight and rather unexciting.' Macmillan's letter seemed fairly ambiguous, and the novel was thrown aside. At William Tinsley's insistence the MS. was given him to read in April 1872 and he promptly offered £30 for the copyright, which Hardy accepted.[2]

---

[1] For Hardy's correspondence with Macmillan and particularly John Morley's discriminating report as reader (first printed, with some interesting omissions, in *Early Life*, pp. 113–14), see Charles Morgan, *The House of Macmillan* (London, 1943), pp. 94–99.
[2] For a calendar of Hardy's correspondence with Tinsley, see Appendix, pp. 329 ff.

Under the Greenwood Tree was published anonymously at 21*s*., in an edition presumably of 500 copies, early in June 1872.[1] Hardy kept four notices of the novel in his scrap-book of reviews, three of which may be identified as the *Athenaeum* (15 June), the *Pall Mall Gazette* (5 July), and the *Saturday Review* (28 September), this last by his patron and friend, H. M. Moule. Tinsley wrote years after that it was one of the 'best press-noticed' books he ever published, but it did not sell. He wrote to Hardy, 4 October 1872, 'I am almost afraid it is no use to advertise "Greenwood Tree" again. However I have put it with my weekly advertisements again, with a quotation from the Saturday. I shall have ready in a few days 1000 rather good bills for railways and street hoardings so that your works will be well before the public.'

Subsequent Editions (*see also* COLLECTED EDITIONS). *Under the Greenwood Tree* was never reprinted in its original two-volume form. Tinsley had the same types repaged and published a 2*s*. edition in August 1873 and an illustrated edition, with frontispiece and plates engraved by R. Knight, for Christmas 1875 (dated 1876). With Tinsley's failure in 1878 the copyright (which he held at £300 when Hardy tried to regain it in 1875), the remaining stock, and the stereotype plates passed to Chatto & Windus, who issued the novel over their imprint in 1878 and subsequently, adding a portrait of Hardy as frontispiece in 1891. Hardy wrote a Preface in August 1896 for Osgood, McIlvaine's edition of the Wessex Novels and a further one in April 1912 for Macmillan's definitive Wessex Edition. The novel was also published by Holt & Williams (New York) in their Leisure Hour Series in June 1873, the first of Hardy's novels published in America.

1873: A PAIR OF BLUE EYES (3 Vols.)

A PAIR OF BLUE EYES. / 𝔄 𝔑𝔬𝔳𝔢𝔩. / BY THOMAS HARDY, / AUTHOR OF / 'UNDER THE GREENWOOD TREE,' 'DESPERATE REMEDIES,' ET . [*ETC. in VOLS. II and III*] / 'A violet in the youth of primy nature, / Forward, not permanent, sweet, not lasting, / The perfume and suppliance of a minute; / No more.' / IN THREE VOLUMES. / VOL. I. [*II.*] [*III.*] / LONDON: / TINSLEY BRO-

---

[1] Though the novel was advertised as early as 18 May, it was not announced as ready until 15 June, on which day it was reviewed in the *Athenaeum*.

THERS, 8 CATHERINE ST. STRAND. / 1873. / [*The right of transla-tion and reproduction is reserved.*]

Collation. VOL. I. π^1, [A]², B–U⁸; pp. [vi]+ 304; [i] half-title; [ii] print-ers' imprint: London: / Robson and Sons, Printers, Pancras Road, N.W. [*The final period may be wanting. Since π1 is independent, it may be found with this variant bound in any of the 3 vols.*] / ; [iii] title-page; [iv] blank; [v] Contents; [vi] Names of the Persons; [1]–303 text, printers' imprint at foot of p. 303: London: Printed by Robson and Sons, Pancras Road, N.W. / ; [304] blank.

VOL. II. π^1, [A]², B–U⁸, X⁴; pp. [vi]+ 312; [i]–[v] as in VOL. 1; [vi] blank; [1]–311 text, printers' imprint at foot of p. 311: London: / Robson and Sons, Printers, Pancras Road, N.W. / ; [312] blank.

VOL. III. π^1, [A]², B–R⁸, S⁴ (–S4); pp. [vi]+ 262; preliminary pages as in VOL. II; [1]–262 text, printers' imprint at foot of p. 262: London: / Robson and Sons, Printers, Pancras Road, N.W.

Tinsley Brothers' catalogue, paged [1]–[16] and dated March 1873, bound in at end.[1]

Binding. Green diagonal-fine-ribbed cloth; blocked in black on front and back with Oxford frame; gold-lettered on spine with bands blocked in black and gold at top and bottom: A Pair / of / Blue / Eyes / [*rule*] / Thomas Hardy / [*rule*] / Vol. I. [*II.*] [*III.*] / Author of / "Under the / Greenwood / Tree" / Tinsley Brothers / .

Cream-white end-papers; top uncut, fore-edge and tail trimmed; leaves measure 5″× 7½″.

Binding Variants. Copies exist in red and plum sand-grain cloth, conform-ing in all other respects to the description above. They are so uncom-mon that they would seem to be trial bindings, and it is worth noting that in both cases they incorporate Tinsley Brothers' catalogue. The 2 copies in Hardy's library were rebound and of comparatively recent acquisition.[2]

Secondary Bindings. The novel also occurs in blue pebbly cloth, blocked in

---

[1] Copies frequently want this catalogue, suggesting that the binders' supply was soon exhausted.

[2] One of these belonged to Coventry Patmore, and Hardy has written on the fly-leaf of Vol. I, 'Thomas Hardy. July: 1922. (Patmore had bought the book, and wrote to the author when a stranger to him. T.H.)'. See *Early Life*, p. 138.

black on front and blind on back with decorative frame; gold-lettered on spine with gold bands at top and bottom: A Pair / of / Blue / Eyes / [*rule*] / Thomas Hardy / [*rule*] / Vol. I. [*II.*] [*III.*] / [*ornament*] / Author of / Under the / Greenwood / Tree. / Tinsley Bros / ; yellow end-papers printed with Chapman and Hall advertisements. And again, in blue sand-grain cloth, blocked in black on front and blind on back with decorative panels; gold-lettered on spine with gold bands at top and bottom: A / Pair of / Blue / Eyes / [*ornament*] / Thomas Hardy. / [*rule*] / Vol. I. [*II.*] [*III.*] / ; plain yellow end-papers. These two styles, from the Chapman and Hall advertisements in the one and the lack of imprint in the other, are almost certainly secondary or remainder bindings and may easily date from Tinsley's failure in August 1878 and the subsequent dispersal of his stock. Still another secondary binding exists, brown cloth, wanting Hardy's name on the spine.

Serial Issue. *A Pair of Blue Eyes* was first printed serially in *Tinsleys' Magazine* from September 1872 to July 1873 as 'By the Author of "Under the Greenwood Tree," "Desperate Remedies," etc.' The monthly instalments, keeping close to the 20 pages Hardy had contracted to supply, ran as follows: September, Chaps. 1–5; October, Chaps. 6–8; November, Chaps. 9–11; December, Chaps. 12–14; January, Chaps. 15–18; February, Chaps. 19–21; March, Chaps. 22–25; April, Chaps. 26–28; May, Chaps. 29–31; June, Chaps. 32–36; July, Chaps. 37–40. With each of the 11 instalments appeared 1 full-page illustration by J. A. Pasquier, and for some if not all of these plates Hardy himself provided sketches. The first chapter was somewhat rewritten and reduced in length before it was reprinted.

The novel was also printed serially in America, apparently by arrangement with Henry Holt, in the *Semi-Weekly New York Tribune* from 26 September to 16 December 1873.

Manuscript. Only a portion of the MS. of *A Pair of Blue Eyes* has survived. This consists of Chaps. 1–8 and 15–18, representing the instalments for September, October, and January in *Tinsleys' Magazine*. The MS. is written on 115 leaves of pale blue ruled paper measuring $7\frac{3}{8}''\times 9\frac{3}{8}''$ and (the later portion) 48 leaves measuring $7\frac{1}{8}''\times 9\frac{1}{4}''$. Some leaves are fragmentary, suggesting cancellations, and $2\frac{1}{2}$ pages are in Miss Gifford's hand. The MS., though printer's copy, shows many alterations; the early chapters have been retitled; and Elfride's song in Chap. 3 was at first a ballad, 'The Banks of Allan Water', from which the novel drew its original title, *A Winning Tongue Had He*. On the September instalment are the instructions to send 2 proofs to the author 'Care of John Gifford, Esq. Kirland House, nr. Bodmin'; on the October instalment the address is '4 Celbridge Place, Westbourne Park'; and on the January instalment, 'Bockhampton, Dorchester'.

The MS. was at one time the property of John Lane[1] and was sold from the library of Mrs. Lane by Hodgson & Co., 16 April 1926 (a page from Chap. 1 is reproduced in facsimile in the sale catalogue). Hardy's recollection of its history (a little at variance with the facts) he wrote to Sydney Cockerell, 24 February 1916: 'As to the MS. of "A Pair of Blue Eyes", there is no doubt that its history is this. When I wrote it in 1872–73 for Tinsleys' Magazine the MS. of each number was not returned with the proof, and its earlier chapters being (as I remember) thought little of by Tinsley, the MS. of them was probably destroyed. But about the middle the story began to excite attention, and so Tinsley must have thought it worth while to preserve the MS. of it on the chance of it being worth something. His business was sold later on, and I suppose Mathews & Lane bought the MS., letters, &c. at the sale.' The MS. is now in the Bliss collection and has been bound in full blue morocco. Another page, the opening of Chap. 6, is reproduced in facsimile in the Kern Sale Catalogue, Part I (New York, The Anderson Galleries, 7–10 January 1929), p. [209].

Notes on Composition and Publication. A Pair of Blue Eyes, under an earlier title, *A Winning Tongue Had He*, was begun, or at least outlined, in the summer of 1871. When Hardy wrote to Tinsley in October of that year 'as to the probable issue of the account between us in "Desperate Remedies"', he added, 'Early in the summer I began, and nearly finished, a little rural story [*Under the Greenwood Tree* which, as a matter of fact, had already been submitted to Macmillan], but owing to the representation of critic-friends who were taken with D.R., I relinquished that and have proceeded a little way with another, the essence of which is plot, *without crime*—but on the plan of D.R. The result of

---

[1] While in his possession it was described as including a fourth instalment, that for July (see Lane's Bibliography in Lionel Johnson, *The Art of Thomas Hardy*, new ed., London, 1923, p. 299). This is presumably an error.

the first venture would of course influence me in choosing which to work up with the most care.'[1] It was not until the July of 1872, however, that Tinsley, in want of a serial for *Tinsleys' Magazine* and encouraged by the reviews of *Under the Greenwood Tree*, which he had issued meanwhile, raised the question of a new story and Hardy agreed (27 July) for £200 to complete his projected novel. The first instalment of 5 chapters was finished in London and published anonymously on 15 August, the writing was continued at Higher Bockhampton and at St. Juliot in Cornwall, so largely the scene of the story, and the conclusion was sent to Tinsley 12 March 1873 (see *Early Life*, pp. 118–21). The novel is of peculiar interest because it was written during Hardy's courtship of Emma Lavinia Gifford, whom he had first met in March 1870, and in several of its characters (notably its heroine) and a number of its episodes is a reflection of actual experience, to a greater extent than the author cared to admit.

A Pair of Blue Eyes was published at 31s. 6d., in an edition presumably of 500 copies, the last week in May 1873. It was the first of Hardy's books to bear his name as author. The reviews of this first edition which he preserved in his scrap-book are: the *Athenaeum* (28 June), the *Spectator* (28 June), the *Graphic* (12 July), the *Saturday Review* (2 August),[2] the *Pall Mall Gazette* (25 October). Again the critical reception was favourable, but Tinsley years later called the novel 'by far the weakest of the three books I published of his' and with it ended his association with Hardy.

Subsequent Editions (*see also* COLLECTED EDITIONS). *A Pair of Blue Eyes* was never reprinted in its original three-volume form. It was first published in America by Holt & Williams in their Leisure Hour Series in July 1873 and reprinted in England by Henry S. King & Co. (and their successors Kegan Paul & Co.) in 1877 with a frontispiece by M. E. E[dwards] (see *Early Life*, p. 149). Hardy added a Preface in March 1895 (for Osgood, McIlvaine's edition of the Wessex Novels) and a Postscript in June 1912 (for Macmillan's definitive Wessex Edition). He revised the novel for the last time in 1919 for the Mellstock Edition, 'to correct the topography a little,' he wrote to Sydney

---

[1] For a calendar of Hardy's correspondence with Tinsley, see Appendix, pp. 329 ff.

[2] Quite probably by Hardy's friend, H. M. Moule, in some respects the original of Henry Knight. He wrote to Hardy, 21 May, that he had received the novel from the editor, though he had 'vowed never to review a friend again'.

Cockerell, 'the reasons that led me to disguise the spot when the book
was written in 1872 no longer existing, the hand of death having taken
care of that.'[1] The reference is to the first Mrs. Hardy, who had died
in 1912, the last of the little group Hardy found at St. Juliot Rectory
in 1870.

1874: FAR FROM THE MADDING CROWD (2 Vols.)

FAR FROM THE MADDING CROWD. / BY THOMAS HARDY, /
AUTHOR OF/"A PAIR OF BLUE EYES," "UNDER THE GREEN-
WOOD TREE," ETC. / *WITH TWELVE ILLUSTRATIONS.* / *IN
TWO VOLUMES.* / VOL. I. [*II.*] / LONDON: / SMITH, ELDER
& CO., 15, WATERLOO PLACE. / 1874. / (*All rights reserved.*)

Collation. VOL. I. [A]², B–Y⁸; pp. iv+336; [i] title-page; [ii] blank;
[iii]–iv Contents and List of Illustrations; [1]–333 text, printers' imprint at foot of p. 333: *Printed by William Moore & Co.* ; [334]–
[336] blank.

VOL. II. [A]², B–Y⁸, Z⁴; pp. iv+344; preliminary pages as in
VOL. I; [1]–342 text, printers' imprint (as above) at foot of p. 342;
[343][344] blank.

Illustrations. Frontispiece and 5 illustrations by H[elen] Paterson, wood-
engraved and separately printed, in each volume. The last 2 in Vol.
II are signed H. Allingham, the artist having married William Allingham in August 1874. Years after, Hardy wrote to Edmund Gosse, 'The
illustrator of Far from the Madding Crowd began as a charming
young lady, Miss Helen Paterson, and ended as a married woman,—
charms unknown—wife of Allingham the poet. I have never set eyes
on her since she was the former and I met her and corresponded
with her about the pictures of the story. She was the best illustrator
I ever had.'[2]

Binding. Green diagonal-fine-ribbed cloth; blocked in black on front with
3-panel design incorporating 2 vignettes, a church and churchyard at

[1] *Friends of a Lifetime*, ed. Viola Meynell (London, 1940), pp. 286–7. See also *Early
Life*, p. 98.
[2] See *Early Life*, p. 128. Hardy later tried to get her to illustrate *A Laodicean*, only
to discover she had entirely given up book-illustration.

top, reproduction of second illustration in Vol. I ('Hands were loosening his neckerchief.' facing p. 32) at bottom, lettered in centre in gold and blind with decorations: Far from / the / Madding Crowd / ; the whole design signed: CSL; blocked in blind on back with 3-rule border; lettered in gold and blind on spine with decorative blocking in gold and black: Far from / the / Madding / Crowd. / By / Thomas Hardy. / Vol. I. [*II*.] / Smith, Elder & C° / .

Chocolate end-papers; top uncut, fore-edge and tail trimmed; leaves measure 5⅜″ × 8⅜″.

Serial Issue. *Far from the Madding Crowd* was first printed serially in the *Cornhill Magazine* from January to December 1874. The monthly instalments, which were anonymous, ran as follows: January, Chaps. 1–5; February, Chaps. 6–8; March, Chaps. 9–14; April, Chaps. 15–20; May, Chaps. 21–24; June, Chaps. 25–29; July, Chaps. 30–33; August, Chaps. 34–38; September, Chaps. 39–42; October, Chaps. 43–47; November, Chaps. 48–51; December, Chaps. 52–57. With each of the 12 instalments appeared 1 full-page illustration and 1 vignette initial by Mrs. Allingham. The former only were published in book form, the October plate, 'Her Tears Fell Fast Beside the Unconscious Pair', being retitled (see Vol. II, facing p. 167).

The novel (without illustrations) was also printed serially in America in several eclectic magazines: *Every Saturday*, 31 January to 24 October 1874 (when the magazine was merged with *Littell's Living Age*); *Littell's Living Age*, 31 January 1874 to 9 January 1875; the *Eclectic Magazine*, March 1874 to February 1875; and (apparently by arrangement with Henry Holt) in the *Semi-Weekly New York Tribune*, 26 June to 15 December 1874.

Manuscript. The MS. of *Far from the Madding Crowd* is written on 605 leaves, measuring 6½″ × 8⅜″, though some are fragmentary. The leaves have been divided in a most unusual way, by Hardy's numbering, into 3 unequal parts: Part 1 (Chaps. 1–21) numbered 1–208 (with 6 scattered supplementary leaves); Part 2 (Chaps. 22–46, as far as 'Meanwhile, Bathsheba remained . . .') numbered 2–1 to 2–263 (with 2 supplementary leaves); and Part 3 (Chaps. 46, concluded, to 57) numbered 3–1 to 3–126. No satisfactory explanation is apparent for this curious foliation—the MS. was submitted to Leslie Stephen in very much smaller sections (perhaps 3 or 4 chapters at a time), and the divisions are too unequal to suggest a projected three-volume form for the novel. The MS., though used by the *Cornhill* printers, shows numerous revisions, many chapters retitled, and some few pencilled bowdlerizations. The word 'parabolic' at the opening of Chap. 15 (MS. f. 147) has been corrected in pencil to 'hyperbolic' and initialed 'L.S.'. Chap. 16, 'All Saints' and All Souls''', is wanting altogether in the MS. since it was an after-thought and written on the proof-sheets. Inserted in the text of Chap. 32 there are 5 drawings of the hoof-marks as Oak and Coggan followed them, which the printers did not find it feasible to reproduce. And there are at least 2 passages of some length which were not printed although left uncancelled in the MS.—perhaps a page in Chap. 43 extending the description of Fanny Robin and her baby in their coffin, and some 3½ pages in Chap. 47 adding an episode or two to Troy's 'Adventures by the Shore'.

The MS., which Hardy imagined had been destroyed at the printers' more than forty years back, was discovered in 1918 by Mrs. Reginald J. Smith after the death of her husband, son-in-law of the publisher and last representative of the firm. At her suggestion Hardy rewrote a missing page (f. 107, end of Chap. 9), and the MS., bound in blue morocco, was sent to the Red Cross Sale at Christie's, 22 April 1918 (Lot 2069). It was subsequently in the collection of the late A. Edward Newton.[1] Referring to it Mrs. Hardy wrote to Mr. Newton, 4 August 1918, 'The afternoon it was sold he and I visited the old home where it was written. We sat in the garden and looked up at the little window under which he sat as he wrote, more than forty years ago.' See *Later Years*, p. 186. The MS. is now the property of Mr. Edwin Thorne.

Two fragments of the first draft of the novel also survive. One, headed 'Chapter [XXIII *added in pencil*]. The shearing-supper', consists of 7 leaves, measuring 6⅝″ × 8⅛″ and numbered 2–18 to 2–24, with the pencilled date '1873' and a later note in red ink, 'Some pages of the first Draft—afterwards revised. T.H.' Perhaps a page of this at most

---

[1] The first page is reproduced in facsimile in the Newton Sale Catalogue, Part II (New York, Parke-Bernet Galleries, 14–16 May 1941), p. [69]. Another page (f. 3) from Chap. 1 is reproduced in A. Edward Newton, *The Amenities of Book-Collecting* (Boston, 1918), p. [14], and the opening of Chap. 46 (f. 2–257), together with Hardy's letter to Mrs. Smith about the MS., 23 January 1918, in the same author's *Thomas Hardy, Novelist or Poet?* (Philadelphia, Privately Printed, 1929), pp. [7]–[9]. A page from Chap. 32 (f. 2–108) is reproduced in the Grolier Club Hardy Exhibition Catalogue, facing p. 15.

has been retained in the present Chap. 23. The alteration was undoubtedly made at the instance of Leslie Stephen, who wrote to Hardy 17 February 1874 that he thought the chapter 'the least good of the three—and therefore the best to abridge.' (See Appendix, pp. 337–8.) The 7 leaves were reduced to 2, and the consequent correction of foliation shows that composition had proceeded at the time as far as Chap. 29. The other fragment, headed simply 'Chapter' (commencing 'Troy soon began to make himself busy about the farm.'), consists of 11 leaves of blue paper, measuring $5\frac{7}{8}'' \times 8''$ and numbered 106^{a-k}, with a later note in red ink, 'Some pages of 1st draft—(Details of Sheep-rot—omitted from MS. when revised) T.H.' These pages are heavily altered and bear no relation (in appearance, foliation, &c.) to the complete MS. as we have it. They would seem to be (as the companion fragment is not) part of a destroyed early MS. of the novel. The two fragments were bound together in blue morocco in 1915 and given by Hardy to his second wife. They are now in the Dorset County Museum.

Notes on Composition and Publication. Under the Greenwood Tree so struck Leslie Stephen that he wrote to Hardy, through H. M. Moule, in November 1872 to inquire about a story for the *Cornhill Magazine*, of which he had become editor the previous year. Hardy was still at work on *A Pair of Blue Eyes* but he sketched for Stephen 'a pastoral tale which I thought of calling "Far from the Madding Crowd," in which the chief characters would be a woman-farmer, a shepherd, and a sergeant in the Dragoon Guards'. 'A few chapters of the story, with some succeeding ones in outline' were submitted in June 1873 and at the end of September perhaps a dozen in tentative form, and Stephen definitely accepted the novel and publication commenced in the *Cornhill* for January of the next year. *Far from the Madding Crowd* was wholly written at Higher Bockhampton and finished by July 1874. No other novel of Hardy's had the benefit of such constant and discriminating criticism as Stephen's, though Hardy confessed at the time to no higher aim than 'to be considered a good hand at a serial.'[1] The novel was anonymous throughout its run in the *Cornhill*, prompting the *Spectator* in its review of the January number (3 January) to remark, 'If "Far from the Madding Crowd" is not written by George

---

[1] For Stephen's letters, see Appendix, pp. 336 ff. See also *Early Life*, pp. 125–33; and, for Hardy's recollections of Stephen as editor, F. W. Maitland, *The Life and Letters of Leslie Stephen* (London, 1906), pp. 270 ff.

Eliot, then there is a new light among novelists.' The authorship was disclosed in the *Spectator*'s review of the February issue (7 February). *Far from the Madding Crowd* was published at 21*s*. in an edition of 1,000 copies on 23 November 1874. The novel was widely noticed, and Hardy preserved eleven reviews in his scrap-book. Almost the only presentation copy known to exist was given to Canon Gifford, who had married the author and his niece Emma Lavinia Gifford scarcely two months before. It bears the inscription in Vol. I, 'To The Revd Dr Gifford—with the Author's kind regards. November 1874.'

American Edition. Far from the Madding Crowd was published in America by Henry Holt & Co. in their Leisure Hour Series in November 1874. This edition, printed from the types of *Every Saturday*, has sometimes been described as the true first edition of the novel,[1] but the claim to priority rests solely on the evidence of advertising end-papers, dated in a few instances 17 November, evidence which is no more conclusive than inserted advertisements. No accession records or deposit copies remain at the Library of Congress nor has any evidence survived at the publishers'. The novel was not advertised by Holt as ready until 28 November (five days after Smith, Elder's edition, as entered in their records), and in default of any further evidence this must be accepted as the date of publication.

Hardy wrote to his American publishers 12 November 1874, '. . . Messrs. Osgood have the right of reprinting in America the articles in the Cornhill Magazine. I do not know anything about the periodical called "Every Saturday". As there seems to have been some misunderstanding with regard to the issue of Far from the Madding Crowd in America I wish you to arrange the publication of your edition of the work so as not to prejudice its issue in the *Atlantic Monthly*.[2] My idea in sending the concluding chapters as you requested is that you wish to get the work in type a little sooner than you would otherwise do—not so soon of course as to prejudice its serial publication by those who have a right to it in that form.' That there was some delay in publication is

---

[1] See I. R. Brussel, *Anglo-American First Editions 1826–1900 East to West* (London, 1935), p. 103.

[2] Hardy seems to have been unaware that James R. Osgood & Co. were formerly the publishers of *Every Saturday* as well as the *Atlantic Monthly*, though they had sold both to H. O. Houghton & Co. at the end of 1873. Osgood had paid the *Cornhill* £75 for advance sheets of the novel.

apparent from a note printed in the *Publishers' Weekly*, 14 November: 'Mr. Hardy's great novel, "Far from the Madding Crowd," is waiting only the arrival of a chapter from England, which has curiously slipped out of the *Cornhill*, and failed also to make its appearance in Mr. Hardy's copy on this side of the water. As soon as Mr. Hardy's missing manuscript arrives, the book will be sent forth, and is likely to make one of the hits of the season. It will be remembered that this novel was at first attributed to George Eliot.' Though no chapter 'slipped out of the *Cornhill*', there may have been complications arising from the merging of *Every Saturday* and *Littell's Living Age* (when the novel still had 13 chapters to run) and some discrepancy in the 'concluding chapters' Hardy had sent direct to Holt.

After the publication of *The Hand of Ethelberta* in 1876 Henry Holt wrote to Hardy that the *Spectator*'s early notice of *Far from the Madding Crowd* was widely quoted and advertised in America and 'stirred up a great initial demand from the dealers' which was not sustained by sales to readers or confirmed by a demand for the later novel.

SECOND IMPRESSION REVISED (CALLED 'SECOND EDITION')

FAR FROM THE MADDING CROWD. / . . . / VOL. I. [*II.*] / SECOND EDITION. / . . .

Collation. As in first impression.

Illustrations. As in first impression.

Binding. As in first impression.

Secondary Binding. Green sand-grain cloth; blocked in blind on front and back with a conventional design; gold-lettered on spine with decorative bands blocked in gold at top and bottom: Far from / the / Madding / Crowd / [*ornament*] / *Thomas Hardy.* / [*rule*] / Vol. I. [*II.*] / .
Pale yellow end-papers; top uncut, fore-edge and tail trimmed; leaves measure 5⅜″ × 8⅜″.
This binding probably dates from 1877 when 125 quires (and 6 copies in cloth) were remaindered to W. H. Smith & Son.

Notes on Revision and Publication. On 15 January 1875 George Smith wrote to Hardy, 'I have the gratification of informing you that we have sold nearly the whole of the first edition of "Far from the Madding

Crowd" and that we propose to print a small second edition. If therefore you wish to make any corrections I must ask you to let me have a note of them as soon as possible.' Hardy sent his corrections immediately, and this 'Second Edition', of 500 copies, was ready in late February. Since superficially this second impression is distinguishable from the first only by the words 'Second Edition' on the title-page (not even the date being altered) and the first signature consists of only 2 leaves easily replaced (I have seen instances of this), it seems worth while to indicate a few of the more significant textual alterations. In some cases these necessitated shifting lines over several pages.

	First impression	*Second impression revised*
VOL. I		
P. 2, l. 1	Sacrament	Communion
73, ll. 13–14	for his mercy endureth for ever	*deleted*
103, l. 4	that had no father at all in the eye of matrimony	*deleted*
201, ll. 12–16	The quiet mean to which we originally found him adhering, and in which, with few exceptions, he had continually moved, was that of neutralization: it was not structural at all.	*deleted*
309, l. 22	These circumambient gleams	These circling gleams
VOL. II		
P. 15, ll. 4–6	The dark rotundity of the earth approached the foreshores and promontories of coppery cloud which bounded	Above the dark margin of the earth appeared foreshores and promontories of coppery cloud, bounding
21, l. 23	Coggan's watch struck one.	Coggan carried an old pinchbeck repeater which he had inherited from some genius in his family; and it now struck one.
40, ll. 20–22	believe in all . . . believe in drab	worship all . . . worship drab
140, l. 22	on this side of respectability	within the pale of respectability

Subsequent Editions (see also COLLECTED EDITIONS*).* Smith, Elder published a one-volume edition of the novel with 6 of the original illustrations (and a modification of the original binding) in 1877, selling the moulds finally to Sampson Low in 1884. Hardy added a Preface in February 1895 for Osgood, McIlvaine's edition of the Wessex Novels, revising and expanding it slightly for Macmillan's first impression in 1902 (see below, pp. 281–2).

1876: THE HAND OF ETHELBERTA (2 Vols.)

THE HAND OF ETHELBERTA / *A COMEDY IN CHAPTERS* / BY / THOMAS HARDY / AUTHOR OF 'FAR FROM THE MADDING CROWD' ETC. / [*rule*] / VITÆ POST-SCENIA CELANT— *Lucretius* / [*rule*] / *WITH ELEVEN ILLUSTRATIONS* / IN TWO VOLUMES / VOL. I. [*II.*] / LONDON / SMITH, ELDER, & CO., 15 WATERLOO PLACE / 1876 / [*All rights reserved*]

Collation. VOL. I. [A]⁴, B–X⁸, Y²; pp. viii + 324; [i] half-title; [ii] blank; [iii] title-page; [iv] blank; [v]–vi Contents; [vii] List of Illustrations; [viii] blank; [1]–322 text, printers' imprint at foot of p. 322: London: Printed by / Spottiswoode and Co., New-Street Square / and Parliament Street / ; [323][324] advertisements of Smith, Elder, & Co.'s publications.

    VOL. II. [A]⁴, B–X⁸; pp. viii + 320; preliminary pages as in VOL. 1; [1]–318 text, printers' imprint (as above) at foot of p. 318; [319] advertisement of *Far from the Madding Crowd*, Second Edition; [320] advertisement of Smith, Elder, & Co.'s publications.

Cancels. In Vol. I the conjugate leaves B4 and B5 (pp. 7–10) and F1 and F8 (pp. 65–66, 79–80) may be cancels, signed *B4 (on p. 7) and *F (on p. 65). I have never seen the leaves in their uncancelled state and I do not know the reason for the cancellation. It occurred while the sheets were printing, making 3 states of signatures B and F (since the alterations were naturally incorporated in the remainder of the impression), i.e. (1) B4 unsigned, F1 signed F, text requiring cancellation; (2) B4 (with B5) a double cancel and signed *B4, F1 (with F8) a double cancel and signed *F, text corrected; (3) B4 unsigned, F1 signed F, text as in (2), not otherwise distinguishable from (1). One signature in the second state, the other in the third, is the rule in copies I have examined.

Illustrations. Frontispiece and 5 illustrations in Vol. I, frontispiece and 4 illustrations in Vol. II by [George] Du Maurier, wood-engraved and separately printed. The illustration facing p. 148, Vol. I, is incorrectly titled, 'Round her, leaning against branches, or prostrate on the ground, were two or three [five or six] individuals', though the title appears correctly in the List of Illustrations. Hardy admired Du Maurier's work, but there was little or no consultation between the two in this case. As Du Maurier wrote to him, 'If we were neighbours and I could have consulted you easily I should have been better able to realise your conceptions'.

Binding. Red-brown diagonal-fine-ribbed cloth; blocked in black on front with conventional design and lettered in gold and blind: The / Hand of / Ethelberta / ; blocked in blind on back with single-rule border; lettered on spine in gold and blind with decorations blocked in black and gold: The / Hand / of / Ethelberta / *by* / *Thomas Hardy* / Vol / I [*II*] / *Smith Elder & C?* / .

Chocolate end-papers; top uncut, fore-edge and tail trimmed; leaves measure $5\frac{1}{2}'' \times 8\frac{1}{4}''$.

Secondary Binding. Green sand-grain cloth; blocked in blind on front and back with a conventional design; gold-lettered on spine with decorative bands blocked in gold at top and bottom: The Hand / of / Ethelberta / [*ornament*] / *Thomas Hardy* / [*rule*] / Vol. I. [*II.*] / .

Dark green end-papers; all edges cut; leaves measure $5\frac{1}{4}'' \times 8\frac{1}{8}''$.

This is obviously a secondary binding and may have been done for W. H. Smith & Son (since it almost duplicates the secondary binding of the Second Impression Revised of *Far from the Madding Crowd*) though Smith, Elder do not record the remaindering of any quires of *The Hand of Ethelberta* (61 cloth copies were remaindered to F. Warne & Co.).

Serial Issue. The Hand of Ethelberta was first printed serially in the *Cornhill Magazine* from July 1875 to May 1876. The monthly instalments ran as follows: July, Chaps. 1–4; August, Chaps. 5–9; September, Chaps. 10–15; October, Chaps. 16–21; November, Chaps. 22–26;

December, Chaps. 27–30; January, Chaps. 31–34; February, Chaps. 35–38; March, Chaps. 39–42; April, Chaps. 43–46; May, Chaps. 47–50. With each of the 11 instalments appeared 1 full-page illustration and 1 vignette initial by George Du Maurier. The former only were published in book form. The text was slightly revised before it was reprinted.

The novel also appeared serially in America in Sunday issues of the *New York Times* from 20 June 1875 to 9 April 1876. It was printed from proofs of the *Cornhill* supplied by Hardy himself and sometimes a little in advance of its publication there, forestalling the eclectic magazines. The first 4 issues described it as 'Written expressly for the New-York Times', subsequent issues, more accurately, as 'Printed by special arrangement with the author.'

Manuscript. A fragment of the MS. of *The Hand of Ethelberta* was discovered among Smith, Elder papers by Mrs. Reginald J. Smith in 1918 at the same time as the MS. of *Far from the Madding Crowd*. It was returned to Hardy at his request and destroyed by him. No other portion of the MS. is known to have survived.

Cornhill *Proof-sheets.* Proof-sheets of *The Hand of Ethelberta* survive and in default of any MS. are of particular importance. They are page proofs of the novel as printed in the *Cornhill* and are complete save for three instalments (February–April). The excisions and additions at a number of points, all in Hardy's hand, are fairly extensive. Most interesting perhaps is the reworking of the rose-leaf incident in Chap. 29 (now 27). This may have been urged by Stephen, since the original version is clumsy and not a little foolish; at least he took occasion to commend the revision.[1] The proof-sheets are now in my possession.

Notes on Composition and Publication. With the success of *Far from the Madding Crowd* Leslie Stephen asked Hardy in December 1874 for another story for the *Cornhill Magazine.* The first chapters of *The Hand of Ethelberta*, 'a plunge in a new and untried direction', were submitted in March 1875, and in spite of Smith, Elder's disappointment at the character of the story, publication commenced in the *Corn-*

---

[1] See F. W. Maitland, *The Life and Letters of Leslie Stephen* (London, 1906), p. 276. A page of the proof at this point is reproduced in facsimile in the Sachs Sale Catalogue (New York, Parke-Bernet Galleries, 1 February 1944), p. [17].

fresh and round as lady-apples—oh, little girl ? But are you disposed to tell me that writer's name ? "

By applying a general idea to a particular case a person with the best of intentions may find himself immediately landed in a quandary. In saying to the country girl before him what would have suited the mass of country lasses well enough, Christopher had offended her beyond the cure of compliment. The expression about lady-apples and little girl was not the kind of thing she cared for.

" I am not disposed to tell the writer's name," she replied, with a dudgeon that was very great for one whose whole stock of it was so small. And she passed on and left him standing alone.

a trifle

Thus further conversation was checked; but perhaps that very flaw in his proceedings for approaching her was what led Christopher to adhere to the re-arranged hours of his lesson; he met her the next Wednesday, and the next Friday, and throughout the following week—no further words passing between them. For a while she went by very demurely, apparently mindful of his offence. But effrontery is not proved to be part of a man's nature till he has been guilty of a second act : the best of men may commit a first through accident or ignorance—may even be betrayed into it by over zeal for experiment. Some such conclusion may or may not have been arrived at by the girl with the lady-apple cheeks ; at any rate, after the lapse of another week a new spectacle presented itself; her redness deepened whenever Christopher passed her by, and embarrassment pervaded her from the lowest stitch to the tip of her feather. She had little chance of escaping him by diverging from the road, for a figure could be seen across the open ground to the distance of half a mile on either side. One day as he drew near as usual, she met him as women meet a cloud of dust—she turned and advanced backwards till he had passed. This was a trifle disconcerting, to say the least, and one curious circumstance alone prevented Christopher from getting out of her way entirely : he had perceived that whenever he was a little later, or she a little earlier, so that the point at which her proper path diverged from the main road that he followed would have been reached too soon for a meeting, she seemed to timidly check her pace until he came up, " If my presence is any source of interest to her, why should I withhold it ? " he said to himself, with the look of a man who knew not vanity. This view of the position, however, was rudely demolished by her meeting him the next afternoon with a parasol over her face, completely screening it from observation. He did not notice that the parasol trembled.

The highly ingenious and womanly device of the parasol had prevailed a few days, when a boy who tended the cows browsing in scores about the meadows asked Christopher the time of day, and afterwards stood regarding him with an arrangement of face in which the eyes dwindled very narrow, and gave up their place as the most noticeable features of the countenance to the upper and lower rows of teeth.

" Well, what makes you merry ? " said Christopher.

216

C

¶ This would have been disconcerting but for one reason : Christopher was ceasing to notice her. He was a man who, often when walking abroad, & looking as it were at the scene before his eyes, discerned successes & failures, friends & relations, episodes of childhood, wedding feasts & funerals, the landscape suffering greatly by these visions, until it became no more than the patterned wall-tints about the paintings in a gallery ; something

necessary to the tone & mood, yet not regarded. Nothing but a special concentration of himself on externals could interrupt this habit, & now that her appearance along the way had changed from a chance to a custom he began to lapse again into the old trick. He gazed once or twice at her form without seeing it : she met him the

hill for July. The novel was begun in Surbiton and London but largely written at Swanage, one of the scenes of the story, where in July the Hardys took lodgings in a sailor's cottage. As with *Far from the Madding Crowd*, though to a lesser extent, Hardy had the benefit of Stephen's critical judgement,[1] and the novel was finished in January 1876.

The Hand of Ethelberta was published at 21*s*. in an edition of 1,000 copies on 3 April 1876. It was not the success its predecessor had been with the reviewers or the libraries, but two years later only 61 copies were left to be remaindered. An unopened copy, inscribed to his wife, 'E. L. Hardy from the Author', was sold with books from Hardy's library in 1938.

Subsequent Editions (*see also* COLLECTED EDITIONS). *The Hand of Ethelberta* was never reprinted in its original two-volume form. Smith, Elder published the novel in a single volume with 6 of the original illustrations in May 1877, but more than half of the edition of 1,000 copies was remaindered (with the moulds) to Sampson Low five years later. Hardy wrote a Preface in December 1895 for Osgood, McIlvaine's edition of the Wessex Novels, and in revision the novel was reduced from 50 to 48 chapters by the excision of much of Chaps. 9 and 12 (the remaining material being included in the present Chaps. 8 and 11). A postscript was added in August 1912 for Macmillan's definitive Wessex Edition.

The novel was published in America in May 1876 by Henry Holt & Co. in their Leisure Hour Series. Hardy wrote to Henry Holt, 18 March 1876, 'I have sent duplicate proof sheets of the conclusion of the story to the New York Times, with a request to them to forward one copy to you, if they are willing to allow you to anticipate them at the finish. As I had disposed of the right to the story to them, till concluded in their pages I could do no otherwise than this: but from what they have told you I conclude that the proofs will be handed over to you at once. I enclose copy[2] for titlepage similar to that which will be prefixed to the English edition.' Though the publishers of the *New York Times* agreed to such anticipation, it seems to have proved impossible.

---

[1] See *Early Life*, pp. 134–7, and F. W. Maitland, loc. cit. 'May' (*Early Life*, p. 136) is a slip for 'July'.

[2] Now inserted in Holt's 'office sample' of the novel.

1878: THE RETURN OF THE NATIVE (3 Vols.)

THE / RETURN OF THE NATIVE / BY / THOMAS HARDY / AUTHOR OF / 'FAR FROM THE MADDING CROWD' 'A PAIR OF BLUE EYES [' *in VOLS. II and III*] ETC. / 'To sorrow / I bade good morrow, / And thought to leave her far away behind; / But cheerly, cheerly, / She loves me dearly; / She is so constant to me, and so kind. / I would deceive her, / And so leave her, / But ah! she is so constant and so kind [' *in VOLS. II and III*] / IN THREE VOLUMES—VOL. I. [*II.*] [*III.*] / LONDON / SMITH, ELDER, & CO., 15 WATERLOO PLACE / 1878 / [*All rights reserved*]

Collation. VOL. I. [A]⁴, B–U⁸; pp. [ii]+vi+304; blank leaf; [i] half-title; [ii] blank; [iii] title-page; [iv] blank; [v]–vi Contents; [1]–303 text, printers' imprint at foot of p. 303: London: Printed by / Spottis-woode and Co., New-Street Square / and Parliament Street / ; [304] blank.

VOL. II. [A]⁴, B–T⁸, U⁴, X²; pp. [ii]+vi+300; preliminary pages as in vol. 1; [1]–297 text, printers' imprint at foot of p. 297: *Spottis-woode & Co., Printers, New-street Square, London.* / ; [298] blank; [299][300] advertisements of Smith, Elder, & Co.'s new novels.

VOL. III. [A]⁴, B–X⁸; pp. [ii]+vi+320; preliminary pages as in vol. 1; [1]–320 text, printers' imprint (as in vol. 1) at foot of p. 320.

Illustration. Inserted in Vol. I as frontispiece is a 'Sketch map of the scene of the story', drawn by Hardy himself and separately printed.[1]

Binding. Brown diagonal-fine-ribbed cloth; blocked in black on front with conventional panel design, in blind on back with 2-rule border; lettered on spine in gold and blind with bands and ornaments blocked in black and gold: The / Return / of / the / Native / Thomas / Hardy / Vol. I. [*II.*] [*Vol III.*] / Smith Elder & Cº / .

Cream-white end-papers; top uncut, fore-edge and tail cut; leaves measure 5″×7⅜″.

Secondary Binding. Cloth usually a slightly redder shade of brown; blocked in blind on back with 3-rule border; imprint on spine (caps. ⅛″ instead

---

[1] See *Early Life*, p. 160. In his own copy of the novel (Dorset County Museum) Hardy has identified Mistover on the map as 'Troytown?' and Blooms End as 'Thornicombe?'.

Portion of a letter from Hardy to Arthur Hopkins, 20 February 1878, with sketches to assist the artist in illustrating *The Return of the Native* in the May *Belgravia*

of $\frac{3}{16}''$): Smith, Elder & C$\underline{o}$ / ; leaves measure $4\frac{7}{8}'' \times 7\frac{1}{4}''$; conforms in all other respects to the description above.

There are a number of reasons for considering this a secondary binding, though it is immediately distinguishable only by its 3-rule border: it is very much less common than the 2-rule binding, which appears on the British Museum, Cambridge, and Bodleian copies (accession dates '19 De 78', '1 Jan 79', and 'Aug 1879' respectively) and Hardy's own copy (though it must be noted that not all the first editions at Max Gate were of contemporary acquisition); copies in the 3-rule binding almost invariably lack the frontispiece in Vol. I; an identical situation prevails in the case of *The Trumpet-Major*, and Smith, Elder records show that 100 quires of *The Return of the Native* and 250 quires of *The Trumpet-Major* were remaindered to W. Glaisher, wholesale bookseller, in the same year, 1882. It seems reasonable to suggest that this is a secondary binding dating from that sale. There were no Smith, Elder binding orders after December 1878.

Serial Issue. The Return of the Native was first printed serially in *Belgravia* from January to December 1878. The monthly instalments ran as follows: January, Bk. I, Chaps. 1–4; February, Bk. I, Chaps. 5–7; March, Bk. I, Chaps. 8–11; April, Bk. II, Chaps. 1–5; May, Bk. II, Chaps. 6–8; June, Bk. III, Chaps. 1–4; July, Bk. III, Chaps. 5–8; August, Bk. IV, Chaps. 1–4; September, Bk. IV, Chaps. 5–8; October, Bk. V, Chaps. 1–4; November, Bk. V, Chaps. 5–8; December, Bk. V, Chap. 9–Bk. VI, Chap. 4. The Books are here untitled but provided with brief arguments, not reprinted. Several chapters were retitled before the novel was published in book form, and there were a number of deletions and additions, notably in Bk. III, Chap. 8 and Bk. IV, Chap. 1.

With each of the 12 instalments appeared 1 full-page illustration by A[rthur] Hopkins. The interest Hardy took in these illustrations, though they were not reproduced in book form, is revealed in his correspondence with the artist, a portion of which has survived. He warned Hopkins that 'the scenes are somewhat outlandish, and may be unduly troublesome to you' and offered rough sketches wherever there might be difficulty with accessories, as in the case of the mummers' dress (in the May illustration), which he drew in detail for the artist. He provided a sketch of Eustacia, but when she first appeared (in the February illustration) he felt that Hopkins had failed and wrote to him, 8 February, 'It is rather ungenerous to criticise; but since you invite me to do so I will say that I think Eustacia should have been represented as more youthful in face, supple in figure, and, in general, with a little more roundness and softness than have been given her. . . . Perhaps it is well for me to give you the following ideas of the story as a guide—Thomasin, as you have divined, is the *good* heroine, and she ultimately marries the reddleman, and lives happily. Eustacia is the wayward and erring heroine—She marries Yeobright, the son of Mrs Yeobright, is unhappy, and dies. The order of importance of the characters is as follows—1 Clym Yeobright 2 Eustacia 3 Thomasin and the reddleman 4 Wildeve 5 Mrs Yeobright.' When Eustacia appeared again in the August illustration (it had been thought unsafe to introduce her in boy's clothes in the mumming scene), Hardy wrote to Hopkins, 3 August, 'I think Eustacia is charming—she is certainly just what I imagined her to be, and the rebelliousness of her nature is precisely caught in your drawing.' Of Clym, who first appears conspicuously in the May illustration, Hardy wrote, 20 February, 'I should prefer to leave Clym's face entirely to you. A thoughtful young man of 25 is all that can be shown, as the particulars of his appearance given in the story are too minute to be represented in a small drawing.'

The novel was also published serially in America in *Harper's New Monthly Magazine* from February 1878 to January 1879. It had been planned to use the Hopkins illustrations, but apparently electrotypes could not be dispatched in time, so after falling a month behind with illustrations for the second and third instalments of the story and publishing two with the fourth instalment *Harper's* abandoned them altogether.

Manuscript. The MS. of *The Return of the Native* is written on 439 leaves, measuring $6\frac{1}{2}'' \times 8''$, though some are fragmentary. The leaves have been numbered 1–429 by Hardy, but there are 13 scattered supplementary leaves and 3 bear double numbers (e.g. 130–131) suggesting excisions. The MS. is divided for use in *Belgravia*, and corrections and additions are not numerous. Portions of it, to an unusual extent, are fair copy (e.g. Chap. 1), and 7 pages are in Mrs. Hardy's hand. The arguments are marked 'For Magazine only' or 'Omit in Vols', and the 'Sketch map of the scene of the story', a late addition, is not present.

The MS., now in a black grained morocco binding with a printed title-page, was given by Hardy to Clement Shorter in 1908 in return for his having had a number of Hardy's MSS. bound. At Shorter's death in 1926 it was bequeathed to the 'Royal University of Dublin' and is now in the Library of University College, Dublin (National University of Ireland).

Notes on Composition and Publication. The Return of the Native was written at 'Riverside Villa', Sturminster Newton, though it must have been concluded at Upper Tooting where the Hardys took a house in March 1878. We have no evidence as to when it was commenced or finished, but the first 7 chapters were written by 28 August 1877 and the first 2 books by 8 November, and publication was begun in Chatto & Windus's *Belgravia* in January of 1878. The novel had been offered Leslie Stephen for the *Cornhill*, 'but, though he liked the opening, he feared that the relations between Eustacia, Wildeve, and Thomasin might develop into something "dangerous" for a family maga-zine, and he refused to have anything to do with it unless he could see the whole.'[1] This was not possible, and Hardy's profitable association with Stephen as editor was ended, though Smith, Elder agreed on 20 September 1878 to publish the finished novel.

The Return of the Native was published at 31*s*. 6*d*. in an edition of 1,000 copies on 4 November 1878. The reviews were not flattering, and in 1882 there were 100 quires and 22 copies in cloth to be remaindered.

Subsequent Editions (see also COLLECTED EDITIONS*). The Return of the Native* was never reprinted in its original three-volume form. In 1880 it passed to Kegan Paul and in 1884 to Sampson Low. Hardy added a Preface in July 1895, when he revised the novel for Osgood, McIlvaine's edition of the Wessex Novels, and a Postscript in April 1912, for Macmillan's definitive Wessex Edition. In the latter edition the provocative note on the original conception of the story was in-serted at p. 473. The novel was published in America by Henry Holt & Co. in their Leisure Hour Series in December 1878.[2]

---

[1] Hardy, in F. W. Maitland, *The Life and Letters of Leslie Stephen* (London, 1906), pp. 276–7.

[2] This edition has sometimes been described as the true first edition of the novel [see *Papers of the Bibliographical Society of America*, vol. 36, no. 1 (New York, 1942), p. 39]. No accession records or deposit copies remain at the Library of Congress nor has any evidence survived at the publishers', but the absurdity of the idea (which rests solely on

[? 1879–80]: THE MISTRESS OF THE FARM

THE MISTRESS OF THE FARM. [*running-title*]

Collation. [ ], B–E⁸, F[ ]; pp. 66+; [*preliminary pages not known*; ? 1–18 Act I]; 19–36 Act II; 37–58 Act III; 59–[ ] Act IV.

Binding. Not known.

All edges cut; leaves measure 4⅝″ × 7″.

Copy. Known from a single, imperfect copy (pp. 19–58, 63–66 only) in the Lord Chamberlain's Office (vol. 510, no. 29).

Notes. Some time in 1879 Hardy undertook to dramatize *Far from the Madding Crowd.*¹ It was his first attempt in a medium that was to attract him repeatedly, though with indifferent success, to the end of his life. What had led him to this particular venture, however, beyond his recognition of 'a promising theme for the stage', or what plan he had for his play, which he called *The Mistress of the Farm*, is unknown. Soon after he finished it J. Comyns Carr and his wife proposed a dramatization of their own. Hardy gave them his version to work with, and a collaboration of sorts followed in the spring of 1880.² In default of any complete copy of *The Mistress of the Farm*, especially its title-page, it is impossible to say whether this printed text is Hardy's original version or Carr's first modification of it. The latter is more probable. Carr, as dramatic critic, had a practical knowledge of the theatre that Hardy lacked and would have been familiar with the device of privately printing plays as manuscript. The dramatization is in four acts, but though the novel has inevitably been much compressed there is only one major alteration in plot, the elimination of Boldwood and the melodramatic substitution of Fanny's half-crazed gipsy brother, a new character, as Sergeant Troy's nemesis.

In this form Carr submitted the play to Hare and Kendal, managers of

the evidence of advertising end-papers in one or two copies, variously dated 18 September and 28 October 1878) is apparent from the fact that Holt's 'priority claim' was not published until 3 December nor was the novel advertised as ready before 14 December. The plate for the map, it may be observed, was not in existence by 18 September.

¹ This is the date he supplied for his biography in *Men of the Time* (11th ed., London, 1884).

² See *J. Comyns Carr*, by His Wife (London, 1920), pp. 83–84, and *Mrs. J. Comyns Carr's Reminiscences*, ed. Eve Adam (London [1926]), pp. 76–79.

the St. James's Theatre, in the summer of 1880. It was provisionally
accepted by Hare but Kendal (or, rather, Mrs. Kendal) did not receive
it favourably and it was finally rejected on 11 November 1880. A year
later, on 29 December 1881, Hare and Kendal came forward with
A. W. Pinero's *The Squire*. A number of critics immediately observed
that this 'new and original play' showed striking resemblances in character and situation to *Far from the Madding Crowd*, and for some days an
angry correspondence followed in the columns of the London papers (in
particular *The Times* and the *Daily News*) in which Carr, Pinero, Hare
and Kendal, and even Hardy himself (see below, pp. 295–6) took part.
Mrs. Kendal was the culprit. Long afterwards Pinero confessed to Carr
that she had given him his plot, he knowing nothing of Hardy's novel
or play. The controversy seems to have revived *The Mistress of the
Farm*. Carr, if not Hardy, was quite shrewd enough to see its value. He
hurried to make a second and drastic revision of the play, excised the first
act altogether as Hardy himself had proposed (reducing the whole to
three acts), and wrote a new last act, and it was finally performed, as
Far from the Madding Crowd by Thomas Hardy and J. Comyns Carr,
at the Prince of Wales Theatre in Liverpool 27 February 1882 with
Marion Terry as Bathsheba and Charles Kelly (Ellen Terry's former
husband) as Gabriel Oak. After further performances in the provinces
and the substitution of Mrs. Bernard-Beere as Bathsheba the play
opened in London at the Globe Theatre on 29 April.[1] It was well
received and ran until 8 July (its 114th performance), though *The
Squire*, partly owing to Mrs. Kendal's popularity, outlasted it one week.

The whole affair was distasteful to Hardy. Revisions he had hoped
Carr could make were not practicable.[2] The controversy over *The
Squire* was acrimonious. It was echoed in half the periodicals of the
time and brought awkward countercharges of plagiarism against Hardy
involving passages in *The Trumpet-Major* and *A Laodicean*. At one
point he tried to dissociate his name and his novel from the play, and in
after years he fostered the impression that the work was wholly Carr's.[3]

No evidence of the dramatization, except a few (mostly undated) letters

---

[1] At this same time Hardy was corresponding with Capt. Bernard-Derosne of Paris
about a possible French production of the play.

[2] Beside a reference to Fanny's having drowned herself Hardy wrote on the MS.,
'Why not died in workhouse, or hung herself in workhouse? I should much prefer keeping
as near the book as possible. T.H.'

[3] See *Men of the Time* (15th ed., London, 1899) and *Early Life*, p. 198.

of Carr's, survives among the Max Gate papers, and no copy of *The Mistress of the Farm* is known beyond the interleaved fragment incorporated in the MS. of *Far from the Madding Crowd* that Carr submitted to the Lord Chamberlain for licensing two days before the Liverpool performance.[1] Hardy's own MS. of *The Mistress of the Farm* and any copies of the printed text he had he must have destroyed. His only references to his share in the play remain his letters to *The Times* and the *Daily News* and, more explicitly, a personal letter to W. Moy Thomas, critic of the *Daily News*, in which he wrote, the day after the first performance of *The Squire*, 'Some time ago I was induced to dramatize [*Far from the Madding Crowd*], which I did alone and unassisted, under the title of "*The Mistress of the Farm*—A pastoral drama.*" Some time after this Mr Comyns Carr asked if I had ever thought of dramatizing the story, when I sent him the play as I had written it. He modified it in places, to suit modern stage carpentry &c, and offered it to the St. James's . . .'

1880: FELLOW-TOWNSMEN

FELLOW-TOWNSMEN / BY / THOMAS HARDY / AUTHOR OF "THE RETURN OF THE NATIVE" "FAR / FROM THE MADDING CROWD" ETC. / [*French rule*] / NEW YORK / HARPER & BROTHERS, PUBLISHERS / FRANKLIN SQUARE / 1880

Collation. [A]–F⁸; pp. 96; [1]–4 advertisement, Harper's Half-Hour Series (132 titles); [5] title-page; [6] blank; [7]–88 text; [89]–[96] advertisements of Harper publications.

Binding. Grey paper wrappers, printed in black and red; front wrapper verso and back wrapper recto and verso, Harper advertisements.

All edges cut; leaves measure $3\frac{1}{8}'' \times 4\frac{3}{4}''$.

Issued simultaneously in flexible green diagonal-fine-ribbed cloth, lettered in black and red.

Notes. This short story was first printed in the *New Quarterly Magazine*, April 1880; and, in America, in *Harper's Weekly* in 5 instalments, 17 April–15 May 1880. While it was still running in their magazine,

---

[1] This MS. is in several unidentified hands, but there are a number of additions and comments by Hardy, often in pencil and partially erased.

Harper & Brothers, using the same types, issued it in this separate edition, to forestall piracy. It was published at 20 cents (15 cents extra for flexible cloth) as No. 136 in Harper's Half-Hour Series at the end of April 1880. Within a fortnight it had been reprinted (together with 'A Strange Guest') in Munro's Seaside Library.

The story was collected in *Wessex Tales*, 1888 (see below, pp. 58 ff.), when the first part and the opening of the second were extensively rearranged and rewritten, with some alteration of incident.

The MS. of 'Fellow-Townsmen' is not known to have survived.

1880: THE TRUMPET-MAJOR (3 Vols.)

THE TRUMPET-MAJOR / *A TALE* / BY / THOMAS HARDY / IN THREE VOLUMES / VOL. I. [*II.*][*III.*] / LONDON / SMITH, ELDER, & CO., 15 WATERLOO PLACE / 1880 / [*All rights reserved*]

Collation. VOL. I. [A]⁴, B–T⁸, U⁴; pp. [ii]+vi+296; blank leaf; [i] half-title; [ii] blank; [iii] title-page; [iv] blank; [v]–vi Contents; [1]–295 text, printers' imprint at foot of p. 295: London: Printed by / Spottis-woode and Co., New-Street Square / and Parliament Street / ; [296] blank.

VOL. II. [A]⁴, B–S⁸, T²; pp. [ii]+vi+276; preliminary pages as in VOL. 1; [1]–276 text, printers' imprint (as in VOL. 1) at foot of p. 276.

VOL. III. [A]⁴, B–R⁸, S²; pp. [ii]+vi+260; preliminary pages as in VOL. 1; [1]–259 text, printers' imprint at foot of p. 259: *Spottiswoode & Co., Printers, New-street Square, London.* / ; [260] blank.

Binding. Red diagonal-fine-ribbed cloth; blocked in black on front with 3-panel design incorporating 2 vignettes, an encampment at top, a mill at bottom, lettered in black in centre panel: *The | Trumpet Major | By the Author of | "Far from the Madding Crowd"* / ; blocked in blind on back with 2-rule border; spine blocked in gold and black with standard, sword, and bugle, and lettered in blind and gold: The / Trumpet / Major / VOL. I. [*II.*][*III.*] / Smith · Elder & Cº / .[1]

[1] The imprint in some cases runs : Smith, Elder & Cº This variation may easily be due to two imprint dies in use simultaneously at the binder's or may be the mark of a second binding order (there were two before the end of 1880, 600 copies and 150 copies). The form I have preferred appears on the Max Gate copy and the copy in the Royal Library. No Smith, Elder file copies of any of Hardy's first editions survive at John Murray's.

Cream-white end-papers; top uncut, fore-edge and tail cut; leaves measure $4\frac{7}{8}'' \times 7\frac{3}{8}''$.

Hardy himself drew the 2 vignettes for the front cover.

Secondary Binding. Blocked in blind on back with 3-rule border; lettered on spine: Vol. I [*II*][*III*]; imprint at foot of spine: Smith, Elder & C$\underline{o}$ / ; conforms in all other respects to the description above.

There are several reasons for considering this a secondary binding. It is less common than the 2-rule binding, which appears on the British Museum, Cambridge, and Bodleian copies (accession dates '17 De 80', '10 Jan 81', 'Feb 1881' respectively) and two copies which one might assume to be early—the Max Gate copy (signed on each title-page 'E. L. Hardy' and 'Thomas Hardy') in which is inserted a letter from Smith, Elder, 27 October 1880, sending 6 copies of the novel, 'which is now ready for publication'; and the copy Hardy sent, without inscription, to Queen Victoria (now in the Royal Library, Windsor Castle), which was acknowledged by Sir Henry Ponsonby on 9 December 1880. Further, an identical situation prevails in the case of *The Return of the Native*, and Smith, Elder records show that 250 quires of *The Trumpet-Major* and 100 quires of *The Return of the Native* were remaindered to W. Glaisher, wholesale bookseller, in the same year, 1882. It seems reasonable to suggest that this is a secondary binding dating from that sale.

Serial Issue. The Trumpet-Major was first printed serially in *Good Words* from January to December 1880. The monthly instalments ran as follows: January, Chaps. 1–4; February, Chaps. 5–7; March, Chaps. 8–10; April, Chaps. 11–14; May, Chaps. 15–17; June, Chaps. 18–21; July, Chaps. 22–24; August, Chaps. 25–27; September, Chaps. 28–30; October, Chaps. 31–34; November, Chaps. 34(*cont.*)–37; December, Chaps. 38–41. Several chapters were retitled before the novel was published in book form, and a few scattered passages were deleted. When Sydney Smith was seeking reminiscences of the editor of *Good Words* in 1925 for his biography, *Donald Macleod of Glasgow*, Hardy wrote to him, 'If I remember my arrangements with him were carried on through Mr. Isbister the publisher, though I met Dr. Macleod whenever he came to London and discussed small literary points with him, all of which I have forgotten except two: that he asked me to make a lover's meeting, which I had fixed for a Sunday afternoon, take place on a Saturday, and that swear-words should be avoided—in both which requests I readily acquiesced, as I restored my own readings when the novel came out as a book.'

With the 12 instalments appeared 32 illustrations (5 of them full-page) by John Collier. Though they were not reproduced in book form, Hardy took considerable pains to ensure their accuracy and provided his illustrator, as he had in the past, with sketches. In thanking him for these, Collier wrote, 20 November 1879, 'They are just what I want the interior of the old kitchen being especially serviceable to me [see February instalment]—I shall very likely adopt your arrangement with only a little compression. I haven't heard anything from Isbister about making a sketch of the trumpet major to serve as an advertisement but I will make one anyhow as it will always serve to introduce into the text. From what source did you get the costume? Pollock's uncle appears to be unable to get us into the U[nited] S[ervice] Museum. If you like we could try to force an entrance for ourselves.'

The novel was also published serially in America (without illustrations) in *Demorest's Monthly Magazine* (New York) from January 1880 to January 1881. Henry Holt arranged the sale, after trying in several other quarters and after Hardy himself had offered the novel to the *Atlantic Monthly*. *Demorest's* paid $500 for the advance sheets, and the instalments exactly paralleled the instalments in *Good Words* until November when (at Hardy's request) the last two instalments were spread over three numbers, possibly to forestall the pirates. There was, however, a pirated serial publication in the *Fortnightly Review* (George Munro, New York) from January to [?] December 1880. This was a short-lived pirated reprint of the London *Fortnightly Review*, to which were added as they appeared the monthly instalments of *The Trumpet-Major*.

Manuscript. The MS. of *The Trumpet-Major* is written on 309 leaves measuring $6\frac{3}{8}'' \times 8''$. The leaves have been numbered 1–306 by Hardy, but there are 17 supplementary leaves and 14 others are missing (ff. 238–51, a portion of the October instalment, Chap. 33 and the first part of 34). Though used for *Good Words*, the MS. shows many cancellations and additions. One page in Chap. 28 (f. 209) is in Mrs. Hardy's hand. At the close of the drilling scene (Chap. 23), which

Hardy has been accused of plagiarizing, there is a footnote (possibly written at a later date) reading, 'partly from a contemporary account.'

The MS., bound in three-quarters plum morocco, was presented to King George V in October 1911 when Hardy, through Sydney Cockerell, was distributing his MSS. among various public collections. The volume bears the king's bookplate and is now in the Royal Library, Windsor Castle. In presenting it Hardy wrote to the Librarian, 14 October 1911, 'I may inform you that Queen Victoria was interested in the book when it came out thirty years or more ago, owing to its being concerned with the time of King George III at Weymouth and Her Majesty thanked me for a copy which I sent her for that reason. This is why the question of presenting the MS. has arisen, though I should never have ventured upon the step but for Mr. Cockerell's suggestion.'[1]

Notes on Composition and Publication. The *Trumpet-Major* was written at Upper Tooting, presumably in 1879–80, but we have little evidence as to when it was begun or finished. It was sketched for Leslie Stephen in February 1879, and there was talk of its appearance in the *Cornhill.*[2] There seems to have been some possibility, too, of *Macmillan's*, but by August of that year arrangements had been completed for its publication in *Good Words* and Collier had agreed to undertake the illustrations. From a letter of Hardy's to Isbister (the publisher of *Good Words*), 6 September 1879, it is apparent Chaps. 1–14 were then in proof and the MS. of Chaps. 15–21 would be ready within the week; and the first instalment appeared in January 1880. Smith, Elder agreed in July 1880 to publish a three-volume edition of the novel, paying the author £200. The pains Hardy took with the historical background of his work are evidenced by a note-book (Dorset County Museum) which he labelled, 'B.<u>sh</u> Museum. Notes taken for "Trumpet Major" & other books of time of Geo III. in (1878–1879–)', and into which he copied passages from contemporary newspapers, drawings of costumes, details from Gillray caricatures, &c.

The Trumpet-Major was published at 31*s*. 6*d*. in an edition of 1,000 copies on 26 October 1880.[3] Though the book was well received, it

---

[1] For a fuller description, with cancelled readings and facsimile pages, see W. G. Bebbington, *The Original Manuscript of Thomas Hardy's "The Trumpet-Major"* (Windsor, 1948).   [2] See *Early Life*, p. 167.

[3] From Smith, Elder records. The date of publication was consistently advertised as 23 October and is so given in *Early Life* (p. 187).

continued the steady decline in sales which marked Hardy's association with Smith, Elder, and in 1882 there were 250 quires and 33 copies in cloth to be remaindered.

Subsequent Editions (see also COLLECTED EDITIONS). *The Trumpet-Major* was never reprinted in its original three-volume form, and in 1881 it passed to Sampson Low. Hardy added a Preface in October 1895 (for Osgood, McIlvaine's edition of the Wessex Novels), which is important for its indication of his sources. The novel was published in America in December 1880 by Henry Holt & Co. in their Leisure Hour Series and by George Munro in his Seaside Library (the types of the *Fortnightly Review* serial issue repaged).[1]

1881: A LAODICEAN

[*in a headpiece*] HARPER'S FRANKLIN SQUARE / LIBRARY. / [*double rule*] / NUMBER 215. PUBLISHED BY HARPER & BROTHERS, NEW YORK. PRICE 20 CTS. / [*double rule*] / *Entered at the Post Office at New York, as Second-class Mail Matter.* / A LAODI-CEAN. / 𝔄 𝔑𝔬𝔟𝔢𝔩. / BY THOMAS HARDY, / AUTHOR OF "THE RETURN OF THE NATIVE," "FAR FROM THE MADDING CROWD," ETC. / BY ARRANGEMENT WITH HENRY HOLT & CO. / [*illustration*] / [*inner margin, printed vertically*] BOOKSELLERS SUPPLIED WITH TRIMMED OR UNTRIMMED COPIES AS THEY MAY INDICATE THEIR PREFERENCE.

Collation. [1]¹⁶, 2¹⁶, 3⁸; pp. [ii]+78; [i] title-page; [ii] Franklin Square Library advertisement; [1]–71 text, 3 columns to a page, with caption title (dated 25 November 1881) and illustration on [1] and advertisement on 71; [72]–[78] advertisements of Harper & Brothers' publications.

N.B. Sig. 3 is placed inside sig. 2 and these two sigs. inside sig. [1].

Illustrations. Two of Du Maurier's illustrations (for the March and July instalments) are reproduced as part of the title-page and caption title.

Binding. Issued unbound (title-page serving as wrapper), fastened with

---

[1] The Munro edition is dated 6 December but was not listed in the *Publishers' Weekly* until 18 December, while the Holt edition was listed 11 December.

2 staples; all edges uncut or trimmed (see note on title-page above); leaves (uncut) measure $8\frac{1}{2}'' \times 11\frac{3}{4}''$.

A LAODICEAN; / OR, / THE CASTLE OF THE DE STANCYS. / *A STORY OF TO-DAY.* / BY / THOMAS HARDY, / AUTHOR OF / "FAR FROM THE MADDING CROWD," "A PAIR OF BLUE EYES," ETC. / *IN THREE VOLUMES.* / VOL. I. [*II.*] [*III.*] / LONDON: / SAMPSON LOW, MARSTON, SEARLE & RIVINGTON, / CROWN BUILDINGS, 188, FLEET STREET. / 1881. / (*All rights reserved.*)

Collation. VOL. I. a^2, B–U^8, X^4; pp. [iv]+312; [i] half-title: A Laodicean; / or, [*wanting in some copies of VOL. I*^{1}] / The Castle of the De Stancys. / ; [ii] blank; [iii] title-page; [iv] printers' imprint: London: / Printed by William Clowes and Sons, Limited, / Stamford Street and Charing Cross. / ; [1]–312 text, printers' imprint at foot of p. 312: London: Printed by William Clowes and Sons, Limited, / Stamford Street and Charing Cross.

VOL. II. a^2, B–S^8, T^2; pp. [iv]+276; preliminary pages as in VOL. I; [1]–275 text, printers' imprint at foot of p. 275: London: Printed by William Clowes and Sons, Limited, / Stamford Street and Charing Cross. / ; [276] blank.

VOL. III. a^2, B–S^8; pp. [iv]+272; preliminary pages as in VOL. I; [1]–269 text, printers' imprint at foot of p. 269: London: Printed by William Clowes and Sons, Limited, / Stamford Street and Charing Cross. / ; [270]–[272] blank.

Sampson Low's 32-page catalogue, dated December 1881, is occasionally bound in at end, the blank leaf [271][272] being removed.

Binding. Slate-grey sand-grain cloth;[2] blocked in blind on front and back with 3-rule border and publishers' circular monogram in centre; gold-lettered on spine, with 3 bands blocked in blind at top and bottom:

[1] The dropping of this word can hardly be said to create an 'issue'. It only indicates a state of sig. *a*, and more probably a late than an early one.

[2] Hardy wrote to the publishers 5 October 1881, 'The binding I should like to be of some shade of green with no gilding except in the lettering.' The grey varies slightly in shade, and I have seen a single copy more accurately described as olive.

A / Laodicean / or / The Castle / of the / De Stancys / [*rule*] / *Hardy* /
Vol. I. [*II.*] [*III.*] / London / Sampson Low & C? /.

Cream-white end-papers; top uncut, fore-edge and tail cut; leaves
measure $4\frac{7}{8}'' \times 7\frac{3}{8}''$.

Binding Variant. Diagonal-fine-ribbed cloth; Vol. I. [*II.*] [*III.*] on spine
placed $\frac{1}{8}''$ higher; conforms in all other respects to the description
above.

The significance of this variant is uncertain, and it may possibly be
part of the original binding order. I have never seen it except in combination with volumes in sand-grain cloth, and W. Bone & Son's ticket
appears on both bindings. It is very much less common, however, than
the sand-grain cloth, which appears on 2 copies one might assume to
be early—the Max Gate copy (bearing Hardy's signature and his
wife's) and a copy Hardy gave the Dorset County Museum in 1889
(undoubtedly one of his 'author's copies'). The diagonal-fine-ribbed
cloth, on the other hand, appears on 1 or 2 volumes of the Cambridge, Bodleian, and British Museum copies, and these show sur-
prisingly late accession dates ('21 Dec 82', '10 Feb 83', '31 My 84'
respectively), though it must be noted the Cambridge and Bodleian
copies of Vol. III (representing both styles of binding) contain the
Sampson Low catalogue of December 1881. There was a remainder
sale to Mudie in February 1882, and this offers a possible explanation.

Serial Issue. *A Laodicean* was first printed serially in the European Edition
of *Harper's New Monthly Magazine* from December 1880 to December
1881. The monthly instalments ran as follows: December, Bk. I, Chaps.
1–4; January, Bk. I, Chaps. 4 (*cont.*)–8; February, Bk. I, Chaps. 9 [8
cont.]–13 [12]; March, Bk. I, Chap. 13 (*cont.*) [13]–Bk. II, Chap. 2;
April, Bk. II, Chaps. 3 [2 *cont.*]–7 [6]; May, Bk. II, Chap. 7 [6]
(*cont.*)–Bk. III, Chap. 3; June, Bk. III, Chaps. 4 [3 *cont.*]–7; July,
Bk. III, Chaps. 8–11; August, Bk. IV, Chaps. 1–5; September, Bk. V,
Chaps. 1–5; October, Bk. V, Chaps. 6–10; November, Bk. V, Chaps.
11–14; December, Bk. VI, Chaps. 1–5. As is apparent from this,
several chapters were redivided before the novel was published in book
form. Other additions and deletions are of little significance.[1]

---

[1] In advertisements of the first instalment the quotation, 'Thou art neither cold nor
hot: I would thou wert cold or hot', was added to the title, but quickly discarded. (See
Athenaeum, 27 November 1880.)

With each of the 13 instalments appeared an illustration (all save the first full-page) by George Du Maurier, who had illustrated *The Hand of Ethelberta*. There was an opportunity for closer collaboration with the artist in this case, however, and Hardy followed work, on the earlier illustrations at least, with some care. Du Maurier wrote to him, for example, 12 July 1880, 'I have adopted your composition of figures for No. 2 and should like you much to see it before the faces are put in; your sketch of furniture &c is most useful to me. . . . I have made two compositions (for No. II) of the luncheon party, from opposite points of view, still keeping to your distribution of the figures. I am particularly anxious that you should see them before selecting one for illustration.' The final illustration, on the beach at Etretat, pleased Hardy specially (he had spent some time there the year before), and Du Maurier gave him the original pen and ink drawing. On the back of its frame Hardy has written, 'From G. Du Maurier to Thomas Hardy March, 1882 (Scene—Etretat, Normandy—portraits of Mr Du Maurier and his dog Chang at right hand of picture.) Illustration to *"A Laodicean"* ' (Dorset County Museum).

The novel was also published serially in America in *Harper's* from January 1881 to January 1882. Though the European Edition of *Harper's* was largely the sheets of the American edition month by month in an English wrapper, the pages containing *A Laodicean* (and some editorial matter of English interest) were printed in England, because of copyright and the exigencies of composition and illustration. The instalments were then entirely reset in America for insertion a month later in the American edition of the magazine. The illustrations were frequently retitled, and one (Sir William De Stancy's funeral procession in the November issue) was not reproduced.

Manuscript. The MS. of *A Laodicean*, undoubtedly because of the peculiar circumstances of its composition, was burned by Hardy.

Harper's *Proof-sheets.* In default of any MS. of *A Laodicean*, the chance survival of proof-sheets of the novel is particularly interesting. These proof-sheets are for the serial publication in the European Edition of *Harper's Magazine*, as printed in London by William Clowes and Sons, Limited. They were preserved, with 16 brief notes and postcards from Hardy relating to them, by Richard Rogers Bowker, the London representative of Harper & Brothers 1880–2, who supervised the printing, and are now in the R. R. Bowker Collection in the Library of Congress.[1] Though all are described as '1st Proof', the first 4 instalments are in galley, the remaining 8 (Part VII is wanting) have been paged. With the exception of Parts I and XIII, they bear numerous corrections in Hardy's hand, in some cases considerable additions (e.g. the 'nobility of talent' passage in Chap. 14). From these dated proofs and the notes to Bowker, it is possible to trace Hardy's progress in the novel. Chaps. 1–4 were in type 3 September 1880, and Hardy wrote from Weymouth, 10 September, 'Parts II and III are nearly ready. They can be in your hands in 10 days—but if Mr. Du Maurier wants Part III immediately I can send a rough copy.' The MS. of Part III was sent 24 September, when Hardy wrote, 'Mr. D. M. has not been instructed for the 3^{d} as yet. Could not printed proof be sent him in time? it would be better than verbal directions or MS. There w^{d} be an advantage in his also having Parts 1 and 2 in print—so as to read the three consecutively.' Parts II and III, Chaps. 5–13, were in type 4 October. Part IV is dated 6 December. The MS. of Part V was promised by 3 January 1881, and the MS. of VI was sent off two days later. Subsequent proofs are dated as follows: Part V, 19 January; VI, 20 January; VII wanting; VIII, 22 March; IX, 9 June; X, 1 July; XI, n.d.; XII, 5 August; XIII, n.d.

Notes on Composition and Publication. A Laodicean was written at Upper Tooting, but we have little evidence as to how early in 1880 it was begun. By 16 April Hardy had opened negotiations with Harper & Brothers and agreed to supply them with a serial (at £100 an instalment) to inaugurate the European Edition of *Harper's New Monthly Magazine*, the first number of which was announced for December 1880, and by 28 July George Du Maurier had finished his illustrations for the first 2 instalments. From the evidence of the dated proof-sheets in the Library of Congress, it is clear that printing was commenced

---

[1] Bowker includes a sketch of Hardy and his work in his *London as a Literary Centre*, Second Paper: The Novelists (*Harper's Magazine*, June 1888, pp. 8–9). 'He is seldom guilty of the little oversights which most writers have now and then to confess ... Yet I recall catching once in proof a curious slip of the pen, by which Mr. Hardy, having brought one of his people to the very summit of a hill, incontinently started him *up* again. On bringing it to Mr. Hardy's attention he corrected it by a post-card of characteristic simplicity: "For 'up' read 'down'." '

in August and that the first 13 chapters (a bit more than 3 instalments) were in type before Hardy fell ill, 23 October. The novel was continued under the gravest handicaps, dictated to Mrs. Hardy from a sick-bed over a period of five months, and a rough draft in pencil completed 1 May 1881 (see *Early Life*, pp. 187–8). Sampson Low, Marston, Searle, & Rivington (who were the publishers of *Harper's* in London) agreed on 17 June to publish the novel in book form.

A Laodicean was first published in America by Harper & Brothers in their Franklin Square Library, 25 November 1881, anticipating the English edition by more than a week.[1] The text was the serial version (reset) as it had been appearing in *Harper's*, without Hardy's final revisions. The novel in its final form was published in England at 31s. 6d., in an edition presumably of 1,000 copies, the first week of December 1881. It was originally announced for 22 November, but its appearance was postponed—possibly because of Hardy's agreement with Harper & Brothers that 'publication of the story here in book-form [should] not be till within a fortnight of its completion in the magazine' and the chances of piracy in the difference of a month between the conclusion of the novel in the European and American editions of *Harper's*. It was not advertised as ready until the week of 4 December. By February 1882 it had been remaindered to Mudie.

Subsequent Editions (*see also* COLLECTED EDITIONS). *A Laodicean*, in America, was almost immediately pirated by George Munro in his Seaside Library and was also published in an authorized edition by Henry Holt & Co. in their Leisure Hour Series (with 8 of the original illustrations). The Munro edition was listed in the *Publishers' Weekly* 10 December, the Holt edition a week later.

Sampson Low never reprinted the novel in its original three-volume form but issued a New Edition (1 vol.) in 1882 and thereafter. Hardy wrote a Preface to the novel in January 1896 (for Osgood, McIlvaine's edition of the Wessex Novels) and added a Postscript in October 1912 for Macmillan's definitive Wessex Edition.

[1] The Franklin Square Library was a weekly publication, the date a part of the collation. The Library of Congress copies of *A Laodicean* were received 26 November 1881.

1882: TWO ON A TOWER (3 Vols.)

TWO ON A TOWER. / 𝔄 Romance. / BY / THOMAS HARDY, / AUTHOR OF "FAR FROM THE MADDING CROWD," / "THE TRUMPET MAJOR," ETC. / IN THREE VOLUMES. / VOL. I. [*II.*] [*III.*] / London: / SAMPSON LOW, MARSTON, SEARLE, & RIVINGTON, / CROWN BUILDINGS, 188, FLEET STREET. / 1882. / [*All rights reserved.*]

Collation. VOL. I. [A]², B–Q⁸, R⁴; pp. [iv]+248; [i] half-title; [ii] printers' imprint: London: / Printed by Gilbert and Rivington, Limited, / St. John's Square, E.C. / ; [iii] title-page; [iv] blank; [1]–246 text; [247] printers' imprint: London: / Printed by Gilbert and Rivington, Limited, / St. John's Square. / ; [248] blank.

VOL. II. [A]², B–Q⁸; pp. [iv]+240; [i] half-title; [ii] printers' imprint: London: / Printed by Gilbert and Rivington, Limited, / St. John's Square. / ; [iii] title-page; [iv] blank; [1]–240 text, printers' imprint at foot of p. 240: Printed by Gilbert & Rivington, Limited, St. John's Square.

VOL. III. [A]², B–P⁸; pp. [iv]+224; preliminary pages as in VOL. II; [1]–223 text; [224] printers' imprint: London: / Printed by Gilbert and Rivington, Limited, / St. John's Square.

Binding. Green diagonal-fine-ribbed cloth; blocked in blind on front and back with 3-rule border and publishers' monogram device in centre; gold-lettered on spine, with 3 bands blocked in blind at top and bottom: Two / on a / Tower / [*rule*] / T. Hardy. / Vol. I. [*II.*] [*III.*] / London. / Sampson Low & C.º /.

Pale yellow end-papers; top uncut, fore-edge and tail cut; leaves measure 4¾″×7⁵⁄₁₆″.

Serial Issue. Two on a Tower was first printed serially in America in the *Atlantic Monthly* (Boston) from May to December 1882. The 8 instalments, without illustrations, ran as follows: May, Chaps. 1–4; June, Chaps. 5–9; July, Chaps. 10–15; August, Chaps. 16–21; September, Chaps. 22–27; October, Chaps. 28–32; November, Chaps. 33–37; December, Chaps. 38–41. Such revision as the novel underwent before its appearance in book form was slight in extent.

The *Atlantic Monthly* was published simultaneously in London, the American sheets in an English wrapper.

Part Issue. Two on a Tower was issued in parts for the purpose of English copyright. When it came to final arrangements for the appearance of the novel in the *Atlantic Monthly*, Hardy wrote to Thomas Bailey Aldrich, 13 January 1882, 'The general opinion here is that the story will be pirated unless one or two numbers of it are nominally published in this country. Half a dozen copies will of course be enough to secure the copyright. I should think that, to save time, it would be better to *print* the first number here for such publication—than to send it over from America and attach a new titlepage, since the latter course will involve such early printing on your side—Mr. Trübner, to whom I have spoken on this copyright question, says that it would be very little trouble and expense to print half a dozen copies here of the first part of the story. This is a matter which Messrs Houghton Mifflin & Co. can settle best, by writing direct to him their instructions—but it is necessary that a part of the story should in some way or other be issued here a few days before the American date of same.'

Only 3 of these parts, registration copies of I, IV, and V in the British Museum, appear to have survived, but they were simply off-prints of the *Atlantic Monthly* instalments month by month, with new (and continuous) pagination, the omission of dates, copyright notices, signatures, &c., that would betray the magazine origin, and the addition of a special title-page:

TWO ON A TOWER. / BY / THOMAS HARDY, / AUTHOR OF "A PAIR OF BLUE EYES," "UNDER THE GREENWOOD TREE," / "FAR FROM THE MADDING CROWD," "THE RE-TURN OF / THE NATIVE," "THE LAODICEAN," / ETC., ETC. / LONDON: / TRÜBNER AND COMPANY, / 57 & 59 LUDGATE HILL, / 1882. / *All rights reserved.* [¹]

Collation. Part I. Pp. 22; [1] title-page; [2] blank; [3]–21 text; [22] blank. Chaps. 1–4 (May instalment); Brit. Mus. accession date '31 MA[RCH] 82'.

---

¹ Line divisions vary slightly in Parts IV and V : . . . / AUTHOR OF "A PAIR OF BLUE EYES," "UNDER THE GREENWOOD TREE," "FAR FROM THE / MAD-DING CROWD," "THE RETURN OF THE NATIVE," / "THE LAODICEAN," ETC., ETC. / . . .

Part IV. Pp. [ii]+20+[ii]; [i] title-page; [ii] blank; [59]–78 text; blank leaf. Chaps. 16–21 (August instalment); Brit. Mus. accession date '14 Jy 82'.

Part V. Pp. [ii]+20; [i] title-page; [ii] blank; [79]–98 text. Chaps. 22–27 (September instalment); Brit. Mus. accession date '28 Au 82'.

Binding. There are traces of a blue paper back or wrapper; all edges cut; leaves measure $6'' \times 9\frac{1}{4}''$.

Stamped on each title-page are the words PART and PRICE, and these have been filled in by hand (the first part was priced 2*s.*, the others 1*s.*). Trübner & Co. were the English publishers of the *Atlantic*, but I have no evidence these parts were advertised or actually sold. It is the more surprising, therefore, that Part I (clearly this part issue and not the May *Atlantic*) received a flattering review in the *Athenaeum*, 22 April 1882.

Manuscript. The MS. of *Two on a Tower* is written on 358 leaves, measuring $6\frac{3}{8}'' \times 7\frac{7}{8}''$ and numbered 1–357 by Hardy (with 1 supplementary leaf). Twenty-eight scattered pages are wholly or in part as copied in Mrs. Hardy's hand. Though used for the serial printing in the *Atlantic Monthly*, the MS. shows numerous additions and excisions and in the earlier pages such tentative names as 'Swithin Cleve' (for Swithin St. Cleeve)[1] and 'Camphill Speer' (for Rings-Hill Speer).

The MS. is bound in three-quarters green leather and was so preserved by Thomas Bailey Aldrich, the *Atlantic*'s editor. It remained with the Aldrich papers in Portsmouth until 1943 when they were given to Harvard University. The MS. is now in the Houghton Library at Harvard.[2]

In sending the second instalment of the novel, Hardy wrote to Aldrich, 8 March 1882, 'A duplicate will follow by the next mail, to guard against accidental loss.' This duplicate MS. is not known to have survived. It was undoubtedly a letter-press copy, the original MS. showing evidences that such a copy was made.

Notes on Composition and Publication. Two on a Tower was written at

---

[1] There was a seventeenth-century rector of Rampisham, Dorset, named Swithin Cleves—a fact Hardy could easily have known.

[2] Four pages (one in Mrs. Hardy's hand) are reproduced in facsimile in *Papers of the Bibliographical Society of America*, vol. 40, no. 1 (New York, 1946), pp. [2] ff.

'Llanherne', Wimborne. Thomas Bailey Aldrich, editor of the *Atlantic Monthly*, wrote to Hardy, 28 September 1881, to inquire about a serial for his magazine, 'to run through six or more numbers', but it was 13 January 1882 before Hardy had received from Henry Stevens, Houghton, Mifflin's confidential literary agent in London, the particulars of the *Atlantic*'s requirements and agreed to meet them. Meanwhile he had made on 26 November his amusing application to inspect the Royal Observatory at Greenwich, in search of details for his story (*Early Life*, p. 195), and in December was corresponding with W. C. Unwin about lens-grinding and telescope-making. Though we have little evidence as to the dates of composition, it is clear from letters to Aldrich that Chaps. 1–9 were finished and sent to Boston by 8 March 1882 (the first instalment was in type that month) and the concluding part had been sent by 19 September. Sampson Low agreed on 14 July to publish the novel in book form. Of his work on it Hardy wrote to Edmund Gosse, 21 January 1883, 'The truth is that, though the plan of the story was carefully thought out, the actual writing was lamentably hurried— having been produced month by month, and the MS. despatched to America, where it was printed without my seeing the proofs. It would have been rewritten for the book form if I had not played truant and gone off to Paris.'

Two on a Tower was published at 31*s*. 6*d*., in an edition of 1,000 copies, at the very end of October 1882. It seems to have been little advertised, and Hardy drew up an advertisement of his own which he sent his publishers, 27 November, describing the novel as 'Being the story of the unforeseen relations into which a lady and a youth many years her junior were drawn by studying the stars together; of her desperate situation through generosity to him; and of the reckless *coup d'audace* by which she effected her deliverance' (see *Athenaeum*, 2 December 1882). Nevertheless, as he admitted, 'the ephemeral printed reviews were not much in its favour.' 'I get most extraordinary criticisms of *Two on a Tower*,' he wrote to Edmund Gosse, 10 December.[1] 'Eminent critics write and tell me in private that it is the most original thing I have done—that the affair of the Bishop is a triumph in tragi-comedy, &c., &c. While other eminent critics (I wonder if they are the same)

---

[1] Hardy had sent Gosse a copy of the novel on 4 December, writing to him, 'You will perceive, if nobody else does, what I have aimed at—to make science, not the mere padding of a romance, but the actual vehicle of romance.'

print the most cutting rebukes you can conceive—show me (to my amazement) that I am quite an immoral person: till I conclude that we are never again to be allowed to laugh and say with Launce—"it is a wise father that knows his own child."' At least one of these rebukes (*St. James's Gazette*, 16 January 1883) Hardy answered (see below, pp. 296–7).

SECOND IMPRESSION REVISED (CALLED 'SECOND EDITION')

TWO ON A TOWER. / ... / VOL. I. [*II.*] [*III.*] / *SECOND EDI-TION.* / ... / 1883. / ...

Collation. VOL. I. As in first impression, save that printers' imprint, p. [ii], has been replaced by a list, within a rule, of four novels 'By the Same Author.'

VOL. II. As in first impression, save that printers' imprint, p. [ii], has been replaced by a list, within a rule, of four novels 'By the Same Author.' Sampson Low's 32-page catalogue, dated November 1882, is occasionally bound in at end.

VOL. III. As in first impression, save that printers' imprint, p. [ii], has been replaced by a list, within a rule, of four novels 'By the Same Author', and the colon in printers' imprint, p. [224], is wanting.

Binding. As in first impression. Where the publishers issued mixed sets, first and second impression, to clear their stock, a slight divergence of alignment in the blocking of the spine is apparent.

Binding Variant. Plum-coloured sand-grain cloth; blocked in blind on front and back with 2-rule border and publishers' monogram device in centre; gold-lettered on spine, with 3 bands blocked in blind at top and bottom: Two / on a / Tower / [*rule*] / T. Hardy. / *Vol. I.* [*II.*] [*III.*] / S. Low, Marston & Cº / London / .
Pale yellow end-papers; top uncut, fore-edge and tail trimmed; leaves measure $5'' \times 7\frac{1}{2}''$.

Notes on Revision and Publication. R. B. Marston of Sampson Low wrote to Hardy on 8 January 1883, 'I am pushing the book all I can but I cannot understand why it does not take hold. I *hope* we may get into a second edition. . . . I should have thought that the six or seven hundred copies sold and now being read would be advertising the work everywhere

amongst novel readers.' This 'Second Edition' must have been undertaken very shortly after, since the first one-volume edition appeared
in April. Though many misprints went unemended, Hardy was permitted several revisions—the enlarging of Swithin's bequest from
£400 to £600 and the correction of a curious slip in Viviette's title.
This last had been pointed out with considerable condescension by
reviewers in the *Athenaeum* and the *Saturday Review* (both 18 November 1882), the former remarking that 'it is quite certain that when
Lady X marries Bishop Y she does not become Lady Y', a kind of
criticism, suggesting unfamiliarity with social custom, that Hardy was
particularly sensitive to. In a letter to Gosse, 21 January 1883, he
wrote, perhaps with some ingenuity, 'The odd blunder about Viviette's
name arose from her having been originally called Lady Viviette Constantine, daughter of an earl, and wife of *Mr.* Constantine. But this of
course is no excuse.'

Since this second impression is distinguishable from the first, superficially
at least, only by the first signature of each volume and that signature
consists of but two leaves easily replaced, it seems worth while to indicate a few of the more significant textual alterations. In several cases
these necessitated the shifting of a number of lines.

	First impression	*Second impression revised*
VOL. I		
P. 24, l. 15	encrustod	encrusted
VOL. II		
Pp. 55, l. 9,		
59, l. 4	400*l.*	600*l.*
P. 75, l. 14	and may therefore be still called here	though she liked to think herself Mrs. St. Cleeve
VOL. III		
P. 17, l. 2	starlight	dark
64, l. 9	four hundred	six hundred [1]
112, l. 10		*adds* [*after* "The Cabin, Rings-Hill.] *July 7th.*
188, l. 5	Lady Helmsdale	the wife of the Bishop of Melchester
197, l. 1	Lady Helmsdale	Lady Constantine [2]

[1] See also pp. 65, l. 1; 69, l. 13; 82, l. 16; 90, ll. 4–5; 108, l. 3.
[2] See also pp. 198, l. 8; 203, ll. 18, 21; 211, l. 18.

Pp. 200, l. 8,
   201, l. 20 Lady Helmsdale   the Bishop's widow
P. 217, l. 6   revenge   revenges

Subsequent Editions (see also COLLECTED EDITIONS). *Two on a Tower* was
published in America early in December 1882 in Holt's Leisure Hour
Series, and pirated in Lovell's Library and Munro's Seaside Library.[1]
Tauchnitz was provided with a list of corrections (acknowledged
15 December 1882) for his edition (1883), and when Sampson Low
issued a one-volume edition in April 1883, Hardy revised the text
in many minor respects and added the quotation from Crashaw's
'Love's Horoscope' to the title-page. The quotation was suggested
by Gosse, to whom Hardy wrote, 21 January 1883, 'I remember
no more of Crashaw's Love's Horoscope than that I have seen it.
Crashaw's "Who e'er she be" is more familiar to me. I'll hunt up the
other, with a view to a motto for the next edition.' A Preface, dated
July 1895, was written for Osgood, McIlvaine's edition of the Wessex
Novels in that year, and slightly modified for Macmillan's definitive
Wessex Edition in 1912.

1883: THE ROMANTIC ADVENTURES OF A MILKMAID

[in a headpiece] HARPER'S FRANKLIN SQUARE / LIBRARY. /
[double rule] / NUMBER 322. PUBLISHED BY HARPER &
BROTHERS, NEW YORK. PRICE 10 CTS. / *[double rule]* / *Entered
at the Post-Office at New York as Second-class Mail Matter.* / THE RO-
MANTIC ADVENTURES / OF A MILKMAID. / 𝕬 𝕹𝖔𝖛𝖊𝖑. / BY
THOMAS HARDY, / AUTHOR OF "A LAODICEAN," "FAR
FROM THE MADDING CROWD," "THE RETURN OF THE
NATIVE." / *ILLUSTRATED.* / *[double rule]* / *[advertisement]* / *[inner
margin, printed vertically]* BOOKSELLERS SUPPLIED WITH
TRIMMED OR UNTRIMMED COPIES AS THEY MAY IN-
DICATE THEIR PREFERENCE.

Collation. Pp. 32; [1] title-page; [2] Franklin Square Library advertise-
    ment; [3]–23 text, 3 columns to a page, with caption title (dated
    29 June 1883) on [3] and advertisement on 23; [24]–[32] advertise-
    ments of Harper & Brothers' publications.

[1] The Holt and Munro editions are listed in the *Publishers' Weekly*, 9 December. The
Lovell's Library edition is not listed at all and may have been a bit earlier. It is dated
14 November, but such dates are hardly trustworthy.

Illustrations. Printed in the text, 4 full-page illustrations by C. S. Reinhart as they had appeared in the *Graphic* and (3 only) *Harper's Weekly*.

Binding. Issued unbound (title-page serving as wrapper), fastened with 2 staples; all edges uncut or trimmed (see note on title-page above); leaves (trimmed) measure 8¼″ × 11⅜″.

Serial Issue. 'The Romantic Adventures of a Milkmaid' was first published in the *Graphic*, Summer Number (pub. 25 June), 1883, with 4 full-page illustrations by C. S. Reinhart. It was also published in America in *Harper's Weekly*, in 7 weekly instalments, 23 June–4 August 1883, with 3 of Reinhart's 4 illustrations.

Manuscript. The MS. of 'The Romantic Adventures of a Milkmaid' is written on 116 leaves of ruled paper, measuring 6¼″ × 8″ and numbered 1–115 by Hardy, with 1 supplementary leaf. Four scattered pages are in Mrs. Hardy's hand. The MS., though used by the *Graphic*'s printers, shows signs of hasty composition. It is much altered, with cancelled passages, and was originally unparagraphed. It was Hardy's first thought to title the chapters, and I was called 'An early journey' and II 'The stranger'.

The MS. is bound in three-quarters blue leather and is now in the Pierpont Morgan Library. It was bought by Mr. Morgan directly from Hardy through Clarence McIlvaine in March 1912.

Notes on Composition and Publication. 'The Romantic Adventures of a Milkmaid' was written at 'Llanherne', Wimborne, in the winter of 1882–3. Nothing further is known of its composition, but Hardy wrote in his diary, 25 February 1883, 'Sent a short hastily written novel to the *Graphic* for Summer Number.' (*Early Life*, p. 205.) It was the first of many contributions to the *Graphic*. Simultaneous publication was arranged in America in *Harper's Weekly*, and Harper & Brothers, to protect themselves from an immediate pirating of the story, published it in their cheap Franklin Square Library 29 June 1883 before more than a single instalment (out of 7) had appeared in the *Weekly*. The types for the two printings, save a little resetting at one or two points, are identical. There was a second impression (called 'Second Edition'). The story was widely pirated, nevertheless, and more frequently and cheaply reprinted in America through many years than perhaps any other work of Hardy's. In 1883 alone it was published in George Munro's Seaside Library (and later in the Seaside Library Pocket Edition) and in Lovell's Library. Hardy was finally forced to collect it in *A Changed Man* in 1913 (see below, pp. 151 ff.), though earlier he had noted, 'This story was written only with a view to a fleeting life in a periodical, and having, moreover, been altered from its original shape, was not deemed worth reprinting.' A few slight verbal changes were made in it at that time, and the scene shifted to Lower Wessex, more to the west, Casterbridge and the Valley of the Swenn giving place to Exonbury and the Valley of the Exe, possibly to remove the story from the scene of *Tess*.

? 1884: THE DORSET FARM LABOURER

THE / DORSET FARM LABOURER / PAST AND PRESENT / BY / THOMAS HARDY. / DORSET AGRICULTURAL WORKERS' UNION, / DORCHESTER. / 1884

Collation. Pp. [iv]+24; [i] half-title: The / Dorset Farm Labourer / by / Thomas Hardy. / ; [ii] blank; [iii] title-page; [iv] blank; [1]–21 text; [22]–[24] blank.

Binding. Issued unbound (half-title serving as wrapper), fastened with one or two staples; all edges cut; leaves measure $4\frac{3}{4}'' \times 7\frac{3}{16}''$.

Copies. *A*, British Museum (wants 'wrapper', i.e. half-title and blank last leaf); *B*, Parrish-Princeton (wants 'wrapper'); *C*, Wilson (wants 'wrapper'); *D*, Adams; *E*, Yale (modern binding, wants 'wrapper' and last leaf of text—replaced by a crude type facsimile).

Notes. In the light of several facts, the authenticity of this pamphlet, where date and imprint are concerned, is open to serious question. These facts may be summarized as follows: (1) There was no copy of the pamphlet at Max Gate, and Hardy described the essay as 'not reprinted' and several times suggested it to the second Mrs. Hardy as something she might issue privately. (2) The pamphlet was unknown until 1931, when 3 copies (*A, B,* and *C*) were offered for sale by a Sussex bookseller. Since then another copy (*E*) has appeared in the same hands

(1939) and a fifth (*D*) in the possession of another Sussex bookseller (1937). This last copy was said to have come from the Frampton Court Sale of 1931. (Hardy, of course, knew the Sheridans and Frampton Court well.) The other copies were said to have been saved when the stock was destroyed in a fire at the printers' (a familiar canard). (3) Nothing is known of a 'Dorset Agricultural Workers' Union' in Dorchester in 1884. On the other hand, it should be pointed out that: (1) The several copies show slight typographical variants, characteristic of a large printing, and a variation in staple marks (one on some sheets, two on others) even within individual copies, suggesting they have been made up from a larger (and imperfect) stock (all copies save *D* are now sewn). Many leaves are foxed, soiled, or damp-stained. (2) A collation of the text with the original version in *Longman's Magazine* reveals several changes of word and phrase (not to mention the altered title), hardly likely in a forgery.[1] A tentative conclusion suggests that Hardy authorized the pamphlet, that it was printed but for some reason never circulated, that in later years he forgot the affair completely, and that in 1931 a cache of copies, mostly imperfect, was discovered, from which the copies here described were salvaged.

Notes on 'The Dorsetshire Labourer'. This essay, under the title 'The Dorsetshire Labourer', was first printed in *Longman's Magazine*, July 1883. Hardy never collected the essay, one reason undoubtedly being that he used it a few years later as a quarry for several passages in *Tess of the d'Urbervilles* (notably the Lady-Day moving, pp. 449–50, 458–60; see also p. 152). It was reprinted in *Life and Art* (New York, 1925), pp. 20–47.

There was a MS. of 'The Dorsetshire Labourer', written on 31 leaves and signed at the end, among the Max Gate papers in 1933. Its present whereabouts is unknown.

1886: THE MAYOR OF CASTERBRIDGE (2 Vols.)

THE / MAYOR OF CASTERBRIDGE: / *THE LIFE AND DEATH OF A* / *MAN OF CHARACTER.* / BY / THOMAS HARDY, / AUTHOR OF / "FAR FROM THE MADDING CROWD," "A

---

[1] Mr. John Carter has kindly examined the British Museum copy at my request and finds no resemblance to the forgeries with which he is familiar.

PAIR OF BLUE EYES," ETC. / *IN TWO VOLUMES.* / VOL. I. [*II.*] / LONDON: / SMITH, ELDER & CO., 15 WATERLOO PLACE. / 1886. / [*All rights reserved.*]

Collation. VOL. I. [A]², B–U⁸, X⁶; pp. [iv]+316; [i] half-title; [ii] printers' imprint: Ballantyne Press / Ballantyne, Hanson and Co., Edinburgh / Chandos street, London / ; [iii] title-page; [iv] blank; [1]–313 text, printers' imprint at foot of p. 313: Printed by Ballantyne, Hanson and Co. / London and Edinburgh / ; [314] blank; [315][316] advertisement of Smith, Elder & Co.'s Popular Library.

VOL. II. [A]², B–U⁸, X⁶; pp. [iv]+316; preliminary pages as in VOL. 1; [1]–312 text, printers' imprint at foot of p. 312: Printed by Ballantyne, Hanson and Co. / London and Edinburgh / ; [313]– [316] advertisements of Smith, Elder & Co.'s publications.

Binding. Smooth blue cloth; blocked in black on front with decorative bands and spray of flowers and lettered in black: The Mayor / of Casterbridge / *Thomas Hardy* / ; back plain; gold-lettered on spine, with decorative bands blocked in black at top and bottom: The Mayor / of / Casterbridge / [*rule*] / *T. Hardy* / Vol. I. [*II.*] / Smith Elder & Cᵒ / . Grey flowered end-papers; top uncut, fore-edge and tail cut; leaves measure 4⅞″×7⅜″.

Binding Variants. Single copies are known bound in red-brown (Cambridge) and bright green cloth (Bodleian), conforming in all other respects to the binding described above. Their accession dates are '18 Jun 86' and '26 Aug 86' respectively. The Cambridge copy wants the leaves of advertisements, and the grey flowered end-papers look to be of a slightly different pattern. These are undoubtedly binders' trial copies, used up on copyright libraries. (The British Museum copy, received '15 My 86', has been rebound.)

Another, presumably trial, binding appears on the Esher-Adams copy (with the blind stamp of W. H. Smith & Son's Library). The cloth is diagonal-fine-ribbed and grey-green, and though the blocking and lettering on front and spine have been laid out as in the binding described above the types and ornaments used are different. Grey flowered end-papers as above.

Serial Issue. The Mayor of Casterbridge was first printed serially in the

Graphic from 2 January to 15 May 1886. The weekly instalments ran as follows: 2 January, Chaps. 1–2; 9 January, Chaps. 3–5; 16 January, Chaps. 5(*cont.*)–7; 23 January, Chaps. 8–9; 30 January, Chaps. 10–12; 6 February, Chaps. 13–15; 13 February, Chaps. 15(*cont.*)–17; 20 February, Chaps. 18–19; 27 February, Chaps. 20–21; 6 March, Chaps. 22–23; 13 March, Chaps. 24–25; 20 March, Chaps. 26–27; 27 March, Chaps. 27(*cont.*)–29; 3 April, Chaps. 30–32; 10 April, Chaps. 33–34; 17 April, Chaps. 35–36; 24 April, Chaps. 37–38; 1 May, Chaps. 39–41; 8 May, Chaps. 41(*cont.*)–43; 15 May, Chaps. 44–45. The novel was considerably rewritten before its publication in book form, with significant alterations in plot and many deletions. Chaps. 12, 18, 34, 43, and 44 particularly show important revisions.[1] These revisions are not, as in the case of several subsequent novels, simply a return to an original unbowdlerized version.

With each of the 20 weekly instalments appeared an illustration by Robert Barnes. Six of the original drawings for these, formerly the property of Lord Leverhulme, and later in the Bliss collection, are now in the Dorset County Museum.

The novel also appeared serially in America in *Harper's Weekly* from 2 January to 15 May 1886. It was set from proofs of the *Graphic* and published simultaneously, though the instalments for 6 (and 13) March and 24 April (and 1 May) differed slightly in length. All the Barnes illustrations were reproduced save 3 (those of 17 April, 8 and 15 May).

Manuscript. The MS. of *The Mayor of Casterbridge*, not now complete, is written on 374 leaves of ruled paper measuring $6\frac{1}{2}'' \times 7\frac{7}{8}''$. The leaves have been numbered 1–479 by Hardy, but some are fragmentary (cancelled material having been cut away), 108 are wanting altogether, and there are 3 supplementary ones not reckoned in the foliation. The MS., with many deletions and additions, presents the text as it was printed in the *Graphic* and gives no indication of the final version. The original title of the novel (restored in the definitive edition) would appear to have been 'The Life and Death of the Mayor of Casterbridge'; Farfrae's name was originally Alan Stansbie, and Michael Henchard

---

1 There is some discussion of these revisions, confused by ignorance of MS. evidence and the chronology of texts, in Mary Ellen Chase, *Thomas Hardy from Serial to Novel* (Minneapolis, 1927), pp. 15–65.

is called Giles and then James throughout. On the last page Hardy has noted '(Written 1884–1885.)'.

The MS. is bound in three-quarters green morocco and, because of its local associations, was presented by Hardy to the Dorset County Museum at Dorchester in November 1911.

Notes on Composition and Publication. The Mayor of Casterbridge was written at Shire Hall Place, Dorchester. We have no evidence as to when the novel was commenced, but Hardy seems to have been at work on it as early as the spring of 1884 and the greater part was finished in that year. The last page was written 17 April 1885 after frequent interruptions (see *Early Life*, p. 223). Though the novel was not to begin publication in the *Graphic* until 2 January 1886, it was in type by 20 October when Arthur Locker the editor wrote to Hardy, 'I find that a complete set of proofs have already been sent to Harper by us, and they were also told that there was *an illustration* for *every three slips*— this appears to have been the instruction given to Barnes the artist, and will make twenty illustrations in all.' Smith, Elder agreed to publish the novel in book form, but apparently not without some misgivings, their reader, James Payn, 'having reported . . . that the lack of gentry among the characters made it uninteresting' (see *Early Life*, pp. 235–6). *The Mayor of Casterbridge* was published at 21*s.*, in an edition of 758 copies, on 10 May 1886. Though the novel was widely noticed, only 650 copies had been bound to December 1886, and in January of the following year Smith, Elder remaindered 108 quires and 37 copies in cloth to Sampson Low for £7. 7*s.* (publication passing to them at this time).

Subsequent Editions (*see also* COLLECTED EDITIONS). *The Mayor of Caster-bridge* was published in America by Henry Holt & Co. in their Leisure Hour Series and their Leisure Moment Series in late May 1886. For their edition Hardy supplied many but not all of his textual revisions. The novel was also widely pirated from the original serial version as it had been appearing in *Harper's Weekly*. Hardy added a Preface for Osgood, McIlvaine's edition of the Wessex Novels in February 1895, on which occasion he restored, 'at the instance of some good judges across the Atlantic, who strongly represented that the home edition suffered from the omission', the material excised from Chap. 44

in the original version.¹ The Preface was slightly rewritten in May 1912 for Macmillan's definitive Wessex Edition.

1887: THE WOODLANDERS (3 Vols.)

THE WOODLANDERS / BY / THOMAS HARDY / *IN THREE VOLUMES* / VOL. I. [*II.*] [*III.*] / 𝕷𝖔𝖓𝖉𝖔𝖓 / MACMILLAN AND CO. / AND NEW YORK / 1887 / *The Right of Translation and Repro-duction is Reserved.*

Collation. VOL. I. [A]², B–U⁸; pp. [iv]+304; [i] half-title; [ii] publishers' device; [iii] title-page; [iv] printers' imprint: Richard Clay and Sons, / London and Bungay. / ; [1]–302 text, printers' imprint at foot of p. 302: Richard Clay and Sons, London and Bungay. / ; [303][304] advertisements of Macmillan and Co.'s publications.

VOL. II. [A]², B–X⁸, Y⁴; pp. [iv]+328; preliminary pages as in VOL. 1; [1]–328 text, printers' imprint at foot of p. 328: Richard Clay and Sons, London and Bungay.

VOL. III. [A]², B–U⁸, X⁶; pp. [iv]+316; preliminary pages as in VOL. 1; [1]–316 text, printers' imprint at foot of p. 316: Richard Clay and Sons, London and Bungay.

Binding. Dark green buckram-grain cloth; blocked in black on front and blind on back with 2-rule border and inner frame with rounded corners; gold-lettered on spine, with decorative band blocked in black at top and bottom: The / Woodlanders / Thomas / Hardy / Vol. I [*II*][*III*] / [*publishers' circular device*] / Macmillan & Cᵒ̲ .

Dark brown end-papers; top uncut, fore-edge and tail trimmed; leaves measure 5″×7½″.²

Secondary Binding. Dark green pebbled cloth; blocked in black on front

---

¹ The copy Hardy used in preparing the text for this edition (Sampson Low's Half-Crown Ed., n.d.), later the property of his niece Lilian Gifford, is now in my possession. The revision also affected 'some shorter passages and names, omitted or altered for reasons which no longer exist, in the original printing of both English and American editions'. 'The Scotch language of Mr. Farfrae' has been corrected, sometimes with comment, in a different hand, which I take to be Sir George Douglas's, the 'professor of the tongue in question' whose 'critical overlooking' Hardy acknowledges in his Preface.

² The whole binding closely duplicates that used by Macmillan for Henry James's *The Bostonians* and *The Princess Casamassima* the previous year.

and blind on back with single-rule border and inner frame with square corners; gold-lettered on spine, with decorative band blocked in black at top and bottom: The / Woodlanders / Thomas / Hardy / Vol. I. [*Vol II.*] [*Vol. III.*] / [*publishers' circular device*] / Macmillan & C̲o̲ / . The leaf of advertisements in Vol. I, pp. [303][304], is wanting.

This is a close approximation to the original binding, though cheaper in detail.[1] It is never found on ex-library copies and is distinctly less common than the buckram-grain binding, which appears on Macmillan's file copy (with the binders' label of Burn & Co.), 2 Max Gate copies, one bearing Hardy's signature with those of his first and second wives (now in the possession of Mr. F. B. Adams, Jr.) and the other unopened (Dorset County Museum), 4 presentation copies, and the registration copies at the British Museum, Cambridge, and the Bodleian. There can be no doubt it is a secondary binding and is to be associated with Macmillan's sale of 170 copies (presumably including 140 in sheets, since only 860 copies of the 1,000 printed were bound up originally) at remainder rates. It is not, however, a binding of recent origin, as sometimes suggested. Hardy put his signature in a copy belonging to Edward Clodd on a visit to Aldeburgh, 'Whitsuntide. 1894.' (Brit. Mus. See *The Ashley Library*, vol. x, London, 1930, p. 121.)

There are no other distinctions of issue in *The Woodlanders*. Typographical variants, which have been carefully examined, show nothing beyond the common, and progressive, degeneration of the type-face through a single impression.

Serial Issue. *The Woodlanders* was first printed serially in *Macmillan's Magazine* from May 1886 to April 1887. The 12 instalments, without illustrations, ran as follows: May, Chaps. 1–4; June, Chaps. 5–8; July, Chaps. 9–13; August, Chaps. 14–18; September, Chaps. 19–22; October, Chaps. 23–25; November, Chaps. 26–29; December, Chaps. 30–33; January, Chaps. 34–37; February, Chaps. 38–40; March, Chaps. 41–43; April, Chaps. 44–48. There were several slight bowdlerizations by the magazine's editor, Mowbray Morris, in Chaps. 20 and 45. After the first of these he wrote to Hardy, 19 September 1886, 'A gentle hint on one small matter—the affair between Miss Damson and the Doctor. . . . I think, if you can contrive not to bring the fair Miss

[1] The two spines are reproduced side by side for comparison in Percy H. Muir, *Points 1874–1930* (London, 1931), facing p. 120.

Suke to too open shame, it would be as well. Let the human frailty be construed mild.' Such revision as the novel underwent before its appearance in book form was limited to scattered passages, particularly in the earlier chapters.

The novel was also published serially in America in *Harper's Bazar*, in weekly instalments from 15 May 1886 to 9 April 1887. Here in the case of Chap. 20, it might be noticed, the text was left untouched. An earlier offer of advance sheets to the *Atlantic Monthly* had been rejected.

Manuscript. The MS. of *The Woodlanders* is written on 498 leaves of ruled paper measuring $7'' \times 8\frac{7}{8}''$. The leaves have been numbered 1–491 by Hardy, but there are 7 scattered supplementary ones. One hundred and six leaves are wholly or in part as copied in the first Mrs. Hardy's hand. Though used by *Macmillan's Magazine*, the MS. shows many alterations, tentative passages, and even some unpublished paragraphs (including a church meeting between Mrs. Charmond and Fitzpiers in Chap. 30). The original title was 'Fitzpiers at Hintock', and there are traces in pencil of 'Book First The Woodlanders'. Giles Winterborne was called Ambrose through the first four chapters, and Edred Fitzpiers, Fitz Rayne at first and Edgar throughout (as also in the serial issue). Cancellations in foliation suggest that Chap. 8, at least in its present position, was an afterthought, inserted when the novel had reached Chap. 15.

The MS. is bound in full blue morocco and remained at Max Gate when Hardy's other MSS. were being distributed in 1911 among various public collections, perhaps because of the large proportion of pages which were not in Hardy's hand. On the death of Mrs. Hardy in 1937 it was deposited in the Dorset County Museum under the provisions of her will.

Notes on Composition and Publication. The Woodlanders, which Hardy sometimes singled out as the best and his own favourite among his novels, was written at Max Gate. A woodland story had been in his mind as early as 1874, but he put it aside for *The Hand of Ethelberta*. In the July of 1884 while he was still at work on *The Mayor of Casterbridge* he promised the Macmillans a story of twelve numbers for their magazine, but it seems to have been November of the following year before writing was actually begun. Under 17–19 November 1885 he wrote in his diary, 'Have gone back to my original plot for *The Woodlanders* after all. Am working from half-past ten A.M. to twelve P.M., to get my mind made up on the details.' (*Early Life*, p. 230.) Publication in *Macmillan's Magazine* was begun in May 1886, but Hardy did not finish the novel until February 1887 when he wrote in his diary, '*February* 4, 8.20 P.M. Finished *The Woodlanders*. Thought I should feel glad, but I do not particularly,—though relieved.' (*Early Life*, p. 243.) In March 1886 he had offered Macmillan the choice of two titles for the novel, 'The Woodlanders' and 'Fitzpiers at Hintock', and Frederick Macmillan and Mowbray Morris, the magazine's editor, promptly chose the former.

The Woodlanders was published at 31s. 6d. in an edition of 1,000 copies on 15 March 1887. Only 860 copies were bound up, and production may have been a little hurried. Frederick Macmillan wrote to Hardy on 24 February, 'I find that it will not be possible to get "The Wood-landers" printed and bound by March 11th and we have therefore arranged to publish on the 15th the date originally suggested by you. I have told Messrs. Harpers' agent.' By the end of June 170 copies had been sold off at remainder rates. The novel was, notwithstanding, a considerable success. Hardy inscribed copies (variously dated in the first months of publication) to Edmund Gosse (March), Swinburne (May), Sir Frederick Leighton (Midsummer), and the Earl of Lytton.

Subsequent Editions (*see also* COLLECTED EDITIONS). Macmillan did not reprint *The Woodlanders* in its original three-volume form but in September 1887 reissued it in one volume in two impressions of 2,000 copies each. Hardy wrote a Preface in September 1895 for Osgood, McIlvaine's edition of the Wessex Novels and added a postscript in April 1912 for Macmillan's definitive Wessex Edition.

The novel was first published in America by Harper & Brothers in their Franklin Square Library (dated 25 March 1887). This paper-bound publication was 'for self-defense' they wrote to Hardy, and it was followed immediately by a more substantial edition in half cloth and by George Munro's pirated Seaside Library pocket edition.

1888: WESSEX TALES (2 Vols.)

WESSEX TALES / 𝔖trange, 𝔏ively, and Commonplace / BY / THOMAS HARDY / AUTHOR OF 'THE WOODLANDERS,' ETC. / IN TWO VOLUMES / VOL. I [*II*] / 𝔏ondon / MACMILLAN AND CO. / AND NEW YORK / 1888 / *All rights reserved*

Collation. VOL. I. [A]⁴, B–Q⁸, R⁴; pp. [viii]+248; [i][ii] blank; [iii] half-title; [iv] publishers' device; [v] title-page; [vi] blank; [vii] Contents; [viii] blank; [1]–247 text ('The Three Strangers', 'The Withered Arm', 'Fellow-Townsmen'), printers' imprint at foot of p. 247: *Printed by* R. & R. Clark, *Edinburgh* / ; [248] blank.

VOL. II. [A]⁴, B–O⁸, P²; pp. [viii]+212; preliminary pages as in VOL. 1; [1]–212 text ('Interlopers at the Knap', 'The Distracted Preacher'), printers' imprint (as above) at foot of p. 212.

Two leaves of advertisements of Macmillan and Co.'s publications bound in at end.

Binding. Smooth dark green cloth; blocked in pale green on front and spine with bands at top and bottom, and on back with publishers' monogram device; gold-lettered on spine: Wessex / Tales / Thomas / Hardy / Vol. I [*II*] / Macmillan & C°. / .

Plain end-papers; top uncut, fore-edge and tail trimmed; leaves measure 4¾″×7⅛″. The Macmillan file copy has inserted the binders' label of Burn & Co.

Remainder Binding. Wessex Tales was remaindered, the 2 volumes bound as one, in dark olive cloth gold-lettered on front and spine: Wessex Tales / Thomas Hardy / .

Serial Issue. The 5 stories collected as *Wessex Tales* had all been published previously in serial form.

'The Three Strangers', *Longman's Magazine*, March 1883; and, in America, *Harper's Weekly*, 2 instalments, 3–10 March 1883. The story was reprinted in *Tales from Many Sources*, Vol. I, Dodd, Mead & Co., New York, 1885.

'The Withered Arm', *Blackwood's Edinburgh Magazine*, January 1888.

'Fellow-Townsmen', first printed in 1880. See above, pp. 30 f.

'Interlopers at the Knap', *The English Illustrated Magazine*, May 1884.

'The Distracted Preacher', as 'The Distracted Young Preacher' in the *New Quarterly Magazine*, April 1879; and, in America, *Harper's Weekly*, 5 instalments, 19 April–17 May 1879. The story was reprinted with 'Hester' by Beatrice May Butt to form No. 41 in Appletons' New Handy-Volume Series, New York, [2 September] 1879.

With the exception of 'Fellow-Townsmen' (q.v.), the stories were only slightly revised for their appearance in *Wessex Tales*.

Manuscript. There was no MS. of *Wessex Tales* as such. Of individual MSS. of the 5 stories, 'The Three Strangers' is the only one that is known to have survived. It is written on 33 leaves measuring $6\frac{1}{8}" \times 7\frac{7}{8}"$. There are numerous alterations and additions, but from compositors' marks it is clear this is the MS. used for the first printing of the story in *Longman's Magazine*.

The MS., with miscellaneous related material, is bound in full blue morocco and was given by Hardy to Sydney Cockerell 29 September 1911 in appreciation of his help in the distribution of Hardy's MSS. among various public collections.

Notes on Composition and Publication. We know almost nothing about the composition of these 5 tales, but it is safe to assume that each was published as soon as possible after it was written. This would suggest that 'The Distracted Preacher' and 'Fellow-Townsmen' were written at Upper Tooting in the interval between *The Return of the Native* and *The Trumpet-Major*; 'The Three Strangers' at Wimborne and 'Interlopers at the Knap' at Dorchester in the much greater interval between *Two on a Tower* and *The Mayor of Casterbridge*; and 'The Withered Arm' at Max Gate after the completion of *The Woodlanders*. The 5 tales cover roughly, therefore, a period of nine years, from the winter of 1878–9 to the end of 1887.

Wessex Tales was published at 12*s.* in an edition of 750 copies on 4 May 1888. Only 634 copies were bound up, however, and unbound sheets were later remaindered. Hardy presented copies, among others, to Browning (on his birthday, 7 May), Meredith, Mrs. Francis Jeune, and Frederic Harrison; the Max Gate copy with his wife's signature in each volume is now in the Dorset County Museum.

In America *Wessex Tales* was published by Harper & Brothers in their Franklin Square Library at the end of May 1888. A portrait of Hardy was included as frontispiece, for the first time in any of his books.

Macmillan reissued the collection in one volume in an edition of 1,500 copies in late February 1889.

Osgood, McIlvaine Edition (1896). The edition of *Wessex Tales* issued by Osgood, McIlvaine in 1896 is of particular importance. Hardy not only wrote a Preface (dated April 1896) as he had done for the other volumes of this edition of the Wessex Novels but to the 5 original stories he added a sixth, 'An Imaginative Woman', to which he gave first place. This story had been written in 1893 (it is so dated in *Wessex Tales* but may be largely earlier work—see *Later Years*, p. 26) and published in the *Pall Mall Magazine* for April 1894, with 7 illustrations by Arthur Jule Goodman.

The MS. of 'An Imaginative Woman' is written on 31 leaves measuring $8\frac{3}{16}'' \times 10\frac{1}{16}''$. It shows a good deal of verbal alteration, especially in the first third, and the title has been altered from 'A Woman of Imagination'. The MS., still in its brown-paper cover with title in blue pencil, is bound in three-quarters brown morocco and was presented to the Aberdeen University Library in 1911 when Hardy was distributing his MSS. among various public collections. Aberdeen had given him the honorary degree of LL.D. in 1905.

Subsequent Editions (see also COLLECTED EDITIONS). In Macmillan's definitive Wessex Edition in 1912 'An Imaginative Woman' was removed to *Life's Little Ironies*, 'as being more nearly its place, turning as it does upon a trick of Nature, so to speak,' and 'A Tradition of Eighteen Hundred and Four' and 'The Melancholy Hussar' were transferred from that volume to *Wessex Tales*, 'where they more naturally belong.' For this edition Hardy revised and extended his original Preface in May 1912 and added a note to 'The Distracted Preacher', suggesting a less conventional ending. He further extended the Preface, with a note on 'A Tradition of Eighteen Hundred and Four', in June 1919 for the Mellstock Edition.

1890: SOME ROMANO-BRITISH RELICS

[*ornament*] / 𝕾𝖔𝖒𝖊 𝕽𝖔𝖒𝖆𝖓𝖔=𝕭𝖗𝖎𝖙𝖎𝖘𝖍 𝕽𝖊𝖑𝖎𝖈𝖘 / 𝕱𝖔𝖚𝖓𝖉 𝖆𝖙 𝕸𝖆𝖝 𝕲𝖆𝖙𝖊, 𝕯𝖔𝖗𝖈𝖍𝖊𝖘𝖙𝖊𝖗. / (*Read at the Dorchester Meeting, 1884; omitted from* / *the Volume of that date*). / BY / MR. THOMAS HARDY. / [*rule*] / [From "Proceedings" Dorset Natural History and Antiquarian / Field Club, Vol. xi., p. 78, 1890.] / [*ornament*] / DORCHESTER: / "Dorset County Chronicle" Printing Works. / [*rule*] / 1890

Collation. Pp. 4; [1]–4 text, caption title on p. [1].

Binding. Stapled in grey paper wrappers; front printed as above. All edges cut; leaves measure $5\frac{7}{16}'' \times 8\frac{7}{16}''$.

Notes. This paper is an account of Romano-British urns and skeletons discovered in digging the foundations of Hardy's new house, Max Gate, in the autumn of 1883 (see *Early Life*, pp. 212–13). It was read by Hardy himself at the Dorchester meeting of the Dorset Natural History and Antiquarian Field Club, 13 May 1884, and printed in the *Dorset County Chronicle* (Dorchester), 15 May, p. 5 (there was an off-print of this among the Max Gate papers in 1933). For some reason the paper, though reported, was not printed in the *Proceedings* of the Club for 1884. It was, however, printed in *Proceedings of the Dorset Natural History and Antiquarian Field Club*, Dorchester, 1890 [January 1891], pp. [78]–81. This pamphlet is an off-print of the *Proceedings*, with new pagination. It is probable that 25 copies were prepared for the author—the current custom of the Club. Over a dozen remained at Max Gate after Hardy's death. The paper was never collected.

1891: A GROUP OF NOBLE DAMES

A GROUP OF / NOBLE DAMES / *BY* / *THOMAS HARDY* / *THAT IS TO SAY* / THE FIRST COUNTESS OF WESSEX / BARBARA OF THE HOUSE OF GREBE / THE MARCHIONESS OF STONEHENGE / LADY MOTTISFONT THE LADY ICENWAY / SQUIRE PETRICK'S LADY / ANNA, LADY BAXBY THE LADY PENELOPE / THE DUCHESS OF HAMPTONSHIRE / AND / THE HONOURABLE LAURA / '. . . Store of Ladies, whose bright eyes / Rain influence.'—L'Allegro. / [*Osgood, McIlvaine & Co.'s decorative device*]

Collation. [A]⁴, B–S⁸; pp. [viii]+272; [i][ii] blank; [iii] half-title; [iv] blank save for words: All Rights / Reserved / ; [v] title-page; [vi] publishers' imprint: James R. Osgood, / McIlvaine, and Co., / 45 / Albemarle Street, / London. / 1891. / ; [vii][viii] Contents; [1]–271 text, printers' imprint at foot of p. 271: *Printed by* R. & R. Clark, *Edinburgh.* / ; [272] blank.

A blank leaf may be bound in at end.

Binding. Smooth whity-brown flecked cloth; front blocked in gold with 6 panels, one filled with 3 conventionalized flowers, back plain; spine blocked in gold with bands and ornaments and lettered in brown: *A / Group / of / Noble / Dames / by / Thomas / Hardy / Osgood, / McIlvaine & Cº. / .*

Plain or yellow end-papers; top uncut, fore-edge and tail trimmed; leaves measure 5″×7½″.

Secondary Binding. Whity-brown diagonal-fine-ribbed cloth, strongly flecked with brown; blocked and lettered exactly as above but in brown throughout.

This has every appearance of being a secondary binding—the cloth is coarse and cheaper in quality, and the blocking operations have been reduced from two to one by the elimination of gold. All Osgood, McIlvaine records have been destroyed, and Hardy himself retained no copy of the book, but three very early presentation copies (with inscriptions dated May and June) and the British Museum, Bodleian, and Cambridge copies (with comparatively late accession dates, however—'9 OC 91', '2 Feb. 92', and '4 Feb 92' respectively) all have the gold-blocked binding.

Serial Issue. The 10 stories collected as *A Group of Noble Dames* had all been published previously in serial form.

'The First Countess of Wessex', *Harper's New Monthly Magazine*, December 1889, with headpiece[1] and 3 illustrations by Alfred Par-

---

[1] The original pen-and-ink drawing for this, a view of the Earl of Ilchester's Melbury House ('King's-Hintock Court'), used to hang in the drawing-room at Max Gate and is now in the Dorset County Museum. Hardy and Parsons had visited the scene together in January 1889.

sons and 4 illustrations by C. S. Reinhart. The last quarter of the story was considerably rewritten before its publication in book form, with fundamental alterations of plot. This may easily represent a return to an original unbowdlerized version, but evidence is wanting.

'Barbara of the House of Grebe'

'The Marchioness of Stonehenge'

'Lady Mottisfont'

'The Lady Icenway'

'Squire Petrick's Lady'

'Anna, Lady Baxby', as *A Group of Noble Dames*: I. Barbara (Daughter of Sir John Grebe), II. The Lady Caroline (Afterwards Marchioness of Stonehenge), III. Anna, Lady Baxby, IV. The Lady Icenway, V. Squire Petrick's Lady, VI. Lady Mottisfont, in the *Graphic*, Christmas Number (pub. 1 December) 1890 (with a French edition, *Noël*); and, in America, *Harper's Weekly*, 4 instalments, 29 November–20 December 1890. All six of these stories were bowdlerized and altered in plot and detail, several (III, V, VI) to a remarkable extent, for their appearance in the *Graphic*. The publication in *Harper's Weekly* is of particular significance because here the stories were printed as originally written and as they were to appear in book form.

The frame used on this occasion, 'Preliminary' and connecting links, was necessarily rewritten when the six tales were rearranged and the group enlarged for book publication.

'The Lady Penelope', *Longman's Magazine*, January 1890.

'The Duchess of Hamptonshire', as 'The Impulsive Lady of Croome Castle' in *Light*,[1] 6 and 13 April 1878; and, in America, *Harper's Weekly*, 11 and 18 May 1878; again, as 'Emmeline; or Passion versus Principle' in the *Independent* (New York), 7 February 1884. The three versions that make up the curious career of this story, as published in 1878, 1884, and finally 1891, are essentially the same save for generous deletions and amplifications. The version of 1884

---

[1] *Light: A Journal of Criticism and Belles Lettres* (London) was a short-lived weekly founded by Robert Buchanan. Fiction was printed in an independent *feuilleton*, 'Belles Lettres', and these were collected and reissued monthly as *Light Magazine*. Hardy's story appeared in the first two numbers, simultaneously with the opening instalments of Trollope's 'The Lady of Launay'. The British Museum has the only file I know of.

is much the longest (and may be the earliest), as the version of 1878 is the shortest.

'The Honourable Laura', as 'Benighted Travellers' in the *Bolton Weekly Journal* (*Christmas Leaves* supplement), 17 December 1881; and, in America, *Harper's Weekly*, 10 and 17 December 1881. The story was sold to Tillotson & Son for their syndicated fiction business (see Appendix, pp. 340 f.) and was widely printed, especially in provincial papers. Even after Hardy had collected it, it appeared under its original title in the *Sphere*, in 2 instalments, 2 and 9 May 1903, with 2 illustrations by Bernard Partridge (see below, p. 308). Beyond changes of names the story was hardly altered at all for *A Group of Noble Dames*.

Manuscript. The MS. of 7 of the stories in *A Group of Noble Dames* was given to the Library of Congress in October 1911, when Hardy, through Sydney Cockerell, was distributing his MSS. among various public collections. It consists of 152 leaves, measuring $8'' \times 10\frac{1}{4}''$ and bound by the Library of Congress in three-quarters leather. Five leaves are wholly or in part in Mrs. Hardy's hand. On a rough paper cover, bound in, Hardy described it in blue pencil as 'A Group of Noble Dames (3 missing) Original MS.' and on the first page of text he wrote, 'To these seven stories three others previously printed were also added —to make up the set of ten in the published volume.' But the MS. is in reality two independent MSS.—the set of 6 tales written for the *Graphic* and 'The Lady Penelope' as printed in *Longman's Magazine*, the 7 arranged to conform to their order in the final collection. To these Hardy has added 2 leaves containing a draft of the title-page and table of contents for the volume of 1891. The MS. as foliated and re-arranged by Hardy runs as follows: 1–2, title-page and table of contents for the volume of 1891; 1–73, 'Preliminary', 'Barbara', and 'The Lady Caroline'; 115–36, 'Lady Mottisfont'; 85–114, 'The Lady Icenway' and 'Squire Petrick's Lady'; 75–83, 'Anna, Lady Baxby'; 1–14, 'The Lady Penelope'; 137–8, conclusion. (The missing leaves 74 and 84 contained links cancelled and rewritten when the stories were collected.) The MS. is dated on the last leaf 'April, 1890'—a date which refers to the *Graphic* portion only.

The MS. shows numerous alterations and additions but (though printers' MS.) few of the bowdlerizations forced on Hardy by the *Graphic's* editor. In 'Squire Petrick's Lady', however, frequent passages have been blue pencilled, and on f. 108 Hardy has written, '[N.B. The above lines were deleted against author's wish, by compulsion of Mrs. Grundy: as were all other passages marked blue.]'. Similar references to 'the tyranny of Mrs. Grundy' appear on ff. 109^v and 110^v. Several alterations in proper names are of some interest in view of the origin of the tales: Barbara was changed for a time to Mabella, then back to Barbara, and Yewsholt was originally Wood Park; the Marchioness of Stonehenge was originally the Marchioness of Athelney, and St. Michael in Bath City was originally St. Fridwell's in Exonbridge City and then Shastonbury. Each of the tales in the *Graphic* MS. was independently foliated by Hardy, and this reveals that 6 pages at the beginning of 'The Lady Icenway' were reduced to a single page after the story was finished.

The MS. of 'The First Countess of Wessex', written on 50 quarto leaves and signed by Hardy, was sold in New York by the Anderson Auction Company 29 May 1906 (Lot 319). Its present whereabouts is not known.

The MS. of 'Emmeline; or Passion versus Principle' (the 1884 version of 'The Duchess of Hamptonshire') is written on 25 leaves of ruled paper measuring 6⅜"× 8". Though printers' MS., it is cleaner than was common with Hardy at this time and there are comparatively few alterations, suggesting it was largely copied from an earlier draft. The sub-title seems to have been an afterthought; at the end has been added, 'Shire-Hall Place, Dorchester, England'. The MS., inlaid and bound in full red morocco, is now in the Pierpont Morgan Library (acquired in 1909).

Notes on Composition and Publication. The nucleus of *A Group of Noble Dames*, the 6 stories which appeared serially under that title, was commissioned by the *Graphic* as a 'short novel' in April 1889 for one of its forthcoming special numbers. Hardy was at work on *Tess of the d'Urbervilles* at the time, however, and it was the end of the year before he could turn to *A Group of Noble Dames*, and the MS. was not sent off until 9 May 1890. The stories reveal in many pages the exhaustion that followed the finishing of the novel. They gave immediate offence to the Directors of the *Graphic*, and Arthur Locker, the editor, wrote Hardy a letter of severe criticism on 25 June, concluding, 'Now, what do you propose to do? Will you write us an entirely fresh story, or will you take the "Noble Dames" and alter them to suit our taste; which means slightly chastening 1, 2, 3, and 4 (Old Surgeon, Rural Dean, Colonel, Churchwarden); and substituting others for 5 and 6 (Maltster, Sentimental Member)?' Hardy entered in his diary, 'Called on Arthur Locker at the *Graphic* office in answer to his letter. He says he does not object to the stories but the Directors do. Here's a pretty job! Must smooth down these Directors somehow I suppose.'[1] He subsequently undertook the drastic bowdlerization referred to above, and the stories were printed in the special Christmas Number of the *Graphic*, published 1 December 1890. When, at the beginning of January 1891, Hardy undertook to arrange *A Group of Noble Dames* for publication in book form, he enlarged the scheme to include two stories written not long before, 'The First Countess of Wessex' and 'The Lady Penelope', which presumably date from 1888–9 (Hardy was discussing possible illustrators for the former in December 1888), and two written many years earlier. 'The Duchess of Hamptonshire' as 'The Impulsive Lady of Croome Castle' dates from the early months of 1878, when Hardy was working on *The Return of the Native* at Sturminster Newton, and 'The Honourable Laura' as 'Benighted Travellers', from a time immediately preceding work on *Two on a Tower* at Wimborne, in the autumn of 1881. The whole collection spans a period of some thirteen years, from 1878 to 1891.

Offering Harper's the American serial rights to the original *Group of Noble Dames*, 7 March 1890, Hardy described it as 'a Tale of Tales— a series of linked stories—of a somewhat different kind from the mass of my work of late, excepting The First Countess of Wessex, which comes near it in character. The scenes, which are numerous, will be laid in the old mansions and castles hereabouts: the characters are to be proportionately numerous, and to be exclusively persons of title of the last century (names disguised, but incidents approximating to fact).' The curious student can easily trace the germ of at least half the stories, as finally collected, in the pedigrees and notes in one of Hardy's favourite books, Hutchins's *History of Dorset*.[2] 'The first Countess of

---

[1] *Early Life*, p. 297. The date 'June 23' would seem to be an error.

[2] John Hutchins, *The History and Antiquities of the County of Dorset*. References are to the 3rd ed., 4 vols., London, 1861–73, a copy of which was in Hardy's library. See, in this connexion, Hardy's Preface to *A Group of Noble Dames*.

Wessex' was Elizabeth Horner, wife of the first Earl of Ilchester (see Hutchins, ii, pp. 663, 667, and 679; see also *Friends of a Lifetime*, p. 282); 'Barbara of the House of Grebe', Barbara Webb, wife of the fifth Earl of Shaftesbury (iii, pp. 298 and 594); 'Squire Petrick's lady', the wife of Peter Walter of Stalbridge House (iii, p. 671); 'Anna, Lady Baxby', Anne, Lady Digby of Sherborne Castle (iv, pp. 269 and 473); and 'the Lady Penelope', the Lady Penelope Darcy, who married in turn Sir George Trenchard, Sir John Gage, and Sir William Hervey (iii, pp. 326 and 329).

A Group of Noble Dames was published at 6s. in an edition of 2,000 copies on 30 May 1891. Hardy inscribed copies (variously dated in the first weeks of publication) to Edward Clodd (May), Sir George Douglas (2 June), Theodore Watts (June), and Edmund Gosse. With this book Hardy commenced almost a decade of association with Osgood, McIlvaine & Co., the London representatives of Harper & Brothers.

Subsequent Editions (*see also* COLLECTED EDITIONS). *A Group of Noble Dames* was published in America by Harper & Brothers early in June 1891. This edition reproduced the headpiece and 6 of the 7 illustrations by Alfred Parsons and C. S. Reinhart for 'The First Countess of Wessex' as they had appeared in *Harper's* a year and a half before. Hardy added a Preface in June 1896 for Osgood, McIlvaine's edition of the Wessex Novels, and in 1912 the book was reprinted in Macmillan's definitive Wessex Edition.

1891: TESS OF THE D'URBERVILLES (3 Vols.)

TESS / OF THE D'URBERVILLES / *A PURE WOMAN* / *FAITH-FULLY PRESENTED BY* / *THOMAS HARDY* / *IN THREE VOLUMES* / *VOL. I* [*II*] [*III*] / '. . . Poor wounded name! My bosom as a bed / Shall lodge thee.'—W. Shakespeare. / [*Osgood, McIlvaine &* *Co.'s decorative device*] / *ALL RIGHTS* / *RESERVED*

Collation. VOL. I. [A]⁴, B–R⁸, S⁴; pp. [viii]+264; [i] half-title; [ii] blank; [iii] title-page; [iv] publishers' imprint: James R. Osgood, / McIlvaine and Co., / 45 / Albemarle Street / London, / 1891 / ; [v] Explanatory Note, dated November, 1891; [vi] blank; [vii] Contents; [viii] blank;

1–[264] text, printers' imprint at foot of p. [264]: *Printed by* R. & R. Clark, *Edinburgh*.

VOL. II. [A]⁴, B–S⁸, T⁴; pp. [viii]+280; [i] half-title; [ii] blank; [iii] title-page; [iv] publishers' imprint as in VOL. 1; [v] Contents; [vi] blank; [vii] divisional title; [viii] blank; 1–[278] text, printers' imprint at foot of p. [278]: *Printed by* R. & R. Clark, *Edinburgh.* / ; [279][280] blank.

VOL. III. [A]⁴, B–S⁸, T⁴; pp. [viii]+280; [i] [ii] blank; [iii] half-title; [iv] blank; [v] title-page; [vi] publishers' imprint as in VOL. 1; [vii] Contents; [viii] blank; 1–[277] text; [278] printers' imprint: *Printed by* R. & R. Clark, *Edinburgh* /; [279][280] blank.

Binding. Smooth tan cloth; blocked in gold on front with conventionalized design of honeysuckle blossoms on two stems running from top to bottom; back plain; gold-lettered on spine: *Tess* / *of* / *the* / *D'Urber·* / *·villes* / [*flower*] / *Thomas* / *Hardy* / *Vol. 1* [2] [3] / *James R.* / *Osgood* / *McIlvaine* / *& Co* / .[1]

Plain end-papers; top uncut, fore-edge and tail trimmed; leaves measure $4\frac{7}{8}'' \times 7\frac{1}{2}''$.

Binding Variant. A peculiar variant has been marked in the blocking on the front cover. In some copies the gold disk in the upper left corner is slightly smaller and the stem at the base of the upper of the two flowers does not widen out but has a small, quite separate, dot on either side. These copies are extremely uncommon and represent, perhaps, a trial form of the blocking.[2]

Serial Issue. Tess of the d'Urbervilles was first printed serially in the *Graphic* from 4 July to 26 December 1891. The weekly instalments (omitted 11 July and 7 November) ran as follows (chapter numbers differing, partly because of omissions, from the book form—here indicated in brackets): 4 July, Chaps. 1–3; 18 July, Chaps. 3(*cont.*)–6[5]; 25 July, Chaps. 6[5](*cont.*)–8[7]; 1 August, Chaps. 9[8]–11[12]; 8 August, Chaps. 12[13]–14[16]; 15 August, Chaps. 15[17]–16[18]; 22 August,

---

[1] I have seen a single copy (Lowell-Harvard) with '*James R.*' wanting. It had, however, been recased, and if the binding is not a freak it may belong to one of the later impressions.

[2] The two forms of the flower are reproduced side by side in A. Edward Newton, *This Book-Collecting Game* (Boston, 1928), p. 231. In the account of the variation (p. 232) the two forms have been reversed, in error, but there is of course no question of 'first edition' and 'second edition' involved.

Chaps. 17[19]–18[20]; 29 August, Chaps. 19[21]–21[23]; 5 September, Chaps. 22[24]–23[25]; 12 September, Chaps. 24[25 *cont.*]–25[26]; 19 September, Chaps. 26[27]–27[28]; 26 September, Chaps. 28[29]–30[31]; 3 October, Chaps. 31[31 *cont.*]–33; 10 October, Chaps. 33(*cont.*)–35; 17 October, Chaps. 35(*cont.*)–37; 24 October, Chaps. 37(*cont.*)–39; 31 October, Chaps. 40–41; 14 November, Chaps. 42–44; 21 November, Chaps. 45–46; 28 November, Chaps. 47–48; 5 December, Chaps. 49–50; 12 December, Chaps. 51–52; 19 December, Chaps. 53–56; 26 December, Chaps. 57–59.

Two episodes, 'more especially addressed to adult readers' as Hardy described them, proved unacceptable to the editor of the *Graphic* and were first printed elsewhere. In each case new material was added to meet the demands of an independent sketch and indications of the real origin of the episode, particularly the name 'Tess', removed. Chaps. 10 and 11, the seduction of Tess by Alec d'Urberville, were printed under the title 'Saturday Night in Arcady' in a Special Literary Supplement of the *National Observer* (Edinburgh), 14 November 1891; Chap. 14, the baptism and death of Tess's baby, was printed under the title 'The Midnight Baptism, A Study in Christianity' in the *Fortnightly Review*, May 1891 (two months, it will be noticed, before serial publication of the novel began).

This temporary dismemberment of the novel necessitated changes in plot, such as the introduction of a mock marriage and the omission of the encounter with the painter of texts (in Chap. 12), and there were numerous scattered bowdlerizations and omissions. When the novel was published in book form the original text was, of course, restored, and Hardy was able 'to piece the trunk and limbs of the novel together, and print it complete, as originally written . . .' though with further revisions in detail.[1]

With each of the 24 weekly instalments appeared an illustration (there were 2 with the instalment of 10 October) by Hubert von Herkomer, R.A., or one of his pupils, Daniel A. Wehrschmidt, E. Borough Johnson, or J. Syddall—a procedure which introduced a curious diversity of interpretation. Herkomer's own illustrations, 6 in number, appeared with the instalments of 4 July, 29 August, 3 and 17 October, 5 and 19

---

[1] There is a full discussion of the text (ignoring MS. evidence, however) in Mary Ellen Chase, *Thomas Hardy from Serial to Novel* (Minneapolis, 1927), pp. 69–112.

December. The original drawings for the first two of these, Tess's return from the dance and Tess in the dry-mead at Talbothays, Herkomer gave Hardy at Christmas 1891. They used to hang in the drawing-room and the study at Max Gate and are now in the Dorset County Museum. Five of the original drawings by Johnson, formerly in the Bliss collection, are also in the Dorset County Museum.

The novel also appeared serially in America in *Harper's Bazar* from 18 July to 26 December 1891. The text is the text of the *Graphic*, though the latter half of the novel shows a number of slight refinements and alterations that did not appear in England until book publication. In the case of the transference of Tess's visit to the tombs of the d'Urbervilles at Kingsbere from Chap. 14 of the serial to Chap. 52 of the book, *Harper's Bazar* presents the episode in *both* chapters. The bowdlerizations of the *Graphic* version are retained throughout, except for Angel's use of a wheelbarrow in carrying the dairymaids over the flooded lane (in Chap. 21)—suggesting this was a last-minute demand of the *Graphic*'s editor (see *Early Life*, p. 315). Only 11 of the 25 illustrations were reproduced. 'The Midnight Baptism' was reprinted from the *Fortnightly Review* in the *Eclectic Magazine* (New York), June 1891.

There was a second serial publication of *Tess* in *John o' London's Weekly*, 24 October 1925 to 10 July 1926, and Hardy described the novel in an introductory note as 'now published serially for the first time complete in all its details as primarily written, a fragment of a chapter here embodied having been discovered but a short while ago' (i.e. the first *serial* publication of the definitive text of 1912—see below).

Manuscript. The MS. of *Tess of the d'Urbervilles* is written on 525 leaves measuring $8\frac{1}{8}'' \times 10\frac{1}{8}''$. The leaves have been numbered 1–565 by Hardy, but 39 (scattered through the first 180) are missing and 1 is incomplete. The MS., though marked for the printer, shows much evidence of alteration, several systems of foliation (suggesting rearrangements of material) and many cancellations.[1] On f. 104 Hardy has written 'Note.—Alterations in blue are adaptations for serial issue only', but such alterations are relatively infrequent (many of them were re-

---

[1] One of the most interesting of these, a paragraph opening the last chapter, has been published in W. R. Rutland, *Thomas Hardy: A Study of his Writings and their Background* (Oxford, 1938), p. 226.

Hardy's draft of the title-page of *Tess of the d'Urbervilles*, 1891

tained in the first edition) and the larger bowdlerizations do not appear in the MS. at all, though pencilled offers of modification are still legible at several points. A projected title for the novel was 'A Daughter of the D'Urbervilles'; the name Durbeyfield was originally Woodrow and then Troublefield, Alec d'Urberville was originally Hawnferne, and Tess's name was successively Love, Cis, Sue, and Rose-Mary. The episode of the d'Urberville portraits does not appear in Chap. 34.

The MS. is bound in three-quarters red morocco and was presented (together with *The Dynasts*) to the British Museum in 1911 when Hardy, through Sydney Cockerell, was distributing his MSS. among various public collections. A portion of the last page is reproduced in facsimile in *Early Life*, facing p. 312.

The MS. of the 'Explanatory Note' prepared for the first edition (where it is dated 'November, 1891') is now in the Bliss collection. Headed 'Prefatory note', it is written on the first page of a folio measuring $5\frac{1}{8}'' \times 8\frac{1}{8}''$, and the numerous cancellations and variants of phrase reveal a considerable softening of tone.[1]

Hardy's draft of the title-page, 'To supersede copy previously sent', incorporating the controversial sub-title and the quotation from *The Two Gentlemen of Verona*, is in the Dorset County Museum. Of the sub-title Hardy wrote at the end of his prefaces to *Tess* (March 1912), 'it was appended at the last moment, after reading the final proofs, as being the estimate left in a candid mind of the heroine's character—an estimate that nobody would be likely to dispute. It was disputed more than anything else in the book. *Melius fuerat non scribere.*'

A fragment only of the MS. of 'Saturday Night in Arcady' (the serial version of Chaps. 10 and 11) has survived. It is written on paper measuring $8\frac{1}{4}'' \times 10\frac{1}{4}''$ and shows numerous alterations. The first 8 leaves (4 in Mrs. Hardy's hand) are in the Bliss collection; f. 10 (in Mrs. Hardy's hand) is inserted in Vol. I of a copy of the first edition of the novel presented to Lady Jeune, now in the Berg Collection.

Notes on Composition and Publication. Tess of the d'Urbervilles was written at Max Gate and seems to have been started as early as the autumn of 1888. It was designed from the first for Tillotson & Son of Bolton and their newspaper syndicate, for which Hardy had already provided three

---

[1] Reproduced in facsimile in the McCutcheon Sale Catalogue (New York, American Art Association, 20–21 April 1925).

short stories.[1] From letters of February 1889 it is apparent the novel was well under way and that serial publication was to begin before the end of the year, under the title 'Too Late Beloved' (or 'Too Late, Beloved!').[2] On 23 August 1889 Hardy sent Tillotson's 'a list of some scenes from the story, that your artist may choose which he prefers', and promised an instalment of the MS. would be sent shortly, and on 9 September he forwarded 'a portion of the MS. of "Too Late Beloved"—equal to about one-half, I think. . . . The remainder to follow as per agreement.' This MS., which included the daring and controversial seduction and midnight baptism scenes, was at once given to the printers, and it was not until proofs were in their hands that Tillotson's realized the nature of the story they had agreed to publish, no prospectus of a forthcoming work being required in their contracts. They were distinctly taken aback. W. F. Tillotson had been a leading Congregationalist and Sunday School worker and held strong views as to the tone of all material in his own papers and the family newspapers that were his clients. Though he had died six months before this time, his firm and particularly his colleague and editor, William Brimelow, faithfully reflected his policies. They at once suggested that the story should be recast and certain scenes and incidents deleted entirely. Hardy would not agree to this, and after a further exchange Tillotson's announced that they could not issue the story although they would pay for it as arranged. On this Hardy suggested that their agreement should be cancelled, and so the matter was settled, with no ill feeling on either side.[3] Tillotson's wrote to him on 25 September that they had returned 'whole of proofs and copy to the point we had in type, being up to Chapter 16 [Book I, as printed in the *Graphic*, or Phase the First and Phase the Second], and now send the remaining manuscript which our printers have not seen. No one beyond ourselves has seen a single line of the story, and we will at once cease our offers of the same. We had already prepared three illustrations for the assistance of our clients, but as these will now be of no use to us, we send them with the manuscript.

[1] See Appendix, pp. 340 f.

[2] This original title is echoed in Tess's desperate words to Angel Clare at Sandbourne, towards the close of Chap. 55.

[3] For much of this information I am indebted to Mr. John Nayler, personal secretary to W. F. Tillotson and long an employee of the firm. Trollope records in his *Autobiography* a strikingly similar experience in the case of *Rachel Ray* and the editor of *Good Words*, Dr. Norman Macleod.

We shall be glad to hear that they are likely to be of service. We will duly advise our American subscriber, in order that you may make your own terms with him when you are ready, if necessary ... We shall be glad to have at your earliest convenience the cancelled agreement relating to the story "Too late, Beloved!" ' No fragment of this first printing of *Tess* with its three illustrations is known to have survived. The whole business must have been distasteful to Hardy, especially in view of his continuing difficulties with the novel, and in the *Early Life* there is no mention of *Tess* before August 1889, when 'Hardy settled down daily to writing the new story he had conceived, which was *Tess of the d'Urbervilles*, though it had not as yet been christened.'[1] The novel, not yet finished, was offered to *Murray's Magazine* in October but refused by Edward Arnold on 15 November, 'virtually on the score of its improper explicitness.' It was next offered to *Macmillan's Magazine*, but Mowbray Morris likewise rejected it ten days later. Hardy then undertook 'with cynical amusement' the dismemberment and modification of the text which made it acceptable to Arthur Locker and the *Graphic* (see *Early Life*, pp. 290–1). Statements in the *Early Life* are conflicting,[2] and it is not clear whether the bowdlerizations were dictated by Locker or were designed to forestall his protests. Hardy had some experience of the *Graphic*'s severe editorial demands in the case of the MS. of *A Group of Noble Dames* in the June of 1890. If *Tess* had not yet been accepted for publication (and it does not seem to have been), that episode would have been instructive. This work was not completed until the latter part of 1890, and it was 4 July 1891 before serial publication commenced, though Hardy had accepted Harper's terms for the serial publication of *Tess* in America as far back as 7 March 1890.

Tess of the d'Urbervilles was published at 31*s.* 6*d.* in an edition of 1,000 copies some time in the week of 29 November 1891. 'The reviews have made me shy of presenting copies of *Tess*,' Hardy later wrote in his diary,[3] but he inscribed copies to his good friend Lady Jeune and to

---

[1] In his sole reference to the affair, in his letter 'A Question of Priority' (see below, p. 304), he wrote, perhaps a little disingenuously, that he had asked to be allowed to withdraw the MS. 'for reasons that had nothing to do with the subject of the story'.

[2] Cf. pp. 291 and 315 ('Henley's *Scots Observer*' is, of course, a slip for the *Fortnightly Review*).

[3] *Later Years*, p. 6. To Gosse he wrote, 20 January 1892, 'As the story was rather a venture into sincerity, I decided not to present you, and some other friends, with a copy, to leave you quite independent. But I shall send the one vol. ed^n when it is published.'

William Morris (both dated December 1891) and to Alfred Austin, adding in the latter case a quotation from 'A Dialogue at Fiesole': '. . . Wrestlers born, Who challenge iron Circumstance—and fail.'[1]

SECOND IMPRESSION REVISED

TESS / OF THE D'URBERVILLES / [. . . *as in first impression*]

Collation. VOL. I. As in first impression, save for date '1892' in publishers' imprint, p. [iv], and final period wanting in printers' imprint at foot of p. [264].[2]

VOL. II. As in first impression, save for date '1892' in publishers' imprint, p. [iv].

VOL. III. As in first impression, save for date '1892' in publishers' imprint, p. [vi], page number present, p. 277, and final period in printers' imprint, p. [278].

Binding. As in first impression.

Notes on Revision and Publication. Hardy wrote to Edmund Gosse 20 January 1892 to thank him for a generous letter about *Tess* and added, 'The same post brings one from the publishers, from which I find that since Saturday the orders have been in larger numbers: so that the review[3] has done no harm. They are reprinting frantically, but unfortunately they will have to keep people waiting a few days I fear.' The publishers advertised on 30 January, 'The large Edition of Thomas Hardy's New Novel, Tess of the D'Urbervilles, having been exhausted, a Second Edition is in rapid preparation, and will be ready immediately', and this second impression of 500 copies was published shortly after (the British Museum copy bears the accession date '8 Fe 92'). Though the printers' records describe the impression as involving 'extensive alterations', these alterations are of little significance, being almost wholly the correction of slips in spelling and typography. One such slip, the misprint 'road' for 'load' (III, p. 198), had been attacked by the *Saturday*

---

[1] From Austin's volume *Love's Widowhood*, which he had sent Hardy two years before with the flattering inscription, 'To the Author of "The Woodlanders" and other Prose Georgics of Our Time, in which are combined with rare felicity, a just observation that never fails, and a romantic imagination that never flags.'

[2] This appears to have dropped out before the first impression was completed.

[3] *The Saturday Review*, 16 January 1892: '. . . Mr. Hardy, it must be conceded, tells an unpleasant story in a very unpleasant way.'

Review with the comment 'Mr. Hardy would do well to look to his grammar', and Hardy referred to it repeatedly in his correspondence[1] and wrote in the Max Gate copy (Dorset County Museum), Vol. III, 'First edition 1891. (misprint on p. 198)', correcting the error with the note '(This misprint is the mark of the first edition)'—and also altering 'piteously' (III, p. 275) to 'pitilessly'. Beyond this the revisions were typographical, particularly in Vol. III, where a good deal of type was pied and had to be reset.

Since, superficially, the first and subsequent impressions of *Tess* are distinguishable only by the dates '1891' and '1892' on the verso of the title-page and there has been a good deal of sophistication of copies, it seems worth while to indicate a few of the revisions.[2]

	First impression	*Second impression revised*
VOL. I		
P. [v], l. 12	have it said	have said
45, ll. 14–15	her skin is / as sumple	her skin is as / sumple
VOL. II		
P. 58, l. 4	Valasquez	Velasquez
155, l. 21	seampstress	sempstress
199	XXV	XXXV
234, l. 14	it's husband's	its husband's
VOL. III		
P. 14, ll. 19–24 (line endings)	towards / but / On / al- / hitherto / a /	folly / they / that / always / been; / true /
112, l. 24	are ye doing	are you doing

[1] He wrote to Edward Clodd, 20 January 1892, 'To think that *you*, of all people, can't see that "road" in the sentence beginning "The Durbeyfield waggon", is a misprint for "load". I read the proofs twice, and yet that "r" slipped in without my perceiving it—in order to afford that mean paper the S.R. an opportunity of attack. You will be surprised to hear (if you have not seen the review) that they alter my preface, omit the second title of the book, which is absolutely necessary to show its meaning, and indulge in innuendoes of indecent intentions on my part, which never entered my mind. Strangely enough however, the review has quickened the sale—I suppose the *animus* was too apparent.' The *Saturday Review* also took exception to the phrase 'to have it said what everybody thinks and feels', in the 'Explanatory Note', and this was quietly altered. Hardy felt the *Saturday Review* attack so keenly that he considered resigning from the Savile Club to avoid encountering the magazine's reviewers.

[2] I have seen at least one copy (Parrish-Princeton) dated '1891' which is apparently unsophisticated but includes some signatures in their revised state [specifically, I D (see p. 45), II Q (see p. 234), III B (see p. 14), and s (see p. 270)]. I do not think this indicates partial revision in the course of the first impression, but simply a clearing of 1891 sheets at the time of the second impression.

P. 160, ll. 6–12 (line endings)	than / deviations / domes- ticity, / vale / curve. / light / was /	Angel; / the / no / moun- /He / from / of /
198, l. 23	summit of the road	summit of the load
252, ll. 1–4 (line endings)	and / foul / bear / And /	he / name; / it. / then /
270, ll. 1–2	sisters-in-law	sister-laws
275, l. 9	piteously	pitilessly

In this form there was a third impression of 500 copies, advertised 20 February 1892 as 'now ready at all Libraries and Booksellers'.' The books of R. & R. Clark, Ltd., record no further printings of the novel in three volumes, but a single advertisement of a 'Fourth Edition' appeared in the *Athenaeum*, 19 March, and this (with the fact that the first one-volume edition was called the 'Fifth Edition') would suggest perhaps two binding orders for the third impression.

American Edition. Tess of the d'Urbervilles was published in America by Harper & Brothers at the end of January 1892. The text was the serial version as it had appeared in *Harper's Bazar*, and the volume contained the same 11 illustrations used on that occasion. In May, Harper's issued a 'New and Revised Edition', expanding the text from 421 to 455 pages, and published the following explanation: 'In view of certain incorrect statements respecting the American edition of Mr. Hardy's "Tess of the D'Urbervilles," the publishers thereof desire to explain that the story was originally published serially in the *Graphic*, of London, and *Harper's Bazar*, of New York, having been revised by the author for such publication, and that while thus appearing serially, it was set up and printed in book form by the American publishers. Afterwards Mr. Hardy made many changes in the story, and these appeared in the English edition in book form, but not in the first issue of the American edition, which had been already printed for reasons connected with the copyright. The new American edition, now on the market, has been thoroughly revised by Mr. Hardy, and is considerably expanded, according to the latest English edition.'[1] The last statement was not wholly true; the major excisions had been restored, but in details the text remained unchanged.[2]

---

[1] *Publishers' Weekly*, 21 May 1892. See also Hardy's letter to the *Critic*, 10 September 1892 (below, p. 301).

[2] There are 62 chapters instead of 59, since 3 remain divided as in the serial, and the

Subsequent Editions (see also COLLECTED EDITIONS). The first one-volume
edition of *Tess*, called the 'Fifth Edition', uniform with *A Group of
Noble Dames* and containing a portrait of Hardy as frontispiece, was
published at 6*s.* in an edition of 5,000 copies, 30 September 1892. In
this form there were five impressions totalling 17,000 copies before the
end of the year. For this edition Hardy prepared an important Preface
dated July 1892, and he inscribed copies of the book to many friends,
including Charles Whibley, Clarence McIlvaine, Grant Allen (in gratitude for his review), Walter Besant, Austin Dobson, Edmund Gosse,
Roden Noel, and Sir George Douglas.

The novel was further revised for Osgood, McIlvaine's edition of the
Wessex Novels and an additional Preface, dated January 1895, prepared.[1] For Macmillan's definitive Wessex Edition Hardy added a note
to his previous Prefaces in March 1912, calling attention in particular
to the fact that a few pages in Chap. 10, overlooked 'when the detached
episodes were collected as stated in the preface of 1891, . . . though
they were in the original manuscript', were now printed in the novel
for the first time. These pages (76–79) contain the episode of the dance
at the hay-trusser's as it had appeared in 'Saturday Night in Arcady'.
Tess being the first volume in this definitive edition, it contains also a
'General Preface to the Novels and Poems', an essay of primary importance dated October 1911. In 1926 Hardy consented to sign an
edition of 325 copies on large paper (printed from the plates of the
Wessex Edition) with 41 wood engravings by Vivien Gribble.

Dramatization. Some time in 1894–5 Hardy made a dramatization of *Tess
of the d'Urbervilles*, in 5 acts 'in the old English manner'. In July
1895 he was discussing with Mrs. Patrick Campbell a possible production for the coming season, but their plans were finally abandoned,
apparently because of the character of the play (see *Later Years*, pp.
32–33). The decision was not unaffected, however, by the reception of
Jude the Obscure at the end of the year. The dramatization was then
sent to Harper & Brothers, and Hardy wrote, 9 February 1896, that he
wished them to act as his agents in arranging an American production.

---

famous last paragraph still opens (as in the serial), ' "Justice" was done, and Time, the
Archsatirist, had had his joke out with Tess.'

[1] The copy used for this revision, labelled on the cover by Hardy 'Corrected for new
edition' and with the MS. of the Preface inserted, is now in the Bliss collection.

Reasonable modifications and adaptations were to be permitted, and on these terms an agreement with Harrison Grey Fiske was signed 3 July 1896. Lorimer Stoddard undertook the necessary revisions (making virtually a new dramatization), and the play, under his name and with Mrs. Fiske as Tess, was produced at the Fifth Avenue Theatre, New York, 2 March 1897, with great success. There was a reading of the play for copyright purposes the same day at the St. James's Theatre, London. In 1924 Hardy himself revised his dramatization for amateur performance by the Hardy Players at Dorchester, and this was followed by professional productions in London in 1925 and again in 1929 (see Appendix, pp. 351 ff., and *Later Years*, pp. 240, 242–4). The texts of these dramatizations are printed in Marguerite Roberts, *Tess in the Theatre* (Toronto, 1950).

Several typescripts of Hardy's play with corrections and additions in his hand survive, in the Dorset County Museum (2) and in the possession of Harper & Brothers and Mr. Frederick B. Adams, Jr. In at least one case the typescript bears the words 'Not to be Printed'. When Macmillan & Co. inquired about possible publication, Hardy wrote, 29 November 1924: 'Owing to the fact that the play is made up more largely from the novel than in many adaptations for the stage—containing pages of the story almost word for word—I feel its publication might injure the novel by being read as a short cut.'

1893: THE THREE WAYFARERS

BOOK OF THE WORDS / [*rule*] / THE THREE WAYFARERS / *A Pastoral Play in One Act* / BY / THOMAS HARDY / NEW YORK / HARPER AND BROTHERS / 1893

Collation. Pp. 32; [1] title-page; [2] copyright notice; [3] Characters, &c.; [4] blank; [5]–30 text; [31][32] blank.

Binding. Sewn, in grey paper wrappers; front printed in black as title-page. All edges cut; leaves measure $3\frac{11}{16}'' \times 5\frac{1}{4}''$.

Copies. Of the half-dozen copies to which this first printing of *The Three Wayfarers* seems to have been limited, five are recorded. Hardy had two copies and in 1918 he inscribed one (now in the Dorset County Museum) to his wife and the other to Sydney Cockerell, 'as you have the MS. of the story', he wrote 28 February. 'About half a dozen copies were printed in New York in 1893 for copyright purposes merely, and the one I enclose is probably the only one in existence except a similar copy my wife has.' In each case Hardy made a note on production and publication to accompany the copy. Two copies were deposited in the Library of Congress to complete copyright (only one is now available), and there is a fifth (formerly the McCutcheon–Wilson copy) in the possession of Mr. Frederick B. Adams, Jr.

Notes on Composition and Publication. The Three Wayfarers is a dramatization of Hardy's short story, 'The Three Strangers' (first published in *Longman's Magazine*, March 1883, and collected in *Wessex Tales* in 1888). It was undertaken at the suggestion of J. M. Barrie, who wrote to Hardy, 19 April 1893, for a companion-piece to a play of his own and one of Conan Doyle's. Hardy was in London for the season and replied (from 70 Hamilton Terrace, N.W. [21 April]), 'I used to think I w^d arrange that little story for the stage: and began doing it—but I do not know what became of my sketch. However the work w^d not be difficult—and I am willing to attempt it again. How many words should it make? About the length of one ordinary act I presume.' The play was produced by Charles Charrington, the actor-manager, at Terry's Theatre, 3 June 1893, as part of a quintuple bill which included *Foreign Policy* by Conan Doyle, *Bud and Blossom* by Lady Colin Campbell, *An Interlude* by Mrs. W. K. Clifford and W. H. Pollock, and *Becky Sharp*, 'a scene from Thackeray arranged by J. M. Barrie'. *The Three Wayfarers* was described by *The Times* as 'unquestionably the best piece of the evening', being 'received . . . with genuine favour', and Hardy thought very well of Charrington's performance as the Hangman, but the production as a whole was no success and lasted only a week.[1]

Hardy had no intention of publishing *The Three Wayfarers*, but for purposes of copyright Harper & Brothers printed this 'Book of the Words' in an edition of some six copies. It was copyrighted in Hardy's name 22 May 1893, and two copies were deposited on 3 June, the date

---

[1] See *Later Years*, p. 20. The play was subsequently produced by the Stage Society (with Stevenson and Henley's *Macaire*), 4 November 1900; by the Dorchester Debating and Dramatic Society (with a dramatization of 'The Distracted Preacher') at Dorchester, 15–16 November (London, 27 November, Weymouth, 15 December) 1911 (see Appendix, pp. 351 ff.); and at the Little Theatre (with Chesterton's *Magic*), 21 November 1913.

of the first performance. Hardy depreciated the work in after years, and described it to Sydney Cockerell (9 November 1911, on the occasion of the Dorchester production) as 'a mere trifle I did for a freak 20 years ago, and should be horrified to write now.' No MS. of *The Three Wayfarers* is known to have survived.[1]

Subsequent Editions. Hardy supplied a revised version of *The Three Wayfarers* in 1926 for amateur performance at Keble College, Oxford, where his fellow townsman, the Rev. Walter Lock, had been Warden. It was produced there (with Gogol's *The Gamblers* and O'Neill's *Ile*) 21–22 June. The revisions, chiefly the addition of some 35 speeches, were designed with much skill to improve the dramatic quality of the play and to lessen the abruptness of its opening and close. Unlike the original version, the new material is largely independent of 'The Three Strangers' and represents fresh invention. Some of these revisions had been made years before, however. Hardy sent them to Charles Charrington, 28 October 1900, on the occasion of the Stage Society production, and wrote, 'They are mainly a slight rearrangement of the opening speeches, which are too artificial in the old copy you have.'

Of this revised version an edition of 542 numbered copies, with 4 illustrations in colour by William H. Cotton, was printed by D. B. Updike at the Merrymount Press, Boston, in February 1930, for publication by the Fountain Press, New York, and the Cayme Press, London.

In April 1935 250 numbered copies of the revised version (with a few very slight variants) were printed for Mrs. Hardy by Henry Ling Ltd., The County Press, Dorchester. The reason for this reprinting, beyond the fact that it constituted the first *English* edition, is not apparent. A cache of 210 copies remained at Max Gate at Mrs. Hardy's death.

A facsimile of the first edition was issued by Scholars' Facsimiles & Reprints (New York, 1943).

---

[1] A portion of a MS. of 'The Hangman's Song' (words and music) is reproduced in facsimile in the programme of the Dorchester production (London and Weymouth issues only) and in Mrs. Hardy's edition of 1935.

1894: LIFE'S LITTLE IRONIES

LIFE'S / LITTLE IRONIES / *A SET OF TALES* / WITH / *SOME COLLOQUIAL SKETCHES* / ENTITLED / A FEW CRUSTED CHARACTERS / BY / THOMAS HARDY / [*Osgood, McIlvaine & Co.'s decorative device*] / ALL RIGHTS / RESERVED

Collation. [A]⁴, B–U⁸; pp. [viii]+304; [i][ii] blank; [iii] half-title; [iv] blank; [v] title-page; [vi] publishers' imprint: Osgood, / McIlvaine and Co., / 45 / Albemarle Street / London, / 1894 / ; [vii][viii] Contents; [1]–301 text, printers' imprint at foot of p. 301: *Printed by* R. & R. Clark, *Edinburgh.* / ; [302] advertisement of *Tess* and *A Group of Noble Dames*; [303][304] blank.

Binding. Sage-green sand-grain cloth; front blocked in brown with 6 panels, one filled with 3 conventionalized flowers, lettered in gold: *Life's / Little Ironies / Thomas / Hardy* / ; back plain; spine blocked in brown with bands and ornaments and lettered in gold: *Life's / Little / Ironies / by / Thomas / Hardy / Osgood, / Mc.Ilvaine & C°.* / .

Plain end-papers; top uncut, fore-edge and tail cut; leaves measure 4⅞″×7⅜″.

The whole format closely resembles *A Group of Noble Dames.*[1]

Serial Issue. The 9 stories collected as *Life's Little Ironies* had all been published previously in serial form.

'The Son's Veto', *The Illustrated London News*, Christmas Number (pub. 1 December) 1891, with 2 illustrations by A. Forestier.

'For Conscience' Sake', as 'For Conscience Sake' in the *Fortnightly Review*, March 1891. The chapters here have titles: I. Sherton Street, W.; II. High Street, Exonbury; III. London Again.

'A Tragedy of Two Ambitions', *The Universal Review*, December 1888, with 6 illustrations by George Lambert. See *Early Life*, p. 279. The walking-stick grown to a silver-poplar at the end was an afterthought and does not appear here.

'On the Western Circuit', *The English Illustrated Magazine*, Decem-

---

[1] The book had originally been announced as uniform with *A Group of Noble Dames* and the one-volume *Tess*, but the publishers wrote to Hardy 9 February 1894, 'We have thought it wise, in deference to the wishes of the trade, to change the cover to the extent of having a dark cloth and adding the title on the side.'

ber 1891, with 4 illustrations by Walter Paget; and, in America, *Harper's Weekly*, 28 November 1891, with 1 illustration by W. T. Smedley. The story was bowdlerized for its serial publication, Mrs. Harnham made a widow, living with her uncle, and Anna simply an infatuated country girl.

'To Please His Wife', *Black and White*, 27 June 1891, with a small portrait of Hardy, and 2 illustrations by W. Hennessy. Reprinted, with portrait and illustrations, in *Stories from "Black and White"*, London, 1893 [December 1892][1] and (from the same plates) *Stories in Black and White*, New York, [February] 1893.

'The Melancholy Hussar of the German Legion', as 'The Melancholy Hussar' in the *Bristol Times and Mirror*, 4 and 11 January 1890. The story was sold to Tillotson & Son for their syndicated fiction business (see Appendix, pp. 340 f.) and was widely printed, especially in provincial newspapers. It was reprinted in *Three Notable Stories* (Spencer Blackett, London, [June] 1890), together with 'Love and Peril' by the Marquis of Lorne and 'To Be, or Not to Be' by Mrs. Alexander, other Tillotson stories.[2] The date 'October 1889' in *Life's Little Ironies* is the date of Hardy's delivering the MS. to Tillotson's (22 October). See *Early Life*, p. 153.

'The Fiddler of the Reels', *Scribner's Magazine* (New York), May 1893, with 1 illustration by W. Hatherell. This was a special 'Exhibition Number' for the Chicago World's Fair, which accounts for Hardy's opening lines and his use of the Great Exhibition of 1851. See *Later Years*, p. 15.

'A Tradition of Eighteen Hundred and Four', as 'A Legend of the Year Eighteen Hundred and Four' in *Harper's Christmas*, December 1882 (a Christmas annual, described as 'Pictures & Papers done by the Tile Club & its Literary Friends', pub. 25 November). The story is called 'Napoleon's Invasion' in advertisements of *Harper's Christmas*. See *Wessex Tales*, p. x, and *Later Years*, p. 195.

'A Few Crusted Characters', as 'Wessex Folk' in *Harper's New Monthly*

[1] There were remainder issues and cheap reprints of this volume (under various titles) by Croome & Co., Richard Butterworth & Co., and others.

[2] The title-page (and contents leaf) is a cancel, with the Marquis of Lorne correctly styled K.T. (instead of K.G.). Sheets were remaindered (with the title-page uncorrected), and plates of 'The Melancholy Hussar' sold to Donohue, Henneberry & Co. (Chicago) and used repeatedly for cheap reprints.

Magazine (American and European editions), March–June 1891, with headpiece (Dorchester High Street) by Alfred Parsons and 7 illustrations by Charles Green. The 4 monthly instalments ran as follows: March, [Introduction], 'Tony Kytes, the Arch-Deceiver', and 'The History of the Hardcomes'; April, 'The Superstitious Man's Story', 'Andrey Satchel and the Parson and Clerk', and 'Andrew Satchel's Experience as a Musician'; May, 'Absent-Mindedness in a Parish Choir' and 'The Winters and the Palmleys'; June, 'Incident in the Life of Mr. George Crookhill' and 'Netty Sargent's Copyhold'. There were a few small bowdlerizations.

With the exception of 'On the Western Circuit', the stories were only slightly revised for their appearance in *Life's Little Ironies*.

Manuscript. There was no MS. of *Life's Little Ironies* as such. Individual MSS. of 6 of the 9 stories here collected are described below. With the exception of 'Wessex Folk', they are printers' MSS. as used for serial publication. No MS. of 'To Please His Wife', 'The Fiddler of the Reels', or 'A Tradition of Eighteen Hundred and Four' is known to have survived.

'The Son's Veto'. Written on 16 leaves measuring $8'' \times 10\frac{1}{4}''$. There are evidences of a considerable excision towards the close of the story. The MS. is bound in three-quarters blue morocco and is now in the Bliss collection.

'For Conscience' Sake'. Written on 24 leaves of cream laid paper measuring $8\frac{1}{8}'' \times 10\frac{1}{8}''$. The MS., a fair copy with a few revisions and alterations, is bound in full brown morocco and is now in Manchester University Library. It is one of three MSS., all of *Life's Little Ironies* (except 'Wessex Folk') that remained in Hardy's possession, sent to Manchester in October 1911, when Hardy, through Sydney Cockerell, was distributing his MSS. among various public collections.

'A Tragedy of Two Ambitions'. Written on 36 leaves measuring $8\frac{1}{8}'' \times 10\frac{1}{4}''$, and bound in full plum morocco. An alternative title was 'The Shame of the Halboroughs'. The MS. was given to the John Rylands Library, Manchester, by Hardy in 1911. See above, 'For Conscience' Sake'.

'On the Western Circuit'. Written on 33 leaves of cream laid paper measuring $8'' \times 10\frac{3}{16}''$ (numbered 1–32 by Hardy with 1 additional fragmentary leaf). This is the original unbowdlerized version of the story. There are two cancelled titles, 'The Amanuensis' and 'The Writer of the Letters', and both the mistaken holding of Mrs. Harnham's hand (in II) and the final glimpse of Anna and Raye appear to have been afterthoughts. The MS. is bound in full brown morocco and was given to the Manchester Central Public Library by Hardy in 1911. See above, 'For Conscience' Sake'.

'The Melancholy Hussar [of the German Legion]'. Written on 27 quarto leaves. The MS. is now in the Henry E. Huntington Library.

'A Few Crusted Characters'. The MS. of these sketches, under the title 'Wessex Folk', which has survived is a very rough hurried first draft (in places hardly more than notes) of a kind Hardy almost invariably destroyed. It is written on 30 leaves (21 measuring $8\frac{1}{8}'' \times 10\frac{1}{4}''$, the rest cut down to varying sizes), numbered 1–31 by Hardy (5 are wanting, and there are 4 supplementary leaves). The MS. is by no means complete: 'The History of the Hardcomes' is called 'Incident at a Wedding Party' and is incomplete; 'Andrey Satchel and the Parson and Clerk' is incomplete; 'Andrew Satchel's Experience as a Musician' is wanting altogether; the first half of 'The Winters and the Palmleys' is wanting; the first half of 'Incident in the Life of Mr. George Crookhill' is wanting, but there is an outline of an alternative version of the story; 'Netty Sargent's Copyhold' is called 'The History [or Strange Trick] of Lucy Serjeant'; and the close of the whole is wanting. There are notes and alterations on the verso of many leaves and at the end a good many trial names. The MS. is bound in full red morocco and was given to Edmund Gosse in July 1913, Hardy noting on it at the time in red ink, 'First Rough Draft of some of the tales afterwards called "A Group of Noble Dames"', a slip he corrected almost immediately in a letter to Gosse. It is now in the Bliss collection.[1]

Galley proofs of *Life's Little Ironies*, variously dated 1 to 30 December 1893, and showing a number of interesting alterations in Hardy's hand, were in the possession of his sister Katharine and have now been deposited in the Dorset County Museum.

[1] A later MS. of 'Wessex Folk' may survive, but its present whereabouts is unknown. One page has been reproduced in facsimile (see *Harper's Monthly Magazine*, July 1925, p. 241).

Notes on Composition and Publication. The majority of tales in this collection ('The Son's Veto', 'For Conscience' Sake', 'On the Western Circuit', 'To Please His Wife', and 'A Few Crusted Characters') date from the latter half of 1890 and the early months of 1891, when work on *Tess* and *A Group of Noble Dames* was largely completed. But 'The Fiddler of the Reels' was not written until 1892 and 'A Tradition of Eighteen Hundred and Four' goes back to the summer of 1882, when Hardy was finishing *Two on a Tower* at Wimborne, so the whole group spans roughly a period of ten years. Hardy was 'hunting up' the stories in the autumn of 1893, and he wrote to Mrs. Henniker, 22 October, 'They are now fastened together to be dispatched to the publisher'.

Life's Little Ironies was published at 6*s*. in an edition of 2,000 copies, 22 February 1894. It had originally been announced for the 16th, but in view of the exceptionally large demand, the first edition being sold out a week in advance, publication was postponed until a second edition could be prepared.[1] The book profited by the great success of *Tess*, then in its twenty-third thousand, and there were 5 large editions (more properly, impressions) before the end of May. Hardy inscribed copies to Gosse, the Earl of Pembroke, Sir Francis Jeune, and to his publisher Clarence McIlvaine. His own copy, labelled 'First Edition' and signed on the half-title, is now in the Dorset County Museum.

Subsequent Editions (*see also* COLLECTED EDITIONS). *Life's Little Ironie* was published in America by Harper & Brothers in March 1894. Hardy added a Preface, dated June 1896, for Osgood, McIlvaine's edition of the Wessex Novels (the volume was printed from the same plates as the first edition two years before). This Preface, with some reflections on the source of 'The Melancholy Hussar' and the original of Parson Toogood in the tale of 'Andrey Satchel', was unfortunately not reprinted in Macmillan's definitive Wessex Edition but replaced with a brief Prefatory Note, dated May 1912. In this definitive edition of *Life's Little Ironies* in 1912, 'An Imaginative Woman' (first collected in the Osgood, McIlvaine edition of *Wessex Tales*, 1896) was added to the group 'as being more nearly its place, turning as it does upon a trick of Nature, so to speak,' and 'A Tradition of

---

[1] See Osgood, McIlvaine's advertisement in the *Athenaeum*, 17 February. The British Museum copy bears the accession date '16 Fe 94', nevertheless, and the book is listed among publications of the week in the *Spectator* and the *Athenaeum*, 17 February.

Eighteen Hundred and Four' and 'The Melancholy Hussar of the German Legion' were removed to *Wessex Tales*, 'where they more naturally belong.'

1896 [1895]: JUDE THE OBSCURE

JUDE / THE OBSCURE / BY / THOMAS HARDY / *WITH AN ETCHING BY* / *H. MACBETH-RAEBURN* / *AND A MAP OF WESSEX* / "The letter killeth." / [*Osgood, McIlvaine & Co.'s decorative device*] / ALL RIGHTS / RESERVED

Collation. π⁴ (π1+1), A–Z⁸, 2A–2I⁸, 2K⁴; pp. ii+1 leaf+vi+520; [i] half-title; [ii] blank; [frontispiece]; leaf not reckoned in pagination, tipped to title-page, recto descriptive letterpress for frontispiece, verso blank; [iii] title-page; [iv] publishers' imprint: Osgood, McIlvaine and Co., / 45 / Albemarle Street / London, / 1896 / ; v–[vi] Preface, dated August 1895; vii–[viii] Contents; 1–[516] text, printers' imprint at foot of p. [516]: *Printed by* Ballantyne, Hanson & Co. / *Edinburgh and London* / ; [517] Map of Wessex; [518]–[520] blank.

Illustration. Frontispiece, 'The "Christminster" of the Story', etched by H[enry] Macbeth-Raeburn and separately printed.

Binding. Dark green bold-ribbed cloth; front blocked in gold with TH monogram medallion; back plain; gold-lettered on spine: Jude / the / Obscure / [*ornament*] / Thomas / Hardy / Osgood, McIlvaine & Cº / . Plain end-papers; top gilt, fore-edge and tail trimmed; leaves measure 5⅜"×7⅞".

The whole format is uniform with the 7 volumes already published of Osgood, McIlvaine's edition of the Wessex Novels.

Binding Variant. White vellum, bevelled edges; blocked in gold on front and back with TH monogram medallion; gold-lettered on spine as in cloth binding.

Plain end-papers; all edges gilt; leaves measure 5"×7 11/16".

This is the binding of Hardy's own copy (now in the Dorset County Museum), in which he has written, '1st edition—early copy.' It is most probably a presentation binding, done to the publishers' special order. I have not seen another like it.

States. The records of neither printer nor publisher have survived in the
case of *Jude*, but from Osgood, McIlvaine's advertisement, '20th
Thousand in England' (*Saturday Review*, 15 February 1896), it is
apparent there was more than one impression of the novel.[1] It is difficult to say if these are distinguishable. Signatures A–H do exist in two
distinct states, however—with page numbers on partially blank pages
and (conforming to usage throughout the remainder of the volume)
without them.[2] These 8 signatures are often found mixed (first and
second state) indiscriminately (and in copies with contemporary inscriptions dated November 1895), but it is to be observed that all are
in the first state in Hardy's own copy, 5 presentation copies inscribed
by him in November 1895, and in the British Museum, Bodleian, and
Cambridge copies (with accession dates '1 No 95', '12.12.1895', and
'13 Dec 95' respectively). Signatures A–H in the first state *may* possibly be an indication, therefore, of the first impression.

Serial Issue. *Jude the Obscure* was first printed serially in *Harper's New
Monthly Magazine* from December 1894 to November 1895. The
American and European editions were published simultaneously in
New York and London, the latter the American sheets bound up with
English advertisements in an English wrapper. The first instalment
appeared under the title *The Simpletons*; with the second instalment
the title was altered to *Hearts Insurgent* and the following note was
published in explanation: 'The author's attention having been drawn
to the resemblance between the title "The Simpletons" and that of
another English novel [presumably Charles Reade's *A Simpleton*, published in *Harper's*, 1872–3], he has decided to revert to the title
originally selected, viz., "Hearts Insurgent," which will therefore be
used in future parts of the story.'[3] The monthly instalments ran as
follows (chapter numbers differing, because of the subsequent division
into Parts, from the book form—here indicated in brackets): December,

---

[1] Wilkinson Sherren in his bibliography (*The Wessex of Romance*, London, 1902,
p. 310) states, on what evidence he cannot now say, 'First Edition, September. Second
Edition, October. Third Edition, November, 1895.' This would suggest 2 impressions
before publication, but it must be noted the novel was still in proof as late as 1 October.

[2] The following pages are involved: Sig. A (pp. 1, 2, 7, 16), B (25, 32), C (38, 47),
D (57, 64), E (72), F (87, 89, 90), G (108), H (116, 126).

[3] Hardy wrote to the publishers, 5 November 1894, asking them to change the title
once more, to *The Recalcitrants*, but the sheets of the January number, with *Hearts
Insurgent*, had already gone to press.

Chaps. 1–6 [I, i–vi]; January, Chaps. 7–11 [I, vii–xi]; February, Chaps. 12–16 [II, i–v]; March, Chaps. 17–21 [II, vi–III, iii]; April, Chaps. 22–25 [III, iv–vii]; May, Chaps. 26–29 [III, viii–IV, ii]; June, Chaps. 30–32 [IV, iii–v]; July, Chaps. 33–36 [IV, vi–v, iii]; August, Chaps. 37–40 [V, iv–vii]; September, Chaps. 41–44 [V, viii–VI, iii]; October, Chaps. 45–48 [VI, iv–vii]; November, Chaps. 48(*cont.*)–51 [VI, vii(*cont.*)–xi]. Chaps. 28 and 49 were divided for book publication, making 53 chapters in all. The novel was 'abridged and modified' to meet the demands of *Harper's*. Jude's relations with Arabella and Sue were fundamentally altered, and numerous passages of considerable extent excised altogether, with amazing sacrifice of art and credibility. This did not pass completely undetected. The *Athenaeum* remarked, 'Complaint has been made by readers of Mr. Hardy's novel in *Harper's Magazine* of the miraculous and perplexing appearance of a child on the scene in the current chapters of the story. We are informed that this was due to an oversight of the author's in modifying the manuscript for the American public, whereby he omitted to substitute some other reason for the child's advent after deleting the authentic reason—its illegitimate birth.'[1]

With each of the 12 monthly instalments appeared an illustration by W. Hatherell. They gave Hardy great satisfaction. He wrote to the artist in admiration of the last, 'Jude at the Mile-stone', that it was 'a tragedy in itself: and I do not remember ever before having an artist who grasped a situation so thoroughly', and he had the whole set of 12 (as reproduced for the American edition) framed and hung over the mantel of his study at Max Gate.[2]

Manuscript. The MS. of *Jude the Obscure* is written on 377 leaves of ruled paper, measuring $8\frac{1}{8}''$(Chaps. 30–40, $7\frac{3}{4}''$)$\times 10\frac{1}{2}''$. These have been numbered 1–436 by Hardy, but some are fragmentary and 59 scattered leaves are wanting altogether. The MS., dated 'March. 1895' at the end, is much altered and revised and does not show the usual marks of the compositor, instalments presumably being set from typescript. Some cancelled passages of interest remain in spite of Hardy's usual procedure of cutting them away. At the head of the MS., but

---

[1] *The Athenaeum*, 19 October 1895, p. 536. Cf. Hardy's letter to the *Daily Chronicle* (25 September 1895) below, p. 305. There is a full discussion of the text of *Jude* in Mary Ellen Chase, *Thomas Hardy from Serial to Novel* (Minneapolis, 1927), pp. 115–77

[2] See *Later Years*, illustration facing p. 76.

deleted, are the words 'The Simpletons / Part First / Hearts Insurgent / A Dreamer.' Jude Fawley's name was at first Jack and Head,[1] Hopeson, Stan, and Stancombe; Marygreen was originally Shawley and Fawn Green. On the first page Hardy has written, 'Note. Alterations and deletions in blue and green are for serial publication only: and have no authority beyond.' This note is repeated at intervals for new instalments, but a few of the alterations are retained in the definitive text nevertheless. Some of the missing leaves correspond to bowdlerizations —8 leaves missing, for instance, at the end of Chap. 32.

The MS. is bound in three-quarters blue morocco and was presented to the Fitzwilliam Museum, Cambridge, in October 1911 when Hardy, through Sydney Cockerell (then Director of the Fitzwilliam), was distributing his MSS. among various public collections.

Notes on Composition and Publication. *Jude the Obscure* was Hardy's last novel and brings to a close, save for a short story or two and the revision of *The Pursuit of the Well-Beloved*, his long career in the field of prose fiction. In the Preface to the first edition, dated August 1895, he is more explicit about the genesis of the novel than was his custom. 'The scheme was jotted down in 1890, from notes made in 1887 and onwards, some of the circumstances being suggested by the death of a woman in the former year.[2] The scenes were revisited in October 1892; the narrative was written in outline in 1892 and the spring of 1893, and at full length, as it now appears, from August 1893 onwards into the next year; the whole, with the exception of a few chapters, being in the hands of the publisher by the end of 1894.' From the date at the end of the MS. it appears the novel was finished in March 1895.

Serial publication had been agreed upon with Harper & Brothers before the end of 1893, Hardy choosing his American publishers and *Harper's Magazine* (with its European edition in the hands of Osgood, McIlvaine) to obviate the difficulties of simultaneous publication. In reply to a gentle stipulation that the proposed novel should 'be in every respect suitable for a family magazine', Hardy had written 'that it would be a tale that could not offend the most fastidious maiden', but

---

[1] Hardy's paternal grandmother was Mary Head of Fawley.

[2] Was this the cousin referred to in 'Thoughts of Phena'? See *Early Life*, p. 293. What may be the germ of the novel is recorded in Hardy's diary under 28 April 1888 (ibid., pp. 272–3).

as composition progressed he had serious misgivings and 7 April 1894 wrote to Harper's asking to be allowed to cancel the agreement altogether, confessing that 'the development of the story was carrying him into unexpected fields and he was afraid to predict its future trend.' The agreement was not cancelled, but with the first instalments in hand[1] H. M. Alden the editor protested, and Hardy consented to revise and bowdlerize, along lines thrice familiar to him by now. Alden wrote to him later (29 August 1894), 'You are right. My objections are based on a purism (not mine, but our readers'), which is undoubtedly more rigid here than in England. Our rule is that the Magazine must contain nothing which could not be read aloud in any family circle. To this we are pledged. You will see for yourself our difficulty, and we fully appreciate the annoyance you must feel at being called upon to modify work conscientiously done, and which is best as it left your hands, from an artist's point of view. I assure you that I felt properly ashamed for every word of protest I had to write to you about the second instalment of "The Simpletons." In the portraiture of the situation there was an artistic excellence surpassing anything I have seen in the fiction of to-day. . . . It is a pity that you should touch a word of the story, but you have been very good to lend yourself so kindly and so promptly to our need, when the task is in itself so ungraceful. I did not much deprecate the pig-killing scene [modified, nevertheless], and my objection was based upon the indignation shown by many of our readers because of a recent sketch by Owen Wister, exposing most frankly the cruelty to animals in our Western ranches.'[2]

The novel was restored to its original form and sent off to the publishers with a Preface in August 1895, Hardy commenting in his diary, 'On account of the labour of altering *Jude the Obscure* to suit the magazine, and then having to alter it back, I have lost energy for revising and improving the original as I meant to do.'[3] The revise of the novel, still in the possession of Ballantyne's reader, Mr. George F. Stewart, shows, however, a number of last-minute additions, most notably the reference to Gibbon among the Christminster voices.

[1] A pencilled note, erased and scarcely legible, on the MS. at the end of Chap. 16 reads : 'End of Part III, About 9,000 words, Sent to Osgood, McIlvaine & Co. July . .. 1894, (Parts I & II sent previously)'.

[2] For this letter and some account of the publication and reception of *Jude*, see J. Henry Harper, *The House of Harper* (New York, 1912), pp. 529–33.

[3] *Later Years*, p. 37.

Jude the Obscure was published at 6s. on 1 November 1895 (post-dated 1896). It was made the 8th volume in Osgood, McIlvaine's edition of the Wessex Novels, volumes of which had been appearing monthly since April of that year. The sale, it was noted a month later, was in advance of *Tess* at the same period after publication (but *Tess* had been published at 31s. 6d.), and by 15 February 1896 the novel was in its twentieth thousand. Hardy inscribed copies to his sister Mary, William Archer, Grant Allen, Edmund Gosse, William Watson, Charles Whibley, and the Duchess of Abercorn (perhaps because of her defence of *Tess*).[1] The bitter attacks on the novel have been often detailed. In America they were characterized by Jeannette Gilder's review in the *New York World* (8 December 1895), which led Hardy to urge Harper's to consider withdrawing the novel from circulation—a review chiefly notable for the letter it drew from Hardy.[2] In England the attacks were characterized by Mrs. Oliphant's review 'The Anti-Marriage League' (in *Blackwood's*, January 1896), at the end of which Hardy has written in his scrap-book, '[The foregoing article is by Mrs Oliphant, who had novels of her own to sell to magazines]'.

Subsequent Editions (*see also* COLLECTED EDITIONS). *Jude* was published in America by Harper & Brothers in mid-November 1895 and post-dated, like the English edition, 1896. The 12 illustrations by Hatherell were reproduced.

The novel was slightly revised, 'errors, particularly of repetition, [being] corrected so far as discovered', when the Osgood, McIlvaine plates passed into Macmillan's hands in 1902. Hardy added an important Postscript to his Preface in April 1912 when the novel was included in Macmillan's definitive Wessex Edition. The MS. of this Postscript, dated 'October: 1911' and still in the envelope in which it was sent to Miss F. E. Dugdale (Mrs. Hardy) to be typed, was given me by her in 1937, shortly before her death. It is written on 8 leaves of folded note-paper (measuring $4\frac{3}{8}'' \times 7''$ and sewn into a quire) and differs in some respects from the printed text.

---

[1] See *Later Years*, p. 6.
[2] See ibid., p. 51, and below, pp. 269–70.

1897: THE WELL-BELOVED

THE WELL-BELOVED / *A SKETCH* / OF *A TEMPERAMENT* /
BY / THOMAS HARDY / *WITH AN ETCHING BY* / H. MAC-
BETH-RAEBURN / AND *A MAP OF WESSEX* / 'One shape of many
names.' / P. B. Shelley. / [*Osgood, McIlvaine & Co.'s decorative device*] /
ALL RIGHTS / *RESERVED*

Collation. $\pi^6(\pi 2+1)$, A–X^8, Y^2; pp. [ii]+ii+1 leaf+viii+340; blank
leaf; [i] half-title; [ii] blank; [frontispiece]; leaf not reckoned in pagination, tipped to title-page, recto descriptive letterpress for frontispiece,
verso blank; [iii] title-page; [iv] publishers' imprint: Osgood, McIl-
vaine and Co. / 45 / Albemarle Street / London, / 1897 / ; v–[vi]
Preface, dated January 1897; vii–[ix] Contents; [x] blank; [1]–[338]
text, printers' imprint at foot of p. [338]: *Printed by* Ballantyne, Hanson & Co. / *Edinburgh and London* / ; [339] Map of Wessex; [340]
blank.

Illustration. Frontispiece, 'The "Isle" of the Story', etched by H[enry]
Macbeth-Raeburn and separately printed.

Binding. Dark green bold-ribbed cloth; front blocked in gold with TH
monogram medallion; back plain; gold-lettered on spine: The / Well-
Beloved / [*ornament*] / Thomas / Hardy / Osgood, McIlvaine & Co / .
Plain end-papers; top gilt, fore-edge and tail trimmed; leaves measure
$5\frac{3}{8}'' \times 7\frac{7}{8}''$.

The whole format is uniform with the 16 volumes already published
of Osgood, McIlvaine's edition of the Wessex Novels.

Serial Issue. The Well-Beloved, under the title *The Pursuit of the Well-
Beloved,* was first published serially in the *Illustrated London News* from
1 October to 17 December 1892. Since this 'experimental issue' (as
Hardy later called it) has independent interest, it is outlined in some
detail, corresponding portions of the book version being indicated in
brackets. The weekly instalments ran as follows:

  1 October: *Part First 'A Young Man of Twenty'*
    Chapter I. 'Relics' [discarded]
    II. 'A supposititious presentment of her' [I, i]
    III. 'The incarnation is assumed to be a true one' [I, ii; one episode
    discarded]
    IV. 'The lonely pedestrian' [I, iii]

8 October: IV (*cont.*) [I, iv]
    V. 'A charge' [I, v]
    VI. 'On the brink' [I, vi]
    VII. 'Her earlier incarnations' [I, vii]

15 October: VII (*cont.*) [I, vii]
    VIII. 'A miscalculation' [I, viii; entirely rewritten]
    IX. 'Familiar phenomena in the distance' [I, ix]
    X. 'The old phantom becomes distinct' [II, i]

22 October: X (*cont.*) [II, i]
    XI. 'She draws close, and satisfies' [II, ii]
    XII. 'She becomes an inaccessible ghost' [II, iii]

29 October: *Part Second 'A Young Man of Forty'*
    XIII. 'She threatens to resume corporeal substance' [II, iv]
    XIV. 'The resumption takes place' [II, v]
    XV. 'The past shines in the present' [II, vi]
    XVI. 'The new becomes established' [II, vii]

5 November: XVI (*cont.*) [II, vii]
    XVII. 'His own soul confronts him' [II, viii]
    XVIII. 'Juxtapositions' [II, ix]

12 November: XIX. 'She fails to vanish when closely confronted' [II, x]
    XX. 'A homely medium does not dull the image' [II, xi]
    XXI. 'A grille descends between the vision and him' [II, xii]

19 November: XXI (*cont.*) [II, xii]
    XXII. 'She is finally enshrouded from sight' [II, xiii]
    Part Third 'A Young Man of Fifty-nine'
    XXIII. 'She returns for the new season' [III, i; partly rewritten]

26 November: XXIV. 'Misgivings on this unexpected re-embodiment'
    [III, i (*cont.*), ii]
    XXV. 'The renewed image burns itself in' [III, iii]

3 December: XXVI. 'He makes a dash for the last incarnation' [III, iv]
    XXVII. 'He desperately clutches the form' [III, v; only half retained,
    with a little of the next chapter. Beyond this point the serial version
    is almost wholly discarded and the closing chapters (III, vi–viii) are
    new.]
    XXVIII. 'He possesses it: he possesses it not'

10 December: XXVIII (*cont.*)
    XXIX. 'The elusiveness continues'
    XXX. 'He becomes retrogressive'

17 December: XXXI. 'The magnanimous thing'
    XXXII. 'The pursuit abandoned'
    XXXIII. 'He becomes aware of new conditions'

When the novel was rewritten for book publication, many scattered passages were excised or added, chapters retitled, &c., but the major alterations were confined to the opening and closing chapters, particularly the latter, where the whole conduct of the plot was changed and an entirely new conclusion substituted. With each of the 12 weekly instalments appeared a headpiece and 2 illustrations by Walter Paget. With the first instalment there was, in addition, a full-page portrait of Hardy and facsimile signature.

The novel was published simultaneously in America in *Harper's Bazar* from 1 October to 17 December 1892, but without illustration (save for a picture of Hardy in his study at Max Gate with the first instalment). Like all Tillotson novels, this was widely reprinted in provincial newspapers (see Appendix, pp. 340 f.).

Manuscript. No MS. of *The Well-Beloved* is thought to have survived. In Hardy's own notes on his MSS. it is not put among those he had himself destroyed but described, rather, as 'unknown'.

Notes on Composition and Publication. When Hardy and Tillotson's cancelled their agreement for the publication of *Too Late Beloved* [*Tess of the d'Urbervilles*] in September 1889, the latter were not long in seeking another and more suitable serial from the same source. Hardy was busy with the finishing of *Tess* and the composition of *A Group of Noble Dames* but he signed an agreement nevertheless on 14 February 1890 to supply Tillotson's at some future date with 'something light' for their syndicate, a 60,000-word serial (less than half the length of *Tess*, that is) capable of division into 12 parts. It was late in the next year before he commenced *The Pursuit of the Well-Beloved*[1] but he wrote to Tillotson's 17 December 1891 that he was at work on the story, had suspended all other writing until it was finished and had 'no doubt of being able to send [it] in within the time specified—though probably not until the end of the time—31 March 1892—owing to my wishing to verify some of the scenes, and the bad weather having hindered getting about.' In view of the difficulties with *Too Late Beloved* he provided them with the following reassuring prospectus:

---

[1] Germs of it are found in Hardy's diary in 1884 and 1889, see *Early Life*, pp. 215, 284. In a defence of the novel in the *Academy* (3 April 1897), he describes it as 'sketched many years before [its serial publication], when I was comparatively a young man.' The title is a curious echo of *Too Late Beloved*.

Title: "The Pursuit of the Well-Beloved."

The novel is entirely modern in date and subject, and, though comparatively short, embraces both extremes of society, from peers, peeresses, and other persons of rank and culture, to villagers.

The principal male characters are: the leading personage—a young sculptor of gradually increasing fame; a landscape painter; one or two [men of rank *deleted*] luminaries of science and law, titled politicians, &c. Those of the opposite sex include an attractive, educated country girl, a rich merchant's daughter of city tastes and habits, the wife of a political peer, her friends, a fashionable London hostess, an aristocratic widow, a village sylph-like creature, &c.

The story, though it deals with some highly emotional situations, is not a tragedy in the ordinary sense. The scenes shift backwards and forwards from London studios and drawing-rooms of fashion to the cottages and cliffs of a remote isle in the English Channel, and a little town on the same.

There is not a word or scene in the tale which can offend the most fastidious taste; and it is equally suited for the reading of young people, and for that of persons of maturer years.[1]

The novel seems to have given Hardy very little satisfaction. He described it to his American publishers (when Harper's were negotiating with Tillotson's for serial rights in February 1892) as 'short and slight, and written entirely with a view to serial publication' and reminded them he reserved the right to withhold *book* publication till it could be rewritten. When the novel had finished its course in the *Illustrated London News*, 17 December 1892, however, Hardy laid it aside for almost four years—years which saw the composition and publication of *Jude*. Then some time in 1896 (the Preface is dated January 1897) he took it up again and revised it, with particular attention to the solution of the plot, as *The Well-Beloved*.

The Well-Beloved was published at 6s. on 16 March 1897. It was made the 17th volume in Osgood, McIlvaine's edition of the Wessex Novels, which had been completed with *Under the Greenwood Tree* in September 1896. It had been announced for February apparently, but the publishers advertised that 'the demand being so exceptionally heavy [they] were compelled to delay the issue.'[2] By 3 April they were advertising a 'Second Edition' and a week later a 'Third Edition in

---

[1] This MS. prospectus, copied by Mrs. Hardy but corrected in Hardy's hand, is still in the possession of the firm.

[2] *Publishers' Circular*, 6 March 1897.

preparation.' Though no printers' or publishers' records survive, it is extremely unlikely that this third impression was required. It was never advertised as ready. Hardy inscribed copies of the novel to his sister Mary, Swinburne,[1] Edward Clodd, Richard le Gallienne, Clement Shorter (then editor of the *Illustrated London News*), and Edmund Gosse. His own copy was included in the sale of books from his library. With this publication Hardy 'ended his prose contributions to literature (beyond two or three short sketches to fulfil engagements)'.[2]

Subsequent Editions (*see also* COLLECTED EDITIONS). *The Well-Beloved* was published in America by Harper & Brothers at the end of March 1897 with the same etching by Macbeth-Raeburn as frontispiece and a format resembling the English edition.

When the novel was included in Macmillan's definitive Wessex Edition, Hardy simply reprinted the original Preface with the addition of a sentence or two and re-dated it 'August 1912'.

1898: WESSEX POEMS

WESSEX POEMS / AND OTHER VERSES / BY / THOMAS HARDY / *WITH THIRTY ILLUSTRATIONS / BY THE AUTHOR* / [*Harper & Brothers' decorative device*]

Collation. π^6, A–O^8, P^2; pp. xii+228; [i] half-title; [ii][iii] blank; [iv] frontispiece; [v] title-page; [vi] publishers' imprint: London and New York / Harper & Brothers / 45 Albemarle Street, W. / MDCCCXCVIII /, and copyright notice; vii–viii Preface, dated September 1898; ix–xi Contents; [xii] blank; [1]–228 text, printers' imprint at foot of p. 228: Printed by Ballantyne, Hanson & Co / Edinburgh & London / .

Illustrations. Frontispiece and 12 full-page illustrations and 18 head- and tailpieces, reproduced from drawings by Hardy and printed with the text.[3]

Binding. Dark green bold-ribbed cloth; front blocked in gold with TH monogram medallion; back plain; gold-lettered on spine: Wessex / Poems / [*ornament*] / Thomas / Hardy / Harpers / .

[1] See *Later Years*, pp. 60–61.   [2] Ibid., p. 60.
[3] The title-page, it will be noticed, calls for only 30 illustrations, apparently ignoring the frontispiece.

Plain end-papers; top gilt, fore-edge and tail trimmed; leaves measure
$5\frac{3}{8}''\times7\frac{7}{8}''$.

The binding is uniform with the 17 volumes of Osgood, McIlvaine's
edition of the Wessex Novels.

Binding Variant. White buckram, bevelled edges; blocked and lettered in
gold as above.

Plain end-papers; all edges gilt; leaves measure $5\frac{3}{16}''\times7\frac{5}{8}''$.

This is a special presentation or gift binding, the book appearing just
at Christmas. The publishers advertised 'A few copies handsomely
bound, for presentation purposes, 7s. 6d. each.' I have never seen a copy
that bore Hardy's inscription nor was there one in his library. The
British Museum copy (accession date '28 De 98') is so bound.

Contents. The Temporary the All   Page [1]
   The headpiece represents a turret at Max Gate with a sun-dial projected by Hardy but not erected until after his death (see *Early Life,*
p. 227). The word '(Sapphics)' was added to the title in subsequent
editions. The MS. shows, faintly pencilled, '(To be thrown out)'.

Amabel   4
   Written at 16 Westbourne Park Villas in 1865 [MS. and *Selected
Poems,* '1866']. The tailpiece represents an hour-glass, the sands
almost run, with two butterflies symbolizing immortality.

Hap   7
   Written at 16 Westbourne Park Villas in 1866. MS. 'Chance'.

'In Vision I Roamed'   9
   Written in 1866.

At a Bridal   11
   Written at 8 Adelphi Terrace in 1866. The sub-title, 'Nature's In-
difference', was added later.

Postponement   13
   Written in 1866.

A Confession to a Friend in Trouble   15
   Written at 16 Westbourne Park Villas in 1866. MS. 'To a Friend
in Trouble (a confession of selfishness)'. The friend was Horace
Moule.

of that year. (See *Early Life*, p. 101.) The line 'Some loves die' was subsequently altered to 'Some forget'.

The Sergeant's Song   43

Written in 1878. Though here described by Hardy as 'Published in "The Trumpet-Major," 1880', only the first stanza (sung by Sergeant Stanner, with twelve other stanzas, not given) and the last (sung by Festus Derriman) were given then (in Chap. 5). Stanzas 2 and 3 were added in later editions. The vignette represents the head of Napoleon in the sky above a rank of bayonets.

Valenciennes   45

Begun in 1878 and finished in 1897. The same episode is recounted very briefly by Corporal Tullidge in *The Trumpet-Major* (Chap. 4, p. 30), as Hardy suggests. See *Early Life*, p. 161. 'S.C. (Pensioner)' [MS. 'Corporal C——'] is perhaps Samuel Clark (1779–1857) of West Stafford, in spite of the date Hardy gives (cf. *The Dynasts*, Part Third, VII, v, p. 224 note). The headpiece represents fortifications at the siege of Valenciennes.

San Sebastian   51

MS. 'In Memory of Sergeant M——. Died 184–.' Hardy drew details from Napier's *History of the War in the Peninsula*, Book XXII, Chap. 2. A penultimate stanza was added in subsequent editions. The illustration represents San Sebastian and Monte Urgull at night.

The Stranger's Song   59

First printed (in 'The Three Strangers') in *Longman's Magazine*, March 1883; and subsequently in *Songs from the Novelists* (ed. W. D. Adams, London, 1885), *Wessex Tales* (1888), and *The Three Wayfarers* (1893), qq.v.

The Burghers   61

MS. 'The Three Burghers'. The headpiece represents 'the High-street to the West' (High West Street, Dorchester) and the 'nearing friend' at sunset.

Leipzig   67

A number of lines were later used in *The Dynasts*, Part Third (1908), see below, p. 130. The full-page illustration represents the Markt-Platz, Leipzig; the tailpiece, the street-fiddler outside the 'Old Ship Inn', Dorchester.

The Peasant's Confession   79
  Written in 1898 (see *Later Years*, p. 74). The quotation is from
  Thiers, *Histoire du Consulat et de l'Empire*, Vol. XX, Book LX,
  'Waterloo', and Hardy has marked the passage in his copy of the
  English translation by D. Forbes Campbell (London, 1862), p. 144.
  Stanza 4 wanting in MS. The full-page illustration represents,
  apparently, the peasant's 'hut ... in a vale recessed' on the rainy
  day of the story.

The Alarm   91
  The reference '*See "The Trumpet-Major"*' (with '1803' [MS.
  '1804'], replaced in subsequent editions by the word 'Traditional')
  is to Chap. 26 ('The Alarm') of that novel, which has for background the same false alarm of Napoleon's landing. 'One of the
  writer's family who was a volunteer during the war with Napoleon'
  is undoubtedly Thomas Hardy the First, the poet's grandfather, and,
  with his wife Mary, the subject of the poem. The headpiece represents the volunteer and 'Barrow-Beacon burning' on the horizon;
  the full-page illustration, the volunteer on Ridgeway Hill with
  Weymouth and Portland in the distance.

Her Death and After   103
  A few lines were rewritten in subsequent editions. The full-page
  illustration represents 'the Field of Tombs' (Dorchester Cemetery)
  with Maumbury Rings and Dorchester beyond; the tailpiece, the
  West Walks, Dorchester.

The Dance at the Phœnix   115
  MS. reads 'Nelly' for 'Jenny' throughout, and stanza 15, 'The
  favourite Quick-step ...', is wanting. Hardy wrote to Edmund Gosse
  that the poem 'is based on fact. The verse beginning "'Twas Christmas" was written first, and quite early—at the time the tradition
  seemed to suggest a ballad. The rest left till later.' The headpiece
  represents a scroll of music with measures of 'Soldier's Joy' (cf. *Far
  from the Madding Crowd*, Chap. 36, pp. 275–6); the tailpiece, the
  King's-Own Cavalry riding over Stinsford Hill.

The Casterbridge Captains   125
  The three captains were John Bascombe Lock (1808–42),[1] Thomas

  [1] For his monument in St. Peter's, Dorchester, see Hutchins, *History of Dorset*, ii,
p. 386.

Henry Gatehouse Besant (1806–?84),[1] and J. Logan (?–1842). The headpiece represents a panel in All Saints, Dorchester, with 'The names, rough-hewn'. The MS. has a naïve tailpiece, not reproduced, representing 'the distant urn' with rays of light streaming from it.

A Sign-Seeker   129
The headpiece represents a comet.

My Cicely   133
Stanzas 10–12 ('Along through the Stour-bordered Forum . . . Or waggoners' jee.') were developed from a single quatrain in the MS. The headpiece represents 'the ancient West Highway' near 'Triple-ramparted Maidon [Castle]'; the tailpiece, the towers of Exeter Cathedral from the north-west.

Her Immortality   143
The full-page illustration represents the pasture of the opening stanza.

The Ivy-Wife   147

A Meeting with Despair   149
MS. shows '(Egdon Heath.)' deleted.

Unknowing   153

Friends Beyond   155
This poem has for illustration the frontispiece, which represents the entrance to Stinsford Churchyard 'at mothy curfew-tide'.

To Outer Nature   159
MS. 'To External Nature'. The headpiece represents a vase of faded flowers.

Thoughts of Ph[en]a   163
Written in March 1890. In his diary, under 5 March 1890, Hardy wrote, 'In the train on the way to London. Wrote the first four or six lines of "Not a line of her writing have I". It was a curious instance of sympathetic telepathy. The woman whom I was thinking of—a cousin [Tryphena Sparks]—was dying at the time, and I quite in ignorance of it. She died six days later. The remainder of the piece was not written till after her death.' (*Early Life*, p. 293.) The title

[1] See V. C. P. Hodson, *List of the Officers of the Bengal Army 1758–1834*, Part I (London, 1927), p. 135.

was altered to 'At News of a Woman's Death' in *Selected Poems* (only). MS. 'T—a. At news of her death. (Died 1890)'. The full-page illustration represents the shrouded body of a woman laid out on a sofa (drawn from a sofa formerly in the dining-room at Max Gate).

Middle-Age Enthusiasms   167
     To M[ary] H[ardy], the poet's sister.

In a Wood   169
     Begun in 1887 and finished in 1896. The reference '*See* "The Woodlanders"' is to Chap. 7 (p. 59) of that novel where a similar thought is suggested: 'Here, as everywhere, the Unfulfilled Intention, which makes life what it is, was as obvious as it could be among the depraved crowds of a city slum. The leaf was deformed, the curve was crippled, the taper was interrupted; the lichen ate the vigour of the stalk, and the ivy slowly strangled to death the promising sapling.'

To a Lady   173
     MS. 'To Lady ——. Offended by something the Author had written.'

To an Orphan Child   175
     The title was altered to 'To a Motherless Child' in subsequent editions.

Nature's Questioning   177
     The headpiece represents a broken key.

The Impercipient   181
     The MS. bears the title 'The Agnostic (Evensong: —— Cathedral.)' and contains an unpublished stanza, following stanza 3:

> But ah, they love me not, although
>   I treat them tenderly,
> And while I bear with them they go
>   To no such [pains] length with me,
> Because—to match their sight I show
>   An incapacity.

The full-page illustration represents the nave of Salisbury Cathedral, a favourite cathedral of Hardy's, the setting for this poem. (See *Later Years*, p. 71.)

Written at the George Inn, Winchester.[1] The poem is, perhaps, to be associated with Mrs. Henniker.

Written in 1894.

Written in 1890. The full-page illustration represents the eweleaze, Coomb near Puddletown, and—superimposed—a pair of spectacles.

ADDITIONS

Written in 1866;[2] first printed in the *Gentleman's Magazine*, November 1875, pp. [552]–555 (and simultaneously, in America, by Henry Holt's arrangement, in *Appletons' Journal*, 6 November 1875, p. 594—though with several slight textual variations), Hardy's earliest appearance as a poet. The poem was considerably bowdlerized, however, and the stanza commencing 'There was one thing to do,' omitted entirely. The original version (described as 'Printed, by permission, from the original MS.') was published in Lionel Johnson, *The Art of Thomas Hardy* (London, 1894), pp. lix–lxiv. The MS. used on this occasion, a copy prepared by Mrs. Hardy with corrections and several lines in Hardy's hand, on 5 leaves measuring $8\frac{5}{16}'' \times 10\frac{7}{16}''$, is now in the Bliss collection. The poem was revised four years later for its appearance in *Wessex Poems* and the dialect heightened, and in subsequent editions the title was altered to 'The Bride-Night Fire' and a glossary of dialectal words added.

Written in 1867 at 8 Adelphi Terrace, office of A[rthur] W[illiam] B[lomfield] the architect, where Hardy was serving as draughtsman at the time. The full-page illustration represents in outline men carrying 'a coffined corpse adown the stairs'.

---

[1] See Hermann Lea, *Thomas Hardy's Wessex* (London, 1913), p. 267. Hardy himself is undoubtedly the authority for this statement, but it may be questioned if he meant the poem was actually composed at the George.

[2] In the Birmingham MS. the date is given as 1867 (as in *The Art of Thomas Hardy*) and the date of printing, 1874—an obvious slip. See *Early Life*, p. 141.

The Two Men   217
>   Written in 1866 at 16 Westbourne Park Villas. MS. 'The World's
>   Verdict. A morality-rime.'

Lines   223
>   Written at the Savile Club at midnight 22 July 1890, at the request
>   of Mrs. Jeune (afterwards Lady Jeune), and spoken by Miss Ada
>   Rehan at the Lyceum Theatre the next day as epilogue to a per-
>   formance on behalf of Mrs. Jeune's Holiday Fund for City Chil-
>   dren (see *Early Life*, p. 299). The lines 'Who has not marked . . .
>   in victims such as these' and 'And yet behind the horizon . . . for
>   ill they cannot cure' were first printed in the *Pall Mall Gazette*, 23
>   July 1890, p. 4 (and the weekly edition, the *Pall Mall Budget*,
>   24 July), but the complete epilogue was first printed in the *Dorset
>   County Chronicle* (Dorchester), 31 July 1890, p. 4. A separate
>   MS. of the poem, written by Hardy on a single leaf (measuring
> $8'' \times 12\frac{1}{2}''$) in an unusually small hand with alterations in pencil
>   and ink, formerly in the Ashley Library, is now in the Bliss col-
>   lection.

'I Look into My Glass'   227
>   There is a fair copy of the poem in the Bliss collection, written on
>   the first page of a folio measuring $6\frac{3}{8}'' \times 8''$.

Manuscript. The MS. of *Wessex Poems* is written on 107 leaves of fine
paper measuring $7\frac{3}{4}'' \times 12\frac{5}{8}''$ (numbered 1–106 by Hardy, with 1
supplementary leaf). Like all Hardy's poetical MSS., this is a fair copy
with relatively few alterations, poems of the 60's in particular frequently set down without a correction—the original MSS. being then
destroyed. There are many divergences from the printed text, but the
more important of these have been indicated above in the treatment
of individual poems. On the last page Hardy has noted in pencil, 'Glossary of Local words (to be sent.)', but such a glossary never appeared,
save for the annotation of 'The Fire at Tranter Sweatley's' in subsequent editions.

Thirty-two drawings lend unique interest to this MS. They are done
in pen and ink with wash and Chinese white and are generally larger
than the reproductions and considerably more effective. They have
been inlaid to size on separate leaves (together with the pencilled in-

structions on separate bits of paper as to placing and reduction of size) and correctly inserted through the MS. One of the drawings, a tail-piece for 'The Casterbridge Captains' (see above), between leaves 60 and 61 was not reproduced.[1]

The MS. is bound in full red morocco and was given to the Birmingham City Museum and Art Gallery in 1911 when Hardy, through Sydney Cockerell, was distributing his MSS. among various public collections.

Notes on Composition and Publication. Wessex Poems marks the final emergence of Hardy's primary interest, verse. The thirty years that remained to him were devoted to the composition of poetry, the resumption of work very dear to him which had been almost wholly laid aside, with the exigencies of novel-writing, since the decade of the 60's. This first collection, like all the others to follow, covers a wide range of years and contains poems which antedate the earliest novels. Of the 51 titles exactly one-third were written in the 60's, for the most part in London lodgings in 1866. Several of the group of Napoleonic poems ('Valenciennes', 'San Sebastian', 'Leipzig', 'The Alarm') may possibly be a portion of that ballad-sequence projected in June 1875 in a note foreshadowing *The Dynasts*, 'Mem: A Ballad of the Hundred Days. Then another of Moscow. Others of earlier campaigns—forming altogether an Iliad of Europe from 1789 to 1815.' (*Early Life*, p. 140.) Beyond 'Valenciennes', begun in 1878 and finished in 1897, we know little of their composition, however. Many other poems, reflecting Hardy's thought and experience in the 90's, are obviously of recent origin (see *Later Years*, p. 66). Only 4 of the collection had been published previously.

'The rough sketches given in illustration,' Hardy is careful to point out in his Preface, are not for the most part contemporaneous with the poems but had 'been recently made, and, as may be surmised, are inserted for personal and local reasons rather than for their intrinsic qualities.' As he wrote to Edward Clodd, '[They] had for me in preparing them a sort of illegitimate interest—that which arose from their being a novel amusement, and a wholly gratuitous performance which could not profit me anything, and probably would do me harm.' They serve,

[1] The earliest announcements of *Wessex Poems* mention 32 illustrations, however.

nevertheless, as a pleasant reminder of Hardy's architectural training and his skill as a draughtsman.

The collection was taking shape early in 1897, before *The Well-Beloved* was fairly off his hands, and under 4 February he set down a title in his diary, 'Wessex Poems: with Sketches of their Scenes by the Author'. (*Later Years*, p. 58, cf. p. 3.) The Preface is dated September 1898.

Wessex Poems was published at 6*s.* in an edition of 500 copies during the week of 11 December 1898. Hardy had offered, in signing the agreement with Harper & Brothers in September, 'to take on his own shoulders the risk of producing the volume, so that if nobody bought it they should not be out of pocket',[1] but it was a risk they were willing to accept. Because of the novelty of the volume, many copies were inscribed to friends at Christmas 1898—among them Swinburne ('whose genius has for more than thirty years been the charm of Thomas Hardy'), Leslie Stephen, William Watson ('with warm congratulations, after reading the reprint of his deathless verse'), Edward Clodd, Edmund Gosse ('Vrom his wold acquaintance'), William Archer, Austin Dobson, Sir James Crichton-Browne, Pearl Craigie, and also his sister Mary.[2] Hardy's own copy with several pencil corrections made in subsequent editions was included in the sale of books from his library and is now in the possession of Mr. F. B. Adams, Jr.

Subsequent Editions (*see also* COLLECTED EDITIONS). *Wessex Poems*, illustrated as the English edition, was published in America by Harper & Brothers at the end of January 1899, though copyrighted 1898. When the volume was included in Macmillan's definitive Wessex Edition in 1912, it was combined with *Poems of the Past and the Present* and the illustrations discarded.[3]

---

[1] *Later Years*, p. 80.

[2] Watson had just sent Hardy his *Collected Poems* (pub. December 1898) 'with admiration flowing into reverence'. Swinburne's and Stephen's acknowledgements are of some interest, see *The Letters of Algernon Charles Swinburne*, ed. Gosse and Wise (2 vols., London, 1918), ii, 253–4, and F. W. Maitland, *The Life and Letters of Leslie Stephen* (London, 1906), pp. 450–1.

[3] They have been retained in Macmillan's Uniform and Pocket Editions.

1902 [1901]: POEMS OF THE PAST AND THE PRESENT

POEMS OF THE PAST / AND THE PRESENT / BY / THOMAS HARDY / [*Harper & Brothers' decorative device*]

Collation. [*a*]², *b*⁴, A–Q⁸, R⁴; pp. xii+264; [i] half-title; [ii] blank; [iii] title-page; [iv] publishers' imprint: London and New York / Harper *& Brothers* / 45 Albemarle Street, W. / MDCCCCII / *All rights reserved* /; [v]–vi Preface, dated August 1901; vii–xi Contents; [xii] blank; [1]–260 text, printers' imprint at foot of p. 260: Printed by Ballantyne, Hanson & Co. / Edinburgh & London / ; [261][262] extracts from reviews of *Wessex Poems*; [263][264] blank.[1]

Binding. Dark green bold-ribbed cloth; front blocked in gold with TH monogram medallion; back plain; gold-lettered on spine: Poems / of the Past / and / the Present / [*ornament*] / Thomas / Hardy / Harpers / . Plain end-papers; top gilt, fore-edge and tail trimmed; leaves measure 5⅜″×7⅞″.

The binding is uniform with *Wessex Poems* and the 17 volumes of Osgood, McIlvaine's edition of the Wessex Novels.

Binding Variant. White buckram, bevelled edges; blocked and lettered in gold as above.

Plain end-papers; all edges gilt; leaves measure 5³⁄₁₆″ × 7¾″.

This is a special presentation or gift binding, as in the case of *Wessex Poems*. The book appeared only a month before Christmas, and the publishers advertised 'a Special Edition, suitable for presentation, bound in white and gold, 7s. 6d.' I have never seen a copy presented by Hardy nor was there one in his library. The British Museum copy (accession date '10 Ja 1902') is so bound.

Contents. V.R. 1819–1901   Page [1]

Written Sunday night, 27 January 1901 and first published in *The Times*, 29 January 1901, p. 9, exactly a week after Queen Victoria's death. Reprinted as the opening poem in an anthology, *The Passing of Victoria*, ed. J. A. Hammerton, London, [March] 1901.

---

[1] An examination of typographical variants in several sigs. shows nothing beyond the common, and progressive, disintegration of the type-face through a single impression.

This sonnet on the departure of troops for the Boer War, which
Hardy had witnessed at Southampton Docks earlier in the month,
was first printed in the *Daily Chronicle*, 25 October 1899, p. 6,
under the title 'The Departure'.

Written in October 1899. Cf. above, 'Embarcation'.

Written in October 1899. Cf. above, 'Embarcation'.

First printed in the *Graphic*, 11 November 1899, p. 662, with the
following explanatory note: '[November 2, 1899. Late at night, in
rain and in darkness, the 73rd Battery, R.F.A., left Dorchester Bar-
racks for the War in South Africa, marching on foot to the railway
station, where their guns were already entrained.]'. Stanzas I and V
were omitted—'not to burden the *Graphic* too heavily', as Hardy
wrote to Mrs. Henniker. The poem was reprinted from the *Graphic*
in the *Academy* just a week later.

Written in December 1899 and first published under the title 'At
the War Office After a Bloody Battle', in a facsimile of Hardy's
MS., in the *Sphere*, 27 January 1900 (vol. i, no. 1), p. 18 (and again
on 17 February). Several separate pulls of the facsimile were made.
The MS. itself, a single leaf measuring 6⅜″ × 8″ and signed at the
end, is now in the Bliss collection. The poem has appeared on one
occasion, in an anthology, *Lest We Forget* (London, 1915), under
the title 'The War-Shadow'.

First printed in the *Westminster Gazette*, 23 December 1899, p. 5,
and so dated in the MS. (though the date of composition is here
given as '*Christmas-eve*, 1899'). Reprinted in *War Against War
in South Africa*, 29 December 1899. The poem was completely revised before being collected, and the last 4 lines were added. For
Hardy's defence of the poem, see below, pp. 306–7.

The Dead Drummer   19

First printed in *Literature*, 25 November 1899, p. 513, with the
following note added to the title: '["One of the Drummers killed
was a native of a village near Casterbridge."]'. The title was subsequently changed to 'Drummer Hodge'.

A Wife in London   21

Written in December 1899. MS. (divisional titles) 'Overnight' and
'Next Day', then 'The Eve' and 'The Morrow'.

The Souls of the Slain   23

Written in December 1899 and first printed in the *Cornhill Magazine*, April 1900, pp. [433]–436, where the following note was
added to the title: 'The spot indicated in the following poem is the
Bill of Portland, which stands, roughly, on a line drawn from South
Africa to the middle of the United Kingdom; in other words, the
flight of a bird along a "great circle" of the earth, cutting through
South Africa and the British Isles, might land him at Portland Bill.
The Race is the turbulent sea-area off the Bill, where contrary tides
meet. "Spawls" are the chips of freestone left by the quarriers [the
word, in stanza II, was altered to "ooze"].' A MS. of the poem
as prepared for the *Cornhill* was discovered in 1918 by Mrs. Reginald
J. Smith at the same time as the MS. of *Far from the Madding Crowd*
(see above, p. 15) and returned to Hardy at his request. Together
with a proof, it is now in the possession of Mr. Frederick B. Adams,
Jr. The MS. is written on 6 leaves, measuring $6\frac{1}{2}'' \times 8''$ and sewn
together, and shows a few alterations, particularly in stanza XI.

Song of the Soldiers' Wives   30

First printed in the *Morning Post*, 30 November 1900, p. 5. In offering
it to the editor, J. Nicol Dunn, Hardy mentioned 'the home-coming
of the Household Cavalry' as occasion for the poem. Several off-
prints were made for Dunn (see Berg Collection and Yale University
Library). The title was subsequently altered to 'Song of the Soldiers'
Wives and Sweethearts'. Under the title 'The Hope Song of the
Soldiers' Sweethearts and Wives' and in a version apparently altered
for the occasion (omitting stanza III), the poem was reprinted in
a soldiers' magazine, *Khaki*, March 1915. This version was reprinted in 1927 by J. A. Allen & Co., London booksellers, as a 4-page
leaflet, limited to 50 numbered copies 'for private circulation only.'

Though Hardy in granting permission (two years before) stipulated the poem must be described as from *Poems of the Past and the Present*, this was not done.

The Sick God   33
The title was altered in subsequent editions to 'The Sick Battle-God'.

POEMS OF PILGRIMAGE

Genoa and the Mediterranean   39
Though Hardy visited Genoa in March 1887, this poem—like most of the 'Poems of Pilgrimage' reflecting his Italian journey of that year—was written 'a long time after' (see *Early Life*, p. 246).

Shelley's Skylark   42
MS. 'March' in the heading altered from 'April'. There is a separate MS. of this poem in the Ashley Library in the British Museum. It is written on 3 leaves of paper measuring $7\frac{7}{8}'' \times 10''$ and watermarked '1913' and is a fair copy made at T. J. Wise's request for his Shelley Collection (for facsimile of first page, see *The Ashley Library*, vol. v, London, 1924, facing p. 134).

In the Old Theatre, Fiesole   44
See *Early Life*, p. 251. An earlier version of this sonnet with several variants appears in the *Academy*, 23 November 1901, p. 476.[1] This version was restored in the second impression of the book.

Rome: On the Palatine   46
See *Early Life*, p. 248.

Rome: Building a New Street in the Ancient Quarter   48
See *Early Life*, pp. 247–8.

Rome: The Vatican—Sala delle Muse   50
See *Early Life*, p. 248.

Rome: At the Pyramid of Cestius   53
MS. '(April, 1887)'. Though Hardy visited the graves of Shelley and Keats 31 March 1887, this poem was 'probably not written till later' (see *Early Life*, p. 248). There is a separate MS. of the poem

---

[1] The review of *Poems of the Past and the Present* in the *Academy*, 23 November 1901 (pp. 475–6), appears to have been based on an early proof of the volume and preserves in its generous quotations a number of interesting discarded readings. The more significant are indicated here. (See also the *Academy*'s quotation from Hardy's Preface a month before its publication, 12 October 1901, p. [331].)

in the Ashley Library in the British Museum. It is written on 3 leaves of paper measuring $7\frac{3}{4}'' \times 10''$ and watermarked '1913' and is a fair copy made at T. J. Wise's request for his Shelley Collection (for fac-simile of first page, see *The Ashley Library*, vol. v, London, 1924, facing p. 135).

Lausanne: In Gibbon's Old Garden   56
    Hardy was stopping at Lausanne on 27 June 1897, and the poem dates from that year. See *Later Years*, pp. 67–69. MS. adds as a note to the closing lines, 'Prose Works: "Doctrine and Discipline of Divorce." '

Zermatt: To the Matterhorn   58
    This sonnet was commenced at Zermatt soon after Hardy's arrival, 28 June 1897, and 'finished some time after'. See *Later Years*, pp. 30–31, 69.

The Bridge of Lodi   60
    MS. '(Visited 23 April, 1887: Battle fought May 10, 1796)'. This 'pleasant jingle' was 'written some time after the excursion to the scene'. See *Early Life*, pp. 256–7.

On an Invitation to the United States   65
    The poem may owe something to a passage from Henry James's *Hawthorne* (London, 1879, p. 12) which Hardy copied into his note-book in 1879 under the heading 'America'.

MISCELLANEOUS POEMS

The Mother Mourns   69
    The germ of the poem appears in Hardy's diary under the date 17 November 1883 (see *Early Life*, p. 213).

'I Said to Love'   75
    A line was added to the last stanza (after l. 2) in subsequent editions.

A Commonplace Day   77

At a Lunar Eclipse   80
    Written in 186–. MS. reproduced in facsimile in W. R. Rutland, *Thomas Hardy* (London and Glasgow, 1938), facing p. 76.

The Lacking Sense   82
    The last 2 lines were a little altered in the second impression (see below, p. 119).

MS. Trial versions of the penultimate line give the poem a Wessex touch now wanting—'On High-stoy Hill or Pilsdon Peak', then 'On Pilsdon Pen or Lewsdon Peak'.

MS. original title, deleted, 'A Peasant's Philosophy'.

MS. adds, ' "She must go to the Union-house to have her baby." *Casterbridge Petty Sessions*.' For an earlier reading of stanzas III, V, and IV (given in that order), see *Academy*, 23 November 1901, p. 475.[1]

Written in February 1899.

Elizabeth B[rowne?] was a gamekeeper's daughter and village beauty of Hardy's boyhood. He set down a word of recollection of her in his diary, 1 March 1888, which might possibly serve as a clue to the date of the poem (see *Early Life*, pp. 33, 270).

MS. 'Young Hope (Song)'.

This poem is closely related in theme to the novel of 1897 and was 'written about this time' (*Later Years*, p. 59). In the Wessex Edition

---

[1] Cf. above, p. 110, note.

(only) the scene was shifted from Bere Regis to Jordon Hill and Weymouth (nearer the scene of the novel).

Written in 1867 at 16 Westbourne Park Villas.

This poem is to be associated with Mrs. Henniker and could not, therefore, have been written before the summer of 1893 at the earliest. The scene is the British Museum.

MS. 'His Love brings little Pleasure'.

Hardy wrote to Edmund Gosse (18 February 1918), 'I am puzzled about the date of "The Widow", (or as it is called in the Wessex Ed^n "The Widow Betrothed"). Anyhow, though I thought of it about 1867 when looking at the house described, which is near here, it must have been written after I had read Wordsworth's famous preface to Lyrical Ballads, which influenced me much, and influences the style of the poem, as you can see for yourself. I am afraid that is all I can recall.' In subsequent editions not only was the title altered to 'The Widow Betrothed' but a penultimate stanza was added and the sole indication of place, 'By Mellstock Lodge and Avenue', removed.

First printed in 'A Changed Man' in the *Sphere*, 21 April 1900, p. 420, where it is described as having been written at the wedding of Captain Maumbry and Laura by the observer of their story, 'the man in the oriel'. 'He could on occasion do a pretty stroke of rhyming in those days, and he beguiled the time of waiting by pencilling on a blank page of his prayer-book a few lines which, though kept private then, may be given here.' The third line of the triolet was rewritten, but it remains unaltered in *A Changed Man* (1913).

The Dream-Follower   149

His Immortality   150
Written in February 1899. For an earlier version, see *Academy*, 23 November 1901, p. 476.[1]

The To-be-Forgotten   152
MS. deleted under title, '(In Stourcastle Churchyard.) "Neither have they any more a reward, for the memory of them is forgotten." ' and at end, 'Feb. 9. 1899?'

Wives in the Sere   155
First printed in the *Tatler*, 31 July 1901, p. 216. The MS. used on that occasion, a fair copy signed on a single leaf measuring 8″ × 10″, is now in the Bliss collection.

The Superseded   157
First printed in *The May Book*, Compiled by Mrs. Aria in Aid of Charing Cross Hospital, London, [May] 1901, pp. 62–63.

An August Midnight   159
Written at Max Gate in 1899.

The Caged Thrush Freed and Home again   161

Birds at Winter Nightfall   163
Written at Max Gate in December 1899. The poem was used by the Hardys as a Christmas card in 1919.

The Puzzled Game-Birds   164
The title was altered in the Wessex Edition (only) to 'The Battue'.

Winter in Durnover Field   165

The Last Chrysanthemum   167

The Darkling Thrush   169
Here described as written 'December 1900'[2] though the MS. suggests an earlier date, 'The Century's End, ~~1899.~~ 1900.' First printed under the title 'By the Century's Deathbed' in the *Graphic*, 29 December 1900, p. 956. The MS. used on that occasion, written

---

[1] Cf. above, p. 110, note.
[2] The date '31st December 1900' in Hardy's final revision he may have felt necessary in view of the altered title.

on the inner sides of a folded sheet of note-paper (measuring $8\frac{7}{8}''$ × $7''$) and signed at the end, is now in the possession of Mr. Frederick B. Adams, Jr. A facsimile of it appeared in Catalogue No. 10 of Barnet J. Beyer, Inc. (New York, 1928), pp. 18–19.

Hardy wrote of this poem, '[The comet] appeared I think, in 1858 or 1859—a very large one—and I remember standing and looking at it as described.' In his final revision the title was shortened to 'The Comet at Yell'ham'.

The Wessex Edition (only) adds the word '(Overheard)'.

MS. 'The Return to Athels-hall'.

MS. 'The Pathetic Fallacy'.

Written in 1882 when Hardy was living at Wimborne. MS. adds to title, '(W——e Minster.)'. The Minster was ruthlessly restored by Wyatt in 1855–7.

Written in 1866 at 16 Westbourne Park Villas. MS. shows '1867' deleted.

Cf. *Early Life*, p. 18.

IMITATIONS, ETC.

After Schiller   246
  A translation of the first stanza of 'Ritter Toggenburg'. Hardy
  wrote a draft of it beside the original in his note-book in 1889.
  Schiller's poem, with interlinear translation, appears in Sonnenschein
  and Stallybrass's *German for the English* (4th ed., London, 1878),
  which he bought and annotated in an effort to learn the language.

Song from Heine   247
  A translation of 'Ich stand in dunkeln Träumen' from the *Reisebilder*
  (*Heimkehr*, 25). Hardy owned at least two volumes of Heine's verse
  in translation, *The Poems of Heine*, trans. E. A. Bowring (London,
  1878), and *Heine's Book of Songs*, trans. C. G. Leland (New York,
  1881), and in both volumes this lyric has been marked. Cf. the
  translation of a quatrain from 'Lieb' Liebschen' in *Two on a Tower*
  (p. 85), probably also Hardy's.

From Victor Hugo   249
  A close translation of 'A une Femme' from *Les Feuilles d'Automne*.

Cardinal Bembo's Epitaph on Raphael   250
  A translation of Pietro Bembo's epitaph,

        Hic ille est Raphael, metuit quo sospite vinci
        Rerum magna parens, et moriendo mori.

RETROSPECT

'I Have Lived with Shades'   253
  Written 2 February 1899.

Memory and I   256

ΑΓΝѠΣΤѠͺ ΘΕѠͺ ['To the Unknown God']   259
  'Automatic' (l. 11) was altered to 'rote-restricted' in the second
  impression.

Manuscript. The MS. of *Poems of the Past and the Present* is written on
  163 leaves of fine paper, measuring 8″ × 10″ and numbered i–vi (Contents, &c.) and 1–157 by Hardy. Like all Hardy's poetical MSS., this
  is a fair copy with late revisions and agrees closely with the printed
  text. Where there are significant divergences, they have been indicated above in the treatment of individual poems. From the table of
  contents it appears that one poem, 'The Complaint of the Common

Man' (placed between 'The King's Experiment' and 'The Tree'), was removed from the collection. It is no longer identifiable, if it appears elsewhere in Hardy's work.

The MS., still in its rough brown paper covers, is bound in three-quarters blue morocco and was given to the Bodleian Library, Oxford, in October 1911, when Hardy, through Sydney Cockerell, was distributing his MSS. among various public collections.

Notes on Composition and Publication. Poems of the Past and the Present is a group of 99 poems, almost twice as many as had comprised Hardy's first volume three years before. Scarcely a quarter of the poems can be dated with any certainty, and these come very largely from 1899 and the opening months of the Boer War. Only two are marked as work of the 60's, and the wide range of years so characteristic of these collections is less noticeable here. The poems are more of the present than the past, where Hardy has been willing to date them. Thirteen had been published previously. Hardy commenced preparing the MS. for the printer in early July 1901, and it was sent off at the end of August. In his agreement with Harper & Brothers (dated 28 May 1901) he set down as title of the volume, 'Poems of Feeling, Dream, and Deed'.

Poems of the Past and the Present (post-dated 1902) was published at 6s. in an edition of 500 copies[1] during the week of 17 November 1901. Hardy inscribed copies to Edmund Gosse, George Douglas ('in long friendship'), Theodore Watts-Dunton, Mrs. Humphry Ward, Arthur Symons, Henley, and Alfred de Lafontaine (owner of Athelhampton Hall, scene of 'The Dame of Athelhall').[2] His own copy, in which he has written 'First edition 1901 (dated 1902)', listed three errata, and made several corrections and alterations, was included in the sale of books from his library and is now in the possession of Mr. F. B. Adams, Jr.

The volume marks the end of Hardy's association with Osgood, Mc-Ilvaine & Co. and their successors, Harper & Brothers (London).

Second Impression Revised (called 'Second Edition'). Clarence McIlvaine of

---

[1] The *edition* was really 1,000 copies, 500 quires being sent to New York for the American edition—more exactly, a second issue.

[2] There were 25 review copies—a large allowance for so small an edition, as the publishers pointed out—but it is characteristic of Hardy's jealousy for his verse that he wanted more distributed.

Harper & Brothers' London office wrote to Hardy 3 December 1901 that only a few copies of *Poems of the Past and the Present* (in the more expensive binding) were left and the publishers proposed to print another edition of 500 copies (half for America). Hardy was urged to send directly such corrections as he wished to make. This second impression revised is described on its title-page as 'Second Edition' but is otherwise indistinguishable in collation or binding from the first edition. It was advertised as ready 18 January 1902. Beyond replacements of type, the following variants may be noticed:

	First impression	*Second impression revised*
P. 45	like gravure	like impress
	The world-imprinting power of perished Rome.	The power, the pride, the reach of perished Rome.
85	dependence gives thee room,	dependence can or may,
	For thou art of her womb."	For thou art of her clay."
260	Thy ancient automatic ways	Thy ancient rote-restricted ways

American and Subsequent Editions (*see also* COLLECTED EDITIONS). *Poems of the Past and the Present* was published in America in an edition of 500 copies by Harper & Brothers in late December 1901. English sheets were used with an altered sig. [*a*]—Harper's London imprint on [*a*]2$^\mathrm{v}$ changed to New York and the date 'December, 1901' added (this last, apparently in New York). When the volume was included in Macmillan's definitive Wessex Edition in 1912, it was combined with *Wessex Poems*.

1903 [1904]: THE DYNASTS, PART FIRST

FIRST ISSUE

THE DYNASTS / A DRAMA / OF THE NAPOLEONIC WARS, / IN THREE PARTS, NINETEEN / ACTS, & ONE HUNDRED AND / THIRTY SCENES / BY / THOMAS HARDY / PART FIRST / *And I heard sounds of insult, shame, and wrong,* / *And trumpets blown for wars.* / 𝕷𝖔𝖓𝖉𝖔𝖓 / MACMILLAN AND CO., LIMITED / NEW YORK: THE MACMILLAN COMPANY / 1903 / *All rights reserved*

Collation. [*a*]^8, *b*^{4}, B–P^8, Q^6; pp. [ii]+xxii+236; blank leaf; [i] half-title;

[ii] publishers' device; [iii] title-page; [iv] copyright notice: *Copyright in the United States of America.* / ; v–xii Preface, dated September 1903; xiii divisional title; [xiv] blank; xv–xvii Contents; [xviii] blank; xix–xxii Characters of Part First; 1–228 text; [229]–[233] Contents of Second and Third Parts, separately paged i–v, printers' imprint at foot of p. [233]: *Printed by* R. & R. Clark, Limited, *Edinburgh.* / ; [234] blank; [235][236] advertisements of Macmillan & Co.'s publications.

Binding. Olive-green cloth; front blocked in gold with TH monogram medallion; back plain; gold-lettered on spine: The / Dynasts / A Drama / [*star*] / Thomas / Hardy / Macmillan & Cº / .

Plain end-papers; top uncut, fore-edge and tail trimmed; leaves measure 5″ × 7$\frac{9}{16}$″.

SECOND ISSUE

THE DYNASTS / . . . / 1904 / . . .

Collation. As in first issue save that [*a*]3 is a cancel, pasted on a stub; recto, title-page as above; verso, copyright notice: *Copyright in the United States of America* / .

Binding. As in first issue.

Manuscript. The MS. of *The Dynasts*, Part First, is written on 247 leaves of fine paper measuring 8″ × 10″. The leaves have been numbered by Hardy i–x and 1–236, with 1 supplementary leaf. Like all Hardy's poetical MSS. this is a fair copy (complete with half-title, table of contents, &c.) with some verbal alterations and a few slight variations from the printed text,[1] and on a rough paper cover Hardy has written, '[The MS. from which the book was printed]'. The speeches of spirits have been underlined in red throughout.

The MS. is bound in three-quarters leather and was presented to the British Museum (together with the MSS. of Parts Second and Third) in October 1911 when Hardy, through Sydney Cockerell, was distributing his MSS. among various public collections. Two pages

---

[1] The note to Act VI, Scene II, reads, 'In attempting to depict this scene, so necessary as a contrast to the night-scene on the French side, the writer . . .' For several other interesting cancellations, see W. R. Rutland, *Thomas Hardy: A Study of his Writings and their Background* (Oxford, 1938), p. 284.

(ff. 168–9, the death of Nelson, Act V, Scene IV) are reproduced in facsimile in *Printers' Pie* (A Festival Souvenir of the Printers' Pension, Almshouse and Orphan Asylum Corporation), London, 1904, pp. 59–60.

A separate MS. of the song, 'The Night of Trafalgar' (Act V, Scene VII), was sent by Hardy to the Red Cross Sale at Christie's, 26 April 1915 (Lot 1537). It is a fair copy, written for the occasion on the first page of a folio of fine paper measuring 8″ × 10″ and signed at the end. The MS. is now in the Bliss collection and is reproduced in facsimile in A. P. Webb, *A Bibliography of the Works of Thomas Hardy* (London, 1916), facing p. 36.

Notes on Composition and Publication. The Dynasts is the culmination of Hardy's lifelong interest in Napoleon and the Napoleonic wars. Through more than thirty years this epic-drama was taking shape in his mind, while in *The Trumpet-Major* (1880), 'A Tradition of Eighteen Hundred and Four' (1882), and some of the poems he touched, in his own phrase, 'the fringe of a vast international tragedy without being able, through limits of plan, knowledge, and opportunity, to enter further into its events'. From entries in his diary it is possible to trace the slow development of his design from the first suggestion in June 1875 of a group of Napoleonic ballads, 'forming altogether an Iliad of Europe from 1789 to 1815',[1] to the completion of *The Dynasts* in the September of 1907. A ballad-sequence was discarded in favour of drama in June 1877, with the note, 'Consider a grand drama, based on the wars with Napoleon, or some one campaign (but not as Shakespeare's historical dramas). It might be called "Napoleon", or "Josephine", or by some other person's name.'[2] Through the 80's, as Hardy's interest in philosophy mounted, the peculiar philosophic framework of the drama held his attention, 'human automatism' and the machinery of 'abstract realisms', spirits and spectral figures.[3] Schemes for the drama that show this new and deepened conception, and an enlarged scope, appear at frequent intervals in the diary. On 21 September 1889 he wrote, 'For carrying out that idea of Napoleon, the Empress, Pitt, Fox, etc., I feel continually that I require a larger canvas. . . . A spectral tone must be adopted. . . . Royal ghosts. . . . Title: "A Drama of

---

[1] *Early Life*, p. 140. Cf. p. 76.   [2] Ibid., p. 150. Cf. p. 188.
[3] See ibid., pp. 191, 197–8, 232.

Kings".'[1] And by September 1896 it had become, 'Europe in Throes. Three Parts. Five Acts each.'[2]

With the publication of *Jude* and the revision of *The Well-Beloved*, Hardy was free at the beginning of 1897 to take up poetry, and 'on a belated day' in that year he seems to have outlined and commenced the composition of *The Dynasts* as we know it.[3] The work was 'taken up now and then at wide intervals', interrupted as it must have been by the preparation of *Wessex Poems* and *Poems of the Past and the Present* for the press, and Part First was finished and sent off to Macmillan 28 September 1903. In a letter to Frederick Macmillan accompanying the MS. Hardy wrote, 'As you will see, it is Part I of a Trilogy. But it is, at the same time, complete in itself, and though I hope to finish the two remaining parts at an early date it is not indispensable that I should do so. I am inclined to wait and see how this part goes off before proceeding further.'[4] From this and other references it is clear that composition had not advanced beyond Part First, though the remaining parts had been outlined and perhaps a few scenes sketched. The 'Contents of Second and Third Parts', published as an appendix to Part First, varies widely from the drama as actually completed. The decision to publish the work piecemeal seems to have been a hurried one and perhaps ill considered. Hardy wrote to Edward Clodd, 22 March 1904, 'I did not mean to publish Part I. by itself until quite a few days before I sent it up to the publishers: and to be engaged in a desultory way on a MS. which may be finished in five years (the date at which I thought I might print it, complete) does not lead one to say much about it. On my return here from London [July 1903] I had a sudden feeling that I should never carry the thing any further, so off it went. But now I am better inclined to go on with it. Though I rather wish I had kept back the parts till the whole could be launched, as I at first intended.'[5]

The Dynasts, Part First, was ready for publication in December 1903,

---

[1] *Early Life*, p. 290. See also pp. 266, 306; *Later Years*, p. 9.

[2] *Later Years*, p. 57.

[3] 'As for the title [from the Magnificat], it was the best and shortest inclusive one I could think of to express the rulers of Europe in their desperate struggle to maintain their dynasties rather than to benefit their peoples.' Hardy to Gosse, 31 January 1904.

[4] Charles Morgan, *The House of Macmillan* (London, 1943), pp. 160–1.

[5] *Later Years*, p. 105.

but the American printers had not finished their edition. The book was therefore kept back because of copyright law, the title-page cancelled, and a new one altering the date to 1904 substituted. In this form it was finally published at 4*s.* 6*d.* in an edition of 1,000 copies, 13 January 1904. Copies with the title-page uncancelled and dated 1903 are less rare than has been assumed,[1] but there is no evidence the book was ever sold in this state. The copies that have survived almost invariably bear Macmillan's blind presentation stamp as copies for review or Hardy's autograph inscription (wherever dated, January 1904). Among the latter are copies inscribed to Swinburne, Gosse (with three corrections in Hardy's hand, made in the second impression), Mrs. Brodrick (Lady St. Helier's daughter), Lady Windsor, and Mrs. Henniker. Hardy's own copy with the pencilled note '1$^{\underline{st}}$ Edition–1903', subsequently inscribed to his wife, 'To Florence Emily, from her husband T.H. October 1916', is now in the Dorset County Museum.

The Dynasts, Part First, marked Hardy's return to Macmillan & Co., who had published *The Woodlanders* and *Wessex Tales* fifteen years back and were to be his last publishers.

SECOND IMPRESSION REVISED

THE DYNASTS / . . . / 1904 / . . .

Collation. As in first impression (first issue) save: [iii] title-page as above; [iv] copyright notice: *Copyright in the United States of America | First Edition 1903. Reprinted 1904 | .*

Binding. As in first impression.

Notes on Revision and Publication. This second impression revised of *The Dynasts*, Part First, numbering 1,000 copies, was printed in the spring of 1904. The reason for it is not apparent, since Macmillan reported a stock of 1,151 copies on 30 June of that year. Hardy made a number of alterations and corrections, the more interesting of which may be noticed.

---

[1] It is impossible to estimate the number of such copies. The notion that there were 12, attributed to Gosse, he repudiated, though the evidence of the sale-room would refute it. Macmillan's statement for the year 1 July 1903–30 June 1904 (covering, however, both impressions of *The Dynasts*, Part First) shows 103 copies presented altogether. It seems highly probable a good proportion of them were of the first issue.

First impression	Second impression revised
P. xii A practicable compromise	In respect of such plays of poesy and dream a practicable compromise
But on this branch of the subject the present writer is unqualified to speak.	But with this branch of the subject we are not concerned here.
26 *Whence an untactical torpid despondency* / *Weighed as with winter the national mind.*	*Whence the grey glooms of a ghost-eyed despondency* / *Wanned as with winter the national mind.*[1]
30 personal influence . . . / Particularly prevails	glamouring influence . . . / Prevails with magic might
106 Within these few weeks past, as you may know	Making us skip like crackers at our heels
225 his past deeds deserve	his vast deeds deserve
Sufficient recognition by the State / To warrant trifling pensions to his kin.	Such size of recognition by the State / As would award wee pensions to his kin.

American Edition. The Dynasts, Part First, was printed in America (from the English sheets) and published by The Macmillan Co. in January 1904, simultaneously with the English edition. Of an edition of 1,314 copies, 105 had been presented and only 161 sold by 30 June.

For subsequent editions, see below, pp. 134-5.

1905 [1906]: THE DYNASTS, PART SECOND

FIRST STATE

THE DYNASTS / A DRAMA / OF THE NAPOLEONIC WARS, / IN THREE PARTS, NINETEEN / ACTS, & ONE HUNDRED AND / THIRTY SCENES / BY / THOMAS HARDY / PART SECOND / *And I heard sounds of insult, shame, and wrong,* / *And trumpets blown for wars.* / 𝕷𝖔𝖓𝖉𝖔𝖓 / MACMILLAN AND CO., LIMITED / NEW YORK: THE MACMILLAN COMPANY / 1905 / *All rights reserved.*

---

[1] This alteration, like so many of Hardy's, seems to have been dictated by a review. 'Phrases like "an untactical torpid diplomacy" [*sic*] and "the free trajection of our entities" are impossible in any music, aerial or otherwise.' (*The Spectator*, 20 February 1904, p. 294.)

Collation. [A]–U⁸; pp. [ii]+xiv+304; blank leaf; [i] half-title; [ii] publishers' device; [iii] title-page; [iv] copyright notice: *Copyright in the
United States of America* / ; v–vii Contents; [viii] blank; ix–xiii
Characters of Part Second; [xiv] blank; 1–302 text; [303][304] Extracts from Reviews of Part First, separately paged [1]–2, printers'
imprint at foot of p. [304]: *Printed by* R. & R. Clark, Limited,
Edinburgh / .

SECOND STATE

THE DYNASTS / . . . / 1906 / *All rights reserved*

Collation. As in first state save that [A]3 is a cancel, pasted on a stub; recto,
title-page as above; verso, blank.

The cancellation, creating these two states, seems to have been required
by a late decision not to print an American edition (as had been done
in the case of Part First) but to send sheets of the English edition to be
bound in America instead. The sale of Part First in America (161 copies
as of 30 June 1904) had shown the demand to be very small indeed.
This decision necessitated the elimination of the American copyright
notice, and since it was the year's end the date, too, was altered. The
cancellation took place not only before publication but apparently while
the book was still in sheets at the printers',¹ so there can be no question
of 'issue'. A very few copies escaped this cancellation and were included
among the 248 sent to America.² There are copies in the Bliss, Parrish-
Princeton, and Wilson collections, all in the American binding.

English Binding. Olive-green cloth; front blocked in gold with TH monogram medallion; back plain; gold-lettered on spine: The / Dynasts /
A Drama / [*two stars*] / Thomas / Hardy / Macmillan *&* Cọ / .

Plain end-papers; top uncut, fore-edge and tail trimmed; leaves measure
5″×7$\frac{9}{16}$″.

¹ Because of this method, it long passed unnoticed. See *The Times Literary Supplement*, 14 February 1929, p. 118.
² From Macmillan's statement to Hardy for the year ended 30 June 1906, the exact
number of Part Second printed was 1,508. It seems very possible that precisely 1,500
copies of the cancel leaf were printed and the 8 copies left uncancelled were included in
the allotment for America. I have never seen a copy in the first state in the English
binding. The Macmillan file copy (second state) contains the following pencilled note:
'They [the American Macmillan Company] printed and copyrighted Part I. / printed Dec.
1905 Cancel title. / pub. Feb. 1906 / Sent 250 to USA in 1905'.

The whole format is uniform with *The Dynasts*, Part First.

American Binding. Green diaper cloth; front lettered in gold: [*within a rule*] The / Dynasts / [*ornament*] / A Drama / of the / Napoleonic / Wars / [*ornament*] / Thomas Hardy / ; back plain; gold-lettered on spine: The / Dynasts / Thomas / Hardy / [*two stars*] / The / Macmillan / Company / .

Plain end-papers; top gilt, fore-edge and tail trimmed; leaves measure $5'' \times 7\frac{1}{2}''$.

Manuscript. The MS. of *The Dynasts*, Part Second, is written on 293 leaves of fine paper measuring $8'' \times 10''$. The leaves have been numbered by Hardy i–vii and 1–284, with 2 supplementary leaves. Like all Hardy's poetical MSS. this is a fair copy (complete with half-title, table of contents, &c.) with some verbal alterations and a few slight variations from the printed text. The speeches of spirits have been underlined in red throughout. There is evidence of cancellation at the opening of Act III, Scene V, f. 131 having been cut away except for the setting and the first 6 speeches of the scene written on leaves 131^A and 131^B inserted at this point.

The MS., dated at the end 'Sept 28. 1905' and still in its rough paper cover, is bound in three-quarters leather and was presented to the British Museum (together with the MSS. of Parts First and Third) in October 1911 when Hardy, through Sydney Cockerell, was distributing his MSS. among various public collections.

Notes on Composition and Publication. Several days after the publication of *The Dynasts*, Part First, Hardy wrote to Edmund Gosse (17 January 1904), 'It is most unlikely that I shall carry the drama any further: for (as I anticipated) in spite of some notable exceptions, the British Philistine is already moved by the *odium theologicum* in his regard of it, though the prejudice is carefully disguised (*vide* Times of Friday).' But notwithstanding the generally unfavourable reception of the work, Hardy proceeded with the composition of Part Second. The MS. was finished 28 September 1905, and Macmillan acknowledged its receipt 12 October. Evidence as to the development of Hardy's design is very largely wanting, but the provisional 'Contents of Second Part' as printed at the conclusion of Part First in 1903 offers a suggestive comparison with the finished work.

As projected (1903)[1]	*As published (1906)*

ACT FIRST

Scene I. The Streets of Berlin.	London. Fox's Lodgings, Arlington Street.
II. London.	The Route between London and Paris.
III. Jena. The French position.	The Streets of Berlin.
IV. The Same. The Prussian Army.	The Field of Jena.
V. Berlin.	Berlin. A Room overlooking a Public Place.
VI. The Same.	The Same.
	VII. Tilsit and the River Niemen.
	VIII. The Same.

ACT SECOND

Scene I. King George's Watering-place, South Wessex.	The Pyrenees and Valleys adjoining.
II. The Shore of Portugal.	Aranjuez. A Room in the Palace of Godoy.
III. Vimiera.	London. The Marchioness of Salisbury's.
IV. Fontainebleau.	Madrid and its Environs.
V. Koenigsberg.	The Open Sea between the English Coasts and the Spanish Peninsula.
VI. Erfurth.	St. Cloud. The Boudoir of Joséphine.
VII. The Same.	Vimiero.
VIII. The Same.	
IX. London.	

ACT THIRD

Scene I. Road between Bembibre and Lugo.	Spain. A Road near Astorga.
II. Road near Astorga.	The Same.
III. Before Coruña.	Before Coruña.
IV. Valladolid.	Coruña. The Jardin de San Carlos.
V. An English Port.	Vienna. A Café in the Stephans-Platz.
VI. Petersburg.	
VII. Vienna.	

[1] Hardy lists among his destroyed MSS., 'Rejected Scene or two of Dynasts (Sarragossa. St. Petersburg)'.

As projected (1903)	*As published (1906)*
ACT FOURTH	
Scene I. Road out of Vienna.	A Road out of Vienna.
II. The Field of Wagram.	The Island of Lobau, with Wagram beyond.
III. The Same.	The Field of Wagram.
IV. London.	The Field of Talavera.
V. Talavera.	The Same.
VI. The Same.	Brighton. The Royal Pavilion.
	VII. The Same. The Assembly-Rooms.
	VIII. Walcheren.
ACT FIFTH	
Scene I. Schönbrünn.	Paris. A Ballroom in the House of Cambacérès.
II. Torres Vedras.	Paris. The Tuilleries.
III. Fontainebleau.	Vienna. A private Apartment in the Imperial Palace.
IV. Vienna.	London. A Club in St. James's Street.
V. Paris. The Tuileries.	The old West Highway out of Vienna.
VI. London.	Courcelles.
VII. The Village of Courcelles.	Petersburg. The Palace of the Empress-Mother.
VIII. Petersburg.	Paris. The Grand Gallery of the Louvre and the Salon-Carré adjoining.
IX. St. Cloud.	
ACT SIXTH	
Scene I. Paris. The Tuileries.	The Lines of Torrès Védras.
II. Albuera.	The Same. Outside the Lines.
III. London. Carlton House.	Paris. The Tuilleries.
	IV. Spain. Albuera.
	V. Windsor Castle. A Room in the King's Apartments.
	VI. London. Carlton House and the Streets adjoining.
	VII. The Same. The Interior of Carlton House.

The Dynasts, Part Second, was published at 4*s*. 6*d*. in an edition of 1,508 copies, 9 February 1906. Of these copies 248 were sent to

America to be bound up as the American edition.[1] Hardy inscribed copies (wherever dated, February 1906) to his sister Katharine, Edmund Gosse ('To my longtime friend . . . 8 Feb. 1906'), Frederic Harrison, Edward Clodd, Mrs. Henniker, Henry Newbolt, Sidney Lee, Arthur Symons, A. M. Broadley ("To the Author of "The Three Dorset Captains at Trafalgar", as a quite inadequate return for his gift of that valuable contribution to English naval history'), and Lorna Bosworth-Smith (with Part First, both inscribed by Hardy and his wife). Hardy's own copy, labelled 'marked', with a number of significant alterations was included in the sale of books from his library and is now in the possession of Mr. F. B. Adams, Jr. (The copy preserved in the Dorset County Museum is one inscribed to his future wife, Florence Emily Dugdale, September 1910.)

Subsequent Editions. There was a second impression of *The Dynasts*, Part Second, in 1909.

For subsequent editions, see below, pp. 134–5.

1908: THE DYNASTS, Part Third

THE DYNASTS / A DRAMA / OF THE NAPOLEONIC WARS, / IN THREE PARTS, NINETEEN / ACTS, & ONE HUNDRED AND / THIRTY SCENES / BY / THOMAS HARDY / PART THIRD / *And I heard sounds of insult, shame, and wrong,* / *And trumpets blown for wars.* / MACMILLAN AND CO., LIMITED / ST. MARTIN'S STREET, LONDON / 1908

Collation. [A]–Z⁸, 2A²; pp. [ii]+xiv+356; blank leaf; [i] half-title; [ii] publishers' device and imprints; [iii] title-page; [iv] blank; v–viii Contents; ix–xiii Characters of Part Third; [xiv] blank; 1–355 text, printers' imprint at foot of p. 355: *Printed by* R. & R. Clark, Limited, *Edinburgh.* / ; [356] blank.

Binding. Olive-green cloth; front blocked in gold with TH monogram medallion; back plain; gold-lettered on spine: The / Dynasts / A Drama / [*three stars*] / Thomas / Hardy / Macmillan & C?. / .

[1] Published in March 1906. Twenty-two copies were presented and only 74 sold as of 30 June.

Plain end-papers; top uncut, fore-edge and tail trimmed; leaves measure
$5'' \times 7\frac{9}{16}''$.

The whole format is uniform with *The Dynasts*, Parts First and Second.

Serial Issue. The closing chorus of the After Scene, commencing 'Last as
first the question rings', was first printed as 'A Latter-Day Chorus
[From "The Dynasts," Part III.]' in the *Nation*, 2 March 1907 (vol. i,
no. 1), p. 13. Some lines were altered and rewritten before their publication in Part Third.

It might be noticed here that a number of lines in the Leipzig scenes of
Act III had already been published in 'Leipzig' in *Wessex Poems* (1898).
The semichoruses of Pities that close Scene IV had been published as
stanzas 26 and 27 of 'Leipzig'; the semichoruses of Pities introduced
near the end of Scene V, as stanzas 30–33 of 'Leipzig'; and scattered
lines from stanzas 6, 11, and 16 reappear in the choruses of Scene II.

Manuscript. The MS. of *The Dynasts*, Part Third, is written on 328 leaves
of fine paper measuring $8'' \times 10''$. The leaves have been numbered by
Hardy i–x and 1–318. Like all Hardy's poetical MSS. this is a fair
copy (complete with half-title, table of contents, &c.) with some verbal
alterations and a few slight variations from the printed text. The
speeches of spirits have been underlined in red throughout.

The MS., still in its rough paper cover, is bound in three-quarters
leather and was presented to the British Museum (together with the
MSS. of Parts First and Second) in October 1911 when Hardy,
through Sydney Cockerell, was distributing his MSS. among various
public collections.

A fragment of an earlier MS. of Part Third has survived and offers
unique evidence as to Hardy's method of composition. This MS.,
with the cancelled date 15 October 1906 on the first page, is written
on 117 leaves of ruled paper measuring $8\frac{1}{16}'' \times 10\frac{3}{16}''$. The leaves have
been numbered 1–116 by Hardy, with 1 supplementary leaf, and
comprise Acts I–IV (to which has been added a fair copy of Act VI,
50 leaves, independently numbered, in the hand of an amanuensis).
Each of the four acts is marked by Hardy 'rough draft' and has been
heavily altered and corrected, sometimes in pencil or red ink, and Acts
III and IV are further described as written—or jotted—on 'Blocking-
in'. It is clear that many speeches and choruses were first set down in

A page of Hardy's rough draft of *The Dynasts*, Part Third (the close of Act IV, Scene II)

prose, often as quotations from Hardy's sources, later to be made into verse. Sometimes this prose 'blocking-in' remains, overwritten with blank verse or converted into verse by insertions and deletions. The opening choruses of Act III, Scene I, for example, have as prose basis a quotation from '*Sloane* IV. 49' [W. M. Sloane, *Life of Napoleon Bonaparte*, 4 vols., New York, 1901] and the speech of the Spirit of the Years at the close of Act IV, Scene II, was built on several sentences from 'Th. XVII. [Bk. LI] end' [A. Thiers, *History of the Consulate and the Empire*, trans. D. Forbes Campbell, 20 vols., London, 1845–62]. Act III, Scenes III and IV, appear as a single scene. This MS., unbound, formed part of the estate of Hardy's sister Katharine and has now been deposited in the Dorset County Museum.

A separate MS. of the song, 'Budmouth Dears' (Act II, Scene I), as copied out for Austin Dobson (8 June 1908), is now in the Bliss collection. It is written on 2 pages of a folio measuring $6\frac{1}{2}'' \times 8\frac{1}{2}''$ and signed at the end.

A separate MS., with signature added, of the closing chorus of the After Scene, commencing 'Last as first the question rings', was sent by Hardy to the Red Cross Sale at Christie's, 22 April 1918. This MS., now in the Bliss collection, is written on a single leaf measuring $8'' \times 10\frac{5}{8}''$ and gives evidence (deleted foliation, marks of sewing, &c.) of having been part of an earlier MS. of the After Scene or perhaps the entire work. It offers little variation from the printed text, however.

Notes on Composition and Publication. Hardy wrote in his diary, 29 March 1907, 'Eve of Good Friday. 11.30 P.M. Finished draft of Part III. of *The Dynasts.*' (*Later Years*, p. 123.) It was 25 September, however, before the MS. was in its final form, and Macmillan acknowledged its receipt 11 October. In default of evidence as to the development of Hardy's design, the provisional 'Contents of Third Part' as printed at the conclusion of Part First in 1903 offers a suggestive comparison with the finished work.

	As projected (1903)	*As published (1908)*
		ACT FIRST
Scene I.	Dresden.	The Banks of the Niemen, near Kowno.
II.	Salamanca.	The Ford of Santa Marta, Salamanca.

	As projected (1903)	*As published (1908)*
III.	Borodino.	The Field of Salamanca.
IV.	Moscow.	The Field of Borodino.
V.	The Same.	The Same.
VI.	Near Moscow.	Moscow.
VII.	The Bridge of the Beresina.	The Same. Outside the City.
VIII.	An English Town.	The Same. The Interior of the Kremlin.
IX.	Paris. The Tuileries.	The Road from Smolensko into Lithuania.
X.	Cadiz.	The Bridge of the Beresina.
XI.		The open country between Smorgoni and Wilna.
XII.		Paris. The Tuileries.

ACT SECOND

Scene I.	The Plain of Vitoria.	The Plain of Vitoria.
II.	The Same.	The Same, from the Puebla Heights.
III.	The Same.	The Same. The Road from the Town.
IV.	The Same.	A Fête at Vauxhall Gardens.
V.	London. Vauxhall.	

ACT THIRD

Scene I.	Vienna.	Leipzig. Napoléon's Quarters in the Reudnitz Suburb.
II.	London.	The Same. The City and the Battlefield.
III.	Leipzig.	The Same, from the Tower of the Pleissenburg.
IV.	The Same.	The Same. At the Thonberg Windmill.
V.	The Same.	The Same. A Street near the Ranstädt Gate.
VI.	London.	The Pyrenees. Near the River Nivelle.
VII.	The Rhine.	
VIII.	Rheims.	
IX.	Paris.	
X.	Fontainebleau.	
XI.	Avignon.	
XII.	Malmaison.	
XIII.	London. The Opera House.	

	As projected (1903)	*As published (1908)*

ACT FOURTH

Scene I.	Elba. The Quay, Porto Ferrajo.	The Upper Rhine.
II.	Vienna.	Paris. The Tuileries.
III.	Near Grenoble.	The Same. The Apartments of the Empress.
IV.	London. On 'Change.	Fontainebleau. A Room in the Palace.
V.	Schönbrunn.	Bayonne. The British Camp.
VI.	London. The House of Commons.	A Highway in the Outskirts of Avignon.
VII.		Malmaison. The Empress Joséphine's Bedchamber.
VIII.		London. The Opera-House.

ACT FIFTH

Scene I.	The Belgian Frontier.	Elba. The Quay, Porto Ferrajo.
II.	A Ballroom at Brussels.	Vienna. The Imperial Palace.
III.	Charleroi.	La Mure, near Grenoble.
IV.	The Streets of Brussels.	Schönbrunn.
V.	Ligny.	London. The Old House of Commons.
VI.	Quatre Bras.	Wessex. Durnover Green, Casterbridge.
VII.	Hôtel de Ville, Brussels.	
VIII.	The Road to Waterloo.	

ACT SIXTH

Scene I.	The Field of Waterloo.	The Belgian Frontier.
II.	The Same.	A Ballroom in Brussels.
III.	The Same.	Charleroi. Napoléon's Quarters.
IV.	Planchenoit.	A Chamber overlooking a main Street in Brussels.
V.	House of the Baron Capellen, Brussels.	The Field of Ligny.
VI.	The Field of Waterloo.	The Field of Quatre-Bras.
VII.	The Same.	Brussels. The Place Royale.
VIII.	The Same.	The Road to Waterloo.
IX.	The Same.	
X.	Near the Field of Waterloo.	
XI.	London. St. James's Square.	

As projected (1903)	*As published (1908)*
	ACT SEVENTH

Scene I.	Rochefort.	The Field of Waterloo.
II.	A Wessex Village.	The Same. The French Position.
	III.	Saint Lambert's Chapel Hill.
	IV.	The Field of Waterloo. The English Position.
	V.	The Same. The Women's Camp near Mont Saint-Jean.
	VI.	The Same. The French Position.
	VII.	The Same. The English Position.
	VIII.	The Same. Later.
	IX.	The Wood of Bossu.
After Scene. The Overworld.		The Overworld.

Though the drama was from the first described as containing 130 scenes, it will be noticed that there are in reality 131 scenes (exclusive of the Fore Scene and the After Scene).

The Dynasts, Part Third, was published at 4*s*. 6*d*. in an edition of 1,500 copies, 11 February 1908. A small portion of the edition (presumably 250 copies) was sent to America to be bound up as the American edition (pub. March 1908). Hardy inscribed copies (wherever dated, February 1908) to his sister Katharine (14 February), Miss F. E. Dugdale, Mrs. Henniker, Edmund Gosse ('in long remembrance'), Edward Clodd, Henry Newbolt, Arthur Symons, Mrs. Crackanthorpe, and William Watson. His own copy, marked in pencil '1st Edition' and containing numerous alterations, was included in the sale of books from his library and is now in the possession of Mr. F. B. Adams, Jr.

Subsequent Editions (*see also* COLLECTED EDITIONS). There was a second impression of *The Dynasts*, Part Third, in 1910. In November of that year the drama as a whole was issued for the first time in a single volume. In 1913 it was included in Macmillan's definitive Wessex Edition, Parts First and Second forming one volume, and Part Third being combined with *Time's Laughingstocks*. In 1927 Macmillan published a special edition of 525 copies on large paper, which Hardy consented to sign (a task he commenced in June 1926). It was in 3

volumes, with a new etched portrait of Hardy by Francis Dodd, made
in April 1927, serving as frontispiece to Vol. I.

Stage Performances. Though he cast *The Dynasts* in dramatic form, Hardy
called it 'a play intended simply for mental performance, and not for
the stage.' When in 1914, however, Harley Granville-Barker proposed
a London production of selected scenes, Hardy agreed to make the
necessary adaptation, and in October of that year he was busy cutting
and rearranging the scenes in question, adding bits of new dialogue,
and composing at Granville-Barker's request a special Prologue and
Epilogue (see below, pp. 172 f.). The play was finally produced at the
Kingsway Theatre, 25 November 1914, 'a splendid failure' though it
ran for 72 performances, closing 30 January 1915 (see *Later Years*,
pp. 164–5). The text (1-vol. ed., 1910) Hardy used in preparing his
adaptation is now in the Dorset County Museum. On the flyleaf he
has written in red ink, 'This abridgment of "The Dynasts", with the
temporary Prologue, Epilogue, and other lines inserted (solely for the
stage performance) is not to be published or reproduced at any time.
T.H.'

A similar production of *The Dynasts*, using the same stage version,
was undertaken by the Oxford University Dramatic Society, 10–14
February 1920 (see *Later Years*, pp. 196–7, 203 ff.), and Wessex
scenes from the play were produced by the Dorchester Debating
and Dramatic Society in 1908 and again in 1916 (see Appendix,
pp. 351 ff.).

1908: SELECT POEMS OF WILLIAM BARNES

SELECT POEMS OF / WILLIAM BARNES / CHOSEN AND
EDITED / WITH A PREFACE AND GLOSSARIAL NOTES /
BY / THOMAS HARDY / LONDON / HENRY FROWDE / 1908

Collation. a⁸, B–N⁸, O²; pp. xvi+196; [i] title-page; [ii] printer's imprint;
[iii]–xii Preface, dated September 1908; [xiii]–xvi Contents; [1]–192
text; [193]–196 Index of First Lines, printer's imprint at foot of p. 196:
Oxford: Horace Hart, Printer to the University / .

Illustration. Photogravure portrait of William Barnes inserted as frontispiece.[1]

Binding. Green cloth; front blocked in gold and back in blind with 6-rule border and conventional decoration; spine gold-lettered, with bands at head and foot: Select / Poems of / William / Barnes / [*ornaments*] / Oxford / .

Plain end-papers; top gilt, fore-edge and tail cut; red ribbon marker; leaves measure $4\frac{1}{2}'' \times 6\frac{3}{4}''$.

The whole format is uniform with other volumes in the Oxford Library of Prose and Poetry (Oxford Miscellany) series.

Secondary Bindings. Copies blocked in blind on front (wholly or in part) and wanting top edge gilt and red ribbon marker are later bindings.

Manuscript. No MS. of Hardy's Preface or the text and glossarial notes as prepared by him is known to survive.

Notes on Composition and Publication. Select Poems of William Barnes is Hardy's most considerable tribute to a Dorset man whom he had known 'well and long', whose friendship he had cherished, and whose poetry had in some measure influenced his own.[2] It entailed uncongenial work of a critical and editorial nature he would hardly have assumed under other circumstances. He undertook the edition at the express invitation of the Delegates of the Clarendon Press. Walter Raleigh laid their proposal before him in a letter of 14 January 1907, offering 25 guineas for advice in the selection of poems and a few pages of introduction. The proposal much interested Hardy because, as he replied, Barnes 'has been badly handled by most of those who have given specimens of his verse—from the point of view of the few of us still left here who know the dialect as Barnes knew it'. But while he offered 'any casual assistance' he demurred at 'the whole work of editing and introducing the poems', being engrossed in *The Dynasts* and feeling perhaps that he had said what he cared to about Barnes in his review of *Poems of Rural Life in the Dorset Dialect* (1879) and his obituary

---

[1] This was from an unpublished photograph by the poet's son, the Rev. W. Miles Barnes. It 'represents him', Hardy wrote, 'just as he used to look when meditating intently.'

[2] For an account of their friendship, see W. R. Rutland, *Thomas Hardy* (London and Glasgow, 1938), pp. 133–43.

notice in the *Athenaeum* (1886). Raleigh was insistent, however, and wrote again, 20 January, 'We can't get, except from you, a preface by one who has as good a right to say what he thinks of the poems as the author had to write them. . . . Where words are laden, as his are, with sentiments and early memories a stranger can do them no justice. My compliments to the poet would resemble international civilities. Yours would please him like the admiration of a brother, from whom one expects only affection and toleration.'[1] A year later, therefore, 29 January 1908, Hardy wrote he 'could now find time' to take up the work. There were vexing and unexpected questions of glossary, text, and copyright, but throughout he showed the most scrupulous concern for Barnes's reputation as an artist. The initial selection was completed and sent to the Clarendon Press 2 March 1908. On 1 July Hardy wrote, 'Having gone through Barnes's poems I find myself in a position to write at least a quite brief preface', and this was in type in September.

Select Poems of William Barnes was published at 2*s*. 6*d*. in an edition of 2,000 copies, 24 November 1908. Hardy inscribed copies to Sir Frederick Treves and to Miss F. E. Dugdale. His own copy, '(Study copy)', is now in the Dorset County Museum. In it he has marked 'Heedless o' my Love' (p. 102) as '(Mary's favourite)', and at the end has inserted a translation in pencil of 'Woone Smile mwore' (p. 76) and a proof of 'The Geäte A-Vallèn To' on which he has written, 'This poem, said to be the last written by Barnes, would have been included in the volume; but at the time of going to press copyright was claimed by the owner, and permission refused.'[2]

Subsequent Editions. There was a second impression (1,000 copies) of *Select Poems of William Barnes* in 1921 (dated 1922) and a third (1,000 copies) in 1933. The imprint of Humphrey Milford replaced that of Henry Frowde, and in copies bound up between 1925 and 1936 the frontispiece was omitted.

---

[1] Raleigh's two letters, both misdated, are printed in Rutland, op. cit., p. 142. Hardy's correspondence with the Delegates is now in the Bodleian Library.
[2] The poem is printed in Lucy Baxter, *The Life of William Barnes* (London, 1887), pp. 316–17.

1909: TIME'S LAUGHINGSTOCKS

TIME'S / LAUGHINGSTOCKS / AND OTHER VERSES / BY / THOMAS HARDY / MACMILLAN AND CO., LIMITED / ST. MARTIN'S STREET, LONDON / 1909

Collation. [A]⁶, B–O⁸, [P]²; pp. [ii]+x+212; blank leaf; [i] half-title; [ii] publishers' device and imprints; [iii] title-page; [iv] blank; v Preface, dated September 1909; [vi] blank; vii–x Contents; [1]–[208] text, printers' imprint at foot of p. [208]: *Printed by* R. & R. Clark, Limited, *Edinburgh*. / ; [209]–[212] publishers' advertisements of Hardy's works, with press opinions of *The Dynasts*.

Binding. Olive-green cloth; front blocked in gold with TH monogram medallion; back plain; gold-lettered on spine: Time's / Laughing- / stocks / Thomas / Hardy / Macmillan & Cº / .

Plain end-papers; top uncut, fore-edge and tail trimmed; leaves measure 5″×7⅝″.

The whole format is uniform with the 3 volumes of *The Dynasts*.

Contents.   TIME'S LAUGHINGSTOCKS

The Revisitation   Page 3

First printed in the *Fortnightly Review*, August 1904, pp. [193]–197, under the title 'Time's Laughingstocks, A Summer Romance'. The MS. used on that occasion is incorporated in the Fitzwilliam MS. of the complete volume.

A Trampwoman's Tragedy   11

Written in April 1902 and first printed in the *North American Review* (New York), November 1903, pp. [775]–778, after the editor of the *Cornhill Magazine* had declined it 'on the ground of it not being a poem he could possibly print in a family periodical' (*Later Years*, p. 101). In the *North American Review* a note at the head of the poem read, '(The incidents on which this tale is based occurred in 1827.)'. The MS. used on this occasion (titled 'The Tramp's Tragedy'), written on 5 leaves measuring 8″×10″ and signed, is now in the Bliss collection (for facsimile of last page, see Kern Sale Catalogue, Part I, New York, The Anderson Galleries, 7–10 January 1929, p. 219), and there are corrected proofs in both the

Bliss and Berg collections. Hardy wrote to Edmund Gosse that the poem was written 'after a bicycle journey I took across the Poldon Hill described, and on to Glastonbury. . . . The circumstances have been known to me for many years. You may like to be told that the woman's name was Mary Ann Taylor—though she has been dust for half a century.' 'Hardy considered this, upon the whole, his most successful poem.' (*Later Years*, p. 93.) See below, pp. 190 f.

The Two Rosalinds   17

First printed in *Collier's* (New York), 20 March 1909, p. 24; and, followed by 'Reminiscences of a Dancing Man' (see below) under the collective title 'London Nights', in the *English Review*, April 1909, pp. 1–3. The two texts are not identical, *Collier's* being clearly the earlier. A MS. of the poem as prepared for the *English Review*, written on 3 leaves of ruled paper measuring 8″× 10″, is now in the possession of Mr. Frederick B. Adams, Jr. (for facsimile of first page, see Maggs Bros. Catalogue No. 312, 1913). See below, 'To an Impersonator of Rosalind', and *Early Life*, p. 298.

A Sunday Morning Tragedy   21

Written in January 1904 and first printed in the *English Review*, December 1908 (vol. i, no. 1), pp. 1–4. The editor, Ford Madox Hueffer [Ford], often said he had founded the *Review* to publish this poem, rejected elsewhere. When he asked for it, Hardy wrote to him, 9 September 1908: 'Since you write so appreciatively I send it on. But please do not feel yourself under any obligation to print it; if you have the slightest doubt or dislike of it return it, and I shall not feel hurt, as it is my intention to open a volume of poems with it when I issue another. The editor of the review [Courtney of the *Fortnightly*], who returned it, merely said that he would have personally liked to print it, but that his review circulated amongst young people. Of course, with a larger morality, the guardians of young people would see that it is the very thing they ought to read, for nobody can say that the treatment is other than moral, and the crime is one of growing prevalence, as you probably know, and the false shame which leads to it is produced by the hypocrisy of the age.' The next year (26 July 1909) Hardy wrote to Galsworthy, 'I wished to produce ["A Sunday Morning Tragedy"] as a tragic play before I printed the ballad form of it; and I went so far as to shape the

scenes, action, &c. But it then occurred to me that the subject ...
would prevent my ever getting it on the boards, so I abandoned it.'
The MS. as prepared for the *English Review*, written on 7 quarto
leaves, is now in the Henry E. Huntington Library. For facsimile
of first page of corrected proof, see McCutcheon Sale Catalogue
(New York, American Art Association, 20–21 April 1925).

The House of Hospitalities   27
First printed in the *New Quarterly*, January 1909, p. 124. The
closing stanza was rewritten before the poem was collected. Hardy
identified the scene as the 'house by the well', Higher Bockhampton.

Bereft   28
Written in 1901; put after 'The Farm-Woman's Winter' in the
Wessex Edition (only).

John and Jane   30

The Curate's Kindness   31

The Flirt's Tragedy   34

The Rejected Member's Wife   40
Written in January 1906 and first printed in the *Spectator*, 27
January 1906, p. 146, under the title 'The Ejected Member's Wife'.
The MS. used on that occasion (titled 'The Rejected One's Wife'),
written on a single leaf measuring 8″ × 10″ and signed, is now in the
Bliss collection. In the Wessex Edition (only) the poem was put
among 'Pieces Occasional and Various', following 'Geographical
Knowledge'.

The Farm-Woman's Winter   42
First printed in the *Pall Mall Magazine*, January 1905, p. 1. A MS.
of the poem, written on a single leaf measuring 8″ × 10″ and signed,
is now in the Bliss collection.

Autumn in the Park   43
Written in 1901 and first printed, under the title 'Autumn in My
Lord's Park', in the *Daily Mail Books' Supplement*, 17 November
1906, p. [1]. After sending it to Edmund Gosse (Director of the
Supplement) Hardy wrote, 'Though the scene as I witnessed it was
a poem, it is quite another question if I had conveyed it to paper.
(It happened in Lady L[ondonderr]y's daughter's park at Melbury
by the way.)' The MS. used on this occasion, a fair copy written

on a single leaf measuring $7'' \times 8\frac{7}{8}''$ and signed, is now in the Bliss collection; a later fair copy was given to Lady Ilchester in 1915. The second stanza was partially rewritten before the poem was collected, and in subsequent editions the title was altered to 'Autumn in King's Hintock Park', to suggest the Earl of Ilchester's Melbury as the setting.

Shut out that Moon   45
     Written in 1904.

Reminiscences of a Dancing Man   47
     First printed in *Collier's* (New York), 27 March 1909, p. 23; and, preceded by 'The Two Rosalinds' (see above) under the collective title 'London Nights', in the *English Review*, April 1909, pp. 4–5. A MS. of the poem as prepared for the *English Review*, written on 2 pages of a folio of ruled paper measuring $8'' \times 10''$ and dated at the end by Hardy '1895', is now in the possession of Mr. Halsted B. VanderPoel. See *Early Life*, p. 56.

The Dead Man Walking   49
     MS. adds '1896' as date of composition.

LOVE LYRICS

[MS. 'Love Poems of Past [Years] Days'. The heading was altered to 'More Love Lyrics' in subsequent editions.]

1967   53
     Written in 1867 at 16 Westbourne Park Villas.

Her Definition   54
     Written in the summer of 1866 at 16 Westbourne Park Villas.

The Division   55
     Written in 1893. This date, added in subsequent editions, suggests that the poem is to be associated with Mrs. Henniker, whom Hardy met in May of that year, and she quotes two stanzas, without author or title, in her novel *Second Fiddle* (London, 1912). A draft of the poem, however, was originally inserted in Miss Dugdale's inscribed copy of *Time's Laughingstocks*, with two other poems of personal significance. This MS., offering a different version of the last stanza, is written on a half-sheet of note-paper measuring $4\frac{1}{2}'' \times 7''$, quite possibly torn from a letter, and is now in my possession.

PIECES OCCASIONAL AND VARIOUS

[MS. deleted, 'Miscellaneous [Verses] Pieces']

The Rash Bride   122
First printed in the *Graphic*, Christmas Number (pub. 24 November)
1902, p. 5. The poem was considerably revised before it was collected. Hardy identified the scene as Higher Bockhampton.

The Dead Quire   128
Written in 1897 and first printed in the *Graphic*, Christmas Number
(pub. 25 November) 1901, p. 16. Before the poem was collected, a
number of lines were revised and the present stanzas XX (wanting in the MS.) and XXIII were added.

The Christening   135
Written in 1904.

A Dream Question   137
MS. deleted, 'An Inquiry. "Thy footsteps are not known."—Ps.
LXXVII. 19.' The rejected title was later used for a not dissimilar
poem in *Human Shows*.

By the Barrows   139

A Wife and Another   140

The Roman Road   144

The Vampirine Fair   145
MS. 'The Fair Vampire'.

The Reminder   150

The Rambler   151

Night in the Old Home   152
Hardy identified the scene as Higher Bockhampton.

After the Last Breath   154
Written in 1904 after the death at Higher Bockhampton on 3 April
of Hardy's mother, Jemima Hardy (b. 1813). Her initials and dates
were added to the poem in subsequent editions.

In Childbed   156

The Pine Planters   158
The second half of the poem, the three 12-line stanzas comprising Part
II, was first printed in the *Cornhill Magazine*, June 1903, pp. [721]–
722, under the title 'The Pine-Planters', without mention of Marty

South but with the following note at the head of the poem, '(*The man fills in the earth; the sad-faced woman holds the tree upright, and meditates*)'. When the poem was collected, the first of these three stanzas was considerably revised and the whole of Part I added. The poem is closely related to the scene between Marty South and Giles Winterborne in Chap. 8 of *The Woodlanders* (pp. 72–74. Cf. *A Pair of Blue Eyes*, p. 80).

The Dear   161

Written in 1901 and first printed as a poem of 4 stanzas in the *Monthly Review*, June 1902, p. [163]. It was, Hardy wrote to the editor, Henry Newbolt, 'made on a real incident that seemed worth recording for its own sake.' The second stanza was added when the poem was collected.

One We Knew   163

Written 20 May 1902 and first printed in the *Tatler*, 2 December 1903, p. 342; and under the title 'Remembrance' (substituted by the editor) in *Harper's Weekly* (New York), 12 December 1903, p. 35. The poem refers to Hardy's grandmother, Mary Head Hardy (1772–1857). See *Later Years*, p. 231.

She Hears the Storm   166

MS. 'The Widow's Thought'. In the Wessex Edition (only) this poem was put among 'Time's Laughingstocks', to stand with 'Bereft' between 'The Farm-Woman's Winter' and 'Autumn in King's Hintock Park'.

A Wet Night   167

Before Life and After   168

New Year's Eve   169

Written in 1906 and first printed in the *Fortnightly Review*, January 1907, pp. [1]–2. A MS. of the poem, as copied out for Edward Clodd, was formerly in the Bliss collection. It is written (and signed) on a folded sheet measuring $4\frac{1}{4}'' \times 6\frac{5}{8}''$.

His Education   171

The title was altered in subsequent editions to 'God's Education'.

To Sincerity   172

Written in February 1899.

Panthera   173

MS. 'Schöttgen' deleted from note. Three scattered lines were added in subsequent editions.

The Unborn   184

First printed, under the title 'Life's Opportunity', in *Wayfarer's Love* (edited by the Duchess of Sutherland and sold for the benefit of the Potteries and Newcastle Cripples' Guild), London, [October] 1904, p. 16. The MS., written on the first page of a folio measuring $7\frac{7}{8}'' \times 10''$ and now in the Berg Collection, was sent to the Duchess in August 1903. The last stanza was discarded when the poem was collected and an entirely different (and less optimistic) one put in its place. In his final revision Hardy added '1905' as the date of composition, a palpable slip—unless he had this preparation of a new close in mind.

The Man he Killed   186

Written in 1902 and first printed in *Harper's Weekly* (New York), 8 November 1902, p. 1649; and in the *Sphere*, 22 November 1902, p. 173a. At the head of the poem appeared the following: 'Scene: *The settle of the Fox Inn, Stagfoot Lane.* Characters: *The speaker (a returned soldier) and his friends, natives of the hamlet.*' The MS. used by the *Sphere*, written and signed on a single leaf measuring $7\frac{7}{8}'' \times 13''$, was preserved by the editor, Clement Shorter, and is now in the Berg Collection. For facsimile, see Shorter Sale Catalogue (Sotheby & Co., 2–4 April 1928), frontispiece.

Geographical Knowledge   187

First printed as a poem of 7 stanzas in the *Outlook* (London), 1 April 1905, p. 454. The 5th stanza, as it appeared there, was not reprinted, possibly because it was reminiscent of the last two lines of 'One We Knew'. 'Christiana C——' was Mrs. Christiana Coward, postmistress at Bockhampton.

One Ralph Blossom Soliloquizes   189

The Noble Lady's Tale   191

First printed (as 'The Noble Lady's Story') in *Harper's Weekly* (New York), 18 February 1905, p. 234; and in the *Cornhill Magazine*, March 1905, pp. 307–12. The MS. used on the latter occasion is incorporated in the Fitzwilliam MS. of the complete volume. Two stanzas in II (12 and 15) were added later when the poem was collected. The noble lady was Lady Susan Fox-Strangways (1743–1827), whose romantic marriage with William O'Brien (1738–1815), an actor, much interested Hardy. The couple lived at Stinsford House and are buried in Stinsford Church. See *Early Life*, pp. 11–12; *Later Years*, pp. 12–13.

Unrealized   201

First printed, under the title 'Orphaned, A Point of View', in *The Queen's (Christmas) Carol* (published by the *Daily Mail* on behalf of Queen Alexandra's Fund for the Unemployed), London, Manchester, and Paris, 1905, p. 58. There was some revision, particularly in the last stanza, before the poem was collected.

Wagtail and Baby   203

First printed, with the sub-title 'An Incident of Civilization', in the *Albany Review*, April 1907 (vol. i, no. 1), p. 34.

Aberdeen   204

First printed in *Alma Mater*, Aberdeen University Magazine, Quater-Centenary Number, September 1906, p. 11. The MS. and a covering note to Theodore Watt of the Editorial Committee dated 30 July 1906 are now in the Aberdeen University Library. April 1905 was the date of Hardy's visit to Aberdeen to receive the honorary degree of LL.D. (see *Later Years*, pp. 108–10).

G.M.   205

Written at the Athenaeum shortly after Meredith's death, 18 May 1909, and first published the day of his funeral, 22 May, in *The Times*, p. 10. See *Later Years*, p. 137.

Yell'ham-Wood's Story   207
Written in 1902.

A Young Man's Epigram on Existence   [208]
Written in 1866 at 16 Westbourne Park Villas. MS. 'Epigram on Existence' (placed after 'Aberdeen', the collection closing with 'Yell'ham-Wood's Story'). See *Later Years*, p. 217.

Manuscript. The MS. of *Time's Laughingstocks* is written on 148 leaves of fine paper measuring $7\frac{1}{2}'' \times 9\frac{3}{4}''$. The leaves have been numbered i–iv (Preface, Contents, &c.) and 1–141 by Hardy, but f. 104 is wanting and there are 4 supplementary leaves. Like all Hardy's later poetical

MSS., this is a collection of fair copies arranged for printing, with few alterations and revisions. Where there are significant divergences from the printed text, they have been indicated above in the treatment of individual poems. Some rearrangement is apparent in the section later headed 'Love Lyrics', and one poem, 'Looking Back', was left un-printed, its place being taken (as the table of contents shows) by 'In the Crypted Way'. It may possibly have been cancelled because of its resemblance in meter and diction to the succeeding poem, 'The Phan-tom' (particularly stanza 4). The verses are here printed for the first time:

Looking Back

When formerly we thought, Dear,
  Of how our souls were set
On spousals doomed to nought, Dear,
  We sickened with regret.

When now we think thereof, Dear,
  Although our eyes are wet,
We know what quenches love, Dear,
  And we do not regret.

The MS., now bound in full blue morocco with all edges gilt, was given to the Fitzwilliam Museum, Cambridge, in October 1911, when Hardy, through Sydney Cockerell (then Director of the Fitzwilliam), was distributing his MSS. among various public collections.

Notes on Composition and Publication. Time's Laughingstocks is a collection of 94 poems, Hardy's first since *Poems of the Past and the Present* in 1901. It is possible to date almost half the poems, and though the volume represents the accumulated work of years when Hardy was largely preoccupied with *The Dynasts* (22 poems are dated 1901 or later, and undoubtedly many more were composed in this period), 18 poems were written before 1900 and 10 of these in the 60's. There is, therefore, a range of more than 40 years in the verses collected here. Twenty-nine of them had been published previously, between 1901 and 1909. Hardy put the volume together in the late summer of 1909 and sent the MS. to Macmillan early in September (the receipt of the first 80 pages was acknowledged 3 September).

Time's Laughingstocks was published at 4*s.* 6*d.* in an edition of 2,000 copies, 3 December 1909. Hardy inscribed copies to his sister Mary, Miss F. E. Dugdale, Edward Clodd, Edmund Gosse, Henry Newbolt, and Dr. T. H. Warren (Vice-Chancellor of Oxford). His own copy, labelled '1ˢᵗ Edition' on the dust wrapper and flyleaf but unopened, is in the Dorset County Museum.

Subsequent Editions (*see also* COLLECTED EDITIONS). There was a second impression revised of *Time's Laughingstocks* in 1910. The revisions were of little consequence, largely alterations of a single word. A third impression called 'Second Edition' appeared in 1915. Meanwhile the volume, combined with *The Dynasts*, Part Third, had been included in Macmillan's definitive Wessex Edition in 1913.

1912: THE CONVERGENCE OF THE TWAIN

THE CONVERGENCE / OF THE TWAIN / BY / THOMAS HARDY / MACMILLAN AND CO., LIMITED / ST. MARTIN'S STREET, LONDON / 1912

Collation. Pp. [16]; [1][2] blank; [3] half-title; [4] Hardy's letter of authorization, July 1912; [5] title-page; [6] printers' certificate: *This poem, first printed in the Covent Garden Souvenir, / May, 1912, and then in the "Fortnightly Review" for / June, 1912, is here first issued in book form, in an edition / limited to ten copies.* / [signed and numbered by Richard Clay & Sons]; [7] divisional title; [8] blank; [9]–[14] text; [15] printers' imprint: Richard Clay and Sons, Limited, / Brunswick Street, Stamford Street, S.E., / and Bungay, Suffolk. / ; [16] blank.

Binding. Blue paper boards; white paper label on front: [*within a rule*] The Convergence of / the Twain / Thomas Hardy / ; back plain. Plain end-papers; all edges uncut; leaves measure 4¹⁵⁄₁₆″×7½″.

Notes. This poem on the sinking of the *Titanic* (15 April 1912) was completed 24 April and first printed in the souvenir programme of the 'Dramatic and Operatic Matinée in Aid of the "Titanic" Disaster Fund' at Covent Garden, 14 May, pp. [2]–[3]. Hardy was a member of the 'Sub-Committee for Programme' of which W. L. Courtney (editor of the *Fortnightly*) was Chairman. The poem was reprinted, with many lines rewritten and stanza V added, in the *Fortnightly Review*, June 1912, pp. [981]–982.

On 2 July Hardy gave Messrs. B. F. Stevens & Brown (representing Messrs. Dodd & Livingston of New York and indirectly George Barr McCutcheon) his permission to print with Macmillan this separate issue. A first proof, dated 29 July, with several typographical corrections in Hardy's hand is now in the Yale University Library. Two sets of a second proof or revise, dated 8 August, with several verbal alterations of significance (especially in stanza V) are now in the Berg Collection. One was formerly the property of McCutcheon himself and is inserted in copy 2 of the finished book, with autograph material relating to it— Hardy's letter of authorization in final form as printed, his receipt for 5 guineas for the right to print the poem, and letters transmitting proof. The 10 copies were finished and dispatched to America by 31 August. None were for sale. Hardy's own copy (No. 10), signed, is now in the Dorset County Museum. The poem was collected in *Satires of Circumstance* (1914), pp. 9–11.

There is a separate MS. of the poem in the Bliss collection. It consists of 4 leaves of fine paper measuring 8″ × 10″, sewn together, the text on 2 of these. Hardy has labelled it 'Replica of Original MS.' and signed and dated it at the end, 'April 24. 1912'. At the head in red ink he has added, '(Written to be sold in aid of the "Titanic" disaster fund, and republished in the Fortnightly Review for June 1912.)'.

1913: A CHANGED MAN AND OTHER TALES

A CHANGED MAN / THE WAITING SUPPER / AND OTHER TALES / CONCLUDING WITH / THE ROMANTIC ADVENTURES / OF A MILKMAID / BY / THOMAS HARDY / MACMILLAN AND CO., LIMITED / ST. MARTIN'S STREET, LONDON / 1913

Collation. [A]⁴, B–Z⁸, 2A–2D⁸; pp. viii+416; [i] half-title; [ii] publishers' device and imprint; [iii] title-page; [iv] blank save for word 'Copyright'; v Prefatory Note, dated August 1913; [vi] blank; vii Contents; [viii] blank; 1–[413] text, printers' imprint at foot of p. [413]: *Printed by* R. & R. Clark, Limited, *Edinburgh.* / ; [414] blank; [415] [416] advertisements of Hardy's works, separately paged 1–2.

Illustrations. Photogravure, 'The Castle of Mai-Dun' [illustrating 'A Tryst at an Ancient Earthwork'], inserted as frontispiece; 2-page 'Map of the Wessex of the Novels and Poems', separately printed and tipped to p. [414].

Binding. Dark green bold-ribbed cloth; front blocked in gold with TH monogram medallion; back plain; gold-lettered on spine: A / Changed / Man / [*ornament*] / Thomas / Hardy / Macmillan & C°. / .
Plain end-papers; top gilt, fore-edge and tail cut; leaves measure 5⅜″× 7⅞″.
The whole format is uniform with the 17 volumes of Osgood, McIlvaine's edition of the Wessex Novels (1895–7), and 'The Wessex Novels Volume XVIII' appears on the half-title.

Serial Issue. The 12 stories here collected had all been published previously in serial form.

'A Changed Man', *The Sphere*, 21 and 28 April 1900, with 2 half-page illustrations by A. S. Hartrick; and, in America, *The Cosmopolitan*, May 1900.

'The Waiting Supper', *Murray's Magazine*, January and February 1888; and, in America, *Harper's Weekly*, 31 December and 7 January 1887–8. A condensation of the closing episodes of the story (the end of VI, and VII and VIII) was published, with no indication of its earlier existence, as 'The Intruder, A Legend of the "Chronicle" Office' in the *Dorset County Chronicle* (Dorchester), 25 December 1890, and again 23 December 1937. Save for an opening paragraph and altered names (Christine and James Bellston become Cecilia and James Belland; Nicholas Long, Nathaniel Arden; and Mrs. Wake, Mrs. Waye) there is nothing which is new. When 'The Waiting Supper' was collected, one episode in VII was changed significantly, and the ominous arrival of Bellston's portmanteau substituted for the appearance of the man himself and his talk with Christine.

'Alicia's Diary', *The Manchester Weekly Times*, 15 and 22 October 1887. The story was sold to Tillotson & Son for their syndicated fiction business (see Appendix, pp. 340 f.) and was widely printed, especially in provincial papers. American rights they sold to S. S. McClure for his similar syndicate in November 1887.

'The Grave by the Handpost', *St. James's Budget*, Christmas Number (pub. 30 November) 1897, with 4 illustrations in the text by George M. Patterson; and, in America (with the sub-title, 'A Christmas Reminiscence'), in *Harper's Weekly*, 4 December 1897, with 3 illustrations unsigned.

'Enter a Dragoon', *Harper's Monthly Magazine* (New York), December 1900, with a full-page illustration by W. Hatherell. When he collected the story, Hardy deleted the quotations at the head of each section (from O'Shaughnessy, Donne, W. Barnes, Ben Jonson, and *King Lear*).

'A Tryst at an Ancient Earthwork', as 'Ancient Earthworks and What Two Enthusiastic Scientists Found Therein' in the *Detroit Post*, 15 March 1885; and as 'Ancient Earthworks at Casterbridge' in the *English Illustrated Magazine*, December 1893, with 4 photographs by W. Pouncy, Dorchester. There were numerous verbal changes and several brief additions when the text of 1885 was prepared for the *English Illustrated Magazine*.

'What the Shepherd Saw', *The Illustrated London News*, Christmas Number (pub. 5 December) 1881. The story was reprinted in America with 5 others (pirated from the Christmas numbers of the *Illustrated London News* and the *Graphic*) in Munro's Seaside Library (No. 1155, 19 December 1881).

'A Committee-Man of "The Terror"', *The Illustrated London News*, Christmas Number (pub. 22 November) 1896, with headpiece and 2 illustrations in the text by H. Burgess.

'Master John Horseleigh, Knight', *The Illustrated London News*, Summer Number (pub. 12 June) 1893, with headpiece and 4 illustrations by W. B. Wollen; and, in America (as 'Mast^r John Horseleigh, Knyght'), in *McClure's Magazine*, July 1893, with head- and tailpiece and 12 vignette illustrations by Harry C. Edwards.

'The Duke's Reappearance', *The Saturday Review*, Christmas Supplement (pub. 14 December) 1896; and, in America, *The Chap-Book* (Chicago), 15 December 1896. When the story was collected, several slight touches were added to identify it as a family tradition. It was privately reprinted in an edition of 89 copies, New York, 1927.

'A Mere Interlude', *The Bolton Weekly Journal*, 17 and 24 October 1885. The story was sold to Tillotson & Son for their syndicated fiction business (see Appendix, pp. 340 f.) and was widely printed, especially in provincial papers. It was pirated in America with 'Mrs. Smith of Longmains' by Rhoda Broughton and 'Oliver's Bride' by Mrs. Oliphant in Munro's Seaside Library Pocket Edition (No. 645, 22 December 1885).

'The Romantic Adventures of a Milkmaid', first printed in 1883. See above, pp. 47 ff.

With the exception of 'The Waiting Supper', the stories were little revised when they were collected.

Manuscript. There was no MS. of the *Changed Man* volume as such. Individual MSS. of 7 of the dozen stories here collected and a portion of an eighth are described below. They are all, except for the fragment of 'What the Shepherd Saw', printers' MSS. as used for English serial publication. No MS. of 'The Waiting Supper', 'Alicia's Diary', 'Enter a Dragoon', or 'A Mere Interlude' is known to have survived.

'A Changed Man'. Written on 27 leaves of ruled paper measuring $7\frac{1}{2}'' \times 10\frac{3}{8}''$, with some alterations throughout. The MS., bound in three-quarters blue morocco, is now in the Bliss collection. Page 1 is reproduced in facsimile in the *Sphere*, 15 November 1913, p. 180.

'The Grave by the Handpost'. Written on 16 leaves of ruled paper measuring $8'' \times 10\frac{9}{16}''$, with some revisions, especially in the earlier pages. 'Luke' has been altered from 'Charl' throughout, and at the head stands a quotation from *Antigone*, 'Consider if thou wilt help me in the work.' The MS., each leaf tipped to a sheet of fine paper and the whole bound in full green morocco, is now in the possession of Mr. Halsted B. VanderPoel. For facsimile of first page, see Sachs Sale Catalogue (New York, Parke-Bernet Galleries, 1 February 1944), p. 13.

'A Tryst at an Ancient Earthwork'. Written on 15 leaves measuring $8'' \times 10\frac{3}{16}''$ and titled 'An Ancient Earthwork'. This is the MS. as prepared for the *English Illustrated Magazine* and preserved by the editor, Clement Shorter. Bound in three-quarters blue morocco, it is now in the Bliss collection. For facsimile of last page, see Shorter Sale Catalogue (Sotheby & Co., 2–4 April 1928), facing p. 37.

'What the Shepherd Saw'. The first 3 leaves only, measuring $6\frac{1}{4}'' \times 8''$. Hardy has noted at the head in red ink, '[First rough draught]

(1881)' and at the end '(*Caetera desunt*.)'. The leaves are sewn in
a folded sheet of fine paper on which Hardy has written, ' "What
the Shepherd Saw" a tale written in 1881, and published in English
and American Periodicals. Recently included in Collected Works
in the volume entitled "A Changed Man". Original MS. being
First Rough Draft (3 pages only—the remainder lost.) Thomas
Hardy.' The fragment was sent to the Red Cross Sale at Christie's,
26 April 1916, by Mrs. Hardy and is now in the Bliss collection.

'A Committee-Man of "The Terror" '. Written on 19 leaves of ruled
paper measuring $7\frac{3}{4}'' \times 9\frac{7}{8}''$, with numerous alterations and a short
cancellation. Hardy has deleted working notes at the head: 'Roy!
Fam. at W[eymou]th Sept. 1801, 2, 4, 5 &c. Peace of Amiens
March 27, '02 Rupture between Fr. & Eng. & arrest of Bsh. travellers: May 12 '03'. The MS., bound in three-quarters blue morocco,
is now in the Bliss collection. Corrected proof-sheets of the story are
in the Henry E. Huntington Library.

'Master John Horseleigh, Knight'. Written on 15 leaves measuring
$8'' \times 10\frac{1}{4}''$ and titled 'Sir John Horseleigh, Knight'. The MS., bound
in three-quarters blue morocco, is now in the Bliss collection.

'The Duke's Reappearance'. Written on 11 leaves of ruled paper
measuring $7\frac{3}{4}'' \times 10\frac{1}{2}''$ and numbered 1–10 by Hardy with 1 supplementary leaf. This is a fair copy with some alterations, and Hardy
has added in red ink as a footnote to the first line, 'Christopher Swet-
man was one of the author's ancestors on the maternal side.' The
MS. was given to Edward Clodd in March 1912 and is so inscribed
by Hardy, who wrote in an accompanying letter (24 March 1912),
'I thought you would be more interested in this particular scrawl
than in many, the tale being a tradition in my mother's family, who
are mentioned in it under their real names.' It is bound in three-
quarters blue morocco and is now in the Bliss collection.

'The Romantic Adventures of a Milkmaid'. See above, p. 48.

Notes on Composition and Publication. A Changed Man and Other Tales is
a group of 'a dozen minor novels' that had lain uncollected in English
and American periodicals, half of them for a quarter of a century or
more. They 'would probably have never been collected by me at this
time of day,' Hardy wrote, 'if frequent reprints of some of them in

America and elsewhere had not set many readers inquiring for them in a volume.'[1] It seemed well, therefore, to make them available as representing all that he consented to preserve of his work in a field he had long abandoned. We know little of the composition of these tales, but it is safe to assume that each was published as soon as possible after it was written. The dates Hardy set to each bear this out, save in the case of 'A Committee-Man of "The Terror"' and 'Enter a Dragoon', both dated a year in advance of publication. 'What the Shepherd Saw', the earliest in the collection, was written at Wimborne in the autumn of 1881, and the two latest, 'A Changed Man' and 'Enter a Dragoon', in the autumn and winter of 1899, marking the close of Hardy's work in prose fiction.

Though the stories are not, perhaps, of a high level, there is much of interest in the volume: the introduction of soldiers and the use of historical setting in the tales written in the 90's, when *The Dynasts* was taking shape; the snatches of reminiscence and family tradition in 'A Tryst at an Ancient Earthwork'[2] and 'The Duke's Reappearance'; the reflection in 'Alicia's Diary' of Hardy's Italian journey a few months before; and the characteristic use of Hutchins's *History of Dorset* as a source for 'Master John Horseleigh, Knight'.[3] The volume was put together in the summer of 1913, and the brief prefatory note is dated August of that year.

A Changed Man was published by Macmillan at 6s. in an edition of 10,000 copies, 24 October 1913. Hardy inscribed copies in October to Edward Clodd and Edmund Gosse and in November to Mrs. Allhusen and to Mrs. Sydney Cockerell. His own copy was included in the sale of books from his library.

Subsequent Editions (see also COLLECTED EDITIONS). *A Changed Man* was published simultaneously in America by Harper & Brothers, with one of Reinhart's illustrations for 'The Romantic Adventures of a

---

[1] *The Times Literary Supplement*, 25 September 1913, p. 402 (a cancelled version of the Prefatory Note, supplied apparently by the publishers from proof). Cf. *Friends of a Lifetime*, p. 276.

[2] Suggested by excavations of Edward Cunnington, a Dorchester antiquary, quite possibly Hardy's reason for not printing the story originally in England.

[3] See Hutchins, vol. i, p. 50 (the 'Havenpool' marriage register), and vol. iv, pp. 426–9 (description of Clifton Maubank and Pedigree of Horsey of Clifton Maubank and Melcombe Horsey).

Milkmaid' replacing the photogravure of Maiden Castle as frontispiece. In 1914 the book was reprinted in Macmillan's definitive Wessex Edition.

1914: SONG OF THE SOLDIERS

[*within a rule*] SONG / OF THE / SOLDIERS / BY / THOMAS HARDY

Collation. Pp. [8]; [1] title-page; [2] blank; [3]–[7] text; [8] letter from Hardy to Shorter, 10 September 1914, granting permission for this printing, reproduced in facsimile, and colophon: *First published in "The Times," September* 9, 1914, *with | the footnote "Neither Mr. Hardy nor 'The Times' reserves | copyright in the poem printed above." This is one of twelve | copies printed for private distribution by Clement Shorter. | It has been corrected by the author and is issued with his | permission, September* 12, 1914.

Binding. Sewn in purple paper wrappers; front printed in black as title-page.

All edges cut; leaves measure $7'' \times 9''$.

Notes. This poem was written 5 September 1914 and first printed in *The Times*, 9 September 1914, p. 9 (*The Times Literary Supplement* and the *New York Times*, 10 September). Since it was expressly stated that copyright was not reserved, the poem was widely reprinted. Clement Shorter's edition, the first of his privately printed pamphlets of Hardy material, was issued with the date 12 September (Hardy acknowledged a copy 22 September). Hardy's 'correction' was limited to the alteration of l. 26 from 'March we . . .' to 'Press we . . .' For a general note on Shorter's pamphlets, see Appendix, pp. 349 f. The poem, under the altered title ' "Men who March Away" (Song of the Soldiers)', was collected two months later in *Satires of Circumstance*, pp. 229–30, a last-minute 'Postscript' to that volume. In subsequent editions it was transferred to *Moments of Vision* and put at the head of the group of 'Poems of War and Patriotism', where it more properly belongs.

A fair copy of the poem (withdrawn from the MS. of *Satires of Circumstance*, where its place is taken by a cutting from *The Times*, see below, p. 171) was sent to the Red Cross Sale at Christie's, 26 April 1915. It is written, with several slight alterations, on pp. 1 and 3 of a folio of fine paper measuring $7\frac{5}{8}'' \times 10''$. This MS., formerly in the possession of Mr. Howard J. Sachs, is reproduced in facsimile in A. P. Webb, *A Bibliography of the Works of Thomas Hardy* (London, 1916), following p. 46. Another and later fair copy (the text in its final form), written on the inner pages of a folio of fine paper measuring $5'' \times 8''$, is now in the Bliss collection.

Hove Editions. The poem was also privately printed, as a 4-page leaflet, by E. Williams, antiquarian bookseller, of 37 New Town Road, Hove (Brighton), 16 September 1914. Mrs. Hardy wrote to Williams 11 September that her husband had no objection to the poem being reprinted, and the leaflet is described as 'Reprinted . . . by permission'. Nothing is discoverable about Williams's activities (he reprinted 'The Oxen' in 1915 in much the same fashion, see below, p. 175), but the edition must have been a large one since the leaflet is common. I do not know the authority for the often repeated statement that these Hove printings were 'issued solely to give away to soldiers on active service abroad'. It first appears in Henry Danielson, *The First Editions of the Writings of Thomas Hardy and their Values* (London, 1916), pp. 20, 26. It seems strange that no similar statement appears in Webb, who had his copies (and presumably any facts that might illuminate them) from Williams himself (Webb, op. cit., p. xii).

Williams seems to have found the poem profitable and reprinted it in a bewildering variety of forms. In the original 4-page leaflet form there are variants indicating at least two distinct editions, the earlier readily identifiable in having '*9th September,*' (instead of '*9th September.*') on p. [1].[1] Of the later edition copies exist printed in gold. In 1915 (after the poem had been collected) Williams again printed it, this time as an 8-page pamphlet sewn in brown printed wrappers. Through all these Hove printings the poem remained unrevised, as it had appeared in *The Times.*

---

1 They are not simply two impressions, I think. The type has been reset, though the result is astonishingly close to the original. The second edition may be a deliberate forgery. Priority is assigned to copies with '*9th September,*' on p. [1] on the evidence of the British Museum copy (received '10 Oc 1914.') and the copies described by Webb and Danielson in their bibliographies (1916). I know of no other copies whose provenance can be dated in any way.

1914: LETTERS ON THE WAR

[*within a rule*] LETTERS / ON / THE WAR / BY / THOMAS HARDY

Collation. Pp. [8]; [1] title-page; [2] blank; [3]–[7] text; [8] colophon: *The first letter was published in "The Times" and certain | other newspapers on October 7th, 1914, and simultaneously in | many journals in the United States of America; the second | letter in "The Manchester Guardian." This is one of twelve | copies of these letters printed for private distribution by | Clement Shorter.—November 9th, 1914.*

Binding. Sewn in purple paper wrappers; front printed in black as title-page.

All edges cut; leaves measure 7″×9″.

Notes. The two letters that compose this pamphlet were first printed in the *Manchester Guardian* (Shorter's colophon is inaccurate in this respect), 'Rheims Cathedral' on 7 October 1914 (p. 7) and 'A Reply to Critics' on 13 October 1914 (p. 6). The first letter appeared simultaneously in the *Daily News,* and portions of it, but not the complete text, in *The Times,* the *New York Times,* &c. For a general note on Shorter's pamphlets, see Appendix, pp. 349 f.

'Rheims Cathedral' was written in September and was commenced at least as a personal letter to Sydney Cockerell, though never sent. Hardy's 2-page rough draft (now in Sir Sydney's possession, together with a later typescript made, at his request, in the form of the personal letter originally intended) shows his own addition of the sentence, 'We are able to publish the following extracts from a letter by Mr. Thomas Hardy on the bombardment of Reims cathedral.' When he authorized Shorter's pamphlet, Hardy made several slight revisions and inserted one sentence of some autobiographical interest (after 'When I was young . . .'), 'Sir Arthur Blomfield, with whom I was working, first set me on the track of early French Gothic, of which he was a great admirer, and I won as an architectural prize the books of Nesfield and Norman Shaw on the same subject.' A cutting from the *Daily News* (now in the Dorset County Museum) was used for this revision.

'A Reply to Critics', dated 11 October, was occasioned by the controversy Hardy's earlier letter provoked in the *Manchester Guardian* because of its contemptuous references to Nietzsche and his school.

Both letters (as they appeared in the *Guardian*) were reprinted in *Life and Art* (New York, 1925), pp. 136–9. Hardy himself never collected them.

1914: SATIRES OF CIRCUMSTANCE

SATIRES / OF CIRCUMSTANCE / LYRICS AND REVERIES / WITH MISCELLANEOUS PIECES / BY / THOMAS HARDY / MACMILLAN AND CO., LIMITED / ST. MARTIN'S STREET, LONDON / 1914

Collation. [A]⁶, B–P⁸, Q⁴; pp. [ii]+x+232; blank leaf; [i] half-title; [ii] publishers' device and imprints; [iii] title-page; [iv] blank save for word 'Copyright'; v–ix Contents; [x] blank; 1–230 text, printers' imprint at foot of p. 230: *Printed by* R. & R. Clark, Limited, *Edinburgh.* /; [231][232] publishers' advertisements of Hardy's works.

Binding. Olive-green cloth; front blocked in gold with TH monogram medallion; back plain; gold-lettered on spine: Satires / of / Circumstance / Thomas / Hardy / Macmillan & C°. / .

Plain end-papers; top uncut, fore-edge and tail trimmed; leaves measure $5\frac{1}{8}'' \times 7\frac{5}{8}''$.

The whole format is uniform with the 3 volumes of *The Dynasts* and *Time's Laughingstocks*.

Contents.   LYRICS AND REVERIES

In Front of the Landscape   Page 3

Channel Firing   7
> Written in April 1914 and first printed in the *Fortnightly Review*, May 1914, pp. [769]–770. See *Later Years*, pp. 161–2.

The Convergence of the Twain   9
> Written and first printed in 1912. See above, pp. 150 f.

The Ghost of the Past   12

After the Visit   15
> First printed in the *Spectator*, 13 August 1910, p. 242. Hardy made

and signed a fair copy of the poem in this form, with several variants, for Miss Dugdale, and it was originally inserted in her inscribed copy of *Time's Laughingstocks* (which suggests 1909 as a possible date of composition). It is written on the first and third pages of a folio of fine paper measuring 5″ × 7½″ and is now in my possession. '(To F[lorence] E[mily] D[ugdale])' was not added until the poem was collected, when Miss Dugdale had become Hardy's second wife. There were a few further alterations.

To Meet, or Otherwise 16
Written to Miss Dugdale and first printed (in a decorative border by Harold Nelson) in the *Sphere*, 20 December 1913, p. 316. There are fair copies of the poem, each made and signed on 2 leaves of fine paper, in the Dorset County Museum and the Yale University Library.

The Difference 18

The Sun on the Bookcase 19
'1870' (MS. '1872') was added to the sub-title in subsequent editions.

'When I Set Out for Lyonnesse' 20
This poem refers to Hardy's journey to St. Juliot in Cornwall, 7 March 1870 when he met his first wife (see *Early Life*, pp. 86–87, 99). The date '(1870)' was added to the title in subsequent editions, and the last stanza a little altered. There is a separate MS. of the poem, as copied out and signed for Sydney Cockerell. It is written on a single leaf measuring 7¾″ × 10″, and 2 lines in the last stanza have been revised.

A Thunderstorm in Town 21
The poem is to be associated with Mrs. Henniker. '1893' was added to the sub-title in later editions.

The Torn Letter 22
First printed in the *English Review*, December 1910, pp. 1–2. The last 2 stanzas were rewritten before the poem was collected.

Beyond the Last Lamp 25
First printed, under the title 'Night in a Suburb', in *Harper's Monthly Magazine* (New York), December 1911, p. [92]. There is a separate MS. of the poem, with this title, in the Bliss collection. It is written on a folio of fine paper measuring 8″ × 10″ and signed and dated

'Sept: 1911.' Hardy was living at Upper Tooting between March 1878 and June 1881.

The Face at the Casement   27

It is not without significance that the one spot identified in this poem, the garth of 'sad Saint Cleather' (or Clether), is in Cornwall close to scenes associated in Hardy's mind with the romance of his first marriage. The episode is reminiscent of Felix Jethway in *A Pair of Blue Eyes* (cf. epigraph, Chap. 38).

Lost Love   30

Cf. *Later Years*, p. 153.

'My Spirit will not Haunt the Mound'   31

First printed in *Poetry and Drama*, December 1913, pp. 395–6.

Wessex Heights   32

The poem was originally designed to open the volume. MS. adds at end, as date of composition, 'December, 1896'.

In Death Divided   35

In Hardy's final revision '189–' was added as date of composition, and the poem is perhaps to be associated with Mrs. Henniker.

The Place on the Map   37

First printed, with the sub-title 'A Poor Schoolmaster's Story', in the *English Review*, September 1913, pp. 161–2.

Where the Picnic Was   39

In subsequent editions this poem was put with 'Poems of 1912–13' where it more properly belongs. It is now the last poem in that group.

The Schreckhorn   41

First printed in F. W. Maitland, *The Life and Letters of Leslie Stephen* (London, 1906), p. 278, where Hardy gives (p. 277) some account of its inspiration. The sonnet was commenced at least in June 1897. See also *Later Years*, p. 67.

A Singer Asleep   42

This tribute to Swinburne was composed on a visit to his grave at Bonchurch, 23 March 1910, not quite a year after his death. Hardy had written to Swinburne in 1897 of 'the buoyant time of 30 years ago, when I used to read your early works walking along the crowded London streets, to my imminent risk of being knocked down', and he often testified to Swinburne's early and abiding influence on his work. He was a 'brother-poet of whom he never spoke save in words of admiration and affection.' (*Later Years*, p. 141. See also pp. 135–7.) The poem was first printed in the *English Review*, April 1910, pp. 1–3 (see below, p. 313). The MS. used on that occasion (now framed and glazed) is written on 3 leaves measuring $7\frac{1}{2}'' \times 9\frac{3}{4}''$ and, though a fair copy, shows a number of verbal alterations and the deleted sub-title, 'A South Coast Nocturne'. It was given (through Sydney Cockerell) to the Newnes Public Library, Putney (close to Swinburne's last home, No. 2 The Pines), in July 1913. Bonchurch had been thought of, but there seemed no place for the MS. there. At T. J. Wise's request Hardy later made and signed a copy of the poem for the Ashley Library Swinburne Collection (now in the British Museum). It is written on 7 leaves of fine paper, measuring $7\frac{3}{4}'' \times 9\frac{7}{8}''$ and watermarked '1920', and is bound in full red morocco. Another MS. was given by Mrs. Hardy to C. H. St. John Hornby.

A Plaint to Man   45
Written in 1909–10. MS. 'The Plaint of a Puppet'.

God's Funeral   47
Begun in 1908 and finished in 1910. First printed, with the sub-title 'An Allegorical Conception of the present state of Theology', in the *Fortnightly Review*, March 1912, pp. [397]–399. An alternative title submitted to the editor was 'The Funeral of Jahveh'. See *Later Years*, p. 147 (the date of publication is incorrectly given). A separate MS. of the poem exists, a fair copy with several slight alterations, written on 4 leaves of fine paper measuring $7\frac{7}{8}'' \times 9\frac{7}{8}''$ and inscribed 'To Edmund Gosse—(To indulge his fancy that these sheets have value.) July: 1913.' Hardy has also noted in red ink '[Original MS.]' and '[First published in the Fortnightly Review from a type-written copy.]'. The MS. is bound in full red morocco and is now in the possession of Mr. Frederick B. Adams, Jr. Hardy wrote to Gosse after he had sent him the MS. that the poem 'would have been enough in itself to damn me for the Laureateship, even if I had tried for or thought of it, which of course I did not.'

Spectres that Grieve   52
First printed, under the title 'The Plaint of Certain Spectres', in the *Saturday Review*, 3 January 1914, p. 16.

'Ah, are you Digging on my Grave?'   54
First printed in the *Saturday Review*, 27 September 1913, p. 396.

SATIRES OF CIRCUMSTANCE

[These fifteen poems are dated '1910' in the MS. Eleven of them were first printed in the *Fortnightly Review*, April 1911, pp. [579]–583. A twelfth printed there, 'On the Doorstep', was afterwards discarded (see below, p. 314). Hardy had used the phrase, 'a satire of circumstance', in *The Hand of Ethelberta*, p. 97. In subsequent editions the whole group was moved to the end of the volume.]

    I. At Tea   59
        First printed in the *Fortnightly Review*.

    II. In Church   60
        First printed in the *Fortnightly Review*. Line 9 was added here.

    III. By her Aunt's Grave   61
        First printed in the *Fortnightly Review*. Several lines were a little altered.

    IV. In the Room of the Bride-Elect   62
        First printed in the *Fortnightly Review*. Line 3 was added here and the closing couplet rewritten.

    V. At a Watering-Place   63
        First printed in the *Fortnightly Review*.

    VI. In the Cemetery   64
        First printed in the *Fortnightly Review*. Lines 5 and 6 were added here.

    VII. Outside the Window   65
        First printed in the *Fortnightly Review*.

    VIII. In the Study   66
        A line was added, after line 15, in subsequent editions.

    IX. At the Altar-Rail   67
        First printed in the *Fortnightly Review*.

    X. In the Nuptial Chamber   68
        First printed in the *Fortnightly Review*.

LYRICS AND REVERIES (*continued*)

St. Launce's Revisited 90
> The poem is dated '1913' in the MS. (and called 'At St. Launce's') and in subsequent editions was put with 'Poems of 1912–13' where it more properly belongs. It is now the last but one in that group.

POEMS OF 1912–13

[The poems in this group, among the most intensely personal Hardy ever wrote, were inspired by the death of his first wife, Emma Lavinia Gifford, 27 November 1912, and a visit to the scenes of their courtship, at St. Juliot in Cornwall, in March 1913 (commenced 6 March, within a day of the 43rd anniversary of his memorable first journey into 'Lyonnesse'). He regretted the later journey and wrote from Boscastle, 'The visit to this neighbourhood has been a very painful one to me, and I have said a dozen times I wish I had not come—what possessed me to do it!' In these first months of his bereavement, however, there was an astonishing recreation of the romance of 1870, long since desperately shattered, and a flood of creative energy to match it (see *Later Years*, p. 156). Hardy sometimes called these poems 'an expiation'.]

The Going 95
> Written in December 1912.

Your Last Drive 97
> Written in December 1912. See *Later Years*, p. 154, and 'A Leaving'.

The Walk 99

Rain on a Grave 100
> Written 31 January 1913. MS. 'Rain on Her Grave'.

'I Found Her out There' 102
> Dated December 1912 in *Selected Poems* (only).

Without Ceremony 104

Lament 105

The Haunter 107
> The last 4 lines were entirely rewritten in subsequent editions.

The Voice 109
> Written in December 1912.

MISCELLANEOUS PIECES

   The MS., which gives the date of composition as 'Autumn: 1910',
has the following cancelled stanza (between stanzas 45 and 46):

     "For really I never knew till now
     What a hero my lord was. Nothing can bow
        Or bend or lower
     A soul so cool! Yes, I'll keep my vow."

> For I am sick of thinking
>   On whither things tend,
>   And will foster hoodwinking
>   Henceforth to the end.

Starlings on the Roof   186
> First printed, with the sub-title '(Moving House, Michaelmas.)', in
> the *Nation*, 18 October 1913, p. 140. There is a proof of the
> poem in this form (dated 10 October), with several autograph
> corrections, in the Yale University Library. Some verbal alterations
> were made when the poem was collected.

The Moon Looks in   187

The Sweet Hussy   188

The Telegram   189
> First printed in *Harper's Monthly Magazine* (New York), December
> 1913, p. [103]. Some verbal alterations were made when the poem
> was collected.

The Moth-Signal   191
> This poem, as the words '(On Egdon Heath)' suggest, is derived
> from a scene in *The Return of the Native* (Bk. IV, Chap. 4, 'Rough
> Coercion is employed', pp. 319–20, 324).

Seen by the Waits   193

The Two Soldiers   194
> MS. 'A Rencounter'.

The Death of Regret   195
> Mrs. Hardy wrote to Lady Hoare from Max Gate in December 1914,
> 'The poem was, in the first place, written about a cat—a little cat
> strangled in a rabbit wire on the barrow in sight of this house . . .
> My husband thought the poem too good for a cat, and so made it
> apply to a man.' Cf. 'The Roman Gravemounds'.

In the Days of Crinoline   197
> Titled 'The Vicar's Young Wife' in the MS., where the date of
> composition is given as 'July: 1911'.

The Roman Gravemounds   199
> Written in November 1910. First printed, under the title 'Among
> the Roman Gravemounds', in the *English Review*, December 1911,
> p. 1. The MS. used on that occasion, with the title 'By the Roman
> Earthworks', and Hardy's corrected proof are now in the possession
> of Professor J. N. Mavrogordato (formerly sub-editor of the *English*

Review). The poem refers to a favourite pet, Kitsy, buried at Max Gate, and the 'mourner' is Hardy himself.

The Workbox   201

The Sacrilege   203
First printed in the *Fortnightly Review*, November 1911, pp. [773]–777. Several lines were rewritten when the poem was collected and the third stanza of Part II added.

The Abbey Mason   210
Written in December 1911, after a visit to Gloucester Cathedral (see *Later Years*, pp. 150–1). First printed (with marginal decorations by Harvey Emrich) in *Harper's Monthly Magazine* (New York), December 1912, pp. [21–25]. A few verbal alterations (in particular, adding frost and icicles to the rain that solved the 'ogive riddle') were made when the poem was collected, and in subsequent editions '(With Memories of John Hicks, Architect)' was added to the title —as tribute to Hardy's first master in architecture. There is a separate MS. of the poem in the Pierpont Morgan Library, written on 13 leaves of fine paper measuring $7\frac{3}{4}'' \times 9\frac{7}{8}''$ and bound in full red morocco. This is a fair copy without alteration, purchased by Mr. Morgan directly from Hardy in March 1912, while the poem still remained unpublished in Harper & Brothers' hands. It preserves one or two readings not found elsewhere. Hardy wrote of the MS. to Clarence McIlvaine, who arranged the sale, 'The Editor [of *Harper's*] has a typewritten copy: this is the original. Thus Mr. Morgan will have one of my earlier ["The Romantic Adventures of a Milkmaid"], and my latest MS. . . . I wonder if they are going to illustrate the poem in the magazine? You will recall the photographs I sent.'

The Jubilee of a Magazine   222
First printed, under the title 'An Impromptu to the Editor', in the *Cornhill Magazine*, January 1910, pp. 6–7. Several lines were rewritten when the poem was collected and the 9th stanza omitted altogether. MS. ' "The Cornhill's" Jubilee'.

The Satin Shoes   224
First printed, with the sub-title 'A Quiet Tragedy' (and an illustration and tailpiece by F. Walter Taylor), in *Harper's Monthly Magazine*

(New York), January 1910, pp. [165]–167. Hardy identified the scene as Higher Bockhampton.

Exeunt Omnes   227

Written 2 June 1913, Hardy's seventy-third birthday. MS. 'Epilogue'.

A Poet   228

Written in July 1914, five months after Hardy's second marriage. The last stanza was rewritten in subsequent editions.

POSTSCRIPT

'Men who March Away'   229

Written and first printed in September 1914. See above, pp. 157 f. The poem was subsequently transferred to *Moments of Vision* and put first among 'Poems of War and Patriotism', where it more properly belongs.

Manuscript. The MS. of *Satires of Circumstance* is written on 189 leaves of fine paper, measuring $7\frac{3}{8}'' \times 9\frac{13}{16}''$ and numbered i–iv (title-page, Contents, &c.) and 1–185 by Hardy. Like all his later poetical MSS., this is a collection of fair copies arranged for printing, with some further alterations and revisions. A good many trial readings in pencil, notes of periodical publication, &c., have been erased. Where there are significant divergences from the printed text, they have been indicated above in the treatment of individual poems. The final poem in the collection, 'Men who March Away', obviously added at the last moment, is wanting in MS., its place being taken by a cutting from *The Times*. Hardy has altered and corrected this text of the poem and written on it, '(A MS. of this song sent to the Red-Cross sale at Christie's.)' and '[Originally printed from type-written copy, the rough draft having been destroyed.]'.

The MS. is bound in full blue crushed levant, all edges gilt. It was given by Hardy to his wife and inscribed to her on her birthday, 12 January 1923. At her death in 1937 it was deposited in the Dorset County Museum under the provisions of her will.

Notes on Composition and Publication. Satires of Circumstance is a collection of 107 poems. In so far as they are dated, they seem to be almost wholly the work of the years 1910–14, and the poems of an earlier time, with the exception of 2 dated in the 90's, are wanting altogether. Thirty-five of the poems, just a third of the contents, had been published previously. The collection is notable for the first appearance, in 'Poems of 1912–13', of a theme dominant in all Hardy's subsequent verse, romance and regret associated with his courtship in Cornwall in the 70's and the death of his first wife (after long estrangement) in 1912. The 18 poems (later 21) grouped as 'Poems of 1912–13' and many others in the collection which belong with them lend a special poignancy and integrity to the volume. No one was more keenly aware than the author, however, of the incongruity of publishing these verses with such sardonic work as 'Satires of Circumstance'. 'So much shadow, domestic and public, had passed over his head since he had written the satires that he was in no mood now to publish humour or irony, and hence he would readily have suppressed them if they had not already gained such currency from magazine publication that he could not do it.' (*Later Years*, p. 164.) The MS. of the volume was in Macmillan's hands in August 1914, and the title was their choice not Hardy's.

Satires of Circumstance was published at 4s. 6d. in an edition of 2,000 copies, 17 November 1914. Hardy inscribed copies to his wife ('Florence Emily in all affection') and (dated November 1914) to Sydney C. Cockerell ('These inconsequent verses'), Edmund Gosse ('the mixture as before, of unstable fancies, conjectures, and contradictions'), and (December 1914) Lascelles Abercrombie. His own copy, marked in pencil '1st edn.', is now in the Dorset County Museum.

Subsequent Editions (*see also* COLLECTED EDITIONS). There was a second impression revised of *Satires of Circumstance* in 1915, introducing minor corrections. The volume, combined with *Moments of Vision*, was included in Macmillan's definitive Wessex Edition in 1919.

[1914]: THE DYNASTS, PROLOGUE AND EPILOGUE

[*within a rule*] .. THE .. / DYNASTS / BY / THOMAS HARDY / THE PROLOGUE AND EPILOGUE

Collation. Pp. [8]; [1] title-page; [2] blank; [3]–[7] text, facsimile of Hardy's signature at end; [8] colophon: *This is the Prologue and Epilogue to Thomas Hardy's | play, "The Dynasts," abridged for the stage*

and pro- | *duced by Granville Barker on November* 25*th,* 1914. | *The Prologue was included in the programme of the* | *play. The Epilogue is here printed with the Author's* | *permission for the first time. This is one of twelve* | *copies privately printed by Clement Shorter for circu-* | *lation among his friends.*

Binding. Sewn in drab paper wrappers; front printed in black as title-page. All edges cut; leaves measure $7\frac{1}{2}'' \times 9''$.

Notes. These two poems were written at Granville-Barker's request for his production of *The Dynasts* at the Kingsway Theatre (see above, p. 135) and were recited by 'The Reader', Henry Ainley. The play ran for seventy-two performances, opening 25 November 1914 and closing 30 January 1915. The Prologue was printed in the programme from the first and was reprinted, under the title 'A Poem on the War', in the *Sphere,* 5 December 1914, p. viii; the Epilogue was first printed here and added to the programme in later (undated) issues.

There is no evidence from which to date this edition of Shorter's. It was presumably produced early in December 1914; the British Museum copy was received 9 January 1915. For a general note on Shorter's privately printed pamphlets, see Appendix, pp. 349 f.

Though the poems appear again in the programme of the Hardy Players' production of *Wessex Scenes from The Dynasts*, Weymouth and Dorchester, 1916 (see Appendix, pp. 351 ff.), Hardy never collected them, occasional as they are and of no distinction.[1] They are both in heroic couplets, the Prologue a poem of 23 lines, the Epilogue of 18 lines.

There are rough drafts of the two poems in the Dorset County Museum (see above, p. 135) and a signed typescript of the Epilogue, supplied for Shorter's edition, in the Bliss collection.

---

[1] The Prologue and the last 6 lines (only) of the Epilogue were reprinted in the *Fortnightly Review*, February 1915, pp. 356–7 (in a review by J. F. Macdonald, 'English Life and the English Stage'); see also Ernest Brennecke, *The Life of Thomas Hardy* (New York, 1925), pp. 241–2, and E. C. Hickson, *The Versification of Thomas Hardy* (Philadelphia, 1931), p. 85.

[1915]: BEFORE MARCHING AND AFTER

[*within a rule*] BEFORE / MARCHING / AND AFTER. / BY / THOMAS HARDY.

Collation. Pp. [12]; [1][2] blank; [3] title-page; [4] photograph of 2nd Lieutenant F. W. George, separately printed and mounted; [5][6] Foreword, signed 'F.E.H.'; [7]–[9] text; [10] colophon: *Of this Poem and Foreword, the former of / which first appeared in the "Fortnightly / Review" for November* [sic]*, 1915, twenty-five / copies only have been privately printed, by / permission of the Author, for distribution / among friends.* / [numbered and signed by Clement Shorter]; [11][12] blank.

Binding. Sewn in stiff purple paper wrappers (lined with white); front printed in black as title-page.

All edges cut; leaves measure $7\frac{7}{16}" \times 8\frac{7}{8}"$.

Notes. This poem was written in September 1915 and first printed in the *Fortnightly Review*, October 1915, p. [609]. Shorter's edition seems to have followed in December (Hardy acknowledged a proof of the poem on 8 December). The verses were collected in *Selected Poems*, pp. 201–2, and later in *Moments of Vision*, pp. 235–6. For a general note on Shorter's pamphlets, see Appendix, pp. 349 f.

The poem is a tribute to 2nd Lieutenant Frank William George of the 5th Dorset Regiment, whose death in action on the Gallipoli Peninsula 22 August was announced in *The Times*, 3 September 1915. Through his mother, a Hardy, he was a cousin of the poet. Hardy wrote of him, 'Frank George, though so remotely related, is the first one of my family to be killed in battle for the last hundred years, so far as I know. He might say Militavi non sine gloria—short as his career has been.' (*Later Years*, p. 169. See also *Friends of a Lifetime*, pp. 280–1.) Mrs. Hardy in her Foreword quotes from one of his last letters.

There is a fair copy of the poem in the Bliss collection, written with signature and date on a single leaf measuring $7" \times 8\frac{7}{8}"$. It is reproduced in facsimile in the Barrie *et al.* Sale Catalogue (Sotheby & Co., 20–22 December 1937), p. 16.

1915: THE OXEN

THE ¶ / [*double rule and ornament*] / OXEN. / [*double rule*] / By THOMAS HARDY. / [*ornament*] / Published in "The Times," 24th December, 1915. / Reprinted at Hove, 28th December, 1915.

Collation. Pp. [4]; [1] title-page; [2] blank; [3] text; [4] blank.

Binding. Sewn in grey paper wrappers; front printed in black: THE ¶ / [*double rule and ornament*] / OXEN. / [*double rule*] / By THOMAS HARDY. / [*ornament*] / HOVE, 1915. / [Private Circulation Only].

All edges cut; leaves measure 5⅛″ × 8″.

Notes. This poem was first printed in *The Times*, 24 December 1915, p. 7, with the express statement, 'No Copyright reserved.' It was reprinted four days later for 'private circulation only' by E. Williams, antiquarian bookseller, of 37 New Town Road, Hove (Brighton), who had reprinted 'Song of the Soldiers' in similar fashion the year before. Hardy acknowledged the receipt of copies 23 January 1916. Nothing further is discoverable about this edition, but it must have been a large one—the pamphlet is common, and Sydney Cockerell noted in his copy, given him by the author, 20 February 1916, 'Fifty copies had been sent to [Hardy] by the reprinter.' For the often repeated statement that it was 'issued solely to give away to soldiers on active service abroad', see above, p. 158. The poem was collected in *Selected Poems*, p. 130, and later in *Moments of Vision*, p. 80. Hardy had used the old belief before, in *Tess of the d'Urbervilles*, Chap. 17 (p. 143), where Angel Clare comments, 'It's a curious story; it carries us back to mediaeval times, when faith was a living thing!' He identified the scene as Higher Bockhampton.

There is a separate MS. of the poem, a fair copy made by Hardy for the occasion, which Mrs. Hardy sent to the Red Cross Sale at Christie's, 26 April 1916. It is reproduced in facsimile in the Folsom Sale Catalogue (New York, American Art Association Anderson Galleries, 6 December 1932), p. 39.

1916: IN TIME OF 'THE BREAKING OF NATIONS'

[*within a rule*] IN TIME OF / "THE BREAKING / OF NATIONS" / BY / THOMAS HARDY

Collation. Pp. [8]; [1][2] blank; [3] title-page; [4] colophon: *Of this Poem, which first appeared in "The | Saturday Review" for January* 29, 1916, / *twenty-five copies only have been printed by | Clement Shorter for private circulation, with | the permission of the Author. | February* 1, 1916. / [numbered and signed by Clement Shorter]; [5][6] text; [7][8] blank.

Binding. Sewn in stiff purple paper wrappers (lined with white); front printed in black as title-page.

All edges cut; leaves measure $7\frac{7}{16}'' \times 9''$.

Notes. This poem was written in 1915 and first printed in the *Saturday Review*, 29 January 1916, p. 108. It was there expressly stated that the copyright was not reserved, and Shorter's edition seems to have followed immediately, though the date 'February 1' is not necessarily trustworthy. For a general note on Shorter's pamphlets, see Appendix, pp. 349 f.

The poem is a reminiscence of St. Juliot in August 1870, during the Franco-Prussian War (see *Early Life*, p. 104, and *Later Years*, p. 178). When Hardy collected it in *Selected Poems* (p. 203) and later in *Moments of Vision* (p. 232), he made several verbal alterations.

Two separate MSS. exist, both fair copies on fine paper. The earlier, written and signed on a folio measuring $8'' \times 10''$, was sent by Mrs. Hardy to the Red Cross Sale at Christie's, 26 April 1916, and is now in the Bliss collection. The later, on a single leaf of the same paper, was made and signed after the poem had been collected. It was formerly in the possession of Paul Lemperly, a gift of Mrs. Hardy in July 1918.

1916: DOMICILIUM

[*within a rule*] DOMICILIUM / BY / THOMAS HARDY

Collation. Pp. [ii]+10; blank leaf; [1] title-page; [2] blank; 3 Note, signed 'C.K.S.' and dated 5 April 1916; [4] blank; 5–7 text; [8] colophon: *Of this poem by Thomas Hardy, twenty-five | copies have been privately*

printed by Clement | Shorter for distribution among his friends. | [num-
bered and signed by Clement Shorter]; [9][10] blank.

Binding. Sewn in stiff purple paper wrappers (lined with white); front
printed in black as title-page.

All edges cut; leaves measure 7½"×9".

Notes. This poem was written between 1857 and 1860 and is 'the earliest
discoverable of young Hardy's attempts in verse'. It describes his birthplace at Higher Bockhampton as he knew it and as his grandparents
had known it fifty years before. Shorter was permitted to print the
poem, presumably in the spring of 1916, 'with the express condition
that it is not to be published in any book or newspaper.' For a general
note on Shorter's privately printed pamphlets, see Appendix, pp. 349 f.
Mrs. Hardy printed the poem privately in 1918 (see below, p. 208),
and it was reprinted in *Early Life*, pp. 4–5.

There is a MS. of the poem in the Dorset County Museum, written
(with several slight alterations) on a single leaf measuring 8"×10".
Hardy has noted on it, '[T. Hardy's [first *del.*] earliest known production in verse]' and, in red ink, '(original written between 1857 and
1860 this being a copy some years later.)'.

1916: TO SHAKESPEARE AFTER THREE HUNDRED
YEARS

TO SHAKESPEARE AFTER / THREE HUNDRED YEARS / BY
THOMAS HARDY / [*ornament*]

Collation. Pp. [8]; [1][2] blank; [3] title-page; [4] blank; [5][6] text;
[7] blank; [8] colophon: *Fifty copies printed for Florence Emily Hardy |
at the Chiswick Press, London, E.C. 1916 | This is No.* [numbered and
initialed by Mrs. Hardy] / .

Binding. Sewn in dark or light blue antique paper wrappers; front printed
in black as title-page.

All edges uncut; leaves measure 6⅞"×8¹³⁄₁₆".

Notes. This poem was written 14 February 1916 and first printed in *A
Book of Homage to Shakespeare*, ed. Israel Gollancz (London, April

1916), pp. [1]–2. Several off-prints were made, in the form of a broadside measuring $9\frac{7}{8}'' \times 14\frac{1}{2}''$, and one in the Bliss collection is signed. With a few alterations the poem was reprinted in the *Fortnightly Review*, June 1916, pp. [927]–928. Mrs. Hardy's edition, the first of her privately printed pamphlets, was sent to the printers in July. The typescript used and three successive proofs, the earliest dated 26 July and with Hardy's corrections, are now in the possession of Sir Sydney Cockerell. The pamphlet was ready for distribution in August, and Hardy inscribed a copy to Cockerell 25 August. The poem, with a few further revisions, was collected in *Moments of Vision*, pp. 24–26. For a general note on Mrs. Hardy's privately printed pamphlets, see Appendix, pp. 349 f.

There is a separate MS. of the poem in the Ashley Library in the British Museum. It is a fair copy (complete with title-page), written out at T. J. Wise's request, on 7 leaves of fine paper measuring $7\frac{7}{8}'' \times 9\frac{15}{16}''$ and bound in full red morocco. The first stanza is reproduced in facsimile in *The Ashley Library*, vol. ii (London, 1922), facing p. 172.[1] In similar fashion the poem was copied for Sydney Cockerell on the fly-leaf of a facsimile First Folio (London, 1910).

1916: SELECTED POEMS

SELECTED POEMS / OF / THOMAS HARDY / [*vignette, Thornycroft's bust of Hardy*] / MACMILLAN AND CO., LIMITED / ST. MARTIN'S STREET, LONDON / 1916

Collation. [A]⁴(A1+2), B–O⁸, P⁴; pp. [ii]+x+216; blank leaf; [i] half-title; [ii] blank; [iii] title-page; [iv] blank save for word 'Copyright'; v–ix Contents; [x] blank; 1 divisional title; [2] blank; 3–214 text, printers' imprint at foot of p. 214: *Printed by* R. & R. Clark, Limited, *Edinburgh.* / ; [215][216] advertisements of Hardy's works, separately paged 1–2.

---

[1] The poem as it appears in the Magdalene Coll. MS. of *Moments of Vision*, the earliest version with subsequent alterations, is reproduced in facsimile in C. J. Weber, *Hardy of Wessex* (New York, 1940), pp. [209–10]. Still another MS. of the poem, stanzas 1, 2, and 6 only, written out for the occasion, is reproduced in the programme of the 'Grand Matinee in Aid of the Shakespeare Memorial Theatre Fund', Theatre Royal, Drury Lane, 9 November 1926.

Half-title and title-leaf are separately printed in photogravure and inserted.

Binding. Blue cloth; front blocked in gold with GTS monogram medallion; front and back blocked in blind with 2 rules at top and bottom; gold-lettered on spine: [*2 rules*] / Selected / Poems / of / Thomas / Hardy / [*rule*] / Macmillan & C.° / [*rule*] / .

Plain end-papers; top uncut, fore-edge and tail trimmed; leaves measure 4⅛″×6¼″.

The whole format is uniform with other volumes in the Golden Treasury Series.

PART II. POEMS NARRATIVE AND REFLECTIVE

Notes on Composition and Publication. Selected Poems is a collection of 120 poems drawn from *The Dynasts* and the four volumes of poetry Hardy had published up to 1916 and including, a fact that lends the book particular importance, nine poems from the unpublished MS. of *Moments of Vision*. Eighteen come from *Wessex Poems*, 28 from *Poems of the Past and the Present*, 6 from *The Dynasts*, 26 from *Time's Laughingstocks*, and 33 from *Satires of Circumstance*. Hardy set great store by the volume (which Macmillan proposed in March 1916), hoping it would bring his poetry to a wider public, and the selections were made, as he wrote to Gosse, with an eye to the 'General Reader'.

Selected Poems was published at 2*s*. 6*d*. in an edition of 2,000 copies, 3 October 1916. Hardy inscribed copies to his wife (4 October, 'this first copy'), Ethel Richardson (his sister-in-law), Galsworthy, Charles Whibley, H. J. C. Grierson ('in remembrance of 1905' [Hardy's visit to Aberdeen]), Shorter ('in whose paper some of these verses first saw the light'), and Evelyn Gifford. His own copy, labelled '[Study copy] 1ˢᵗ Edⁿ (marked as to be corrected in reprint)' and containing many corrections and a list of titles 'Some at first chosen: afterwards omitted', is now in the Dorset County Museum.

Subsequent Editions, Chosen Poems. There was a second impression of *Selected Poems* in the month of publication and further impressions in 1917, 1922, &c. In 1921 the Medici Society published an edition with wood-engraved portrait of Hardy and title-page vignette by William Nicholson. This was limited to 1,025 copies, with 14 copies on vellum signed by Hardy.

The preparation of a new edition of *Selected Poems* formed almost the last literary activity of Hardy's life. The work was done in September 1927, 'in case anything should happen', he wrote to Macmillan, and 'the last entry but one in his notebook refers to the sending of the copy to the publishers.' (*Later Years*, p. 258.) This was 18 September. In a letter of 10 November acknowledging proof, he suggested 'Select' or 'Chosen' for the title because of the confusion between 'Selected' and 'Collected', concluding, 'Perhaps Chosen is most distinctive.' The selection was enlarged from 120 to 161 poems. Eight were discarded (as indicated above); 'Hap' (*Wessex Poems*), 'The Fiddler' and 'A Tramp-woman's Tragedy' (*Time's Laughingstocks*), and 'Albuera' (*The Dynasts*) were added and, from the volumes published since 1916, 45 poems (11 from *Moments of Vision*, 15 from *Late Lyrics and Earlier*, 2 from *The Queen of Cornwall*, and 17 from *Human Shows*). *Chosen Poems* was not published until August 1929.

1916: 'WHEN I WEEKLY KNEW'

"WHEN I WEEKLY KNEW" / BY THOMAS HARDY / [*ornament*]

Collation. Pp. 8; [1] title-page; [2] blank; 3–5 text; [6][7] blank; [8] colophon: *Twenty-five copies printed for Florence Emily Hardy / at the Chiswick Press, London, E.C. 1916 / This is No.* [numbered and initialed by Mrs. Hardy] / .

Binding. Sewn in light or dark blue antique paper wrappers; front printed in black as title-page.

All edges uncut; leaves measure $5\frac{5}{8}'' \times 8\frac{13}{16}''$.

Notes. This poem, under the title 'In Time of Slaughter', was first printed in the *Spectator*, 19 August 1916, p. 212. Mrs. Hardy's edition was sent to the printers 29 September and seems to have been ready in late October. The typescript used and a first proof dated 5 October are now in the possession of Sir Sydney Cockerell. For this edition the poem was not only retitled but extensively revised, 12 scattered lines being added. It was collected in *Moments of Vision* (pp. 27–29) under the title 'Quid Hic Agis?' For a general note on Mrs. Hardy's pamphlets, see Appendix, pp. 349 f.

The poem recalls St. Juliot Church in the 70's and Hardy's first wife.
The 'chapter from Kings' (1 Kings xix) was a special favourite of
the poet's and was appropriately chosen for his memorial window in
Stinsford Church. See *Early Life*, pp. 50, 203, and *A Pair of Blue
Eyes*, p. 202.

1917: ENGLAND TO GERMANY, ETC.

ENGLAND TO GERMANY. / THE PITY OF IT. I MET A /
MAN. A NEW YEAR'S EVE / IN WAR TIME / BY THOMAS
HARDY / [*ornament*]

Collation. Pp. 12; [1] title-page; [2] blank; 3–8 text; [9] blank; [10] colophon: *Twenty-five copies printed for Florence Emily Hardy / at the Chiswick Press, London, E.C. February* 1917 / *This is No.* [numbered and
initialed by Mrs. Hardy] / ; [11][12] blank.

Binding. Sewn in dark or light blue antique paper wrappers; front printed
in black as title-page.

All edges uncut; leaves measure $6\frac{7}{8}'' \times 8\frac{3}{4}''$.

Notes. With the exception of 'England to Germany', the four war poems
which compose this pamphlet had been printed previously.

'England to Germany' was written in October 1914 and first printed
here. It was collected, with some alteration, as 'England to Germany
in 1914', in *Moments of Vision*, p. 227.

'The Pity of It' was written in February 1915 and first printed in the
Fortnightly Review, April 1915, p. [567]. The sonnet was suggested
by a contemporary article by Dr. Caleb Williams Saleeby on 'Eugenics',
and Hardy presented a MS. of it to Dr. Saleeby (for facsimile, see Elkin
Mathews Catalogue 100, Bishops Stortford, 1945). Cf. *Early Life*,
p. 290. The poem was collected in *Moments of Vision*, p. 230.

'I Met a Man' was written in 1916 and first printed in the *Fortnightly
Review*, February 1917, pp. [187]–188. A number of verbal altera-
tions were then made for its appearance here. It was collected in
Moments of Vision, pp. 246–7.

'A New Year's Eve in War Time' was written in 1915–16 and first
printed in the *Sphere*, 6 January 1917, p. 10. The poem was slightly

revised for its appearance here and one line deleted. It was collected in *Moments of Vision*, pp. 244–5. The incident described was an actual one (see *Friends of a Lifetime*, p. 284).

The inclusion of 'The Pity of It' in this collection was an afterthought, and there is a proof of the pamphlet without it, corrected by Hardy and dated 8 February 1917, in the possession of Sir Sydney Cockerell. Preserved with it are a typescript of 'The Pity of It', and 'A New Year's Eve in War Time' as cut from the *Sphere* and revised by Hardy. The pamphlet as finally printed was not ready for distribution until March 1917 (Hardy inscribing a copy to Sydney Cockerell with that date, Mrs. Hardy inscribing one to him with the date 10 March). For a general note on Mrs. Hardy's privately printed pamphlets, see Appendix, pp. 349 f.

1917: A TRAMPWOMAN'S TRAGEDY

A TRAMPWOMAN'S / TRAGEDY / BY THOMAS HARDY / [*ornament*]

Collation. Pp. [ii]+10; blank leaf; [1] title-page; [2] blank; 3–8 text; [9] blank; [10] colophon: *Twenty-five copies printed for Florence Emily Hardy / at the Chiswick Press, London, E.C. March 1917 / This is No.* [numbered and initialed by Mrs. Hardy] / .

Binding. Sewn in dark or light blue antique paper wrappers; front printed in black as title-page.

All edges uncut; leaves measure $5\frac{11}{16}'' \times 8\frac{7}{8}''$.

Notes. This poem, written in April 1902 and first printed in the *North American Review* (New York), November 1903, had been collected in *Time's Laughingstocks*, 1909 (see above, pp. 138–9). The reason for this edition is not apparent, unless it be the fact that 'Hardy considered this, upon the whole, his most successful poem.' (*Later Years*, p. 93.) It is included here solely to complete the record of Mrs. Hardy's privately printed pamphlets, which must be considered authoritative (this offers one or two very slight variant readings). There are two proofs in the possession of Sir Sydney Cockerell, the first (21 February

1917) corrected by Hardy but without the notes, the second dated 3 March 1917. For a general note on these pamphlets, see Appendix, pp. 349 f.

1917: A CALL TO NATIONAL SERVICE, ETC.

A CALL TO NATIONAL SERVICE / AN APPEAL TO AMERICA / CRY OF THE HOMELESS / BY THOMAS HARDY / [*ornament*]

Collation. Pp. 8; [1] title-page; [2] blank; 3–6 text; [7] blank; [8] colophon: *Twenty-five copies printed for Florence Emily Hardy | at the Chiswick Press, London, E.C. May* 1917 *| This is No.* [numbered and initialed by Mrs. Hardy] / .

Binding. Sewn in dark or light blue antique paper wrappers; front printed in black as title-page.

All edges uncut; leaves measure $6\frac{7}{8}'' \times 8\frac{3}{4}''$.

Notes. The three war poems which compose this pamphlet had all been printed previously.

'A Call to National Service' was written in March 1917 and first printed (without title) in *The Times*, 12 March 1917, p. 9 (and simultaneously in the *Morning Post*—with the title 'For National to Service'— and elsewhere). The MS. used on that occasion is incorporated in the Magdalene Coll. MS. of *Moments of Vision*. When Hardy was considering the inclusion of the sonnet in this pamphlet, he wrote to Sydney Cockerell, 31 March 1917, that it was 'written in a great hurry at the request of the N.S. Depart^t and no proof was sent. I rewrote one line [8] after they had gone, which I will insert if you do print the sonnet.' The poem was collected in *Moments of Vision*, p. 240.

'An Appeal to America on behalf of the Belgian Destitute' was written in December 1914 and first printed, as 'An Appeal to America', in the *New York Times*, 4 January 1915, p. 10, and in other American papers. It was accompanied by the following introductory note: 'This poem, written as an appeal to the American people on behalf of the destitute people of Belgium by Thomas Hardy, the English writer, was given out by the American Commission for Relief in Belgium yesterday.' The poem was subsequently reprinted in *The Need of Belgium, Hand*

Book, and other publications of the Commission. It was collected in *Moments of Vision,* p. 229.

'Cry of the Homeless' was written in August 1915 at the request of Henry James (representing Mrs. Wharton) and first printed in *The Book of the Homeless,* ed. Edith Wharton, New York and London, 1916, p. 16. (There seems to have been a Paris edition, in translation, under the title *Le Livre des Sans-Foyer,* dated 1915.) The poem was accompanied by a reproduction of one of Jacques-Émile Blanche's portraits of Hardy (now in the Tate Gallery). There was a special edition of 50 copies de luxe which contained, among others, a facsimile reproduction of Hardy's MS. The poem was collected in *Moments of Vision,* pp. 233–4.

From proofs in the possession of Sir Sydney Cockerell it is apparent the scheme of the pamphlet was twice altered. The earliest proof (27 March 1917) shows 'For National Service' [*sic*] and 'Men who March Away', altered and corrected in Hardy's hand, with the colophon dated March 1917. This was followed by a proof (13 April) in which 'Before Marching and After' was added and the colophon altered to April 1917. A third proof (28 April), with corrections in Hardy's hand, shows the three poems as finally printed. The pamphlet was ready for distribution in May. For a general note on Mrs. Hardy's privately printed pamphlets, see Appendix, pp. 349 f.

1917: THE FIDDLER'S STORY, ETC.

THE FIDDLER'S STORY / A JINGLE ON THE TIMES / BY THOMAS HARDY / [*ornament*]

Collation. Pp. [ii]+10; blank leaf; [1] title-page; [2] blank; 3–8 text; [9] colophon: *Twenty-five copies printed for Florence Emily Hardy | at the Chiswick Press, London, E.C. October* 1917 | *This is No.* [numbered and initialed by Mrs. Hardy] / ; [10] blank.[1]

Binding. Sewn in dark or light blue antique paper wrappers; front printed in black as title-page.

All edges uncut; leaves measure 6$\frac{15}{16}$″ × 8$\frac{7}{8}$″.

[1] In some copies the outside half-sheet was folded in reverse, and the collation runs: [i] colophon; [ii] blank; ... [9][10] blank.

Notes. These two poems are here printed for the first time.

'The Fiddler's Story', with the addition of a new stanza (inserted after stanza 1), was reprinted under the title 'The Country Wedding', with 2 illustrations in colour by C. E. Brock, in *Cassell's Winter Annual*, 1921–2 [November 1921], pp. 67–68. In this form the poem was collected in *Late Lyrics and Earlier*, pp. 187–9.

'A Jingle on the Times' was written in December 1914 and sent to Elizabeth Asquith for an 'album' she was proposing to publish early the following spring in aid of the Arts Fund. The volume seems never to have appeared, and the MS. prepared for her, sheets of note-paper sewn together into a quire, was among the Max Gate papers in 1937. The poem, a satiric work of nine 8-line stanzas, was never collected by Hardy (for some reason Mrs. Hardy, in presenting copies of the pamphlet, described *both* poems as unlikely to be reprinted).

A typescript of the poems with Hardy's additions and a first proof (25 September 1917) corrected by Hardy are in the possession of Sir Sydney Cockerell. For a general note on Mrs. Hardy's privately printed pamphlets, see Appendix, pp. 349 f.

1917: MOMENTS OF VISION

MOMENTS OF VISION / AND / MISCELLANEOUS VERSES / BY / THOMAS HARDY / MACMILLAN AND CO., LIMITED / ST. MARTIN'S STREET, LONDON / 1917

Collation. [A]⁶, B–R⁸, [S]²; pp. xii+260; [i] half-title; [ii] publishers' device and imprints; [iii] title-page; [iv] blank save for word 'Copyright'; v–xi Contents; [xii] blank; 1–256 text, printers' imprint at foot of p. 256: *Printed by* R. & R. Clark, Limited, *Edinburgh.* / ; [257]–[260] publishers' advertisements of Hardy's works, separately paged [1]–4.

Binding. Olive-green cloth; front blocked in gold with TH monogram medallion; back plain; gold-lettered on spine: Moments / of / Vision / Thomas / Hardy / Macmillan & Cᵒ. / .

Plain end-papers; top uncut, fore-edge and tail trimmed; leaves measure 5″×7⅝″.

The whole format is uniform with the 3 volumes of *The Dynasts*, &c.

Contents. Moments of Vision   Page 1
There is a separate MS. of the poem in the Bliss collection. It is a fair copy with several alterations, written on a single leaf of fine paper measuring 8″×10″, and signed by Hardy. It was one of his contributions to the Red Cross Sale at Christie's, 22 April 1918.

The Voice of Things   2
This poem would seem to date from Hardy's journey to Cornwall in March 1913 or, better, his last visit to these scenes in September 1916 (see *Later Years*, pp. 172–3).

'Why be at Pains?'   3

'We Sat at the Window'   4
The poem is obviously a personal recollection—Hardy and his wife were at Bournemouth in July 1875 (not quite a year after their marriage).

Afternoon Service at Mellstock   5
See *Early Life,* p. 23.

At the Wicket-Gate   6

In a Museum   7
Written (?) at Exeter, possibly in June 1915 (see *Later Years*, p. 169).

Apostrophe to an Old Psalm Tune   8
Written Sunday, 13 August 1916.

At the Word 'Farewell'   11
First printed in *Selected Poems.* See above, p. 180.

The Day of First Sight   13
First printed, as 'The Return from First Beholding Her', in *Selected Poems.* See above, p. 179. The title was altered in subsequent editions to 'First Sight of Her and After'.

The Rival   14

Heredity   15
The germ of this poem appears in Hardy's diary under date of 19 February 1889 (see *Early Life*, p. 284).

'You were the Sort that Men Forget'   16

She, I, and They   17
Written in 1916 (MS. adds 'August 1').

Near Lanivet, 1872   18
> MS. deleted, 'From an old note.' Lanivet is near Bodmin in Corn-
> wall, and the handpost was on the St. Austell road. The scene, an
> actual one, occurred between Hardy and his first wife before their
> marriage.

Joys of Memory   20
> The 'certain day' is presumably 7 March, anniversary of Hardy's
> meeting with his first wife.

To the Moon   21
> MS. 'Questions', a tentative title (or addition to the title), deleted.

Copying Architecture in an Old Minster   22
> Hardy was living in Wimborne from June 1881 to June 1883.

To Shakespeare   24
> Written and first printed in 1916. See above, pp. 177 f.

Quid Hic Agis?   27
> First printed in 1916. See above, 'When I Weekly Knew', pp. 188 f.

On a Midsummer Eve   30
> First printed in *Selected Poems*. See above, p. 182.

Timing Her   31

Before Knowledge   34

The Blinded Bird   35

'The Wind blew Words'   36

The Faded Face   37

The Riddle   38

The Duel   39
> The poem recalls the notorious duel in which the Earl of Shrews-
> bury was killed by the second Duke of Buckingham at Cliveden in
> 1668. Hardy found the story in the Countess of Cardigan's *My
> Recollections* (London, 1909, pp. 124–5) and copied it into his note-
> book.

At Mayfair Lodgings   42
> MS. deleted, 'At Lodgings in London'. The poem was suggested
> by an experience of December 1894 (see *Later Years*, p. 35).

To my Father's Violin 44
> Written in 1916 (Hardy's father had been dead since 1892). The third stanza does not appear in the MS. (where the first form of the title is 'To my Father's Fiddle'). The violin hung in the study at Max Gate.

The Statue of Liberty 47
> MS. shows a cancelled stanza, now illegible, between stanzas 8 and 9.

The Background and the Figure 50

The Change 51
> Written in January–February 1913 and, like the poems of that period, a recollection of Hardy's courtship and first marriage.

Sitting on the Bridge 54
> Grey's Bridge, where the poem was suggested, is on the edge of Dorchester.

The Young Churchwarden 56
> MS. 'At an Evening Service [Sunday] August 14, 1870' (note, deleted). The poem is a reminiscence of St. Juliot Church and Hardy's courtship.

'I Travel as a Phantom now' 57
> Written in 1915.

Lines to a Movement in Mozart's E-Flat Symphony 58
> The poem was begun, at least, in November 1898. MS. shows that 'Movement' was originally 'Minuet'.

'In the Seventies' 60

The Pedigree 62
> Written in 1916.

His Heart. A Woman's Dream 65

Where They Lived 68
> MS. indicates the poem was written '[March *del.*] Oct. 1913.' It refers, therefore, to St. Juliot Rectory.

The Occultation 69

Life Laughs Onward 70

The Peace-Offering 71

'Something Tapped'   72
  Written in August 1913. (Mrs. Hardy had died 9 months before.)

The Wound   73
  First printed (with the succeeding poem) in 1916 and already collected in *Selected Poems*. See above, p. 180.

A Merrymaking in Question   74
  First printed (with the preceding poem) in 1916 and already collected in *Selected Poems*. See above, p. 180.

'I Said and Sang her Excellence'   75
  Rushy-Pond is a pool on the heath within sight of Dorchester (see
  Wessex Tales, p. 99).

A January Night. 1879   77
  The poem recalls an experience at Upper Tooting, where the Hardys
  were living in 1879 and 'where they seemed to begin to feel that
  "there had past away a glory from the earth".' See *Early Life*,
  p. 163.

A Kiss   78

The Announcement   79
  MS. adds under the title, '(January 1879)', which suggests the poem
  is to be associated with 'A January Night. 1879' above. Elsewhere,
  however, Hardy identifies the scene as Higher Bockhampton.

The Oxen   80
  First printed in 1915. See above, p. 175. The poem had already
  been collected in *Selected Poems*.

The Tresses   81

The Photograph   82
  Hardy identified the scene as Max Gate.

On a Heath   84

An Anniversary   85
  The poem was suggested in 'Kingston-Maurward Ewelease'. See
  below, 'In Her Precincts'.

'By the Runic Stone'   87
  '(*Two who became a story*)' was added at the head of the poem in
  subsequent editions, presumably a reference to Hardy's courtship in
  Cornwall and its reflection in *A Pair of Blue Eyes*.

The Pink Frock 88
The poem was suggested by some words of Marcia, Lady Yarborough, in May 1894 (see *Later Years*, p. 31).

Transformations 89
MS. shows 'In a Churchyard' as an earlier title (or perhaps subtitle). Hardy identified the scene as Stinsford Churchyard. Cf. 'Voices from Things Growing in a Churchyard'.

In Her Precincts 90
This poem (Hardy called it 'an experience'), suggested in 'Kingston-Maurward Park', is apparently to be associated with Julia Augusta Martin, whose husband, Francis P. B. Martin, owned Kingston Maurward House, Stinsford, the 'manor' of Hardy's childhood, from 1845 to 1853, and whose curious relations with the poet are several times referred to in the *Early Life* (see pp. 23–25, 53–54, 134), or more probably with one of the daughters of James Fellowes, who bought the estate in 1853. Cf. above, 'An Anniversary'.

The Last Signal 91
This poem is a recollection of 'the singular incident' which occurred as Hardy walked by Winterborne-Came Path to the funeral of William Barnes, the Dorset poet, 11 October 1886 (see *Early Life*, p. 240). There is some imitation of *Barnes's metrics*.

The House of Silence 93
There is a facsimile of the MS. in the *Strand Magazine*, October 1924, p. 341. Hardy identified the house as Max Gate.

Great Things 95

The Chimes 97
The chimes are those of St. Peter's, Dorchester.

The Figure in the Scene 98
The poem is described as 'From an old note' and is a memory of Hardy's courtship in Cornwall (see *Early Life*, p. 104).

'Why did I Sketch' 99
This poem, like the preceding, is described as 'From an old note' and seems to have derived from the same episode. It is a memory of Hardy's courtship in Cornwall (see *Early Life*, p. 104).

Old Furniture 116

Stanza 6 does not appear in the MS., where its place is taken by the
following:

> [And] From each curled eff-hole the ghosts of ditties
>   Incanted there by his skill in his prime
> Quaver in whispers the pangs and pities
>   They once could language, and in their time
>   Would daily chime.

A Thought in Two Moods 118

The Last Performance 119

Written in 1912. In the autumn of that year, very shortly before her
death, Mrs. Hardy 'one day suddenly sat down to the piano and
played a long series of her favourite old tunes, saying at the end she
would never play any more.' (See *Later Years*, p. 153.) MS. deleted,
'From old notes.'

'You on the Tower' 120

The Interloper 122

MS. 'One Who Ought Not to be There', earlier title, deleted. 'The
interloper' was the threat of madness which hung over Hardy's first
wife, at St. Juliot, Sturminster Newton, &c. The meaning was made
clearer in Hardy's final revision by the addition of the quotation,
'And I saw the figure and visage of Madness seeking for a home.'

Logs on the Hearth 124

Written in December 1915, with thoughts of Hardy's favourite
sister Mary, who had died 24 November. In subsequent editions,
'A Memory of a Sister' was added as sub-title and the refrain excised.

The Sunshade 126

The poem is to be associated with 'Swanage Cliffs'. Hardy lived at
Swanage in 1875–6 and had revisited the place as recently as the
summer of 1916.

The Ageing House 128

The house is Max Gate. The sycamore tree is described as 'little'
(stanza 1) and then 'long-limbed' (stanza 2) in subsequent editions.

The Caged Goldfinch 129

The third stanza was suppressed in subsequent editions because of

the unconscious humour of the last line (a slang phrase Hardy had
not been familiar with).

At Madame Tussaud's in Victorian Years   130
    MS. 'At Madame Tussaud's and Later', tentative title deleted.

The Ballet   132

The Five Students   133
    Horace Moule ('dark He') was one of these students (see *Later
    Years*, pp. 211–12). MS. adds two stanzas, labelled by Hardy
    '[Omitted from first edition]':

> And what do they say in that yon Pale Land
>   Who trod the track with me,
> If there they dwell, and watch, and understand?
>   They murmur, it may be,
> "All of us—how we strode, as still does that lean thrall
>   For nought at all!"
>
> The Years may add: "Peace, know ye not,
>   Life's ashy track hence eyeing,
> That though gilt Vanity called your eyes somewhat,
>   And ye were torn in trying,
> All of you, while you panted, saw aureola'd far
>   Heaven's central star?"

The Wind's Prophecy   135
    Described by Hardy as 'Rewritten from an old copy.' The poem is
    to be associated with his first journey into Cornwall and the drive
    from Launceston to St. Juliot (7 March 1870).

During Wind and Rain   137
    The poem seems to be a memory of St. Juliot Rectory and Hardy's
    courtship.

He Prefers Her Earthly   139
    MS. 'He Prefers the Earthly'.

The Dolls   140

Molly Gone   141
    'Molly' here may possibly represent Hardy's first wife rather than
    his sister Mary (both were dead, however, when this volume was
    published).

Written in November 1893. In the MS. the closing lines read:

> Bend a hairsbreadth creature-courses [. . . forces],
> And a fain desire fulfil?

Hardy has noted opposite them, '[Incorrectly printed in some Editions]', but the printed text was never altered.

See *Early Life*, p. 20.

The MS. has a third stanza never printed save in *Pages from the Works of Thomas Hardy*, ed. Ruth Head (London, 1922), p. 171, where it is described as 'specially communicated for this Selection.' There is a separate MS. of the stanza in the possession of Sir Sydney Cockerell.

The same 'journeying boy', undoubtedly a figure Hardy had seen and recorded, appears as Little Father Time in the down train to Aldbrickham, *Jude the Obscure*, pp. 331–2.

'Rou'tor Town' suggests Rough Tor (or Row Tor), a hill in Cornwall not far from Camelford and scenes associated with Hardy's first wife. The poem is a pendant to 'When I Set Out for Lyonnesse' (see above, p. 161), closely reproducing its metrical pattern in particular. In subsequent editions '(She, alone)' was added at the head.

In the MS. the last 16 lines (commencing 'Him I followed . . .') are wanting, apparently having been added when the poem was in proof.

in his diary under date of 23 November 1893 (see *Later Years*, p. 26). The poem is a little reminiscent of *Jude* which he was at work on at this time.

Written in the spring of 1913 (MS. shows 'March' deleted from the date of composition). The anniversary was 7 March, the day on which Hardy met his first wife.

MS. 'The Choirmaster's Funeral', earlier title.

The poem seems to have been suggested by Hardy's revisiting St. Juliot Rectory and the scenes of his courtship, in March 1913.

MS. 'While Drawing Architecture in a Churchyard', earlier title.

POEMS OF WAR AND PATRIOTISM

Written in 1913. The concluding stanza and gloss were cancelled in subsequent editions (as also the obvious footnote to the title).

Written in 1914 and first printed in March 1917. See above, pp. 189 f.

Written 18 October 1914 and first printed, as 'Sonnet on the Belgian Expatriation', in *King Albert's Book* [London, 1914], p. 21 (a volume edited by Hall Caine and sold for the benefit of the *Daily Telegraph* Belgian Fund). The last 3 lines were rewritten when the poem was collected.

Written in 1914 and first printed in 1915. See above, pp. 191 f.

Written and first printed in 1915. See above, pp. 189 f.

Written in 1915 and first printed, as 'In the Time of War and

Tumults', in the *Sphere*, 24 November 1917, p. 164. There is a signed off-print of the poem in this form in the Bliss collection.

Manuscript. The MS. of *Moments of Vision* is written on 201 leaves of fine
   paper, measuring 8″ × 10″ and numbered 1–199 by Hardy with 2
   supplementary leaves. To these have been added a title-page and 7 type-
   written pages of Contents. Inlaid on a preliminary leaf is a fragment
   with the title in blue pencil and traces of earlier titles written in red and
   erased, 'Moments from the Years' and 'Moments of Vision and other
   Poetry'. Like the MSS. of all Hardy's later volumes of verse, this is
   a collection of fair copies arranged for printing, with final alterations
   and revisions only. Where there are significant divergences from the
   printed text, they have been indicated above in the treatment of individual poems. 'The Tree and the Lady', on the evidence of the Table
   of Contents, seems to have replaced a poem called 'The Sound of Her',
   no longer identifiable.

   The MS., still in its brown paper wrappers but with each leaf mounted
   on a stub, is bound in full blue crushed morocco. It remained at Max
   Gate until Hardy's death when it was given to Magdalene College,
   Cambridge, by Mrs. Hardy, 7 February 1928, 'in accordance with my
   husband's direction' (see below, pp. 251–2). Hardy had been elected
   an Honorary Fellow of Magdalene in 1913.

Notes on Composition and Publication. Moments of Vision is a collection of
   159 poems, the largest such collection Hardy ever published. Where
   it is possible to date the poems, they seem to be almost wholly the
   product of the years 1913–16, and only 5 (with varying dates 1871–
   98) give any evidence of earlier work. Nine had already appeared in
   Selected Poems the year before. The recurring theme, excluding the
   war poems, is the theme of 'Poems of 1912–13', the death of Hardy's
   wife and the recreation of their old romance, and the size of this collection and the brief interval of three years that had elapsed since *Satires
   of Circumstance* are witness to its hold on the poet. The personal character of the verse is further emphasized by the fact that, barring 14 'Poems
   of War and Patriotism', designed for widest circulation, only 6 poems
   in the volume had been published previously (save in *Selected Poems*).
   Very rarely if ever did Hardy permit periodical publication of poems
   of so intimate a nature. The MS. of the volume was sent to Macmillan
   in August 1917.

   Moments of Vision was published at 6*s.* in an edition of 3,000 copies,
   30 November 1917. Hardy inscribed his wife's copy, 'From Thomas

Hardy, this first copy of the first edition, to the first of women Florence
Hardy. Nov: 1917.' Other copies (dated November) were inscribed
to Edmund Gosse ('these late notes of a worn-out lyre') and Sydney
Cockerell (with corrections on 11 pages in Hardy's hand) and (dated
December) to John Galsworthy. See *Later Years*, p. 179.

Subsequent Editions (*see also* COLLECTED EDITIONS). *Moments of Vision*,
combined with *Satires of Circumstance*, was included in Macmillan's
definitive Wessex Edition in 1919.

1918: DOMICILIUM

DOMICILIUM / BY THOMAS HARDY / [*ornament*]

Collation. Pp. 8; [1] title-page; [2] blank; 3 note, signed 'F. E. H.'; [4]
blank; 5–6 text; [7] blank; [8] colophon: *Twenty-five copies printed for
Florence Emily Hardy / at the Chiswick Press, London, E.C. July* 1918 /
This is No. [numbered and initialed by Mrs. Hardy] / .

Binding. Sewn in light or dark blue antique paper wrappers; front printed
in black as title-page.

All edges uncut; leaves measure $6\frac{7}{8}'' \times 8\frac{3}{4}''$.

Notes. This poem had already been privately printed by Clement Shorter
in 1916 (see above, pp. 176 f.) and is included here solely to complete
the record of Mrs. Hardy's privately printed pamphlets, which must
be considered authoritative. The typescript used (with Hardy's corrections in Mrs. Hardy's note, which he had dictated) and a proof (dated
June 1918) are in the possession of Sir Sydney Cockerell. In sending
'*our* "Domicilium", which my husband has inscribed as you wished',
Mrs. Hardy wrote to T. J. Wise, 9 December 1918, 'I know that Mr.
Shorter thinks that *my* edition is valueless in comparison with the one
he produced, but friends of ours have thought it of interest.' For a
general note on Mrs. Hardy's privately printed pamphlets, see Appendix, pp. 349 f.

1918: [APPEAL FOR MRS. ALLHUSEN'S CANTEENS]

[*No title-page*]

Collation. Pp. [4]; [1] text; [2] blank; [3] text; [4] blank.

Binding. Issued unbound; all edges cut; leaves measure $8\frac{1}{8}'' \times 10''$.

Notes. This appeal was written (the first draft in September 1918) at the request of Mrs. Henry Allhusen, on behalf of her canteens for French soldiers at Vertus and Cires-lès-Mello. Mrs. Allhusen, as Dorothy Stanley, daughter of Lady St. Helier, had known Hardy since her childhood. The appeal, signed and dated 'October: 1918' at the end, is a reproduction in facsimile of Hardy's manuscript, to which has been added the printed heading (as from his note-paper): 'Max Gate / Dorchester.' About 300 copies were made, as nearly as Mrs. Allhusen recollects, and sent out with a personal letter of her own to people who had already helped her with the work she was doing in France. She wrote to Hardy 13 November 1918, 'I am sending you a copy of your letter to show you how nice it looks, and already I have sent out several copies with photographs of my new Canteen.' The appeal, a tribute to France and a picture of the work of the canteens, was never reprinted, and indeed there is some reason to believe it was in part the work of Mrs. Hardy. Mrs. Allhusen's own copy (together with the original MS. from which the facsimile was made) is now in my possession. I know of no other that has survived.

1919: JEZREEL, ETC.

JEZREEL / THE MASTER AND THE / LEAVES / BY THOMAS HARDY / [*ornament*]

Collation. Pp. 8; [1] title-page; [2] blank; 3–6 text; [7] blank; [8] colophon: *Twenty-five copies printed for Florence Emily Hardy* / *at the Chiswick Press, London, E.C. September* 1919 / *This is No.* [numbered and initialed by Mrs. Hardy] / .

Binding. Sewn in blue or grey antique paper wrappers; front printed in black as title-page.

All edges uncut; leaves measure $6\frac{7}{8}'' \times 8\frac{3}{4}''$.

Notes. These two poems had both been printed previously.

'Jezreel' was written 24–25 September 1918 and first printed in *The Times*, 27 September 1918, p. 7. Copyright was not reserved, and the poem was reprinted in *Air Pie*, The Royal Air Force Annual, London, (April) 1919, p. 44. It was collected in *Late Lyrics and Earlier*, pp. 15–16, when the sub-title was added to clarify the subject. See 2 Kings ix.

'The Master and the Leaves' was written in 1917 and first printed in *The Owl*, A Miscellany, May 1919, p. 5. Twenty-four copies were autographed by the contributors (see Siegfried Sassoon, *Siegfried's Journey*, London, 1945, pp. 147–8). When the poem was collected in *Late Lyrics and Earlier*, pp. 199–200, several lines were rewritten.

A first proof for this pamphlet with Hardy's corrections (11 September 1919) and the typescript used are now in the possession of Sir Sydney Cockerell. For a general note on Mrs. Hardy's privately printed pamphlets, see Appendix, pp. 349 f.

[? 1920]: PREFATORY NOTE TO *A DULL DAY IN LONDON*

"A DULL DAY IN LONDON" / BY / DORA SIGERSON SHOR-TER. / A PREFATORY NOTE / BY / THOMAS HARDY.

Collation. Single leaf; recto, caption title as above, text signed 'T.H.', and note: '*Twelve copies only.*'; verso, blank.

Binding. Issued unbound; all edges cut; leaf measures 8″ × 10$\frac{5}{16}$″; watermark: 'Royal / Vellum' surmounted by a crown.

Notes. This brief Prefatory Note was written by Hardy at Clement Shorter's request for a posthumous volume of Dora Sigerson Shorter's sketches. Dora Sigerson had married Shorter in 1896 and died 6 January 1918. The note was published in *A Dull Day in London*, by Dora Sigerson, London, 1920, pp. 7–8.

There is no evidence for the dating of this leaf. It is not an off-print of the note as published but represents an independent setting of type (presumably, from the paper used, by Eyre & Spottiswoode). Considering Shorter's known propensities as a collector, it is safe to say this private printing preceded the publication of the volume in June 1920. By 1920, however, Hardy had ceased permitting Shorter to print his work in this fashion, and I suspect he was unaware of the existence of this leaf. There was no copy at Max Gate, though Shorter inscribed a copy of the book to Hardy, 24 June 1920. For a general note on Shorter's privately printed pamphlets, see Appendix, pp. 349 f.

1920 [1921]: 'AND THERE WAS A GREAT CALM'

"AND THERE WAS A / GREAT CALM" / 11 NOVEMBER 1918 / BY THOMAS HARDY / [*ornament*]

Collation. Pp. 8; [1] title-page; [2] blank; 3–5 text; [6] colophon: *Twenty-five copies printed for Florence Emily Hardy / at the Chiswick Press, London, E.C. December* 1920 / *This is No.* [numbered and initialed by Mrs. Hardy] / ; [7][8] blank.

Binding. Sewn in blue or grey antique paper wrappers; front printed in black as title-page.

All edges uncut; leaves measure $6\frac{7}{8}'' \times 8\frac{3}{4}''$.

Notes. This poem was written in November 1920 at the request of *The Times* and first printed in a special Armistice Day Section (p. iii) of *The Times*, 11 November 1920 (the day of the burial of the Unknown Soldier). See *Later Years*, pp. 214–15. Mrs. Hardy's edition was not ready for distribution until January 1921 (Hardy putting that date in the first and last copies, which he signed as his custom was). The typescript used and a first proof (16 December 1920) with Hardy's corrections are in the possession of Sir Sydney Cockerell. The poem was collected in *Late Lyrics and Earlier*, pp. 55–58. For a general note on Mrs. Hardy's privately printed pamphlets, see Appendix, pp. 349 f.

There is a separate MS. in the Bliss collection, the earliest version of the poem with subsequent alterations, written on 2 leaves of fine paper measuring $8'' \times 10''$. It was formerly in the possession of T. J. Wise and is reproduced in full in *The Ashley Library*, vol. ii (London, 1922), at pp. 176–7.

1921: THE PLAY OF 'SAINT GEORGE'

THE PLAY OF / 'SAINT GEORGE' / AS AFORETIME ACTED / BY THE DORSETSHIRE / CHRISTMAS MUMMERS / BASED ON THE VERSION IN / 'THE RETURN OF THE NATIVE,' / AND COMPLETED FROM OTHER / VERSIONS, AND FROM LOCAL / TRADITION. COLLOCATED AND / REVISED BY THOMAS HARDY /

Collation. Pp. [ii]+10; [i] title-page; [ii] blank; [1]–8 text; [9] colophon: *Twenty-five copies printed for private cir- | culation by Florence Emily Hardy at the | University Press, Cambridge, April* 1921 | *This is No.* [numbered and initialed by Mrs. Hardy] / ; [10] blank.

Binding. Green paper wrappers, printed on front in black: The Play of / 'Saint George' /.

Fly-leaf at front and back; all edges cut; leaves measure $4\frac{3}{4}'' \times 7\frac{7}{16}''$.

Notes. Hardy undertook this recension of the traditional play of 'Saint George' in the autumn of 1920, when the Hardy Players were preparing their dramatization of *The Return of the Native* (see Appendix, pp. 351 ff.). It was introduced into Act II, Scene 2 of that dramatization, 'The Kitchen of Mrs. Yeobright's House at Bloom's End', a scene based on Bk. II, Chaps. 5 and 6 of the novel where fragments only of the mummers' speeches are given. The Hardy Players produced their play in Dorchester 17 and 18 November 1920 and in London 27 January 1921; 'Saint George' by itself they acted for Hardy in his drawing-room, Christmas night 1920 (see *Later Years*, p. 220; *Friends of a Lifetime*, p. 307).

Mrs. Hardy's edition was sent to the printers in March 1921 and was ready for distribution the following month. There is a first proof (31 March), with Hardy's corrections and the colophon written out in his hand, in the possession of Sir Sydney Cockerell. Two typescripts with Hardy's alterations are now in the Dorset County Museum. For a general note on Mrs. Hardy's privately printed pamphlets, see Appendix, pp. 349 f.

The play was reprinted, together with a modernized version by Roger S. Loomis, in an edition of 1,000 copies by Samuel French, New York, 1928. In Hardy's letter of authorization, there reproduced, he refers to the play as something 'I managed to concoct from my memories of it as acted in my boyhood.' Some of these memories are recorded in William Archer, *Real Conversations* (London, 1904), pp. 34–36.

1922: HAUNTING FINGERS, ETC.

HAUNTING FINGERS / VOICES FROM THINGS GROWING / TWO PHANTASIES / BY / THOMAS HARDY / [*ornament*]

Collation. Pp. 12; [1] title-page; [2] blank; 3–9 text; [10] colophon: *Twenty-five copies printed for Florence Emily Hardy | at the Chiswick Press, London, E.C. February 1922 | This is No.* [numbered and initialed by Mrs. Hardy] /; [11][12] blank.

Binding. Sewn in dark or light blue antique paper wrappers; front printed in black as title-page.

All edges uncut; leaves measure $6\frac{7}{8}'' \times 8\frac{3}{4}''$.

Notes. These two poems had both been printed previously.

'Haunting Fingers' was first printed, under the title 'The Haunting Fingers', in the *New Republic* (New York), 21 December 1921, p. 103. A number of lines were revised when the poem was reprinted here; it was collected in *Late Lyrics and Earlier*, pp. 59–62. There is a separate MS. of the poem in the Dorset County Museum, an early draft showing the cancelled title 'The Dead Fingers', written on 2 leaves of fine paper measuring $7\frac{3}{4}'' \times 10''$.

'Voices from Things Growing' was written *c*. June 1921 and first printed in the *London Mercury*, December 1921, pp. 119–20. The poem was collected in *Late Lyrics and Earlier*, pp. 127–9, when the title was expanded to 'Voices from Things Growing in a Churchyard' and the note on 'Eve Greensleeves' added. For the 'voices', see *Later Years*, p. 223; *Early Life*, p. 122; Hutchins, *History of Dorset*, ii. 567.

The typescript for this pamphlet with some additions in Hardy's hand, a proof with his corrections (24 January 1922), and a revise (31 January) are in the possession of Sir Sydney Cockerell. Hardy seems to have had some fears the pamphlet would be anticipated by *Late Lyrics and Earlier*. He wrote to Cockerell, 14 February 1922, '... the proofs have begun to come for the volume: yet I imagine that the "Two

Fantasies" will be able to be put about before the volume appears.' The pamphlet was ready in February, Mrs. Hardy inscribing a copy to Cockerell 22 February 1922, but, quite inexplicably, Hardy did not sign and date the first and last copies, as his custom was, until July. For a general note on Mrs. Hardy's privately printed pamphlets, see Appendix, pp. 349 f.

1922: LATE LYRICS AND EARLIER

LATE LYRICS / AND EARLIER / WITH MANY OTHER VERSES / BY / THOMAS HARDY / MACMILLAN AND CO., LIMITED / ST. MARTIN'S STREET, LONDON / 1922

Collation. [*a*]⁴, *b*⁸, B–T⁸; pp. xxiv+288; [i] half-title; [ii] publishers' device and imprints; [iii] title-page; [iv] blank save for words: Copyright / Printed in Great Britain / ; v–xviii Apology; xix–xxiv Contents; 1–288 text, printers' imprint at foot of p. 288: *Printed in Great Britain by* R. & R. Clark, Limited, *Edinburgh.*

Binding. Olive-green cloth; front blocked in gold with TH monogram medallion; back plain; gold-lettered on spine: Late / Lyrics / and / Earlier / Thomas / Hardy / Macmillan & Cᵒ / .

Plain end-papers; top uncut, fore-edge and tail trimmed; leaves measure 5″×7⅝″.

The whole format is uniform with *The Dynasts* and succeeding volumes of verse.

Contents. Apology   Page v

Written in January and February 1922. Though this is his most significant and extended utterance on poetry and criticism, Hardy had grave doubts as to the wisdom of printing it, and in the end the text was somewhat abridged. It was written during an illness and had come into his mind, as he wrote to Sydney Cockerell (15 February), 'mostly while lying in bed during the late weeks, and seemed then almost necessary.' In subsequent editions a few verbal alterations of interest were made. See *Later Years*, p. 225; *Friends of a Lifetime,* pp. 288–9.

Weathers   1
>   First printed in *Good Housekeeping* (London), May 1922, p. 5.

The Maid of Keinton Mandeville   3
>   Written in 1915 or 1916 and first printed in the *Athenaeum*, 30
>   April 1920, p. [565], with the note '(A tribute to Sir Henry Bishop
>   on the sixty-fifth anniversary of his death: April 30, 1855)'. Hardy
>   wrote in his diary, 5 March 1878, 'Concert at Sturminster. A Miss
>   Marsh of Sutton [Keinton?] Mandeville sang "Should he upbraid",
>   to Bishop's old tune. She is the sweetest of singers—thrush-like in
>   the descending scale, and lark-like in the ascending—drawing out
>   the soul of listeners in a gradual thread of excruciating attenuation
>   like silk from a cocoon.' See *Early Life*, p. 156; *A Pair of Blue Eyes*,
>   p. 17.

Summer Schemes   5

Epeisodia   6
>   The episodes may be taken to represent courtship at St. Juliot,
>   marriage in London, and burial at Stinsford.

Faintheart in a Railway Train   8
>   First printed, under the title 'A Glimpse from the Train', in the
>   *London Mercury*, January 1920, p. 265. The MS. used on that occa-
>   sion, pasted to a proof of 'Going and Staying' (see below), was
>   formerly in the possession of Crosby Gaige. The editor (J. C.
>   Squire) has written in the margin, 'Hardy first sent one poem to
>   the London Mercury and then added the other, which was pasted
>   to the proof.'

At Moonrise and Onwards   9

The Garden Seat   11
>   Hardy identified the scene as Max Gate.

Barthélémon at Vauxhall   12
>   First printed in *The Times*, 23 July 1921, p. 11. The note there
>   continues, 'To-day is the anniversary of his death in 1808. The cir-
>   cumstances of the following lines have no claim to be more than
>   supposititious.' See *Later Years*, pp. 223–4.

'I Sometimes Think'   14
>   The poem is addressed to Mrs. Hardy, and the MS. is reproduced
>   in facsimile in *Later Years*, facing p. 225.

Jezreel 15
> Written and first printed in 1918. See above, pp. 209 f.

A Jog-trot Pair 17
> The poem refers, apparently, to Hardy's second marriage.

'The Curtains now are Drawn' 19
> Written in 1913, with thoughts of Hardy's courtship at St. Juliot (I) and the death of his wife in 1912 (II). MS. '(Song: Major and Minor)', the 2 stanzas so denominated.

'According to the Mighty Working' 21
> Written in 1917 and first printed in the *Athenaeum*, 4 April 1919, p. [129]. See *Later Years*, p. 190.

'I Was not He' 22

The West-of-Wessex Girl 23
> The poem was begun in Plymouth in March 1913 and belongs in spirit with 'Poems of 1912–13'. Plymouth was Mrs. Hardy's birthplace, and the poet paused in the city on his return from Cornwall and the scenes of their courtship. He gave the Plymouth Free Public Library a MS. of the poem in 1923. Cf. above, 'Places', p. 167.

Welcome Home 25

Going and Staying 26
> First printed, stanzas I and II only, in the *London Mercury*, November 1919, p. 7 (see above, 'Faintheart in a Railway Train'); and in *Modern British Poetry*, ed. Louis Untermeyer (New York, 1920), p. 4. The third stanza was added when the poem was collected.

Read by Moonlight 27

At a House in Hampstead 28
> Written in July 1920 and first printed in *The John Keats Memorial Volume* (London, 23 February 1921), pp. 89–90. The MS. of the poem as printed on that occasion (for which it was composed) is now in the Ashley Library, British Museum. It is written, with several alterations, on 2 leaves of fine paper measuring 8″ × 10″ and is reproduced in facsimile in *The Ashley Library*, vol. ii (London, 1922), following p. 176. A few verbal alterations were made in the first half of the poem before it was collected. When the Keats House (Wentworth Place), Hampstead, was opened in 1925, Hardy, who had

been on the Committee for Acquisitions, made a fair copy of the verses in their final form to be framed and hung in Keats's sitting-room. This MS. has been reproduced in a separate facsimile for sale.

'And there was a Great Calm'   55
    Written and first printed in 1920. See above, p. 211.

Haunting Fingers   . 59
    First printed in 1921. See above, pp. 213 f.

The Woman I met   63
    Written in London in 1918 and first printed in the *London Mercury*,
    April 1921, pp. 584–6. The 4-page typewritten MS. used on that
    occasion, with several autograph alterations, is now in the Bliss
    collection. The poem, at least stanza 7, recalls an episode of April
    1891 (see *Early Life*, p. 308).

'If it's ever Spring again'   67

The Two Houses   68
    First printed in the *Dial* (New York), August 1921, pp. [127]–129.
    Hardy sent Sydney Cockerell 'as a New Year's card', 28 December
    1921, a proof (or possibly an off-print) of the poem in a different
    setting, which has not been identified. There were a few verbal
    alterations when the poem was collected.

On Stinsford Hill at Midnight   72
    The poem is based on an experience Hardy described in his diary
    4 February 1894 (see *Later Years*, p. 28). In subsequent editions a
    note was added, 'It was said that she belonged to a body of religious
    enthusiasts.'

The Fallow Deer at the Lonely House   74
    A fair copy of the poem was sent to Cheltenham College in 1925.

The Selfsame Song   75

The Wanderer   76
    MS. tentative title deleted, 'The Benighted Traveller'.

A Wife Comes Back   78

A Young Man's Exhortation   81
    Written in 1867 at 16 Westbourne Park Villas. MS. 'An Exhorta-
    tion'.

At Lulworth Cove a Century back   83
    Written in September 1920.

A Bygone Occasion   85

Though 'outwardly referring to the crucifixion', the poem was 'in reality inspired by the news of the clearance of the wooden crosses on the old Western Front' (Edmund Blunden, *Thomas Hardy*, London, 1941, p. 167).

The poem refers to Helen Paterson (Mrs. William Allingham, 1848–1926), whom Hardy first met in May 1874 (see *Early Life*, p. 132). She was married in August of that year as he was married in September. When Edmund Gosse inquired about her, Hardy wrote to him (25 July 1906), 'The illustrator of Far from the Madding Crowd began as a charming young lady, Miss Helen Paterson, and ended as a married woman,—charms unknown—wife of Allingham the poet. I have never set eyes on her since she was the former and I met her and corresponded with her about the pictures of the story. She was the best illustrator I ever had. She and I were married about the same time in the progress of our mutual work, but not to each other, which I fear rather spoils the information. Though I have never thought of her for the last 20 years your inquiry makes me feel "quite romantical" about her (as they say here), and as she is a London artist, well known as Mrs. A. you might hunt her up, and tell me what she looks like as an elderly widow woman. If you do, please give her my kind regards, but you must not add that those two almost simultaneous weddings would have been one but for a stupid blunder of God Almighty.'

Written on the death of Evelyn Gifford of Oxford, 6 September 1920. She was Hardy's cousin by marriage, daughter of Archdeacon Gifford, who had married Hardy and his first wife in 1874. See *Later Years*, p. 214.

Written and first printed in 1921. See above, pp. 213 f.

The Inscription   244
  Written 30 October 1907. MS. 'The Words on the Brass'. The
  poem is reminiscent of 'The Memorial Brass: 186–' (1917).

The Marble-streeted Town   251
  Written at Plymouth in (?)1914, with thoughts of Hardy's first wife
  whose birthplace it was. MS. '(1913?)', date of the other Plymouth
  poems (cf. above, 'Places', p. 167, and 'The West-of-Wessex Girl',
  p. 216). Hardy gave the Plymouth Free Public Library a MS. of
  the poem in 1923.

A Woman Driving   252
  Cf. 'The Phantom Horsewoman'.

A Woman's Trust   254

Best Times   256
  Described as 'Rewritten from an old draft.' MS. 'Not Again'. The
  'times' are associated with Hardy's first wife.

The Casual Acquaintance   258

Intra Sepulchrum   260

The Whitewashed Wall   262
  First printed in *Reveille*, November 1918, p. [175]. Several lines
  were revised when the poem was collected.

Just the Same   264

The Last Time   265
  The poem was altered to the first person in subsequent editions.

The Seven Times   266
  The poem seems to refer to seven journeys to St. Juliot, the seventh
  after Mrs. Hardy's death.

The Sun's Last Look on the Country Girl   269
  Written in December 1915, with thoughts of Hardy's favourite sister
  Mary, who had died the month before.

In a London Flat   270
  MS. 'In a London Lodging'.

Drawing Details in an old Church   272

Rake-hell Muses   273
  Written in 189–. MS. 'The Seducer Muses'.

Manuscript. The MS. of *Late Lyrics and Earlier* is written on 205 leaves
of fine paper measuring 7¾″× 10″. These have been numbered i–xii
('Apology') and 1–193 by Hardy, and to them have been added 4 type-
written pages of Contents. Like the MSS. of all Hardy's later volumes
of poetry, this is a collection of fair copies, made at varying dates and
put together for printing, with final alterations and revisions only. Many
trial readings in pencil have been erased. Where there are significant
divergences from the printed text, they have been indicated above in
the treatment of individual poems.

The MS., still in its rough cardboard covers, has been bound in full
blue crushed levant. It remained at Max Gate until Mrs. Hardy's
death in 1937, when it was deposited in the Dorset County Museum
under the provisions of her will.

Notes on Composition and Publication. Late Lyrics and Earlier is a collection
of 151 poems, to which Hardy added a notable 'Apology' addressed
to his critics and to all those, like himself, 'concerned to keep poetry
alive'. This 'Apology', which presents the author in an unfamiliar role,
lends particular distinction to the volume. 'About half the verses', Hardy
remarks, 'were written quite lately.' As for the remainder, the earlier
lyrics, in so far as they are dated, there is the same surprising range that
marked *Wessex Poems* and *Time's Laughingstocks.* The earliest is dated
1866, the latest 1921, and every decade between (save the 80's) pro-
vides some verse. In many respects the volume is the most representative of Hardy's whole career. Twenty-two of the poems had been
printed previously in the years 1917–22. The MS. of the volume was

sent to Macmillan 23 January 1922, and a new MS. of the 'Apology' as modified and revised was forwarded 21 February. In handling the proofs Hardy was much assisted by Sydney Cockerell, and there are numerous letters in the latter's possession which deal with the work (for four of these, see *Friends of a Lifetime*, pp. 288–91).

Late Lyrics and Earlier was published at 7*s.* 6*d.* in an edition of 3,250 copies, 23 May 1922. Hardy inscribed copies (dated May) to his wife and to Sydney Cockerell. The volume was twice reprinted before the end of the year.

Subsequent Editions (*see also* COLLECTED EDITIONS). *Late Lyrics and Earlier*, combined with *The Famous Tragedy of the Queen of Cornwall*, was included in Macmillan's definitive Wessex Edition in 1926.

1923: THE FAMOUS TRAGEDY OF THE QUEEN OF CORNWALL

THE FAMOUS TRAGEDY / OF THE / QUEEN OF CORN-WALL / AT TINTAGEL IN LYONNESSE / A NEW VERSION OF AN OLD STORY / ARRANGED AS A PLAY FOR MUM-MERS / IN ONE ACT / REQUIRING NO THEATRE OR SCEN-ERY / BY / THOMAS HARDY / "Isot ma drue, Isot m'amie, / En vos ma mort, en vos ma vie!" / Gottfried von Strassburg. / MACMILLAN AND CO., LIMITED / ST. MARTIN'S STREET, LONDON / 1923

Collation. [A]⁴, B–F⁸; pp. [viii]+80; [i][ii] blank; [iii] half-title; [iv] publishers' device and imprints; [v] title-page; [vi] blank save for words: Copyright / Printed in Great Britain / ; [vii] dedication; [viii] blank; 1 divisional title; [2] blank; 3–[77] text; [78] printers' imprint: *Printed in Great Britain by* R. & R. Clark, Limited, *Edinburgh.* / ; [79][80] blank.

Illustrations. Frontispiece and 1 illustration, reproduced from drawings by Hardy and separately printed.

Binding. Smooth green cloth; front blocked in blind with panel design, circular design reproducing portion of frontispiece blocked in gold, gold-lettered: The Famous Tragedy / *of the* / Queen of Cornwall / *by* / Thomas Hardy / ; back plain; spine blocked in gold with bands and ornaments and gold-lettered: The / Famous / Tragedy / *of the* / Queen / of / Cornwall / Thomas / Hardy / Macmillan / .

Plain end-papers; all edges cut; leaves measure 6″×8 1/16″.

Manuscript. The MS. of *The Famous Tragedy of the Queen of Cornwall* is written on 47 leaves of fine paper measuring 7 7/8″×9 15/16″. It is a fair copy prepared for the printers, with some late alterations (though none of the revisions for the second edition). Iseult's song in Scene VII is wanting. Hardy has identified the initials on the leaf of dedication as: 'Caddell Holder, M.A. Rector of St. Juliot, Cornwall, Helen Catherine Holder, née Gifford, Emma Lavinia Hardy, née Gifford, Florence Emily Hardy, née Dugdale'. On 2 preliminary leaves are mounted a reduced photograph of the drawing that serves as frontispiece (see below) and a replica on yellow tracing-paper of the 'Imaginary Aspect of the Great Hall at the Time of the Tragedy', differing slightly from the original.

The MS. is sewn in brown paper wrappers, bearing the title in Hardy's hand and '*Original MS.*', and preserved in a full red morocco case. It remained at Max Gate until Mrs. Hardy's death in 1937, when it was deposited in the Dorset County Museum under the provisions of her will. The title-page of the MS. was reproduced in facsimile on the dust wrapper of the first edition.

The original drawing for the frontispiece, 'Imaginary View of Tintagel Castle at the Time of the Tragedy', formerly in the Bliss collection, is now in the Dorset County Museum. It is an exquisite piece of draughtsmanship, measuring 16¾″×13″, and is dated May 1923 (see *Later Years*, p. 230). The original of the second illustration, a pencil and wash drawing on yellow tracing-paper measuring 7″×6″, mounted with a floor plan of the scene and adjacent rooms, is also in the Dorset County Museum.

The corrected proofs of the book were given to George A. Macmillan.

Notes on Composition and Publication. The Famous Tragedy of the Queen of Cornwall is closely linked with the romance of Hardy's first marriage. He visited Tintagel and King Arthur's Castle with Miss Gifford and the Holders during his second stay at St. Juliot in August 1870,[1] and

---

[1] *Early Life*, p. 103. There is mention of Tintagel in his diary under 9 March 1870 (p. 98). See also p. 120.

the poetry of the scene and its associations lingered in his mind through more than fifty years. 'The place is pre-eminently (for one person at least)', he wrote of this North Cornish coast, 'the region of dream and mystery',[1] and it was inevitable these scenes and legends should return with new power in the years following Mrs. Hardy's death in 1912, when he sought to recreate the romance of their courtship. Hardy revisited Tintagel with his second wife in September 1916 (*Later Years*, pp. 172–3) and on his return he wrote to Sydney Cockerell, 20 September, 'We went to Cornwall—and saw the tablet at St. Juliot, Boscastle; and thence to Tintagel. Alas, I fear your hopes of a poem on Iseult—the English, or British, Helen—will be disappointed. I visited the place 44 years ago with an Iseult of my own, and of course she was mixed in the vision of the other.' (*Friends of a Lifetime*, p. 284.) Nevertheless, *The Queen of Cornwall*, which had been shaping in his mind since the 70's, was begun in this autumn, only to be laid aside for some seven years. Work was resumed in 1923, and the rough draft was finished in April of that year.[2] In sending the MS. to Macmillan, 30 August 1923, Hardy added, 'I have written it, or rather finished it (for it has been more or less in existence for a long time) for our local dramatic society, who are going to act it about the middle of November.'[3] And it is clear he had little thought, originally, of publication. The same was true of the drawings. The carefully finished view of Tintagel Castle he had done for his own pleasure; of the other, he wrote to his publishers, 10 September, 'The rough sketch of the interior, which was also attached to the MS. was made merely for the use of the scene-painter here, but Mr. Granville Barker, who happened to see it, says it is a great help to reading the play; hence I don't know whether it ought not to be included as a second illustration, even though so badly drawn.' How personal were the associations of the play he indicated by his dedication of it (the only one of his works to bear a dedication of any sort) to the family at St. Juliot Rectory in the 70's and to his second wife.

[1] Preface to *A Pair of Blue Eyes*, p. viii. It will be recalled that the title of Elfride's ill-fated novel was *The Court of King Arthur's Castle: a Romance of Lyonnesse*.

[2] For Hardy's own comments on his design, see *Later Years*, pp. 235–6. It is clear from the markings in his copy of Malory (ed. Ernest Rhys, 2 vols., The Scott Library, London, n.d.) that he had carefully familiarized himself with that version of the story.

[3] The Prologue and Epilogue were written solely to provide one of the Hardy Players with a part.

The Famous Tragedy of the Queen of Cornwall was published at 6s. in an edition of 3,000 copies, 15 November 1923. Publication had originally been planned to coincide with the Hardy Players' production of the play at Dorchester, 28 November,[1] but the book was ready 29 October and the date was advanced. Hardy inscribed an early copy to his wife, 'Florence Emily Hardy, from Thomas Hardy. Oct. 30: 1923. (1st Edition: 1st copy.)', identifying in this copy the initials on the dedication page. Other copies (dated November) were inscribed to Mr. and Mrs. Edward Dugdale (Mrs. Hardy's parents), Sydney Cockerell, and Edmund Gosse. The book was twice reprinted in November 1923, and an American edition of 1,000 numbered copies was published by The Macmillan Company (New York) in the same month.

Second and Subsequent Editions (*see also* COLLECTED EDITIONS). A 'second and revised edition' of *The Queen of Cornwall*, in the format of the first edition, was printed (1,000 copies) in September 1924. It was marked not only by a detailed revision of text but by the enlarging of the play from 22 to 24 scenes, with the addition of 50 new lines of verse. Some of the verbal alterations and new stage directions were undoubtedly a result of the actual experience of production, Hardy having followed the Hardy Players' rehearsals with a good deal of pleasure, but other changes were made at the instance of Rutland Boughton, who was setting the play to music.[2] In reply to his suggestions, Hardy wrote, 16 January 1924, 'I have always meant to revise it a little, to bring it roughly to the average length of Greek plays. The enlargements are already written, the chief one being at page 46, after "O knight of little cheer". I don't know about page 47, the expression there seeming full enough. But two verses can certainly be added at page 27, and a verse at page 65.' As this letter indicates, the major additions were a second verse for Iseult's song (Scene VII), a

[1] Dorchester, 28–30 November 1923, and London, 21 February 1924 (see *Later Years*, pp. 236–7, and Appendix, pp. 351 ff.). The personal associations of the play were further emphasized in the programme by the reproduction of one of the first Mrs. Hardy's water-colours of Tintagel, identified simply as 'From a Water Colour Drawing in the possession of the Author.' This water-colour was in Hardy's mind when he drew his frontispiece.

[2] See *Later Years*, pp. 237–9, and Rutland Boughton, 'A Musical Association with Thomas Hardy', *Musical News*, February 1928, pp. 33–34. The score was published in 1926.

second verse for Tristram's song (Scene XIX), and the expansion of Scene XIII into three scenes. The new text was sent to Boughton early in February and to Macmillan before the end of that month.

The Famous Tragedy of the Queen of Cornwall, combined with *Late Lyrics and Earlier*, was included in Macmillan's definitive Wessex Edition in 1926, the original frontispiece being retained. Such was Hardy's fondness for the play that he had pages 527–69 of the Pocket Edition (1924), in which it had been printed with *The Dynasts*, Part Third, bound in grey paper wrappers for private distribution.

1924: COMPASSION

COMPASSION / AN ODE / IN CELEBRATION OF THE CEN-TENARY OF THE / ROYAL SOCIETY FOR THE PREVEN-TION / OF CRUELTY TO ANIMALS. / BY / THOMAS HARDY. / [*ornament*]

Collation. Pp. [8]; [1] title-page; [2] blank; [3]–[5] text; [6] colophon: *Twenty-five copies only printed for Mrs. Thomas Hardy, | by Henry Ling, Dorchester, Dorset, June 16th, 1924. | This is No.* [numbered and initialed by Mrs. Hardy] / ; [7][8] blank.

Binding. Sewn in cream cover-paper wrappers; front printed in black as title-page.

All edges uncut; leaves measure $7'' \times 9''$.

Notes. This poem was written 22 January 1924 at the request of the Royal Society for the Prevention of Cruelty to Animals (see *Later Years*, p. 238). It was first printed in the Society's centenary volume (for which it had been designed), Edward G. Fairholme and Wellesley Pain, *A Century of Work for Animals* (London, 1924), pp. xv–xvi, and also in *The Times*, 16 June 1924, p. 15. Hardy's own copy of the former, inscribed by the authors, is dated 16 June (the centenary day), and publication of the poem in these two forms seems to have been simultaneous. The two texts, however, are not identical. There were a number of verbal alterations in proof (4 April), but *The Times* (by some error) was provided with the unrevised version.

It was expressly stated in *The Times* that there was no copyright, and immediate moves were made to reprint the poem privately. Mrs. Hardy wrote to Sydney Cockerell, 21 June 1924, 'I wonder if you noticed his ode *Compassion* in *The Times*. As soon as it appeared we had a long telegram from Shorter, reply prepaid, asking if he might print it privately, and pointing out that "No rights reserved" gave him authority to print it. I at once telephoned to our local printer, Mr. Ling, who was Mayor last year, and explained the situation, and he rushed up and got the poem in print in less than an hour. Then I telegraphed to Shorter that it was already in print. Meanwhile another prepaid telegram had come from a society for producing first editions [the First Edition Club], saying that they intended printing fifty copies and they would be pleased if T.H. would autograph them. I sent them the same reply [17 June]. I had not time to consult you, and I knew you were busy. It was a question of getting it done there and then.' (*Friends of a Lifetime*, p. 312.) For a general note on Mrs. Hardy's privately printed pamphlets, see Appendix, pp. 349 f.

Mrs. Hardy's edition did not, however, prevent other separate printings of the poem. These are derived from *The Times* and dated 16 June, but their actual dates are dubious and there is no question of priority. Fifty copies (16 pp.), numbered and signed by A. J. A. Symons (of the First Edition Club), were printed at the Morland Press. Five hundred numbered copies (8 pp.) were printed by the *First Edition and Book Collector* for the first subscribers to that periodical. Of this there was a large paper issue of 50 numbered copies.

The poem was collected in *Human Shows*, pp. 261–2.

1925: WINTER NIGHT IN WOODLAND

WINTER NIGHT IN / WOODLAND / BY THOMAS HARDY / [*ornament*]

Collation. Pp. [ii]+6; [i][ii] blank; [1] title-page; [2] blank; 3–4 text; [5] blank; [6] colophon: *Twenty-five copies printed for Florence Emily Hardy / at the Chiswick Press, London, E.C. January* 1925 / *This is No.* [numbered and initialed by Mrs. Hardy] / .

Binding. Sewn in grey or blue cover-paper wrappers; front printed in black as title-page.

All edges uncut; leaves measure $6\frac{7}{8}'' \times 8\frac{5}{8}''$.

Notes. This poem was first printed, with 2 small photographs of foxes, in *Country Life*, 6 December 1924, p. 865. Mrs. Hardy's edition was sent to the printers very soon thereafter, and there is a first proof dated 22 December (with the colophon reading '*December* 1924') in the possession of Sir Sydney Cockerell. The pamphlet was ready the following month (the Cockerell copy, inscribed by Mrs. Hardy, is dated 11 January 1925), but for some reason unknown almost no copies were distributed. At Mrs. Hardy's death in 1937 a cache of 18 of the 25 copies remained at Max Gate. The poem was collected, with some verbal alterations (chiefly in the second stanza), in *Human Shows*, pp. 73–74. For a general note on Mrs. Hardy's privately printed pamphlets, see Appendix, pp. 349 f.

1925: NO BELL-RINGING

NO BELL-RINGING / A BALLAD OF DURNOVER / BY / THOMAS HARDY / [*ornament*]

Collation. Pp. [8]; [1] title-page; [2] blank; [3]–[5] text; [6] photograph, The Tower, Fordington St. George, Dorchester; [7] colophon: Twenty-five copies printed for Mrs. Thomas Hardy / by Henry Ling, Dorchester, February 28th, 1925. / This is No.................[numbered and initialed by Mrs. Hardy] / ; [8] blank.

Binding. Sewn in blue paper wrappers; front stamped in black with TH monogram medallion.

All edges cut; leaves measure $7\frac{1}{8}''\times 9\frac{5}{16}''$.

Notes. This poem was printed here for the first time. For a general note on Mrs. Hardy's privately printed pamphlets, see Appendix, pp. 349 f. The poem was reprinted, with pictorial headpiece and 2 vignettes by V. Cooley, in the *Sphere*, 23 November 1925 (Special Christmas Number), p. 14; and, in America, in the *Ladies' Home Journal*, December 1925. Copy for the *Sphere* was sent to Clement Shorter, the editor, in February and seems to have been put in type some time before it was required. When final corrections had been made, but before the addition of headpiece and vignettes, the printers, Eyre & Spottiswoode, supplied Shorter (presumably for distribution among collectors) with 6 proofs in the form of a broadside, 11″×11″. See *The Ashley Library*, vol. ix (London, 1927), pp. 84–85 and reproduction facing p. 84. The date is there given as the spring of 1925.

The poem was collected in *Winter Words*, pp. 165–7. The MS. (bound up in *Winter Words* after 'The Tarrying Bridegroom') shows that stanza 6 was a late addition.

1925: HUMAN SHOWS

HUMAN SHOWS / FAR PHANTASIES / SONGS, AND TRIFLES / BY / THOMAS HARDY / MACMILLAN AND CO., LIMITED / ST. MARTIN'S STREET, LONDON / 1925

Collation. [A]⁶, B–S⁸, T⁶; pp. [ii]+x+284; blank leaf; [i] half-title; [ii] publishers' device and imprints; [iii] title-page; [iv] blank save for words: Copyright / Printed in Great Britain / ; v–x Contents; 1–279 text; [280] printers' imprint: *Printed in Great Britain by* R. & R. Clark, Limited, *Edinburgh.* / ; [281]–[283] publishers' advertisements of Hardy's works, separately paged 1–3; [284] blank.

Binding. Olive-green cloth; front blocked in gold with TH monogram medallion; back plain; gold-lettered on spine: Human / Shows / Far / Phantasies / Thomas / Hardy / Macmillan & C?. / .

Plain end-papers; top uncut, fore-edge and tail trimmed; leaves measure 5″×7½″.

The whole format is uniform with *The Dynasts* and succeeding volumes of verse.

Contents. Waiting Both   Page 1
First printed, together with 'An East-End Curate', in the *London Mercury*, November 1924, p. 7. For a possible source, see *Later Years*, p. 194. There was a separate MS. of the poem in the possession of Paul Lemperly, a fair copy written on a leaf of fine paper measuring 5¼″×7¹⁵⁄₁₆″ and designed for a projected postcard reproduction (apparently never made). It was a gift of Mrs. Hardy in August 1927. A facsimile of this MS. appears in Shun Katayama, *Thomas Hardy* (Tokyo, 1934), p. 129.

A Bird-Scene at a Rural Dwelling   2
First printed in *Chambers's Journal*, January 1925 (6 December
1924), p. [1]. The poem was introduced by an editorial comment,
' 'Tis Sixty Years Since', and followed by a reprinting of 'How I
Built Myself a House' from *Chambers's Journal*, 18 March 1865.
The 'rural dwelling' is presumably Hardy's birthplace at Higher
Bockhampton.

'Any Little Old Song'   3

In a Former Resort after Many Years   4
MS. 'In an Old Place of Resort after Many Years'.

A Cathedral Façade at Midnight   5
MS. gives date of composition as '1897'. For the germ of the poem,
see Hardy's diary, Salisbury, 10 August 1897 (*Later Years*, p. 71).

The Turnip-Hoer   7
First printed, with 3 illustrations (the originals of which are in the
Bliss collection) in the text and a fourth on the cover, in *Cassell's
Magazine*, August 1925, pp. [28]–33. MS. shows that stanza 17
was a late addition to the poem.

The Carrier   13

Lover to Mistress   14
Described as 'From an old copy.'

The Monument-Maker   15
Written in 1916, and suggested by Hardy's journey in September
of that year to St. Juliot Church to inspect the tablet he had designed
and erected in memory of his first wife. Cf. 'The Marble Tablet'.

Circus-Rider to Ringmaster   17
First printed in *Harper's Monthly Magazine* (New York), June 1925,
p. [10]. MS. adds '(Casterbridge Fair: 188–)'. See *Early Life*,
p. 217.

Last Week in October   19

Come not; yet Come!   20

The Later Autumn   21
First printed in the *Saturday Review*, 28 October 1922, p. [633].
MS. gives date of composition as '1921'.

'Let Me' 23
In subsequent editions, 'Let Me Believe'.

At a Fashionable Dinner 24
MS. 'Lavine' originally 'Emleen' (suggesting the episode is to be associated with Hardy's wife, Emma Lavinia).

Green Slates 26
The poem recalls a drive to Penpethy slate-quarries, 9 March 1870, during Hardy's first visit to St. Juliot (see *Early Life*, p. 98).

An East-End Curate 27
First printed, together with 'Waiting Both', in the *London Mercury*, November 1924, p. 7.

At Rushy-Pond 29
The poem may be associated with 'I Said and Sang her Excellence', see above, p. 197.

Four in the Morning 31
The poem is to be associated with Bockhampton and Hardy's youth.

On the Esplanade 33
The poem, though not dated, is reminiscent of other verses associated with Weymouth in 1869—'At a Seaside Town in 1869', &c.

In St. Paul's a While Ago 35
MS. 'In St. Paul's: 1869'.

Coming up Oxford Street: Evening 37
First printed in the *Nation and the Athenaeum*, 13 June 1925, p. 324. When the poem was collected, the second stanza was altered from first to third person (as, the MS. shows, it had been originally). The scene is to be dated 4 July 1872.

A Last Journey 39

Singing Lovers 42
The poem is to be associated with Weymouth, and MS. adds to the title '(in 1869.)'.

The Month's Calendar 44

A Spellbound Palace 45
MS. 'A Sleeping Palace'.

When Dead 47

Sine Prole   48
> This poem was suggested, in form, by the sequences of Adam of
> S. Victor. In the spring of 1900 Hardy spent some time 'in hunting
> up Latin hymns at the British Museum, and copies that he made
> of several have been found, of dates ranging from the thirteenth to
> the seventeenth century, by Thomas of Celano, Adam of S. Victor,
> John Mombaer, Jacob Balde, etc. That English prosody might be
> enriched by adapting some of the verse-forms of these is not un-
> likely to have been his view.' (*Later Years*, pp. 85–86.) These
> transcripts, dated 'B.M. 28 Ap!', are inserted in his copy of *Sequences
> from the Sarum Missal*, trans. C. B. Pearson (London, 1871).

Ten Years Since   49
> Written in November 1922, ten years since the death of Hardy's
> first wife. See *Later Years*, p. 229.

Every Artemisia   50

The Best she Could   52
> Written 8 November 1923. MS. deleted, 'The Fall of the Leaf'.

The Graveyard of Dead Creeds   54

'There Seemed a Strangeness'   56
> MS. deleted, 'The Great Adjustment'.

A Night of Questionings   57

Xenophanes, the Monist of Colophon   61
> Written in 1921 and first printed in the *Nineteenth Century*, March
> 1924, pp. 315–17.

Life and Death at Sunrise   64
> MS. 'A Long-Ago Sunrise at Dogbury Gate'.

Night-time in Mid-Fall   66
> MS. 'Autumn Night-time'.

A Sheep Fair   67

Snow in the Suburbs   69
> MS. tentative title erased, 'Snow at Upper Tooting' (where Hardy
> had lived 1878–81).

A Light Snow-fall after Frost   71
> The poem is to be associated with Surbiton (where Hardy was

living in the winter of 1874–5). MS. shows that stanza 2 was a late addition.

Midnight on Beechen, 187–   144
> The poem recalls a journey to Bath in June 1873 while Miss Gifford was visiting there. See *Early Life*, pp. 123–4.

The Aërolite   145

The Prospect   147
> Written in December 1912, the month following Mrs. Hardy's death (with a reference to her last garden party in July).

Genitrix Laesa   148
> See above, 'Sine Prole'. The measure here used is that of Adam of S. Victor's 'Officium Beatae Mariae' (*Sequences from the Sarum Missal*, pp. 152–4).

The Fading Rose   150

When Oats were Reaped   152
> Written in August 1913, with thoughts of Mrs. Hardy who had died the year before.

Louie   153
> Written in July 1913, with thoughts of Hardy's first wife and 'a farmer's daughter named Louisa [Harding]' (see *Early Life*, pp. 33–34), both buried in Stinsford Churchyard.

'She Opened the Door'   154
> Written in 1913. The reference is, of course, to Hardy's first wife.

'What's there to Tell?'   155
> Written in 190–.

The Harbour Bridge   157
> The poem is to be associated with Weymouth and is reminiscent of others written there in 1869 or recalling episodes of that time and place.

Vagrant's Song   159
> First printed, in a decorative illustration by Arthur Wragg, in *Nash's and Pall Mall Magazine*, January 1925, p. 39. The last 2 lines of each stanza were added when the poem was collected, extending the 'old Wessex refrain'.

Farmer Dunman's Funeral   161
> MS. shows stanza 2 (originally in the first person) was a late addition to the poem.

First printed, with 2 illustrations by C. E. Brock, in the *New Magazine*, December [November] 1925, pp. 308–9. There were a number of revisions when the poem was collected. In its background at least, it is a boyhood recollection of a harvest-supper and dance at Kingston Maurward (see *Early Life*, pp. 24–26).

Written 6 January 1923 and first printed in the *London Mercury*, February 1923, p. 344. The woman was Mrs. Thompson, hanged for murder at Holloway Jail, 9 January 1923, a *cause célèbre* of the day.

First printed in the *Chapbook*, March 1923, p. 26. A proof of this, with several alterations in Hardy's hand, was formerly in the Bliss collection. The last 2 stanzas were partially rewritten when the poem was collected.

The Hardys were living at Swanage in the autumn and winter of 1875–6. See Hardy's note, *Early Life*, p. 142.

MS. adds as date of composition, 'About 1910.'

First printed in *The Owl* (a miscellany, ed. Robert Graves and William Nicholson), Winter [November] 1923, p. 3. There were several verbal alterations when the poem was reprinted in *The Best*

Poems of 1924, ed. L. A. G. Strong (Boston, 1924), p. 111, and others when it was collected.

Under High-Stoy Hill 186

Hardy wrote in his diary, 11 August 1922, that he walked to the top of High Stoy, 'probably for the last time'—a clue, perhaps, to the date of this poem (*Later Years*, p. 227).

At the Mill 187

Alike and Unlike 189

Hardy and his wife stopped in Llandudno 18 May 1893 on their way to Dublin, and Hardy wrote in his diary, 'After arrival at Llandudno drove around Great Orme's Head. Magnificent deep purple-grey mountains, the fine colour being on account of an approaching storm.' (*Later Years*, p. 18.) MS. adds '*She speaks.*'

The Thing Unplanned 190

The Sheep-Boy 191

The poem is to be associated with Rainbarrows on Puddletown Heath.

Retty's Phases 193

Described as 'From an old draft of 1868.' This 'old draft', called simply 'Song', is now in the Dorset County Museum, the earliest MS. of a poem by Hardy that survives. It is written on a single leaf, measuring $3\frac{3}{4}'' \times 6\frac{1}{4}''$, torn from a diary or note-book and headed 'June 22. 1868'. The MS. offers unique evidence as to the significance of Hardy's familiar phrase, 'from an old draft', and reveals something of his treatment of these poems of the 60's when he came to publish them. As he wrote to Edmund Gosse, 'Many of the poems were temporarily jotted down to the extent of a stanza or two when the ideas occurred, and put aside till time should serve for finishing them—often not till years after.' 'Song' is a poem of 7 stanzas, though stanzas 1, 4, and 6 are unfinished, suggested only by a line or so. As printed here 57 years later (with 'Retty' altered from 'Hetty'), I is a recasting of stanza 2; II, of stanzas 4 (fragmentary) and 5; and IV, of stanza 7. MS. stanza 3 was not used at all; and 'Retty's Phases' III is wholly new.

A Poor Man and a Lady 195

Hardy's own note suggests something of the unusual significance

The first draft of 'Retty's Phases', the earliest MS. of a poem by Hardy

of this poem as preserving material from his first, unpublished novel.
See below, pp. 275-6.

An Expostulation   198

To a Sea-Cliff   199
For the setting of the poem, see above, 'Once at Swanage'.

The Echo-Elf Answers   201
MS. adds '(Impromptu)'.

Cynic's Epitaph   202
First printed, with 'Epitaph on a Pessimist', in the *London Mercury*,
September 1925, p. 456.

A Beauty's Soliloquy during her Honeymoon   203
Suggested, if not written, 'In a London Hotel, 1892.'

Donaghadee   205

He inadvertently Cures his Love-pains   207

The Peace Peal   208
Written 'At the end of the War.' MS. '1918'.

Lady Vi   210
MS. 'Lady Clo'.

A Popular Personage at Home   212
Written in 1924 and first printed, with head- and tailpiece by
Harold Earnshaw, in *The Flying Carpet*, ed. Cynthia Asquith,
London [September 1925], pp. 9–10. Several lines were revised
when the poem was collected. For 'Wessex', see below, 'Dead
"Wessex" the Dog to the Household', p. 260.

Inscriptions for a Peal of Eight Bells   214

A Refusal   216
Written in August 1924. Hardy, with a number of eminent men
of letters and statesmen, had signed a communication in *The Times*,
14 July 1924, urging in this centenary year a tablet be erected to
Byron's memory in Poets' Corner. The Dean of Westminster,
Bishop Herbert E. Ryle, rejected the proposal in a letter published
19 July—a rejection that roused considerable comment. MS. shows
that lines 38–47 (' 'Tis urged . . . mean distortion.'), reminiscent
incidentally of the Dean's letter, were a late addition.

To C.F.H.   239
The poem is addressed to Caroline Fox Hanbury of Kingston Maurward House at whose christening in early September 1921 Hardy
served as godparent. A parchment MS. of the poem in a silver box
was his christening gift (*Later Years*, p. 224).

The High-School Lawn   240

The Forbidden Banns   241

The Paphian Ball   243
First printed, under the title 'The Midnight Revel', with a 2-page
illustration by N. C. Wyeth, in *McCall's Magazine* (New York),
December 1924, pp. 8–9. Several lines were revised when the poem
was collected. MS. adds, 'Note. The foregoing was composed
several years ago; but being cast in a familiar mediaeval mould was
not printed till now, when it has been considered to have some
qualities worth preserving.'

On Martock Moor   248
Written in 1899. MS. 'On Durnover Moor'.

That Moment   250
MS. 'The Misery of that Moment'.

Premonitions   251
MS. deleted, 'Forebodings'.

This Summer and Last   252
Written in (?)1913, with thoughts of Mrs. Hardy's death.

'Nothing Matters Much'   254
The poem refers to Judge Benjamin Fossett Lock, born at Dor-
chester in 1847 and died at Bridlington (near Flamborough Head),
Yorkshire, 11 August 1922. He was an early friend of Hardy's,
younger brother of the Warden of Keble College, Secretary of the
Positivist Society, and one of Leslie Stephen's 'Sunday Tramps'.
Mrs. Lock ('she who sat there') had died two years before him.

In the Evening   256
First printed, as a poem of 4 stanzas, in *The Times*, 5 January 1924,
p. 11. It was then considerably rewritten, and the last stanza expanded into 2 stanzas. In this 'amended version' it was printed
in *The Dorset Year-Book* (pub. Society of Dorset Men in London),

1924, p. 3, and a number of off-prints were made. Sir Frederick Treves, friend and fellow-townsman of Hardy, had died at Vevey, 7 December 1923. See *Later Years*, pp. 236–7. The last 3 lines of the original version of the poem appear on the Treves monument in Dorchester Cemetery.

The Six Boards · 258

Before my Friend Arrived · 260
The reference is most probably to Horace Moule, who took his life at Cambridge, 21 September 1873, and was buried at Fordington St. George, Dorchester, five days later.

Compassion: An Ode · 261
Written and first printed in 1924. See above, pp. 231 f.

'Why She Moved House' · 263

Tragedian to Tragedienne · 264

The Lady of Forebodings · 266

The Bird-catcher's Boy · 267
Written 21 November 1912 and first printed, as a poem of 15 stanzas, in a pictorial border by T. C. Dugdale, in the *Sphere*, 4 January 1913, p. 21. The MS. used on that occasion is now in the Bliss collection. It is a fair copy without alteration, written on 4 leaves measuring 5″×8″ and bound in three-quarters brown morocco. There is also in the collection a proof of the poem with corrections and alterations in Hardy's hand. When the poem was collected, it was extensively rewritten and lengthened by 2 stanzas.

A Hurried Meeting · 271

Discouragement · 275
Written in 1863–7 (MS. '1865–7') at 16 Westbourne Park Villas (described as 'From old MS.').

A Leaving · 276
There is a separate MS. of the poem, with the title 'A Last Leaving' and several variants, in my possession, the gift of Mrs. Hardy in 1933. It is written on a single leaf of fine paper measuring 8″×10″. This MS. is reproduced in facsimile in Roger Fry and E. A. Lowe, *English Handwriting* (S.P.E. Tract no. xxiii), Oxford, 1926, Plate 22. The poem recalls the last time the first Mrs. Hardy went out,

five days before her death (see *Later Years*, p. 154, and 'Your Last Drive').

Manuscript. The MS. of *Human Shows* is written on 196 leaves of fine paper, measuring 7⅞″× 10″ and numbered 1–196 by Hardy. To these have been added a draft of the title-page in his hand and 4 type-written pages of Contents. Like the MSS. of all Hardy's later volumes of poetry, this is a collection of fair copies, made at varying dates and put together for printing, with final alterations and revisions only. Pencilled notes on previous printings, trial readings, &c., have been largely erased. Where there are significant divergences from the printed text, they have been indicated above in the treatment of individual poems.

The MS., with its rough paper cover, has been bound in full blue crushed morocco. It remained at Max Gate until after Mrs. Hardy's death, when it was presented (in April 1939) to Yale University, 'The Gift of Miss Eva Dugdale in fulfilment of the wish of her sister Mrs. Thomas Hardy.'

Notes on Composition and Publication. Human Shows, the last of his volumes published during Hardy's lifetime, is a collection of 152 poems. Two are marked as work of the 60's, five as work of the 90's, but for the rest, where they have been dated, they are of more recent composition. In subject they bear frequent evidence of Hardy's examination of old diaries and letters, the ordering of his papers for work on the *Early Life* (seen to some extent in *Late Lyrics and Earlier* as well). Twenty-five of the poems had been printed previously. The MS. was sent to Macmillan 29 July 1925 and 'called for want of a better title "Poems Imaginative and Incidental: with Songs and Trifles" ', as Hardy wrote at the time. On 25 August he suggested to the publishers *Human Shows* as an alternative title, 'not quite so commonplace'. Again Sydney Cockerell assisted with the proofs (see *Friends of a Lifetime*, p. 293). *Human Shows* was published at 7s. 6d. in an edition of 5,000 copies, 20 November 1925. Macmillan wrote to Hardy the day before publication that practically the whole of the first edition was sold. He inscribed copies (dated November) to his wife (on the day of publication),

Sydney Cockerell, and Howard Bliss; and in December to Lascelles Abercrombie and Henry Newbolt.

Subsequent Editions (*see also* COLLECTED EDITIONS). Macmillan wrote Hardy 25 November 1925 (five days after publication) that a second impression was in hand and errors he had noted would be corrected. A third impression followed in December, making 7,000 copies in all by the end of the year.

Human Shows was published in America by The Macmillan Company in December 1925, in a trade edition and also a special edition limited to 100 numbered copies. It was the first time since *Wessex Poems* in 1898 that a publisher had felt justified in printing (and copyrighting) a volume of Hardy's lyrics in America.

Human Shows, combined with *Winter Words*, was included in Macmillan's definitive Wessex Edition in 1931.

1927: DORCHESTER GRAMMAR SCHOOL ADDRESS

ADDRESS / DELIVERED BY / THOMAS HARDY / ON LAYING / THE COMMEMORATION STONE / OF THE NEW / DORCHESTER GRAMMAR SCHOOL / TWENTY-FIRST JULY / 1927

Collation. Pp. [4]; [1]–[3] text; [4] colophon: *Twelve copies printed for Florence Emily Hardy / at the University Press, Cambridge, August 1927 / This is No.*............... [numbered and initialed by Mrs. Hardy] / .

Binding. Sewn in grey antique paper wrappers; front printed in black as above.

All edges uncut; leaves measure $7\frac{5}{8}'' \times 10\frac{1}{16}''$.

Notes. This address, delivered 21 July 1927, was the occasion of Hardy's last public appearance. As he wrote to Sydney Cockerell two days later, '. . . it was only intended for local consumption, and in fulfilment of a rash promise made months ago.' It was printed, nevertheless, in *The Times*, 22 July, p. 11, the *Dorset County Chronicle* (Dorchester), 28 July, p. 2, and elsewhere. Mrs. Hardy's pamphlet was set from *The Times*. A proof (dated 26 July) with revisions by Hardy and also the original typescript (with autograph additions) used at the stone-laying, the pages cut in half for ease in handling, are now in the possession of Sir Sydney Cockerell. For a general note on Mrs. Hardy's privately printed pamphlets, see Appendix, pp. 349 f.

There was an unauthorized edition of the address, under the title 'The Two Hardys', printed from a newspaper account of the occasion (which was included) by Joseph A. Allen of J. A. Allen & Co., London booksellers (cf. above, 'The Hope Song of the Soldiers' Sweethearts and Wives', pp. 109–10). This is a 4-page leaflet, with 'an instantaneous photo of Mr. Hardy reading the address' on the title-page, limited to 50 numbered copies 'for private circulation only.' It was produced in August 1927 (according to J. A. Allen & Co.'s catalogues) and may conceivably have anticipated Mrs. Hardy's edition, though evidence is wanting.

The address was reprinted in *Later Years*, pp. 254–6. Hardy had been a Governor of the Dorchester Grammar School from 1909 to 1926.

[1927]: YULETIDE IN A YOUNGER WORLD

YULETIDE | IN A | YOUNGER WORLD | [vignette] | BY THOMAS HARDY | Drawings by ALBERT RUTHERSTON

Collation. Pp. [8]; [1][2] blank; [3] coloured illustration; [4][5] text; [6] list of 8 titles; [7] colophon: *This is Number 1 of | THE ARIEL POEMS | Published by Faber & Gwyer Limited | at 24 Russell Square, London, W.C. 1 | Printed at The Curwen Press, Plaistow |* ; [8] certificate: *This edition on Zanders' hand-made | paper is limited to 350 copies | This is No.* [numbered by hand] | .

Binding. Green paper boards, lined with white; front printed in black as above; back plain.

Fly-leaf at front and back; all edges cut; leaves measure 4¾″×7¼″.

Ordinary Edition. Collation as above save that pp. [7] and [8] are blank. Sewn in green paper wrappers with folded fore-edges; front printed in black as above; back, colophon as above, p. [7].

All edges cut; leaves measure as above.

Notes. This poem is here printed for the first time. It was sent to the publishers in May 1927 at the request of Richard de la Mare, son of the poet, to inaugurate a series of gift booklets. It was published 25 August 1927 in two forms simultaneously, a limited edition of 350 copies at 5*s*. and an ordinary edition of 5,000 copies at 1*s*. The poem (like the others in the series) was also printed in an edition of 27 copies (12 only for sale) by William Edwin Rudge, Mount Vernon, New York, December 1927. It was collected in *Winter Words*, pp. 57–58.

1927: G.M.: A REMINISCENCE

G.M.: *A Reminiscence* / BY / THOMAS HARDY

Collation. Pp. [8]; [1]–[5] text; [6] colophon: *Twelve copies printed for Florence Emily Hardy / at the University Press, Cambridge, 21st November 1927 / This is No.* .... [numbered and initialed by Mrs. Hardy] / ; [7][8] blank.

Binding. Sewn in grey antique paper wrappers; front printed in black as above.

All edges uncut; leaves measure $7\frac{5}{8}'' \times 10\frac{1}{16}''$.

Notes. This brief reminiscence of Meredith was written in October 1927, at the request of Meredith's son and the editor of the *Nineteenth Century and After*, for publication in February 1928, the centenary of Meredith's birth. It was in proof 31 October, and from this proof (corrected by Hardy, with the important addition of 'the only words of his that I remember') Mrs. Hardy's pamphlet was prepared. This *Nineteenth Century* proof and two proofs for the pamphlet (9 and 14 November), showing several corrections of fact, are now in the possession of Sir Sydney Cockerell. For a general note on Mrs. Hardy's privately printed pamphlets, see Appendix, pp. 349 f.

The article was printed as planned in the *Nineteenth Century and After*, February 1928, pp. 146–8, together with a brief note by the editor on Hardy's death, which had intervened. The reminiscence is slight, adding nothing to the account of Hardy's first meeting with Meredith in March 1869 (here dated, in error, January) as given in *Early Life*, pp. 80–82. Hardy had written to the editor, 4 October, before undertaking the task, 'Unfortunately I am not physically able to write anything that can be dignified by the title of an article! But, as I say, I will get it ready when wanted. It will be a poor thing, I fear, much as I could have wished, for the late Mr. Meredith's sake, that I could have done something worthy of his memory.'

The MS. of the article is now in the Dorset County Museum. It is a fair copy, with a few alterations, written on 5 leaves of fine paper measuring 8″ × 10″ and signed and dated at the end 'October: 1927: (for Feb: 1928.)'.

1927: CHRISTMAS IN THE ELGIN ROOM

CHRISTMAS IN THE ELGIN ROOM. / BRITISH MUSEUM: / EARLY LAST CENTURY. / BY / THOMAS HARDY. / [*ornament*]

Collation. Pp. [8]; [1] title-page; [2] blank; [3]–[6] text; [7] colophon: *25 copies only printed for Mrs. Thomas Hardy, by | Henry Ling, Ltd., Dorchester, Dorset, 24th December, 1927. | This is No.* [numbered and initialed by Mrs. Hardy] / ; [8] blank.

Binding. Sewn in grey cover-paper wrappers; front printed in black as title-page.

All edges cut; leaves measure 7⅛″ × 9⅜″.

Notes. 'Christmas in the Elgin Room' was the last of Hardy's works to be published in his lifetime, and his concern for it is a touching detail that marks the close of his career (see *Later Years*, p. 264). The poem was written in 1905 and 1926 and published, not three weeks before his death, in *The Times*, 24 December 1927, p. 9. Mrs. Hardy's pamphlet was arranged to coincide with this publication. For a general note on these privately printed pamphlets, see Appendix, pp. 349 f. The poem was reprinted in the *Daily Telegraph*, 11 June 1928 and collected in *Winter Words*, pp. 197–9.

There is a separate MS. of the poem in Magdalene College, Cambridge. This is a fair copy (with revisions in 2 lines only), written on 2 leaves of fine paper measuring 8″ × 10″ and now framed and glazed. The first 2 stanzas are reproduced in facsimile in *The Times*, 1 February 1928, p. 8, where the revisions are called 'Mr. Hardy's final contribution to literature'. The MS. was presented to Magdalene by Hardy's literary executors, Mrs. Hardy and Sydney Cockerell, under a mis-understanding of his instructions, corrected by the subsequent gift of *Moments of Vision* (see above, p. 207). The MS. of 'Christmas in the Elgin Room' bound up in *Winter Words* is an earlier draft of the poem with numerous revisions.

1928: WINTER WORDS

WINTER WORDS / IN VARIOUS MOODS AND METRES / BY / THOMAS HARDY / MACMILLAN AND CO., LIMITED / ST. MARTIN'S STREET, LONDON / 1928

Collation. [A]⁶, B–N⁸, O⁶; pp. xii+204; [i] half-title; [ii] publishers' device and imprints; [iii] title-page; [iv] copyright notice; v–vi Introductory Note; vii–xi Contents; [xii] blank; 1–202 text; [203] printers' imprint: *Printed in Great Britain by* R. & R. Clark, Limited, *Edinburgh.* / ; [204] blank.

Binding. Olive-green cloth; front blocked in gold with TH monogram medallion; back plain; gold-lettered on spine: Winter / Words / Thomas / Hardy / Macmillan *&* Cᵒ. / .

Plain end-papers; top uncut, fore-edge and tail trimmed; leaves measure 5″×7½″.

The whole format is uniform with *The Dynasts* and succeeding volumes of verse.

Contents. Introductory Note   Page v
> There is a draft of the last 2 paragraphs in the possession of Sir Sydney Cockerell.

The New Dawn's Business   1
> First printed in the *Daily Telegraph*, 20 March 1928.

Proud Songsters   3
> First printed in the *Daily Telegraph*, 9 April 1928. There is a separate MS. of the poem in the possession of Sir Sydney Cockerell. It is written on a leaf of fine paper measuring 6″×7½″ and shows some 5 verbal alterations.

Thoughts at Midnight   4
> Written in part 25 May 1906.

It was written by March 1924 when it was sent to Macmillan to market.

First printed in the *Saturday Review*, 3 December 1927, p. 769.

Written in 1925 and first printed, under the title 'The Lady in the Christmas Furs', in the *Saturday Review*, 4 December 1926, p. 669 (and subsequently in the *Daily Telegraph*, 26 July 1928).

First printed in the *Daily Telegraph*, 29 March 1928. The MS., omitted from the gift to Queen's College, is now in the possession of Sir Sydney Cockerell. It is written on a leaf of fine paper measuring 8″×10″, with alterations in the last line. The poem recalls Hardy's own childhood and offers a close parallel to passages in the *Early Life* (pp. 19–20) and *Jude the Obscure* (p. 15).

Written in 1884.

First printed in the *Daily Telegraph*, 2 July 1928.

Written in 192–. MS. shows stanza 7 written tentatively, with variants, in pencil. Hardy worked in Clement's Inn in Raphael Brandon's architectural offices during the summer of 1870. Cf. *A Pair of Blue Eyes*, pp. 141–2.

A separate MS. of this poem, under the title 'The Thrown Elm', was given by Hardy himself to Mrs. St. John Hornby. It is an earlier draft with alterations and alternative readings.

First printed in the *Daily Telegraph*, 17 May 1928. A separate MS. of the poem is now in the possession of Sir Newman Flower. It offers a number of variant readings and is marked by Hardy in pencil '[best]'. The MS. is reproduced in facsimile in *English Poetical Autographs*, ed. Desmond Flower and A. N. L. Munby (London, 1938), Plate 38.

So Various   80
First printed in the *Daily Telegraph*, 22 March 1928. There is a rough draft of the last 3 stanzas in the possession of Sir Sydney Cockerell.

A Self-Glamourer   83

The Dead Bastard   85
First printed in the *Daily Telegraph*, 7 September 1928.

The Clasped Skeletons   86
First printed in the *Daily Telegraph*, 2 August 1928. There is a separate MS. of the poem in the Dorset County Museum. It is an earlier draft with numerous alterations made in pencil, written on a folio of fine paper measuring $7\frac{3}{4}'' \times 10''$.

In the Marquee   89
First printed in the *Daily Telegraph*, 16 July 1928. Hardy's rough notes for the poem are headed, 'The party at W[estbourne] P[ark] V[illas].'

After the Burial   91
There is a separate MS. of the poem, written on a leaf of ruled paper measuring $8'' \times 10''$ and showing alterations in 6 lines. It was a gift of Mrs. Hardy to Mrs. Allhusen and is now in the Dorset County Museum.

The Mongrel   93
First printed in the *Daily Telegraph*, 25 June 1928.

Concerning Agnes   95
First printed in the *Daily Telegraph*, 21 May 1928. Agnes was Lady Grove, who died 7 December 1926. The poem recalls particularly Hardy's meeting with her at Rushmore in *September* 1895 (*Later Years*, pp. 37–38; see also p. 53). The two kept up a friendship and correspondence, Lady Grove consulting Hardy about her writing and dedicating her book *The Social Fetich* (1907) to him.

Henley Regatta   97

An Evening in Galilee   98

The Brother   101

We Field-Women   103
There is a separate MS. of the poem in the Bliss collection. It is
written on a single leaf of fine paper measuring 8″ × 10″ and shows
several alterations in the first stanza. The poem recalls scenes in *Tess
of the d'Urbervilles* (particularly Chap. 43).

A Practical Woman   104

Squire Hooper   105
First printed in the *Daily Telegraph*, 12 April 1928.

'A Gentleman's Second-Hand Suit'   108
First printed in *Harper's Monthly Magazine* (New York), March
1928, p. [443]. Hardy himself sent the poem in December 1927.

'We Say We shall not Meet'   110
First printed in the *Daily Telegraph*, 11 September 1928.

Seeing the Moon Rise   111
Written in August 1927.

Song to Aurore   112
First printed in the *Daily Telegraph*, 3 May 1928.

He Never Expected Much   113
Written *c.* 2 June 1926 and first printed in the *Daily Telegraph*,
19 March 1928.

Standing by the Mantelpiece   115
The speaker is Hardy's early and devoted friend, Horace M. Moule,
who took his life at Cambridge, 21 September 1873. It is a woman
addressed.

Boys Then and Now   117

That Kiss in the Dark   118
First printed in the *Daily Telegraph*, 13 September 1928.

A Necessitarian's Epitaph   119

Burning the Holly   120
First printed in the *Daily Telegraph*, 20 August 1928.

Suspense   124

The Second Visit   125
First printed in the *Daily Telegraph*, 31 May 1928.

Lorna the Second   151
The poem was suggested by an unusual marriage in 1927 in the
family of Hardy's old friend, Bosworth Smith. A disappointed
suitor of 'Lorna the First' married, eight years after her death, her
young daughter. The reminiscence of *The Well-Beloved* could not
have escaped the poet.

A Daughter Returns   152
Written 17 December 1901.

The Third Kissing-Gate   154
First printed, in its present form, in the *Daily Telegraph*, 30 July
1928. Four of the 5 stanzas (excepting stanza 4) are derived, with
some revision, from 'The Forsaking of the Nest', a poem of 9 stanzas
printed, with head- and tailpiece and full-page illustration by Edward Blampied, in *Nash's Magazine*, February 1912, p. 584. The
MS. of 'The Forsaking of the Nest', a fair copy written on pp. 1
and 3 of a folio of note-paper measuring $5'' \times 7\frac{7}{8}''$, is now in the
possession of Mr. Halsted B. VanderPoel. Hardy never reprinted
the poem in this form and may even have forgotten its existence until
a query about the MS. in 1924.

Drinking Song   155
First printed in the *Daily Telegraph*, 14 June 1928. MS. suggests
as sub-title, 'on Great Thoughts belittled'.

The Tarrying Bridegroom   159

The Destined Pair   160
First printed in the *Daily Telegraph*, 7 June 1928.

A Musical Incident   161

June Leaves and Autumn   163
Written 19 November 1898 and first printed in the *Daily Telegraph*, 28 June 1928 (the last 6 lines omitted in error).

No Bell-Ringing   165
First printed in 1925. See above, pp. 233 f.

'I Looked Back'   168
First printed in the *Daily Telegraph*, 24 May 1928.

The Aged Newspaper Soliloquizes   170
First printed, under the title 'The Newspaper Soliloquises', in the

Observer, 14 March 1926, p. 16. The MS. is reproduced in facsimile in the *New York Times*, 11 April 1926.

Christmas: 1924   171
Written at Christmas 1924 and first printed, under the title 'Peace upon Earth', in the *Daily Telegraph*, 18 June 1928.

The Single Witness   172

How She Went to Ireland   174
The poem presumably refers to Dora Sigerson, Clement Shorter's wife, who died 6 January 1918 and was taken to Dublin for burial. See above, pp. 210 f.

Dead 'Wessex' the Dog to the Household   175
First printed (2 stanzas only) in the *Daily Telegraph*, 10 May 1928. 'Wessex', the Hardys' wire-haired terrier, already celebrated in the poem 'A Popular Personage at Home', died 27 December 1926. See *Later Years*, pp. 250–1; *Friends of a Lifetime*, p. 314 (for '*Dec. 26th*' read '*Dec. 29th*').

The Woman who went East   177
First printed in the *Daily Telegraph*, 14 May 1928. MS. deleted, 'The Woman of the West'.

Not Known   179
MS. deleted at end, '1914: After reading criticism.'

The Boy's Dream   180
First printed in the *Daily Telegraph*, 12 July 1928.

The Gap in the White   182

Family Portraits   184
First printed, as a poem of 7 stanzas under the title 'The Portraits', in *Nash's and Pall Mall Magazine*, December 1924, pp. 26–27. It was subsequently much revised, the present fifth stanza added and the last 3 stanzas in particular rearranged and rewritten. This final version was first printed in the *Daily Telegraph*, 6 August 1928.

The Catching Ballet of the Wedding Clothes   187
Written in 1919. MS. shows stanza 7 was a late addition to the poem.

A Winsome Woman   192

Serial Issue. Hardy's literary executors, Mrs. Hardy and Sydney Cockerell,
sold the serial rights in 50 of the poems to the *Daily Telegraph*, where
they appeared at irregular intervals between 19 March and 26 September 1928 (as indicated above). The entire volume was reprinted,
but with the poems wholly rearranged, in the *Book League Monthly*
(New York), December 1928, pp. [9]–142.

Manuscript. The MS. of *Winter Words* is written on 136 leaves of fine
paper measuring $7\frac{3}{4}'' \times 9\frac{15}{16}''$. The leaves are unnumbered, showing that
Hardy had not yet fastened on the order of the poems, and pencilled
notes as to first printings, trial readings, &c., have not been erased as
in the case of other MSS. Like the MSS. of all his later volumes of
verse, this is a collection of fair copies made at varying dates, with
some further alterations and revisions. Hardy has marked it on the
title-page, however, '[unrevised.]'. Where there are deletions or alterations of significance they have been indicated above in the treatment
of individual poems. 'Childhood among the Ferns' (see above, p. 255)
and 'He Resolves to Say No More' are wanting.

The MS. is bound in full blue crushed morocco and was presented
by Mrs. Hardy to Queen's College, Oxford, in the summer of
1928, 'in accordance with the wish of her husband, Thomas Hardy,

expressed during his lifetime.' Hardy had been elected an Honorary Fellow of Queen's College in 1922.

There is a draft of the title-page in the possession of Sir Sydney Cockerell, showing such trial titles as 'Wintry Things', 'A Wintry Voice', and 'Winter Flowers'.

Notes on Composition and Publication. Winter Words is a collection of 105 poems, which Hardy had been assembling at the time of his death in January 1928. From the 'Introductory Note' which he had drafted, it would appear he had planned to bring out the volume on his birthday in June 1928, but already he foresaw it as 'probably my last appearance on the literary stage' and had chosen for its close 'He Resolves to Say No More'. The poems had not yet been set in order or finally revised, and several he had questioned in the MS. would undoubtedly have been rejected altogether and others (unfinished and so destroyed by his instructions) would have been included. He had brought together, however, the work of over sixty years, 2 poems of 1866 and 1868 having been gathered with work of every subsequent decade (save the 70's), and in nothing is this last collection more characteristic of its author. Eleven of the poems had been printed previously, 4 of these also being included in the group of 50 printed in the *Daily Telegraph*.

Winter Words was published at 7*s.* 6*d.* in an edition of 5,000 copies, 2 October 1928. There was a second impression the same month.

Subsequent Editions (*see also* COLLECTED EDITIONS). *Winter Words* was published in America by The Macmillan Company in November 1928, in a trade edition and also a large-paper edition limited to 500 numbered copies.

Combined with *Human Shows*, it was included in Macmillan's definitive Wessex Edition in 1931.

1928: THE EARLY LIFE OF THOMAS HARDY

THE EARLY LIFE OF / THOMAS HARDY / 1840–1891 / COMPILED LARGELY FROM / CONTEMPORARY NOTES, LETTERS, DIARIES, AND / BIOGRAPHICAL MEMORANDA, AS WELL AS FROM / ORAL INFORMATION IN CONVERSATIONS

EXTENDING / OVER MANY YEARS / BY / FLORENCE EMILY HARDY / MACMILLAN AND CO., LIMITED / ST. MARTIN'S STREET, LONDON / 1928

Collation. [A]⁶, B–X⁸, Y⁴; pp. xii+328; [i] half-title; [ii] publishers' device and imprints; [iii] title-page; [iv] copyright notice; v dedication; [vi] blank; vii–viii Prefatory Note; ix–xi Contents; xii List of Illustrations; 1 divisional title; [2] blank; 3–315 text; [316] blank; 317–27 Index, printers' imprint at foot of p. 327: *Printed in Great Britain by* R. & R. Clark, Limited, *Edinburgh.* / ; [328] blank.

Illustrations. Frontispiece and 14 illustrations, all save one (p. 13) separately printed.

Binding. Olive-green cloth; front blocked in gold with TH monogram medallion; back plain; gold-lettered on spine: The / Early Life / of / Thomas / Hardy / 1840–1891 / Macmillan & Cᵒ / .

Plain end-papers; top gilt, fore-edge and tail cut; leaves measure $5\frac{3}{4}'' \times 8\frac{5}{8}''$.

The binding is uniform with *The Dynasts* and succeeding volumes of verse.

Notes on Contents. The following letters, sketches, &c., previously published in books and periodicals, are here collected for the first time. That Hardy chose them for preservation from a mass of such materials is not without significance. Few personal letters of this early period, however, were accessible, save those in print.

'Domicilium' (pp. 4–5)

First printed in 1916. See above, pp. 176 f.

Letter on Adelphi Terrace (p. 49)

First printed in Austin Brereton, *The Literary History of the Adelphi* (London, 1907), p. 216. The original letter (in the Bliss collection) is addressed to Clement Shorter and dated 24 January 1906.

Letter to William Tinsley (pp. 109–10)

First printed in A. Edward Newton, 'The Amenities of Book-Collecting', the *Atlantic Monthly* (Boston), March 1915, p. 339. Reproduced in facsimile in the same author's *The Amenities of Book-Collecting* (Boston, 1918), p. [12].

Recollections of Leslie Stephen (pp. 130–1, 139)
> First printed in Frederic William Maitland, *The Life and Letters of Leslie Stephen* (London, 1906), pp. 275, 263–4. Some use is made in the *Early Life* of the remainder of Hardy's important contribution to Maitland's book (pp. 270–8, including the sonnet, 'The Schreckhorn', q.v.) but without direct quotation.

Letter to Frederick Locker (pp. 174–5)
> First printed in Augustine Birrell, *Frederick Locker-Lampson* (London, 1920), pp. 139–40.

Letter to Handley Moule (p. 176)
> First printed in J. B. Harford and F. C. Macdonald, *Handley Carr Glyn Moule* (London [1922]), pp. 75–76.

Letter to A. A. Reade (pp. 204–5)
> First printed in *Study and Stimulants*, ed. A. Arthur Reade (Manchester and London, 1883), p. 66. Hardy's contribution to this symposium is there dated 5 December 1882. The first half of the letter—on tobacco—is not reprinted, and the remainder has been a little rewritten.

[Descriptions of Max Gate and Hardy in 1886 (pp. 226–7)
> These passages are quoted from an unsigned sketch, 'Mr. Thomas Hardy at Max Gate, Dorchester', No. 440 of a series called 'Celebrities at Home', in the *World*, 17 February 1886, pp. 6–7. Copies of an off-print were found among the Max Gate papers (a leaflet with text printed on pp. 1 and 3), and this fact, together with some internal evidence of style, has suggested Hardy himself as the 'careful observer'. The series, however, was the work of Edmund Yates and his staff, and there is little reason to suppose the present sketch an exception.]

Letter, 'The State Recognition of Authors' (p. 315)
> First printed in the *Bookman*, December 1891, p. 98. One of several letters written at the request of Robertson Nicoll, the editor, as comment on a recent controversy between Walter Besant and the *Spectator*.

Serial Issue. Portions of Parts I and II of the *Early Life* were published serially in *The Times* through the week preceding the appearance of the volume. There were 6 instalments, running from 22 October to

27 October 1928 and introduced by a long and perceptive leader, 'Thomas Hardy's Life', on the 22nd. Chapters were much compressed and given new titles, and selections were drawn together, where necessary, by editorial comment. The 6 instalments ran as follows: 22 October, 'Birth and Childhood' (Chap. 1); 23 October, 'Student and Architect' (Chaps. 2 and 3); 24 October, 'A First Novel' (Chap.4); 25 October, 'A Cornish Expedition' (Chaps. 4 and 5); 26 October, 'Between Two Arts' (Chap. 6); 27 October, 'Success Confirmed' (Chaps. 7, 9, and 10).

Notes on Composition and Publication. The Early Life of Thomas Hardy is in reality an autobiography. Though Mrs. Hardy's name stands on the title-page, her work was confined to a few editorial touches, and the writing is throughout Hardy's own. It was not a task to which he had looked forward nor one he could find congenial. His constant intention was 'not to produce my reminiscences to the world',[1] his 'feeling for a long time was that he would not care to have his life written at all',[2] and his natural reticence and modesty made impossible any acknowledgement of the work. From the first the 'exactness' of 'Mr. Hardy's own reminiscent phrases'[3] was recognized, but Mrs. Hardy loyally preserved the fiction of her authorship to the end, and her known experience as journalist and writer assisted this innocent deception.[4] Mrs. Hardy (almost certainly Hardy himself) remarks in her Prefatory Note that her husband's hand was forced, in the matter of a biography, he 'having observed many erroneous and grotesque statements advanced as his experiences, and a so-called "Life" published as authoritative'. This is undoubtedly a reference to F. A. Hedgcock's *Thomas Hardy, Penseur et Artiste* (Paris, 1911) and Ernest Brennecke, Jr.'s *The Life of Thomas Hardy* (New York, 1925). Both books angered and pained Hardy. He refused to sanction an English translation of the one, though it had many merits, and through Macmillan repudiated the other and threatened an injunction for breach of copyright.[5]

---

[1] *Later Years*, p. 142.   [2] *Early Life*, p. vii.   [3] Ibid., p. viii.

[4] A possible alternative seems to have been an offer to T. E. Lawrence 'to edit or "ghost" ' Hardy's diary. 'The existence of the materials is not known, even to Macmillan's', Lawrence wrote, 'indeed only five people do know of it.' *The Letters of T. E. Lawrence*, ed. David Garnett (London, 1938), pp. 474–5.

[5] See *The Times*, 11 April 1925, p. 11. Hardy's copy of Hedgcock's book is heavily and caustically annotated.

The actual composition of the *Early Life* (and the *Later Years*), though evidence is wanting, probably lies midway between the appearance of these two volumes. There is a noticeable pause in publication after *Moments of Vision* (1917), and there are references in letters of this time to the ordering of Hardy's papers. Mrs. Hardy wrote to Sydney Cockerell, 6 February 1919, 'The letter sorting is still going on—nineteen years more to do. When they are all sorted I am going to arrange them under initials, instead of dates. A most interesting letter of Swinburne's has come to light—in praise of *Jude the Obscure* which ought to have been included in Swinburne's Letters.'[1] And Hardy wrote to Sir George Douglas, 7 May 1919, 'I have not been doing much—mainly destroying papers of the last 30 or 40 years, and they raise ghosts.' And again 11 September 1919, 'I have been occupied in the dismal work of destroying all sorts of papers which were absolutely of no use for any purpose, God's or man's.' The writing proceeded with a good deal of secrecy, Hardy destroying his MS. as fast as Mrs. Hardy completed a typescript (work she first mentions in her diary 11 February 1918).[2] Letters were sorted and tied in bundles by years, those introduced into the biography and some others being preserved, many more being destroyed. Excerpts were taken from diaries and note-books, and then these were destroyed (or marked 'To be destroyed') with almost no exception. As a result the Max Gate papers today contain little private and personal material that Hardy did not wish to survive. The *Early Life*, if no more of the biography, was near completion by 1926. Barrie (in a letter to Mrs. Hardy, 18 March 1926) was offering to read 'the first part of the book [? the whole of the *Early Life*] in type-writing', and Col. Lawrence had already read with great admiration 'the early, formative, life'.[3]

The unusual circumstances in which the *Early Life* was written mean that it wants, as every autobiography, objectivity—even such objectivity as Mrs. Hardy could have given it. It is immensely valuable as

---

[1] *Friends of a Lifetime*, p. 301. The Swinburne letter appears in *Later Years*, pp. 39–40.

[2] The typescript now among the Max Gate papers, with the title 'The Life and Work of Thomas Hardy, Vol. I', is marked by Hardy 'Mrs. Hardy. (Personal Copy)' and '2nd. Copy'. The many additions and corrections are printed in a calligraphic hand, as a kind of disguise. The hand is sometimes Hardy's and sometimes Mrs. Hardy's (copying his alterations as made on a duplicate typescript).

[3] Lawrence to Mrs. Hardy, 21 June 1926 (*The Letters of T. E. Lawrence*, p. 498). It is not clear what portion of the MS. Hardy had destroyed.

a personal and intimate document and preserves diaries and papers no longer available in any other form, but it has naturally many significant silences and some characters in the story are never mentioned at all. As Trollope wrote in his own *Autobiography*, 'That I, or any man, should tell everything of himself, I hold to be impossible.' The conditions of Hardy's birth and childhood are idealized. The bitterness of his struggle for an education and a profession and the suffering of his first marriage find no reflection. The facts of many episodes (the dramatization of *Far from the Madding Crowd* and the rejection of *Too Late Beloved*, for example) are not recalled. This is only to say that Hardy set down what he chose, free from the obligations of formal biography. The measure of detachment he achieved is remarkable.

The MS. of the *Early Life* was complete at Hardy's death and in less than three weeks had been dispatched to Macmillan.

The book was published at 18*s*. in an edition of 3,000 copies, 2 November 1928.

Subsequent Editions. A 'New Edition' of the *Early Life*, under the title *The Life of Thomas Hardy*, Vol. I, 1840–1891, was published in 1933. This was in reality a second impression, with altered title-page, from which all inserted illustrations save the frontispiece were omitted.

The *Early Life* was published in America by The Macmillan Company in November 1928.

1929: OLD MRS. CHUNDLE

OLD MRS. CHUNDLE / 𝔄 𝔖𝔥𝔬𝔯𝔱 𝔖𝔱𝔬𝔯𝔶 / BY / THOMAS HARDY / [*vignette*] / NEW YORK / CROSBY GAIGE / 1929

Collation. Pp. [viii]+32; [i][ii] blank; [iii] half-title; [iv] blank; [v] title-page; [vi] copyright notice; [vii] divisional title; [viii] blank; 1–[27] text, with head- and tailpiece; [28] blank; [29] colophon: *Of this story—written about 1880–1890 and prob-* | *ably intended to be included in the volume entitled* | *"Life's Little Ironies," or "Wessex Tales,"—* | *742 copies have been printed on Zanders hand-* | *made paper, and 13 on gray French Ingres paper,* | *by D. B. Updike, The Merrymount Press, Boston,* | *January, 1929. Of these, 700 copies, numbered from* | *1 to 700, inclusive, are for sale, and will be distrib- | uted by Random House. | This is copy number* [numbered by hand]. / ; [30]–[32] blank.

Binding. Decorated paper boards; green cloth spine, gold-lettered, between ornamental bands: *Old | Mrs. | Chundle |* ˙.˙ *| Thomas | Hardy |* . Plain end-papers, blank leaf inserted at beginning and end; all edges uncut; leaves measure 6″ × 8⅜″.

Notes. Old Mrs. Chundle is a discarded short story, never printed in Hardy's lifetime. It was first published in *Ladies' Home Journal* (Philadelphia), February 1929, pp. 3–4, 142, with 2 illustrations in the text by Edward Ryan and an Editor's Note: 'This is the only unpublished short story by the late Thomas Hardy.' The Crosby Gaige edition followed immediately (never copyrighted, in spite of the notice on p. [vi]). Both printings were by arrangement with Mrs. Hardy but, on account of the inferiority of the story, contrary to the strong objection of her co-executor, Sydney Cockerell (see *The Times Literary Supplement*, 14 March 1935, p. 160).

The story, a true one, Hardy had from Henry Moule (original of the sketching curate) and often repeated. Beyond this all we know is contained in his note on the MS. (inaccurately printed in the colophon above): '(Written about 1888–1890. Probably intended to be included in the volume entitled "Life's Little Ironies", or "Wessex Tales".)'. This 13-page MS. '[Copied from the original rough draft]' remained among the Max Gate papers at Mrs. Hardy's death and is now in the Dorset County Museum.

1930: THE LATER YEARS OF THOMAS HARDY

THE LATER YEARS OF | THOMAS HARDY | 1892–1928 | BY | FLORENCE EMILY HARDY | MACMILLAN AND CO., LIMITED | ST. MARTIN'S STREET, LONDON | 1930

Collation. [A]⁶, B–T⁸; pp. xii+288; [i] half-title; [ii] publishers' device and imprints; [iii] title-page; [iv] copyright notice; v note; [vi] blank; vii–ix Contents; [x] blank; xi List of Illustrations; [xii] blank; 1 divisional title; [2] blank; 3–276 text; 277–86 Index, printers' imprint at foot of p. 286: *Printed in Great Britain by* R. & R. Clark, Limited,

Edinburgh. | ; [287][288] advertisements of Hardy's works, separately
paged 1–2.

Illustrations. Frontispiece and 11 illustrations, separately printed.

Binding. Olive-green cloth; front blocked in gold with TH monogram
medallion; back plain; gold-lettered on spine: The / Later Years / of /
Thomas / Hardy / 1892–1928 / Macmillan & C⁰ / .

Plain end-papers; top gilt, fore-edge and tail cut; leaves measure
5¾″× 8⅝″.

The whole format is uniform with *The Early Life of Thomas Hardy.*

Notes on Contents. The following notes, letters, &c., previously published
in books and periodicals, are here collected for the first time. As in the
case of the *Early Life,* Hardy's choice of them for preservation from
a mass of such materials is significant. For this later period drafts and
copies among the Max Gate papers were often used, and these (and
Hardy's habits of revision) account for some divergences of text.

Letter, 'Contrainte et liberté' (p. 23)

First printed in *L'Ermitage* (Paris), November 1893, p. 260.
Hardy's draft of his brief contribution to this symposium (here
translated into French) is dated 14 August 1893.

Letters to [Edmund Gosse] (pp. 40–43)

These 3 letters, inserted at this point by Mrs. Hardy, were first
printed from the originals in his possession by T. J. Wise as *A Defence
of Jude the Obscure . . . In Three Letters to Sir Edmund Gosse, C.B.*
(Edinburgh, 1928), a pamphlet 'for private circulation only' limited
to 30 copies.

Letter to W. T. Stead (p. 45)

The letter was not printed with other replies to Stead's query in
'The Penny Hymnal for the People', the *Review of Reviews,* January
1896, but Hardy's three choices were listed, without comment, in
Hymns That Have Helped, ed. W. T. Stead (London [1896]), p. 117.

Letter to Miss Jeannette Gilder (p. 51)

First printed from the original in his possession by Paul Lemperly
in *Jude the Obscure, A Letter and a Foreword* (Lakewood, Ohio,
1917). The pamphlet was limited to 27 copies for private circulation, the foreword written by Clement Shorter. Hardy's letter is

reproduced in facsimile, with related material, in A. Edward Newton, *Thomas Hardy, Novelist or Poet?* (Philadelphia, Privately
Printed, 1929).

Letter, 'The Well-Beloved' (pp. 59–60)
First printed in the *Academy*, 3 April 1897, p. 381. The letter, only
partially reprinted, is dated 'Dorchester: March 29' and is in retort
to a review of the novel in the *Academy*, 27 March (pp. 345–6).

Letter to Swinburne (pp. 60–61)
The entire letter, dated 1 April 1897, is reproduced in facsimile in
The Ashley Library, vol. ii (London, 1922), following p. 168.

Letter, 'The Best Scenery I Know' (pp. 70–71)
First printed in the *Saturday Review*, 7 August 1897, p. 140. The
letter is dated 9 July and is a contribution to a symposium on the
subject running at this time.

Letter, 'A Plea for the Horses' (p. 81)
First printed in *War against War*, 20 January 1899, p. 21, where
the letter is dated 10 January.

Letter, 'The American National Red Cross Society' (p. 86)
Written 3 October 1900 to F. D. Higbee, a promoter employed
by the American Red Cross, as part of a scheme for raising funds.
The scheme (watch-night gatherings in large cities to open the new
century with greetings from sovereigns and prominent men) fell
through in most instances, and Hardy's letter was apparently not
printed until the *Biblio* (Pompton Lakes, New Jersey), November–
December 1925, p. 857.

Letter, 'La Littérature anglaise et la guerre du Sud-Africain' (p. 92)
First printed in *Revue Bleue* (Paris), 16 August 1902, p. 213. The
letter (translated into French) is included with others in an article
by Gilbert Giluncy. It is not reprinted entire.

Tribute to Victor Hugo (p. 92)
First printed (in Italian) in *Il Piccolo della Sera* (Trieste), 26
February 1902.

Letter to Rider Haggard (pp. 93–96)
First printed in H. Rider Haggard, *Rural England* (2 vols., London,
1902), vol. i, pp. 282–5. The letter is accompanied by several brief
excerpts from 'The Dorsetshire Labourer'.

Letter, 'M. Maeterlinck's Apology for Nature' (pp. 97–98)
First printed in the *Academy and Literature*, 17 May 1902, pp. 514–15. The letter was a comment on a review of Maeterlinck's *The Buried Temple* (3 May 1902, pp. 451–2) and was headed 'M. Maeterlinck's Apology for Nature' (which accounts for Hardy's later confusion of titles).

Letter, 'Edmund Kean in Dorchester' (1) (pp. 98–99)
First printed in the *Dorset County Chronicle* (Dorchester), 29 May 1902, p. 11. Signed 'History'.

Letter, 'Edmund Kean in Dorchester' (2) (p. 99)
First printed in the *Dorset County Chronicle* (Dorchester), 12 June 1902, p. 10. Signed 'History'. Several sentences were not reprinted. For a third letter in the series, not reprinted, see below, p. 308.

Letter, 'La France est-elle en décadence?' (p. 101)
First printed (in French) in *L'Européen* (Paris), 26 March 1904, p. 4, as a contribution to a symposium on this question. Reprinted in the *Daily Chronicle*, 31 March 1904.

Letter to Edward Clodd (pp. 104–6)
First printed in 1929 (see below).

Letter, 'Tolstoy on War' (p. 107)
First printed in *The Times*, 28 June 1904, p. 9. Dated from the Athenaeum, 27 June.

Letter to Israel Zangwill (pp. 115–16)
First printed in the *Fortnightly Review*, April 1906, pp. 638–9. One of a number of comments by men of letters on the programme of the Ito (Jewish Territorial Organization), forming a symposium 'Letters and the Ito'.

Letter, 'A Glimpse of John Stuart Mill' (pp. 118–19)
First printed in *The Times*, 21 May 1906, p. 6.

Letter, 'The Poe Centenary' (p. 134)
First printed in *The Times*, 15 January 1909, p. 11; and subsequently in *The Book of the Poe Centenary*, ed. C. W. Kent and J. S. Patton (University of Virginia, 1909), pp. 196–7. The letter was written 4 January.

Letter on Vivisection (pp. 138–9)
First printed in a pamphlet, *Vivisection from the Viewpoint of Some*

Great Minds (Vivisection Investigation League, New York [?1909]), p. [16], where Hardy's comment is dated May 1909.

Letter to the Secretary of the Humanitarian League (pp. 141–2)
First printed in the *Humanitarian*, May 1910, p. 35.

Speech on receiving the Freedom of the Borough (pp. 143–7)
First printed in *The Times*, 17 November 1910, p. 12; also in the *Morning Post*, 17 November, and the *Dorset County Chronicle* (Dorchester), 24 November.

Letter on Anatole France (p. 159)
First printed in *The Times*, 11 December 1913, p. 9; and subsequently in a pamphlet, *Dinner Given in Honour of M. Anatole France at the Savoy Hotel, December 10, 1913* (London, Privately Printed, December 1913), p. 4. The letter was written 7 December.

Letter to Bishop Moule (pp. 193–4)
First printed, in part, in J. B. Harford and F. C. Macdonald, *Handley Carr Glyn Moule* (London [1922]), pp. 4, 76.

Note on International Disarmament (p. 219)
First printed as a cablegram in the *World* (New York), 29 December 1920, p. 1.

Address at the Dorchester Grammar School (pp. 254–6)
First printed in 1927. See above, pp. 248 f.

Letters to Edward Clodd (pp. 274–6)
These 3 letters were first printed from the originals in his possession by T. J. Wise in *Notes on "The Dynasts" ... In Four Letters to Edward Clodd* (Edinburgh, 1929), a pamphlet 'for private circulation only' limited to 20 copies. The fourth letter (22 March 1904) was cancelled when the volume was in proof, Mrs. Hardy not having noticed until then that Hardy himself had already included it (from a draft) at pp. 104–6.

Serial Issue. Portions of the *Later Years* were printed serially in *The Times* in advance of publication of the volume. There were 2 instalments, largely a series of extracts from letters and diaries: 8 April 1930, 'The Making of "The Dynasts"'; 9 April, 'Life in Old Dorset'.

Notes on Composition and Publication. The Later Years of Thomas Hardy was largely written by Hardy himself under the same circumstances

Mem:
Vol II. might begin here – if 2 vols.

[*Number of typoscript pages in the whole, probably about 650 or under, when finished, which at 230 words each page makes 150,000 - (a fair length for a biography.)*]

PART V.

Tess, Jude, and the end of Prose.

Chapter XX.

The Reception of the Book.

1892. Aet. 51 - 52.

As ~~the novel~~ *Tess of the d'Urbervilles* got into general circulation it attracted an attention that Hardy had apparently not foreseen, for at the time of its publication he was planning something of quite a different kind, according to an entry he made:

"Title:- 'Songs of Five-and-Twenty Years'. Arrangement of the songs: Lyric Ecstacy inspired by music to have precedence."

However, reviews, letters, and other intelligence speedily called him from these casual thoughts back to the novel, which the tediousness of the alterations and restorations had made him weary of. From the prefaces to later editions can be gathered more or less clearly what happened to the book as, passing into great popularity, an endeavour was made *by some critics* to change it to *scandalous* notoriety – the latter kind of clamour, raised by a certain small section of the public and the press, being quite inexplicable to *its just* ~~any fair~~ judge*s*, and to the writer himself. (It would have been amusing if it had not revealed such antagonism at the back of)

(The sub-title of the book, added as a casual afterthought, seemed to be especially exasperating. All this)

The first page of Hardy's 'rough copy' of the typescript of *The Later Years of Thomas Hardy*, with additions in his calligraphic hand as the *Early Life* (see above, pp. 265–7). It was not carried beyond the year 1918, however, which may give some clue to the date of composition, and the four concluding chapters are Mrs. Hardy's work.[1] Even here Hardy provided frequent paragraphs and continued to select detail—on the draft, for example, of a letter to Galsworthy, 20 April 1923 (see *Later Years*, p. 230), he has written '[may be inserted in *Materials* at date]'. Mrs. Hardy had the advice and criticism of Sir James Barrie in preparing the MS. for the printers, but her difficulties in finishing a book she had not written and in editing material with which she was not always familiar are suggested by the letters to Dr. Saleeby and Edward Clodd in Appendixes II and III. These letters were not made available until after Hardy's death and they were in type before it was discovered that one letter in each group already appeared in the body of the book (Hardy having kept drafts of each). In the case of the Saleeby letter a footnote (p. 272) was hastily improvised; the Clodd letter was cancelled (though it remains in the American edition).

The *Later Years* was published at 18*s*. in an edition of 3,000 copies, 29 April 1930.

Subsequent Editions. A 'New Edition' of the *Later Years*, under the title *The Life of Thomas Hardy*, Vol. II, 1892–1928, was published in 1933. This was in reality a second issue, sheets of the first edition being bound up with an altered title-page and (in most copies) no illustrations save the frontispiece.

The *Later Years* was published in America by The Macmillan Company in April 1930.

Though Mrs. Hardy often spoke of revising and compressing the whole work, she never did so.

---

[1] There are two typescripts of the *Later Years*, under the title 'The Life and Work of Thomas Hardy, Vol. II', now among the Max Gate papers. Hardy has marked one 'Mrs. Hardy. (Personal Copy.)' and '2nd. Copy' and the other (not now complete) '3rd.-(Rough) Copy.' The former, very like the typescript of the *Early Life* in character, ends with Chap. 15, the remaining four chapters being represented by a brief synopsis carrying the biography as far as September 1926. A number of passages relating to Hardy's critics and his social engagements were deleted at the time of publication. The 'rough copy' would seem to have been Hardy's own, and its additions and corrections are almost wholly in his calligraphic hand.

1934: AN INDISCRETION IN THE LIFE OF AN HEIRESS

AN INDISCRETION / IN THE / LIFE OF AN HEIRESS / BY / THOMAS HARDY / LONDON / PRIVATELY PRINTED / 1934

Collation. [A]–F⁸; pp. [vi]+90; [i] half-title; [ii] blank; [iii] title-page; [iv] printers' imprint; [v] note [numbered and initialed by Mrs. Hardy]; [vi] blank; [1]–89 text; [90] colophon: 100 copies of this book / have been printed at the / Curwen Press, Plaistow, / for private distribution /.

Binding. Limp vellum; spine gold-lettered vertically: An Indiscretion in the Life of an Heiress by Thomas Hardy /.

Plain end-papers, blank leaf inserted at beginning and end; all edges gilt; leaves measure $5\frac{1}{2}'' \times 8\frac{5}{8}''$.

Issued in black board case.

Notes. *An Indiscretion in the Life of an Heiress* was first printed in the *New Quarterly Magazine,* July 1878, pp. [315]–378. It was published simultaneously in America in *Harper's Weekly* (New York) in 5 instalments, 29 June–27 July 1878, and reprinted (as from the *New Quarterly Magazine*) in *Littell's Living Age* (Boston), 5 and 12 October 1878. The *Harper's* text has independent value and is of particular interest. It was presumably set from unrevised sheets of the *New Quarterly* and shows many variants, the most notable of which is an entirely different account in Chap. I of the first meeting of Egbert and Geraldine, brief and quite wanting the melodrama of the threshing-machine episode. Hardy never collected this story (much the most considerable piece of his writing he so ignored);[1] it is not mentioned in his biography nor is any MS. of it known to have survived. The reason for this willingness to let it be forgotten must be sought in its relation to *The Poor Man and the Lady* (see below) and the unmistakably autobiographical cast of both works.

Mrs. Hardy's edition, reprinted from the *New Quarterly Magazine* and seen through the press by Desmond Flower, was ready for distribution 5 October 1934.[2] A cache of 35 of the 100 copies remained at

[1] Henry Holt wrote to Hardy, 8 June 1878, that he had sold the story to Harper's for the *Weekly* for £20 but added, 'I shall probably myself publish it later in a little volume'.

[2] See Desmond Flower, 'Hardy's "First Novel"', *The Times,* 4 March 1935, p. 15. An application by Paul Lemperly in 1929 to reprint the story had been denied (see Sydney

Max Gate at her death. The story has also been reprinted in America, ed. Carl J. Weber, Baltimore, 1935.

The Poor Man and the Lady. What had led Mrs. Hardy to reprint *An Indiscretion* she suggested in a brief note to her edition. '*An Indiscretion in the Life of an Heiress* is an adaptation by the author of his first novel, *The Poor Man and the Lady,* which was never published. The manuscript of the latter was destroyed by Thomas Hardy some years before his death, and no copy remains.'[1] The story has, therefore, an interest which far outweighs its intrinsic merits.

All that we know about *The Poor Man and the Lady* is derived from three sources: Hardy's own account of the novel as given in the *Early Life* (pp. 75–83);[2] John Morley's report as reader and Alexander Macmillan's detailed criticism of the MS. in a letter to the author, 10 August 1868 (see Charles Morgan, *The House of Macmillan,* London, 1943, pp. 87–91); and Edmund Gosse's recollections (remarkably circumstantial and to be accepted with caution) of a conversation with Hardy about the novel in 1921 ('Thomas Hardy's Lost Novel', *The Sunday Times,* 22 January 1928, p. 8).

The novel was begun at Bockhampton in the late summer of 1867 and largely finished that year, the fair copy occupying Hardy from 16 January to 9 June 1868. The MS. was first submitted to Alexander Macmillan, 25 July 1868, when it was read by John Morley and the publisher himself. In the light of their comments (forwarded by Macmillan 10 August) some pages were rewritten, but when it was apparent Macmillan would not publish the book it was submitted to Frederic Chapman, 8 December 1868. Chapman and Hall rejected the MS. 8 February 1869, 'the principal [reason] being that you have not got an interesting story to work upon and thus some of your episodic scenes are fatally injured', but there seems to have been some possibility of their publishing it with a guarantee from Hardy of £20. It was not put in hand, however, and finally he was asked to meet 'Mr. Chapman and the gentleman who read your manuscript.' There followed, in

Cockerell, 'Early Hardy Stories', *The Times Literary Supplement,* 14 March 1935, p. 160).

[1] Such a relation between the two works had long been suspected. See Sir George Douglas, 'Thomas Hardy, Some Recollections and Reflections', *The Hibbert Journal,* April 1928, p. 392.

[2] Here supplemented by one or two unpublished letters among the Max Gate papers.

March 1869, the remarkable interview with Meredith which ended in Hardy's withdrawal of his MS. It was in the hands of one further publisher, Tinsley,[1] through the summer of 1869, but the terms offered were rather beyond Hardy and the novel was finally laid aside in favour of *Desperate Remedies*.

With great thrift Hardy apparently used the MS. of *The Poor Man and the Lady* as quarry for a number of subsequent works. The core of the novel was adapted for *An Indiscretion in the Life of an Heiress*. Beyond that there is reason to believe that descriptions of Kingston Maurward House were used in *Desperate Remedies*; scenes of rural life (the tranter scenes and possibly much more) went into *Under the Greenwood Tree*; and satiric details of London society into *A Pair of Blue Eyes* and possibly *The Hand of Ethelberta*.[2] As late as 1925 and *Human Shows* Hardy published a poem, 'A Poor Man and a Lady', 'intended to preserve an episode in the story of "The Poor Man and the Lady"'. 'It was', he said of the novel long after, 'the most original thing (for its date) that I ever wrote.'

No portion of the MS. of *The Poor Man and the Lady* has survived. A fragment, perhaps 80 leaves, existed in 1916, and Sydney Cockerell undertook to have it handsomely bound for Hardy, to ensure its preservation. It was given to Mrs. Hardy on the third anniversary of her marriage but subsequently destroyed by Hardy himself.[3]

[1] See Appendix, p. 329.
[2] For a detailed study of *The Poor Man and the Lady* and some of these textual relations, see W. R. Rutland, *Thomas Hardy: A Study of his Writings and their Background* (Oxford, 1938), pp. 111–33.
[3] See Rutland, op. cit., p. 113; *Friends of a Lifetime*, p. 295.

PART II

COLLECTED EDITIONS

1895–6: THE WESSEX NOVELS (16 Vols.)

FIRST UNIFORM AND COMPLETE EDITION

London: Osgood, McIlvaine & Co.

Vol. I. *Tess of the D'Urbervilles*: 1895
Frontispiece, etched portrait of Hardy with facsimile signature.
Illustration, 'Wellbridge Manor House'.
Preface, January 1895.
Note: Plates of the first one-volume edition were used (see above,
p. 77).

II. *Far from the Madding Crowd*: 1895
Frontispiece, 'Weatherbury'.
Preface, February 1895.

III. *The Mayor of Casterbridge*: 1895
Frontispiece, 'The High Street, Casterbridge'.
Preface, February 1895.
Note: Excised material was restored to Chap. 44 (see above,
pp. 53–54).

IV. *A Pair of Blue Eyes*: 1895
Frontispiece, 'Castle Boterel'.
Preface, March 1895.

V. *Two on a Tower*: 1895
Frontispiece, 'Welland House and Park' (see *Later Years*, pp.
35–36).
Preface, July 1895.

VI. *The Return of the Native*: 1895
Frontispiece, 'Egdon Heath'.
Preface, July 1895.

VII. *The Woodlanders*: 1896 [1895]
Frontispiece, 'The Country of "The Woodlanders"'.
Preface, September 1895.

VIII. *Jude the Obscure*: 1896 [1895]
Frontispiece, 'Christminster'.
Preface, August 1895.
Note: This is the first edition of the novel (see above, pp. 86 ff.).

IX. *The Trumpet-Major*: 1896 [1895]
    Frontispiece, 'Budmouth Harbour'.
    Preface, October 1895.

X. *The Hand of Ethelberta*: 1896
    Frontispiece, 'Corvsgate Castle'.
    Preface, December 1895.
    Note: The novel was reduced from 50 to 48 chapters (see above, p. 23).

XI. *A Laodicean*: 1896
    Frontispiece, 'Stancy Castle'.
    Preface, January 1896.

XII. *Desperate Remedies*: 1896
    Frontispiece, 'Knapwater House'.
    Preface, February 1896.

XIII. *Wessex Tales*: 1896
    Frontispiece, 'Higher Crowstairs'.
    Preface, April 1896.
    Note: 'An Imaginative Woman' is here first collected (see above, p. 60).

XIV. *Life's Little Ironies*: 1896
    Frontispiece, 'A View in "Melchester"'.
    Preface, June 1896.
    Note: Plates of the original edition were used. The Preface was subsequently discarded in the definitive Wessex Edition (see above, p. 85).

XV. *A Group of Noble Dames*: 1896
    Frontispiece, 'King's-Hintock Court'.
    Preface, June 1896.
    Note: Plates of the original edition were used.

XVI. *Under the Greenwood Tree*: 1896
    Frontispiece, 'Mellstock Church'.
    Preface, August 1896.

Binding, &c. The volumes are bound in dark green bold-ribbed cloth, the front blocked in gold with TH monogram medallion. For a detailed description of the format, see above, p. 86. Each volume contains an etched frontispiece by H. Macbeth-Raeburn, a scene from the novel drawn on the spot, and a map of 'The Wessex of The Novels' drawn by Hardy himself.

The Well-Beloved (Osgood, McIlvaine & Co., 1897), *A Changed Man* (Macmillan & Co., 1913), *Wessex Poems* (Harper & Brothers, 1898), and *Poems of the Past and the Present* (Harper & Brothers, 1902), qq.v., were all first issued in a matching format, the first two as Vols. XVII and XVIII of the Wessex Novels. A. P. Webb's *Bibliography of the Works of Thomas Hardy* (Frank Hollings, 1916) was also published in this format.

Notes on Revision and Publication. Osgood, McIlvaine & Co. had become Hardy's publishers with the appearance of *A Group of Noble Dames* in 1891. On the expiration of Sampson Low's rights in the earlier novels in June 1894 these passed into Osgood, McIlvaine's hands, and they immediately undertook the publication of the first uniform and complete edition of Hardy's works. Though Sampson Low had bought up (largely from Smith, Elder) the plates and the rights of 8 novels and issued them in frequent popular impressions between 1881 and 1893, 4 books were controlled elsewhere (*Desperate Remedies* by Heinemann, *Under the Greenwood Tree* by Chatto & Windus, and *The Woodlanders* and *Wessex Tales* by Macmillan) and there had been no attempt at such an edition before.

Osgood, McIlvaine's edition is an important one. The text of every novel was thoroughly and carefully revised, the topography (names and distances) corrected where necessary, chapters frequently retitled, and much rewriting done. In addition Hardy prepared a special preface for each volume (prefaces which have a peculiar interest when read consecutively as the work of 1895–6) and assumed the drudgery of proof-reading. The first volume of the edition was published at 6s., 4 April 1895, and subsequent volumes followed at monthly intervals, the last appearing in September 1896.

Sheets of the Osgood, McIlvaine edition of the Wessex Novels with an altered title-page were published in America by Harper & Brothers, except for the copyright volumes they already had in type. The plates were used for a number of impressions by Osgood, McIlvaine, their successors Harper & Brothers (London), and after 1902 by Macmillan & Co. for their Uniform Edition. When the plates passed into Macmillan's hands, however, Hardy stipulated that changes be made before they were used again. According to his own note on the transaction, 'The corrections . . . were to rewrite the Preface to F. M. Crowd and change some words in Chaps. 2 and 51—change some words in Tess Chap. 46—and change some words in one chap. of Jude [errors of repetition].'

1912–31: WESSEX EDITION (24 Vols.)
London: Macmillan & Co., Ltd.

THE WESSEX NOVELS

I. NOVELS OF CHARACTER AND ENVIRONMENT

Vol. I. *Tess of the d'Urbervilles*: 1912
  Frontispiece, 'The Froom Meadow'.
  General Preface to the Novels and Poems, October 1911 (incorporating all but the first paragraph of the *Tess* Preface of January 1895).
  Preface, March 1912.
  Note: A few pages in Chap. 10 are here included for the first time (see above, p. 77).

 II. *Far from the Madding Crowd*: 1912
  Frontispiece, 'Village of Weatherbury'.
  Preface, 1895–1902 (the Preface to Osgood, McIlvaine's edition as revised for Macmillan's impression of 1902, see above, pp. 281–2).

 III. *Jude the Obscure*: 1912
  Frontispiece, 'Christminster'.
  Preface, April 1912 (see above, p. 91).

 IV. *The Return of the Native*: 1912
  Frontispiece, 'Egdon Heath'.
  Preface, April 1912.
  Note: An important note on the original conception of the story appears on p. 473.

 V. *The Mayor of Casterbridge*: 1912
  Frontispiece, 'Looking up the High Street of Casterbridge'.

Preface, February 1895–May 1912 (the Preface to Osgood, McIlvaine's edition, almost unchanged).

VI. *The Woodlanders*: 1912
Frontispiece, 'The Country of the Woodlanders'.
Preface, April 1912.

VII. *Under the Greenwood Tree*: 1912
Frontispiece, 'Mellstock Church'.
Preface, April 1912.

VIII. *Life's Little Ironies*: 1912
Frontispiece, 'The White Hart at Casterbridge'.
Preface, May 1912 (replacing the Preface of June 1896 which was discarded).
Note: There are several alterations in contents (see above, pp. 85–86).

IX. *Wessex Tales*: 1912
Frontispiece, 'The Hangman's Cottage at Casterbridge'.
Preface, April 1896–May 1912 (the Preface to Osgood, McIlvaine's edition revised and extended).
Note: There are several alterations in contents (see above, p. 60). A note on the ending of 'The Distracted Preacher' appears on pp. 286–7. For a further addition to the Preface, see below, p. 287.

II. ROMANCES AND FANTASIES

X. *A Pair of Blue Eyes*: 1912
Frontispiece, 'Harbour of Castle Boterel'.
Preface, June 1912.
Note: For the final revision of this novel, see below, p. 287.

XI. *The Trumpet-Major*: 1912
Frontispiece, 'Budmouth Harbour'.
Preface, October 1895 (the Preface to Osgood, McIlvaine's edition).

XII. *Two on a Tower*: 1912
Frontispiece, 'Welland House and Tower'.
Preface, July 1895 (the Preface to Osgood, McIlvaine's edition, slightly modified).

XIII. *The Well-Beloved*: 1912
>Frontispiece, 'The Isle of Slingers'.
>Preface, August 1912 (the original Preface of January 1897, a little enlarged).

XIV. *A Group of Noble Dames*: 1912
>Frontispiece, 'Wintoncester Cathedral (in "Lady Mottisfont")'.
>Preface, June 1896 (the Preface to Osgood, McIlvaine's edition).

III. NOVELS OF INGENUITY

XV. *Desperate Remedies*: 1912
>Frontispiece, 'Knapwater House'.
>Preface, August 1912.

XVI. *The Hand of Ethelberta*: 1912
>Frontispiece, 'Corvesgate [*sic*] Castle'.
>Preface, August 1912.

XVII. *A Laodicean*: 1912
>Frontispiece, 'Stancy Castle'.
>Preface, October 1912.

IV. MIXED NOVELS

XVIII. *A Changed Man*: 1914
>Frontispiece, 'The Castle of Mai-Dun' (frontispiece to the original edition).
>Preface, August 1913 (original preface).
>Note: This volume was actually published after Verse, Vols. I–III (numbered in error XVIII–XX).

VERSE

Vol. I. *Wessex Poems, Poems of the Past and the Present*: 1912
>Frontispiece, portrait of Hardy with facsimile signature.
>Note: No new prefaces were written for the volumes of verse.

II. *The Dynasts*, Parts First and Second: 1913
>Frontispiece, 'The English Channel from Ridgeway Hill'.

III. *The Dynasts*, Part Third, *Time's Laughingstocks*: 1913
>Frontispiece, 'Wynyard's Gap (in "A Trampwoman's Tragedy")'.

IV. *Satires of Circumstance, Moments of Vision*: 1919

> Frontispiece, 'When I set out for Lyonnesse . . . the rime was on the spray' (Hardy's birthplace at Higher Bockhampton).

V. *Late Lyrics and Earlier, The Famous Tragedy of the Queen of Cornwall*: 1926

> Frontispiece, 'Imaginary View of Tintagel Castle at the Time of the Tragedy' (frontispiece to the original edition).
>
> Note: C2 (and C7, pp. 19–20 and 29–30) was cancelled to alter the reading of 'Welcome Home', stanza 3, line 2, from 'I once heard' to 'Said they'. In some copies the leaves are present in both states.

VI. *Human Shows, Winter Words*: 1931

> Frontispiece, facsimile of the MS. of 'He Resolves to Say No More'.

Binding, &c. The volumes are bound in maroon cloth gilt, and each contains a photogravure frontispiece and a 'Map of the Wessex of the Novels and Poems' (made from Hardy's own drawing, now in the Dorset County Museum).[1] Vols. I–XX only are numbered on the spine. Hermann Lea's *Thomas Hardy's Wessex* (Macmillan, 1913) was issued in a matching format.

Notes on Revision and Publication. Macmillan & Co. became the publishers of Hardy's works on the expiration of his agreements with Osgood, McIlvaine & Co. and Harper & Brothers in 1902. As he wrote to Frederick Macmillan, 'The unexpected vicissitudes of the firm [the taking over in 1897 of Osgood, McIlvaine & Co. by Harper & Brothers, whose London representatives they had been], owing to which it befalls that my publisher here has become only a subordinate member of a New York house, make it necessary—from obvious considerations of convenience—that I transfer the English edition of the books to a publisher whose headquarters are London.'[2] Macmillan's had held Hardy's colonial rights since 1894 and were quick to accept his new offer. At first they printed the Wessex Novels from Osgood, McIlvaine's plates (with the alterations Hardy had stipulated, see above,

---

[1] Reproduced in facsimile in the *Countryman* (Idbury), July 1936, pp. [488–9].

[2] For Hardy's correspondence with Frederick Macmillan at this time, see Charles Morgan, *The House of Macmillan* (London, 1943), pp. 154–60.

pp. 281–2), but in 1912 they undertook a new and definitive edition, called (at Frederick Macmillan's suggestion) the 'Wessex Edition'.

For this edition Hardy revised his novels throughout for the last time, correcting a few errors and adding an occasional footnote or brief postscript to the earlier prefaces. The task was a fairly exacting one (see *Later Years*, pp. 151–2). The revisions and notes, with a few exceptions, are by no means so important, however, as those of 1895–6. In a 'General Preface to the Novels and Poems', dated October 1911 and printed in Vol. I, he explained the classification of his novels here adopted for the first time (revealing his estimate of their relative merits) and offered a brief *apologia* for his work. This is an essay of primary importance. The revise of these pages (in the Bliss collection) shows it was much worked over.

The first 2 volumes of the Wessex Edition were published at 7*s*. 6*d*., 30 April 1912, and 2 volumes were issued monthly until the original 20 had appeared. Four volumes were published at irregular intervals thereafter (the last, posthumously) to complete the series. Later impressions incorporate the slight revisions made for the Mellstock Edition in 1919 and some 4 pages of trifling corrections submitted in April 1920. The Wessex Edition is in every sense the definitive edition of Hardy's work and the last authority in questions of text.

American Edition. Harper & Brothers issued the first 21 volumes of the Wessex Edition in America as the 'Autograph Edition' in 1915. This edition, limited to 153 sets with Hardy's signature on an inserted leaf, was in 20 volumes (*The Well-Beloved* and *A Group of Noble Dames* being combined in a single volume) and was partly printed from the English plates and partly reset in America (in the case of volumes already copyright there). The 'Map of the Wessex of the Novels and Poems' appears in Vol. I only, and the illustrations (4 to a volume) are derived from Lea's *Thomas Hardy's Wessex*. Hardy inscribed his own set to his wife, June 1915.

The edition was reissued in 1920 as the 'Anniversary Edition' (recalling Hardy's eightieth year), limited to 1,250 sets. A twenty-first volume was included, *Satires of Circumstance* and *Moments of Vision*, a makeshift printed from plates of the original editions.

1919: COLLECTED POEMS
London: Macmillan & Co., Ltd.

Pp. xx+524; bound in green cloth, with a photogravure portrait of Hardy as frontispiece. The whole format matches the one-volume edition of *The Dynasts* (1910), the 2 volumes making up 'The Poetical Works of Thomas Hardy'. The contents comprise the 5 collections of verse Hardy had published up to this time, *Wessex Poems* through *Moments of Vision*. The book was issued 10 October 1919 at 8s. 6d. in an edition of 3,000 copies. On 22 November 1919 Hardy sent Macmillan a list of 14 errata, and these were promptly printed on a slip and inserted in copies still unsold. In sending the errata slip to friends Hardy wrote in still another erratum: 'Page 5 under the title "The Temporary the All" insert "(Sapphics)"'.

In subsequent editions the later collections of verse were added, *Late Lyrics and Earlier* in 1923, *Human Shows* in 1928, and *Winter Words* in 1930.

1919–20: MELLSTOCK EDITION (37 Vols.)
London: Macmillan & Co., Ltd.

Vols. I, II. *Tess of the d'Urbervilles*: 1919
III, IV. *Far from the Madding Crowd*: 1919
V, VI. *Jude the Obscure*: 1920
VII, VIII. *The Return of the Native*: 1920
IX, X. *The Mayor of Casterbridge*: 1920
XI, XII. *The Woodlanders*: 1920
XIII. *Under the Greenwood Tree*: 1920
XIV. *Life's Little Ironies*: 1920
XV. *Wessex Tales*: 1920
Note: There is an addition to the Preface, dated June 1919 (see above, p. 60).
XVI, XVII. *A Pair of Blue Eyes*: 1920
Note: There are a few textual changes (see above, pp.12–13).
XVIII, XIX. *The Trumpet-Major*: 1920
XX. *Two on a Tower*: 1920
XXI. *The Well-Beloved*: 1920
XXII. *A Group of Noble Dames*: 1920
XXIII, XXIV. *Desperate Remedies*: 1920
XXV, XXVI. *The Hand of Ethelberta*: 1920

XXVII, XXVIII. *A Laodicean*: 1920
XXIX, XXX. *A Changed Man*: 1920
XXXI–XXXIII. *The Dynasts*: 1920
XXXIV. *Wessex Poems, Poems of the Past and the Present*: 1920
XXXV. *Time's Laughingstocks*: 1920
XXXVI. *Satires of Circumstance*: 1920
XXXVII. *Moments of Vision*: 1920

Binding, &c. The volumes are bound in blue cloth, the front blocked in gold with a solid TH monogram medallion of acorns and oak leaves. The paper bears Hardy's initials as watermark. Vol. I is signed by Hardy on a preliminary leaf and has an etched portrait by William Strang as frontispiece. Vol. II has the 'Map of the Wessex of the Novels and Poems'. There are no further illustrations or maps in the edition. Large-paper copies of A. P. Webb's *Bibliography of the Works of Thomas Hardy* (Frank Hollings, 1916) were bound in a matching format.

Notes on Revision and Publication. This is an *édition de luxe*, limited to 500 copies and published in a format Macmillan had already used for similar editions of Tennyson, Arnold, Kipling, &c. It was projected as early as July 1914, when Hardy suggested 'The Casterbridge Edition' or 'The Mellstock Edition' as a possible title, but production was interrupted by the First World War. The edition was printed from the plates of the Wessex Edition and, save for *A Pair of Blue Eyes*, is of little textual importance. Hardy sent the publishers 5 pages of corrections and additions, 18 June 1919, but saw no proofs except those of *A Pair of Blue Eyes* and the volumes of verse. Publication began with the first 2 volumes in December 1919, the remainder following at intervals the next year.

1928: THE SHORT STORIES OF THOMAS HARDY
London: Macmillan & Co., Ltd.

Pp. viii+1,080; bound in maroon cloth, with a map of 'Thomas Hardy's Wessex' (from the Wessex Edition) as end-papers. This is simply a reprinting in one volume of Hardy's 4 collections of short stories. It was published posthumously 23 March 1928 at 7*s.* 6*d.*

PART III

UNCOLLECTED CONTRIBUTIONS TO BOOKS, PERIODICALS, AND NEWSPAPERS

(Personal letters, not intended for
publication, have been excluded.)

? Letter: 'A Pump Complaining'

The Southern Times (Weymouth edition of the following), 1 March 1856, p. 140.

The Dorset County Chronicle (Dorchester), 6 March 1856, p. 614.

'During the years of architectural pupillage [1856–62] Hardy . . . began writing verses, and also a few prose articles, which do not appear to have been printed anywhere. The first effusion of his to see the light of print [he was sixteen he recalls elsewhere] was an anonymous skit in a Dorchester paper on the disappearance of the Alms-House clock, which then as now stood on a bracket in South Street, the paragraph being in the form of a plaintive letter from the ghost of the clock. (It had been neglected, after having been taken down to be cleaned.) As the author was supposed to be an alderman of influence the clock was immediately replaced. He would never have been known to be Hardy but for the conspiracy of a post-office clerk, who watched the handwriting of letters posted till he had spotted the culprit. After this followed the descriptive verses "Domicilium", and accounts of church-restorations carried out by Hicks, which Hardy prepared for the grateful reporter of the *Dorset Chronicle*.' (*Early Life*, pp. 42–43.) Though these words are Hardy's own, painstaking and repeated search of all Dorchester papers for this period has failed to reveal this 'anonymous skit'. It has revealed, however, one not too dissimilar, 'a plaintive letter' not from the neglected Dorchester Alms-House clock but the neglected Wareham town pump. The Shakespeare tags and the reference to 'Purbeck Portland' are characteristic, though Hardy's connexion at this time with Wareham (fifteen miles from Dorchester) is unknown. Mrs. Hardy, to whom I showed this letter, came to believe it was Hardy's and that his memory had played him false after sixty years. In the last conversation I had with her before her death, she told me she was convinced of its authenticity. Nevertheless for want of any proof its acceptance must be tentative. Since it is not readily accessible, the letter may be reproduced here (as reprinted in the *Dorset County Chronicle* the letter was made into a paragraph headed 'A Pump Complaining' and the two errors were corrected):

To the Editor of the "Southern Times."

Sir,—Will you allow a much-abused public servant a corner in your pages, in order that, should his just remonstrance catch the eye of the proper functionary, or any other good Samaritan who may pour oil over his aching limbs, he may cease to wail his complaints upon ungrateful ears. For the past twelve months I have suffered the most dreadful—rheumatic, I suppose it is—twitchings and pains, and, although unable to help myself, or move a limb, yet am I daily set in motion, and compelled to supply the wants of the others, though every and the slightest move puts me in an agony of pain, and I screech, and am heard by all around; the pains I speak of thrilling through and through me, and as the arterial process, which, (like the bipeds that daily and nightly, too, torment me), ramify my whole system, become gorged by the accelerated motion, I bleed plentifully at the nose, as long as my friends (save the mark!), are pleased with the wail of my aching limbs.

My constitution, Sir, was originally *very good*, my parentage equally un-questionable (for I trace my origin to one of the first houses in the metropolis of this great kingdom), though doomed to waste my *stream* of life in the almost unknown locality in which I am unhappily placed, and although all are beholden to me, yet am I treated with carelessness and neglect. My misery commenced the moment my parents suffered me to leave their skilled and polished circle, and the house I was designed to occupy, though con-structed of the best "Purbeck Portland" was, alas, too confined and small for my stalwart limbs; and, would you believe it, Mr. Editor, rather than enlarge my future abode, a wretch, who ought to have known better, actually amputated my arm at the wrist, and, to suit his own construction, said I was too *cranky*, and still not content with thus mutilating my fair proportions, he further hamstrung me, and cut and docked my tail, thus destroying the proper beverage [leverage] so necessary to carry on the daily *motion* of my *stationary* existence, and though thus shorn of my pristine fair proportion, and "crabbed [cabined], cribbed, confined" in a nutshell, I became abused by some for not shedding more tears the harder they thumped me.

I wonder, Mr. Editor, the authorities do not look to my wants, for though so many are beholden to me, yet none will help: perhaps a word in season from you, in addition to my own, may do much for me. I hate self-praise, yet the man to whom I was consigned from my London parentage delights to speak of me as the best, most useful, most skilfully contrived, and the hardest worked pump in the whole town; and would you, or any other consistent person believe me, I have worked incessantly for the past five years, and not cost my tormentors *one penny!* and all I ask for my long ser-vitude, is a little oil to prevent my aching limbs from being prematurely consigned to the "tomb of all the capulets."

I know the danger of rushing heedlessly into print—yet, Mr. Editor, do gratify my ambition this time, and should you ever pass me, I will shed tears of joy, pure as crystal, and be eternally grateful.

Your misused and much abused Servant,

THE WAREHAM TOWN PUMP.

Of the other pieces mentioned in this description of Hardy's beginnings as a writer, 'Domicilium' does not appear to have been printed before 1916 (see above, pp. 176 f.) and the 'accounts of church-restorations' are not identifiable. It may be noted, however, that the following such accounts (specifically mentioning Hicks as architect) appeared in the *Dorset County Chronicle* during Hardy's years in Hicks's office: St. Peter's, Dorchester (17 July 1856, pp. 985–6; 4 June 1857, p. 865), Rampisham (10 March 1859, p. 625), Powerstock (3 November 1859, pp. 267–8), St. Mary's, Bridport (19 July 1860, p. 1011), Combe Keynes (29 August 1861, p. 84), and new churches at Athelhampton (2 January 1862, p. 449) and Bettiscombe (3 April 1862, pp. 705–6).

1862

[Essay: 'On the Application of Coloured Bricks and Terra Cotta to Modern Architecture'
Unpublished.

This essay, on a subject chosen from four set by the Council of the Royal Institute of British Architects for their annual competition, was written in 1862 and submitted under the motto, 'Tentavi quid in eo genere possem.' It was awarded the Silver Medal of the Institute 16 March 1863, and this was presented to Hardy at the Ordinary General Meeting of the Institute 18 May, with 'a few appropriate remarks' from the President, T. L. Donaldson. For the text of the judge's criticism, see A. P. Webb, *A Bibliography of the Works of Thomas Hardy* (London, 1916), p. 41. The essay was never printed, and no MS. is known to survive.]

1865

Sketch: 'How I Built Myself a House'
Chambers's Journal, 18 March 1865, pp. [161]–164.

Unsigned. This sketch, for which the publishers paid £3. 15s., was written to amuse the pupils of Arthur Blomfield, the architect, in whose office at 8 Adelphi Terrace Hardy was working at the time. The architect of the 'house' was Mr. Penny, a name used afterwards in *Under the Greenwood Tree*. The sketch has been frequently reprinted; see *Chambers's Journal*, January 1925, pp. 2–5, where it is preceded by editorial comment, ' 'Tis Sixty Years Since', and a new poem by Hardy, 'A Bird-Scene at a Rural Dwelling'; *Life and Art* (New York, 1925), pp. 9–19; &c.

1874

Story: 'Destiny and a Blue Cloak'
The New York Times, Sunday, 4 October 1874, pp. 2–3.

This story was sent to the editor of the *New York Times* 12 September 1874 from 4 Celbridge Place, Westbourne Park, 'at the request of Mr. J. H. Fyfe, Saville Club, on terms probably known to yourself.' Hardy left it uncollected because he had used material from it in writing *The Hand of Ethelberta* the following year. Farmer Lovill, the 'aged youth' of sixty-five, might be called a first crude sketch for Lord Mountclere, and the cruel trick by which Agatha Pollin is frustrated in her attempt to escape marrying Lovill is closely duplicated in Ethelberta's unsuccessful attempt to leave Mountclere in Chap. 47 of the novel. The very slight portrait of the hero of the story, Oswald Winwood, has some interest since it was clearly suggested by Hardy's friend T. W. H. Tolbort (see below, p. 297). Like Tolbort, Winwood studies for the Indian Examination; his name leads all the rest when the results are published in *The Times*, though he has been educated at 'some obscure little academy'; he proceeds to a successful career in the Indian Civil Service and occupies himself with a translation from 'Hindostani'. When a reprinting of the story was proposed to Hardy a few months before his death, he called it 'an impromptu of a trivial kind and of no literary value'.

1877

Story: 'The Thieves Who Couldn't Help Sneezing'
Father Christmas, London, 1877, pp. 1–3.

This Christmas annual for children, edited by Miss N. D'Anvers, was published early in December 1877 at the Office of the *Illustrated London News*. There can be no question of Hardy's authorship, unlikely as it seems, since the title appears as an addition in his own hand, with the comment 'child's story', on a list of his works drawn up by Mrs. Hardy *c.* 1880. There is a copy of this extremely scarce annual in the Bodleian Library. Hardy's story has been reprinted, ed. Carl J. Weber, Waterville, Maine, 1942.

1878

? Sketch: 'Thomas Hardy'
    The Literary World (Boston), 1 August 1878, p. 46.

    This is an anonymous sketch of particular interest, one of a series
headed 'World Biographies'. The editor wrote to Hardy 18 April 1878,
asking for material for a biographical sketch, indicating the points to be
covered, and a clipping of the sketch as published appears in Hardy's
'Personal' scrap-book. It is ascribed to Hardy himself on internal
evidence of style and intimate detail.

Letter: 'Dialect in Novels'
    The Athenaeum, 30 November 1878, p. 688.

    Retort to a review of *The Return of the Native* (23 November, p. 654).
Reprinted in Lionel Johnson, *The Art of Thomas Hardy* (London,
1894), p. xvii; and in *Life and Art* (New York, 1925), p. 113.

1879

Review: *Poems of Rural Life in the Dorset Dialect* by William Barnes
    The New Quarterly Magazine, October 1879, pp. 469–73.

    Unsigned. This is the only review Hardy ever wrote. It was solicited
by C. Kegan Paul, publisher of the volume and of the *New Quarterly*.
Though it was never collected, several paragraphs (largely critical in
nature) reappear in Hardy's obituary notice of Barnes seven years later
(see below, p. 297) and one in *Tess* (pp. 9–10).

1881

Letter: 'Papers of the Manchester Literary Club'
    The Spectator, 15 October 1881, p. 1308.

    Retort to a review of an essay, 'George Eliot's Use of Dialect' (in
Papers of the Manchester Literary Club), in the *Spectator*, 8 October,
pp. 1277–8, which contained a passing (unfavourable) reference to
Hardy's use of dialect. Dated 'The Avenue, Wimborne, Dorset, October 11th'. Reprinted in *Life and Art* (New York, 1925), pp. 114–15.

1882

Letter: *The Squire* at the St. James's Theatre
    The Daily News, 2 January 1882, p. 2.

    A protest at the similarity of Pinero's play to *Far from the Madding*

Crowd, a dramatization of which had been in the hands of the managers of the St. James's Theatre. Dated 'Wimborne, Dorset, Saturday [December 31].' The letter is accompanied by others from J. W. Comyns Carr, Hardy's collaborator in the dramatization, and Pinero and followed the next day by a retort from Hare and Kendal, the managers in question.

Letter: ' "The Squire" at the St. James's Theatre'
  The Times, 2 January 1882, p. 6.

A further protest at the similarity of Pinero's play to *Far from the Madding Crowd*, dated 1 January and fuller than the letter to the *Daily News*. Letters from Comyns Carr and Hare and Kendal appeared here also, and in both papers a considerable controversy followed. See above, pp. 28 ff.

[Poem: 'Two Roses'
  London Society, August 1882, p. 151.

These 'wretched ungrammatical verses', three 6-line stanzas, though signed with his name are not by Hardy. In response to an inquiry, Mrs. Hardy wrote to me, 'That poem was never written by my husband—it was written by a worthless young man, a pupil of Sir Arthur Blomfield's who was at 8 Adelphi Terrace at the same time as T.H. He used to borrow money from my husband, and he wrote the poem and obtained a cheque for it which he cashed—forging T.H.'s name as an endorsement and keeping the money.' The poem was not unnoticed and caused Hardy some embarrassment. 'I have been ridiculed in the magazine notices,' he wrote, 'as "stronger in prose than in verse".' A disclaimer was published in *Figaro* (London), 19 August 1882. See Frederick B. Adams, Jr., 'Another Man's Roses', *The New Colophon* (New York), June 1949, pp. 107–12.]

Letter: 'English Authors and American Publishers'
  The Athenaeum, 23 December 1882, pp. 848–9.

One of several communications in defence of Harper & Brothers' treatment of English authors. Dated 'Savile Club, Dec. 19, 1882'.

1883

Letter: 'Two on a Tower'
  The St. James's Gazette, 19 January 1883, p. 14.

Retort to a review of *Two on a Tower* (16 January), denying that an insult to the Church was intended in making a Bishop a victim in the story. Dated 'Savile Club, Jan. 18'. The letter is indirectly referred to in Hardy's 1895 Preface to the novel.

Obituary: 'The Late Mr. T. W. H. Tolbort, B.C.S.'
The Dorset County Chronicle (Dorchester), 16 August 1883, p. 10.

A tribute to 'a friend of Hardy's from youth', dated 'Dorchester, August 14th, 1883.' See *Early Life*, pp. 42–43, 211. There was an off-print among the Max Gate papers. Portions of the notice are reproduced in W. R. Rutland, *Thomas Hardy* (London and Glasgow, 1938), pp. 131–3. It does not appear that Hardy was able to publish the MS. of Tolbort's work on the Portuguese in India as Tolbort had commissioned him to do just before his death.

1886

Obituary: 'The Rev. William Barnes, B.D.'
The Athenaeum, 16 October 1886, pp. 501–2.

Reprinted in Lionel Johnson, *The Art of Thomas Hardy* (London, 1894), pp. xlix–lviii; and in *Life and Art* (New York, 1925), pp. 48–55; see also *Early Life*, p. 211. Several paragraphs, largely critical in nature, are derived from Hardy's unsigned review of Barnes's *Poems of Rural Life in the Dorset Dialect* (see above, p. 295).

1887

Symposium: 'Fine Passages in Verse and Prose; Selected by Living Men of Letters'
The Fortnightly Review, August 1887, p. 304.

Written in reply to a request for 'the one passage in all poetry which seems the finest, and also the one passage in prose which appears of its kind the best.' Hardy chooses, with significant comments, Shelley's 'Lament', *Childe Harold*, III. 85–87 (a passage which seems to have had personal associations for him, since he set the date '14.5.66' opposite it in his copy of Byron), passages from *The French Revolution* (vol. i, bk. ii, ch. i) and *Sartor Resartus* (bk. i, ch. iii), and 2 Sam. xviii. The symposium was continued through three subsequent issues and included among its contributors Arnold, Meredith, and Swinburne.

1888

Essay: 'The Profitable Reading of Fiction'
The Forum (New York), March 1888, pp. [57]–70.

This essay, for which Hardy was paid £40, was solicited 18 August 1887. Reprinted in *Life and Art* (New York, 1925), pp. 56–74.

Letter: 'The Waterloo Ball'
The Times, 17 December 1888, p. 4.

Written from the Savile Club and undated. The letter is a contribution to an intermittent correspondence about the site of the Duchess of Richmond's ball, initiated by Sir William Fraser, 25 August. It was a subject of perennial interest to Hardy, especially during visits to Brussels in 1876 and 1896 (see *Early Life*, p. 146, *Later Years*, p. 57, and *The Dynasts*, Part Third, p. 167, note). This may possibly, by some confusion, be the lost letter referred to in the *Early Life*, p. 146, but (apart from the twelve years' discrepancy in date) it deals rather with the contradiction in the testimony of the Duchess's two daughters than the site itself.

1889

Letter: 'How Authors Write'
The Phonographic World (New York), July 1889, p. 252.

Written from the Savile Club, 6 April 1889. The letter is one of a number in answer to queries from the editor. Hardy states that he writes in longhand and has occasionally dictated but not to a shorthand writer. '. . . Several years ago [1863, see *Early Life*, p. 53] I studied shorthand with a view to taking notes . . . The two systems which most attracted me were Taylor's and Pitman's. I found that Taylor's *un*improved—*i.e.*, as published by Taylor himself in the last century—was a good old system; but as improved by more recent stenographers it was completely ruined.' Hardy's copy of *Taylor's System of Stenography* (1856), one of seven of his shorthand books now in the Dorset County Museum, he has labelled 'the best system'.

Letter: 'A British "Théatre Libre"'
The Weekly Comedy, 30 November 1889, p. 7.

Written from the Savile Club and undated. The letter, one of a number solicited by the editors, discusses faults of the contemporary stage and the possibility of simplification of costume and setting.

1890

Symposium: 'Candour in English Fiction'
The New Review, January 1890, pp. [15]–21.

Hardy's contribution was the third and last in a series begun by Walter Besant and Mrs. Lynn Linton. It was written in the midst of his difficulties over the serial publication of *Tess*. Reprinted in *Life and Art* (New York, 1925), pp. 75–84.

Symposium: 'The Art of Authorship'
The Art of Authorship, compiled and edited by George Bainton, London, [May] 1890, pp. 320–1.

Hardy's contribution, derived from a letter of 11 October 1887 and printed in a section headed 'Truthfulness to One's Self', is very slight.

1891

Story: 'The Doctor's Legend'
The Independent (New York), 26 March 1891, pp. 35–37.

This story is based on incidents in the life of Joseph Damer (Lord Milton, afterwards Earl of Dorchester, 1718–98) of Milton Abbey, his wife, Lady Caroline Sackville, and their son John Damer, who married in 1767 Anne Seymour Conway, sculptress and protégée of Horace Walpole, and took his life nine years later. It owes much to Hutchins's *History of Dorset*, iv, pp. 386–8, 395, 406. Though the scenes and even the characters, except for 'Lady Cicely', are nowhere explicitly named, the subject was unmistakable. The episode of the transplanted village, which had made Lord Milton notorious, would alone have revealed it. Remembering the displeasure of Lord Ilchester at 'The First Countess of Wessex' in 1889, Hardy may have wished to avoid offending collateral descendants of Lord Milton and 'the tragic Damers' (see *Early Life*, p. 311), the Dawson-Damers of Came House, among his nearest neighbours. To this and the general inferiority of the story we owe the fact that it was printed only in America and never collected. From its use of a frame, its dependence on Hutchins, and its prevailingly sardonic tone, the story would seem to belong to the early months of 1890, when Hardy was preparing *A Group of Noble Dames* for the *Graphic*, and it may even be a rejected portion of that work. In some details it is slightly reminiscent of the Old Surgeon's story, 'Barbara of the House of Grebe'.

The MS. of 'The Doctor's Legend' is now in the Bliss collection. It is written on 16 leaves measuring $8\frac{1}{4}"\times 10\frac{1}{8}"$ and is wholly in Mrs. Hardy's hand, save for the heading and occasional alterations made by the author. It was long the property of Bliss Carman, office editor of the *Independent* at the time. The first page is reproduced in facsimile (as in Hardy's hand) in the Kern Sale Catalogue, Part I (New York, The Anderson Galleries, 7–10 January 1929), p. 220.

Symposium: 'The Science of Fiction'
The New Review, April 1891, pp. 315–19.

Hardy's contribution was the third and last in a series begun by Paul Bourget and Walter Besant. Reprinted in *Life and Art* (New York, 1925), pp. 85–90, and in *Life and Letters*, June 1928.

Letter: 'The Merry Wives of Wessex'
The Pall Mall Gazette, 10 July 1891, p. 2.

Dated 'Mandeville-place, W., July 8'. Retort to an unfavourable review of *A Group of Noble Dames*, published under the above title 8 July and attacking in particular 'Barbara of the House of Grebe' as 'a hideous and hateful fantasy'. Hardy's letter is answered in turn by the reviewer.

1892

? Interview: 'Mr. Thomas Hardy at Max Gate, Dorchester'
Cassell's Saturday Journal, 25 June 1892, pp. 944–6.

There is nothing in style or content to suggest that this is not a genuine interview by 'the representative of the *Saturday Journal*', like others in the series, 'Representative Men at Home'. In writing to Hardy for an illustration, 3 February 1892, the editor referred to it, however, as 'your article on yourself'.

? Obituary: Thomas Hardy, Sen.
The Dorset County Chronicle (Dorchester), 28 July 1892, p. 16.

Unsigned notice, in briefest form, of the death of Hardy's father, 20 July at Bockhampton 'in the house of his birth' (cf. *Later Years*, p. 10). For the authorship of these family obituaries, see below, p. 309. For the service at Stinsford Church Hardy prepared a leaflet containing 'the grave-side hymn' and a Latin legend recording his father's connexion with the choir.

Symposium: 'Why I Don't Write Plays'
The Pall Mall Gazette, 31 August 1892, p. [1].

Hardy's contribution is the first in a series of answers to three questions on 'the present divorce of fiction from the drama', put to a number of contemporary novelists. Reprinted in the *Pall Mall Budget* (weekly edition of the above), 1 September 1892, p. 1313, with the addition of a facsimile of Hardy's MS. Also reprinted in *Life and Art* (New York, 1925), pp. 116–17 (with facsimile).

Letter: The American Edition of *Tess*
The Critic (New York), 10 September 1892, p. 134.

Dated 'Max Gate, Dorchester, Aug. 26th, 1892'. Reply to a review of *Tess* (9 July) which complained of the omission of the Explanatory Note, even in the new and revised American edition. Declaring the omission unintentional and about to be corrected, Hardy points out the difficulty of giving final touches to a text when 'simultaneous publication in America of English books' is necessary. See above, p. 76. Reprinted in *Life and Art* (New York, 1925), p. 129.

Story: 'Our Exploits at West Poley'
The Household (Boston), November 1892–April 1893 (vol. xxv, no. 11–vol. xxvi, no. 4).

The 6 monthly instalments of this story for boys ran as follows: November (pp. 343–4), Chap. I (no title); December (pp. 384–6), Chap. II, 'How We Shone in the Eyes of the Public'; January (pp. 5–6), Chap. III, 'How We Were Caught in Our Own Trap'; February (pp. 41–42), Chap. IV, 'How Older Heads than Ours Became Concerned'; March (pp. 78–79), Chap. V, 'How We Became Close Allies with the Villagers'; April (pp. 114–15), Chap. VI, 'How all Our Difficulties Came to an End'. With each instalment there was an illustration, though none appeared in January and there were two in March. This irregularity, together with the fact that the story was at first described as in eight chapters and that Chaps. IV and V are noticeably shorter than the others, would suggest that Hardy's MS. may have been abridged by the editor. This is not apparent, however, in the narrative.

The history of this long-lost story is a curious one. In a letter of 5 April 1883 Hardy agreed to supply the *Youth's Companion* (Boston) with a story for serial publication, the MS. to be delivered 'not later than the end of the present year.' 'I have', he wrote, 'roughly thought out a plot which at present seems promising. But I should prefer not to commit myself to a title till later on in the year. The general scope, or subtitle, however, might be announced as "A rural tale of adventure in the West of England." You may depend upon my using my best efforts to please your numerous readers; and that the story shall have a healthy tone, suitable to intelligent youth of both sexes.' The MS., under the title 'Our Exploits at West Poley', was dispatched 5 November 1883, and Hardy wrote of it, 'In constructing the story I have been careful to avoid making it a mere precept in narrative—a fatal defect, to my thinking, in tales for the young, or for the old. That it carries with it, nevertheless, a sufficiently apparent moral, will I think be admitted. The important features of plot and incident have received my best attention. The end of each chapter will probably form a sufficiently striking point for breaking off the weekly instalment; but equally good places may be discovered elsewhere, if your editor should desire a different division. Should you wish to give the story a second title, "A tale of the Mendips" would suit.'

'A Story of English Rustic Life, by Thomas Hardy' was duly announced in the *Youth's Companion*, 22 November 1883, heading a list of 'Illustrated Serial Stories' promised for 1884, but the editors seem not to have been wholly satisfied. On 14 March 1884 Hardy returned 'the copy you were good enough to send for correction' and added, 'The story seems to me to go naturally enough now, and I hope you will think the same—still more that your numerous young readers will think so. I shall be much obliged if you will send the numbers of the Companion in which the story appears, as I have no correct copy from which it could be printed in England afterwards, should I desire to do so.' The story was not published, however, and as late as 13 December 1886 Hardy wrote to William H. Rideing, one of the editors, 'With regard to the short story I wrote for the Companion please do not pay any attention to the fact that I cannot avail myself of it here as long as you keep it unpublished. The proprietors of the Companion treated me very courteously in the matter, and I should much prefer that you hold it back as long as there is any chance of your having room for it, to your publishing it elsewhere to oblige me. Possibly if you have no space for it at length you may some day think fit to produce it in a somewhat abridged form—it being a story of an imaginative kind suitable for a Christmas number, or such like. Our children here are younger for their age than yours; and possibly the story is too juvenile for your side of the sea. I fancy you may be mistaken in that; but of course I do not know as well as yourselves.'

For the final chapter in the history of 'Our Exploits' I am indebted to the late Charles Miner Thompson (associate editor and later editor-in-chief of the magazine). 'I did not join the staff of the Youth's Companion', he wrote to me, 'until 1890, and consequently have no first-hand knowledge of the serial story by Thomas Hardy. All that I can tell you is what I heard about it later [from Rideing], for the action that Mr. Daniel S. Ford, then editor and proprietor of the Companion, took in regard to it amazed his sub-editors and became an office legend. Mr. Ford's daughter married a Mr. Hartshorn, for whom Mr. Ford bought a small story-paper entitled "The Household". I think that it never prospered greatly, and, to help things along, Mr. Ford would now and then give his son-in-law MSS. from the ample stock of the Youth's Companion. Among those MSS. was Hardy's story. I think that Mr. Hartshorn did not fully appreciate the importance of Thomas Hardy as a writer; if he printed it at all, and the legend says that he did, you will find "Our Exploits at West Poley", perhaps under a different title, but surely under Hardy's name, in some volume of the Household after [1886].'

That so considerable a piece of prose (over 20,000 words) could have lain in MS. at a publisher's for nearly a decade and then, though printed when Hardy's reputation was at a peak in the year after *Tess*, have gone unnoticed and disappeared from memory (obscure as this monthly 'Devoted to the Interests of the American Housewife' seems to have been) are facts as surprising as any in Hardy's bibliography. The story, with its adventures in a cave in the Mendip Hills (a bit removed from the familiar Wessex scene, it will be observed), is well calculated to interest boys, and in the character of Leonard the narrator, thirteen years old 'though rather small for my age', courageous yet prudent and thoughtful, there may be a reflection of Hardy himself and his boyhood. No MS. of 'Our Exploits at West Poley' is known to survive, and there is no evidence that Hardy was aware of its publication. The Oxford University Press reprinted the story in 1952, with an Introduction by R. L. Purdy and illustrations by Lynton Lamb.

1893

Letter: 'A Question of Priority'
  The Westminster Gazette, 10 May 1893, p. 2.

Dated 9 May. The question had been raised in a letter by William Archer and involved a baptism scene in the anonymous and controversial play, *Alan's Wife* (derived from a Swedish story published in January 1891), and the similar scene in *Tess*. Hardy's retort reveals the important fact that 'the chapters of "Tess" containing this incident were in the hands of Messrs. Tillotson and Sons, the syndicate-publishers of Bolton, so early as September, 1889, and were partly put into type by their printers at that date . . .' See above, pp. 71–73. The letter was reprinted in *Alan's Wife*, ed. J. T. Grein (London, 1893), p. [55].

1894

Symposium: 'The Tree of Knowledge'
  The New Review, June 1894, p. 681.

Hardy's contribution to this symposium on sex education and marriage was written, it may be noticed, when he was at work on *Jude*. Reprinted in *Life and Art* (New York, 1925), pp. 118–19.

Sketch: 'The Hon. Mrs. Henniker'
  The Illustrated London News, 18 August 1894, p. 195.

Unsigned. A brief sketch of Florence Henniker as a writer, designed to accompany her portrait. Hardy had first met her in May of the previous year, and the two had already collaborated in 'The Spectre of the Real'. For further details of Hardy's friendship with Mrs. Henniker, see Appendix, pp. 342 ff. The 1-page MS. of this sketch, formerly in the possession of Clement Shorter, editor of the periodical at the time, now belongs to Mr. Frederick B. Adams, Jr.

Story (with Florence Henniker): 'The Spectre of the Real'
  To-Day, Winter Number (17 November) 1894, pp. [5]–15.

With 5 illustrations by H. R. Millar. The story was written by Hardy and Mrs. Henniker in October 1893 and subsequently collected by Mrs. Henniker in July 1896 in her volume, *In Scarlet and Grey* (Stories of Soldiers and Others by Florence Henniker, and The Spectre of the Real by Thomas Hardy and Florence Henniker, London: John

Lane, Boston: Roberts Bros., 1896), pp. 164–208. A 'Second Edition' of *In Scarlet and Grey* was advertised. For details of the composition of this story and Hardy's friendship with Mrs. Henniker, see Appendix, pp. 342 ff.

1895

Note: 'The Duchy of Cornwall and Mr. Thomas Hardy'
The Dorset County Chronicle (Dorchester), 17 January 1895, p. 4.

A paragraph denying a story of Hardy's difficulties in purchasing (in 1883) the site for Max Gate.

Letter: 'Hearts Insurgent'
The Daily Chronicle, 25 September 1895, p. 3.

Written 24 September in reply to a letter printed that day which protested against Harper's apparent bowdlerizing of *Hearts Insurgent* [*Jude the Obscure*]. Hardy remarks, '. . . little or nothing has been omitted or modified without my knowledge, though I failed to see the necessity for some of the alterations, if for any. However, as abridged in the magazine I venture to think the novel a not uninteresting one for the general family circle, to which the magazine is primarily addressed—to use the editor's own words to me—while the novel as originally written, addressed mainly to middle-aged readers, and of less interest than as now printed to those young ladies for whose innocence we are all so solicitous, will be published in a volume a month hence, under a new title.'

1896

Letter: *The Trumpet-Major*
The Critic (New York), 4 July 1896, p. 8.

Dated 'London, June 9, 1896'. Retort to a revival (9 May) of the old charge of plagiarism in Chap. 23 (the drilling scene) of *The Trumpet-Major* (see *The Critic*, 28 January 1882). Hardy's letter largely rehearses statements in his recent Preface to the Osgood, McIlvaine edition of the novel (which had revived the charge).

1897

Letter: 'The Disappearance of an Englishman at Zermatt'
The Times, 8 July 1897, p. 10.

Written from 'Hôtel de la Paix, Geneva, July 3' and relating to the mysterious disappearance of a Mr. Cooper on 24 June (four days before Hardy himself arrived at Zermatt). For the circumstances of the letter, see *Later Years*, pp. 69–70. 'Mr. Cooper' was James Robert Cooper, father of the Edith Cooper of 'Michael Field'.

1899

Symposium: 'Les Écrivains français jugés par les écrivains anglais'
Le Gaulois du dimanche ('Supplément hebdomadaire littéraire et illustré' of *Le Gaulois*, Paris), 11–12 February 1899, p. [1].

Hardy's letter (here translated into French) is dated January 1899 and is in answer to the question, 'Which French authors now dead best represented in their works the distinctive genius of France?' The question was put by *Le Gaulois* to a number of English writers, including Conan Doyle, Saintsbury, Meredith, and Pinero. The replies were published simultaneously in the *Morning Post*, 11 February 1899, p. 5, under the title 'British Authors on French Literature'.

Interview: 'Shall Stonehenge Go?'
The Daily Chronicle, 24 August 1899, p. 3.

Although ostensibly an interview with Hardy at Max Gate by 'Our Special Correspondent' (James Milne), this is largely Hardy's own composition and of some interest. It is apparent from a 5-page rough draft in the Bliss collection that Hardy wrote out his reflections on Stonehenge in the form of a letter or article, which is here printed almost verbatim but cast by Milne in the form of an interview with the addition of setting, questions, and colloquialisms. The interview is part of a considerable campaign to rouse the public over the projected sale of Stonehenge. The following day the *Daily Chronicle* reprinted the Stonehenge scene from *Tess*. Portions of the interview are reprinted in James Milne, *A Window in Fleet Street* (London, 1931), pp. 253–64.

Letter: 'A Christmas Ghost-Story'
The Daily Chronicle, 28 December 1899, p. 8.

A fine letter, written 25 December, in reply to a leader of that date which had taken exception to the character of the soldier's phantom in the poem 'A Christmas Ghost-Story' (*The Westminster Gazette*, 23 December 1899) as unheroic. Letter and poem are reprinted in

War Against War in South Africa (ed. W. T. Stead), 29 December 1899, p. 166.

1900

Letter: ' "Tess" at the Coronet Theatre'
  The Times, 21 February 1900, p. 4.

  Written from Dorchester, 20 February, to disclaim any authorization or knowledge of an adaptation of *Tess* produced the previous night (and poorly reviewed by *The Times*). It was the work of H. A. Kennedy, who published a reply 8 March.

1901

Symposium: 'The Curse of Militarism'
  The Young Man, June 1901, p. 191.

  Brief comment on an article, 'The Curse of Militarism' by William Clarke, in the May issue. Among other contributors were Clodd and Walter Crane.

Letter: The Royal Buckhounds
  Humanity (Journal of the Humanitarian League), August 1901, pp. 155–6.

  Written from Max Gate, 27 June 1901, for a meeting to celebrate the fall of the Royal Buckhounds.

Letter: The Beauty of Wessex
  The Sphere, 7 September 1901, p. 288.

  Retort, printed in Clement Shorter's 'Literary Letter', to a statement in the *New York Times Saturday Review* that a party of London pilgrims on a visit to Hardy 'found that the Wessex country was not intrinsically romantic and beautiful, but could only move as viewed through the illusions produced by the novelist'. See *Later Years*, p. 89. Printed simultaneously in the *Academy*, p. [183]. Reprinted in *Life and Art* (New York, 1925), p. 135.

1902

Letter: 'The Wessex of Thomas Hardy'
  The Guardian, 16 April 1902, p. 551.

  Dated 11 April 1902. The letter corrects misstatements in an ill-natured review (9 April) of B. C. A. Windle's *The Wessex of Thomas Hardy*, touching Hardy's use of the term 'Wessex' and the burial of Roman soldiers at Dorchester. Hardy's letter is followed by an answer from 'The Reviewer'.

Letter: 'Edmund Kean in Dorchester'
The Dorset County Chronicle (Dorchester), 10 July 1902, p. 11.

Third in a series of three letters contributed by Hardy to a local controversy over Edmund Kean's connexion with Dorchester, signed like its predecessors with the pseudonym 'History'. The earlier letters, printed 29 May and 12 June, are collected in *Later Years*, pp. 98–99 (see above, p. 271). The present letter is a retort to suggestions as to the scene of Kean's performance. '. . . The conclusion, therefore, is that Kean in 1813 acted in a theatre built fifteen years after he visited the town. This seems a more wonderful performance of Kean's than the play itself. All things may be possible in the eyes of some newspaper correspondents; but one would like to know how Kean achieved his feat. Like Miss Rosa Dartle I only ask for information.'

Letter: 'Recollections of "Leader Scott"'
The Dorset County Chronicle (Dorchester), 27 November 1902, p. 5.

A letter of some autobiographical interest, dated from Max Gate, 24 November. Lucy Baxter (1837–1902), writer on art under the pseudonym 'Leader Scott', was a daughter of William Barnes and a friend of Hardy's since her girlhood in Dorchester. She had died at Florence, 10 November. The letter appeared simultaneously in *The Times* (p. 11) as 'contributed to the *Dorset County Chronicle* of today'.

1903

Letter: 'Serial Rights in Stories'
The Athenaeum, 16 May 1903, p. 626.

A brief letter disclaiming responsibility for the 'publication as if new' of 'a resuscitated old story' ['Benighted Travellers'] in the *Sphere* for 2 and 9 May and 'reminding inexperienced writers of fiction' of the necessity of limiting serial rights.

1904

Letter: ' "The Dynasts": A Rejoinder'

The Times Literary Supplement, 5 February 1904, pp. 36–37.

Written from Max Gate, 2 February, in reply to ' "The Dynasts": A Suggestion' (29 January), an unsigned article (by A. B. Walkley, dramatic critic of *The Times*) objecting to the dramatic form of the work. The first of two important letters on this subject.

Letter: ' "The Dynasts": A Postscript'

The Times Literary Supplement, 19 February 1904, p. 53.

Written from Max Gate, 16 February, in reply to ' "The Dynasts" and the Puppets' (12 February), an unsigned article (by A. B. Walkley, dramatic critic of *The Times*) continuing the controversy inaugurated 29 January. The second of two important letters on this subject.

? Obituary: Jemima Hardy

The Dorset County Chronicle (Dorchester), 7 April 1904, p. 4.

Unsigned. A brief account of Hardy's mother, who had died on Easter Sunday, 3 April. The ascription of these family obituaries to Hardy is made on the basis of Mrs. Hardy's belief and her remark to me, 'If anything was written, he must have done it.' The notice in *The Times*, 6 April, p. 4, may also, therefore, be his.

Note: Jemima Hardy

The Daily Chronicle, 9 April 1904, p. 4.

A note correcting erroneous statements about Hardy's mother which had appeared in various places since her death. Reprinted, with an account of her funeral, among Stinsford items in the *Dorset County Chronicle* (Dorchester), 14 April 1904, p. 6.

Obituary: 'Laurence Hope'

The Athenaeum, 29 October 1904, p. 591.

Unsigned. A brief tribute to Adela Florence (called 'Violet') Nicolson (1865–1904), writer of verses under the pseudonym of 'Laurence Hope', who took her life at Madras, 4 October. See *Later Years*, p. 108. Hardy seems to have approved the 'tropical luxuriance and Sapphic fervour' of her work. His 3-page rough MS. (with presentation copies of Mrs. Nicolson's 2 volumes, *The Garden of Kama* and *Stars of the Desert*) was in the possession of the late Carroll A. Wilson.

1905

Letter: A *Daily Chronicle* Interview
The Daily Chronicle, 9 February 1905, p. 3.

Written 8 February and disclaiming an offensive interview published by W. Smithard in the *Daily Chronicle* of that date.

Letter: '"Far from the Madding Crowd": A Correction'
The Spectator, 29 April 1905, p. 638.

Written from the Athenaeum to deny a statement in Edmund Downey's *Twenty Years Ago*, quoted in the *Spectator*'s review of the book on 22 April (p. 596), that *Far from the Madding Crowd* 'was offered to the late Mr. W. Tinsley, and withdrawn because he would not "give a rise" on another publisher's price for it.' Downey replied on 6 May (p. 672).

Letter: Walter Tyndale's Water-Colours
Catalogue of an Exhibition of Water-Colours of Wessex (*Thomas Hardy's Country*), *by Walter Tyndale*, The Leicester Galleries, London, June–July 1905, pp. 5–6.

An 'introductory letter' of appreciation and brief reminiscence, written 5 June 1905 from Hyde Park Mansions, W. The water-colours, some of which Hardy had suggested, were reproduced in Walter Tyndale and Clive Holland, *Wessex*, London, 1906.

Preface: *Dorchester (Dorset), and its Surroundings*
F. R. and Sidney Heath, *Dorchester (Dorset), and its Surroundings*, Dorchester and London, 1905–6, p. [7].

Vol. 46 of The Homeland Handbooks, published in October 1905. Hardy sent his 'few forewords' 23 September, and the copy of the cloth-bound issue inscribed to him is dated 20 November.

1906

Preface: 'H.J.M. Some Memories and Letters'
H. J. Moule, *Dorchester Antiquities*, Dorchester, 1906, pp. [7]–13.

The quiet record of 'a friendship of between forty and fifty years' with Henry Joseph Moule (1825–1904), elder brother of Hardy's great friend Horace Moule and long the Curator of the Dorset County Museum. Published in January 1906. The drawing, on p. 76, of 3 fibulae 'taken from the forehead of a skull exhumed at Max Gate' is by Hardy and had appeared in an earlier edition of the book in 1901.

Essay: 'Memories of Church Restoration'

The Society for the Protection of Ancient Buildings. The General Meeting of the Society; Twenty-Ninth Annual Report of the Committee; and Paper Read by Thomas Hardy, Esq. June, 1906, London, 1906, pp. 59–80.

An important paper, written for the Society for the Protection of Ancient Buildings, of which Hardy was a member, and read at the General Meeting of the Society, 20 June 1906, by Col. Eustace Balfour (in the author's absence). See *Later Years*, pp. 119–20. The essay was also printed in the *Cornhill Magazine*, August 1906, pp. 184–96. In this connexion Reginald Smith of Smith, Elder & Co. wrote to Hardy, 4 July 1906, 'The "Cornhill Magazine" likes your paper so much that it will wink at the concurrent appearance of it in the Transactions of the Society for the Protection of Ancient Buildings on the 26th.' The *Cornhill* text shows several revisions and omits the marginal glosses of the original. The MS., a fair copy on 20 leaves of ruled paper measuring $8'' \times 10\frac{1}{8}''$, signed and dated April 1906 at the end, is now in the Bliss collection. Reprinted in *Life and Art* (New York, 1925), pp. 91–109.

Note: A Commission on Spelling Reform

The Daily Chronicle, 29 August 1906, p. 4.

Comment on a proposed Commission on Spelling Reform, a telegram sent in reply to a query.

Letter: Henry Mills Alden

Harper's Weekly (New York), 15 December 1906, p. 1814.

A letter of congratulation for the seventieth birthday of Henry Mills Alden, editor of *Harper's Magazine*. Written from Max Gate, 11 November 1906, and printed with other tributes as a souvenir of the occasion.

1907

Preface: *The Society of Dorset Men in London*

The Society of Dorset Men in London (Year-book, 1907–8), London, 1907, pp. [3]–4.

Hardy had been elected second President of the Society at its annual meeting, 15 November 1907. In his 'Forewords' there are several reminiscences of his early days in London.

1908

Note: George Meredith
The Daily News, 12 February 1908, p. 4.

A sentence of tribute for Meredith's eightieth birthday, one of a number of 'appreciative messages' printed.

Article: 'Maumbury Ring'
The Times, 9 October 1908, p. 11.

An important article, combining personal recollections and history (with a good deal of space devoted to the execution of Mrs. Channing, a story Hardy often recalled). It was solicited by Moberly Bell (manager of *The Times*), 30 September, because of the general interest roused at this time by excavations at Maumbury Rings, Dorchester.

Note: ['Louis Napoleon, and the Poet Barnes']
F. H. Cheetham, *Louis Napoleon and the Genesis of the Second Empire*, London, 1909 [November 1908], unpaged leaf inserted between pp. 378 and 379.

Hardy's note is introduced as a 'Postscript' with the explanation, 'At the moment of going to press the following interesting anecdote has reached me from Mr. Thomas Hardy; it seems far too interesting to omit altogether, and is consequently printed as a postscript, being too belated to take its proper place in the text or to be included in the index.' The anecdote, with the title 'Louis Napoleon, and the Poet Barnes', was written out in a letter to John Lane, publisher of the book. In briefer form, as Hardy set it down in his diary after a conversation with Barnes, 17 October 1885, it appears in the *Early Life*, pp. 229–30.

Address: 'Dorset in London'
The Society of Dorset Men in London (Year-book, 1908–9), London, 1908, pp. [3]–7.

Hardy's address as President of the Society, prepared for the annual dinner in May 1908 but never delivered (see *Later Years*, p. 131). As in the case of his 'Forewords' of the previous year, there are remini-

scences of the London of his youth. A portion of the MS. is reproduced in facsimile on p. [i]. Hardy continued as President for a second
term, 1908–9.

1909

Letter: The Censorship of Plays
The Times, 13 August 1909, p. 4.

Written 26 July 1909 at the request of John Galsworthy and read by
him as part of his testimony before a Joint Committee of Lords and
Commons appointed to inquire into the censorship of plays. The letter
has special reference to 'A Sunday Morning Tragedy'. Reprinted in
the *Academy*, 14 August 1909; *Life and Art* (New York, 1925), p. 128;
Edmund Blunden, *Thomas Hardy* (London, 1941), p. 127.

Letter: 'Mr. Hardy's Poems'
The Daily News, 15 December 1909, p. 6.

Written 13 December in reply to a review of *Time's Laughingstocks*
that day, which complained that 'throughout . . . the outlook [is] that
of disillusion and despair.' Hardy retorts that more than half the ninety-
odd poems 'do not answer to the description at all'.

1910

Note: 'Mr. Hardy's Swinburne Poem'
The Daily Mail, 5 April 1910, p. [5].

Unsigned. A news item reproducing the first stanza of 'A Singer Asleep'
from the current number of the *English Review* and describing the
poem as 'in commemoration of Swinburne' and identifying the 'fair
niche' as Bonchurch graveyard, 'now in all its budding beauty'. There
had been some doubt as to the subject of the poem, and Hardy sent
this explanatory paragraph to Lindsay Bashford (literary editor of the
Daily Mail) 3 April for publication, 'as Swinburne's memory is so
important in poetry.'

Note: 'Some Old-Fashioned Psalm-tunes Associated with the County of
Dorset'
The Society of Dorset Men in London (Year-book, 1910–11), London,
1910, pp. [103–6].

Ten tunes transcribed with notes by Hardy and reproduced in a facsimile of his MS. He had collected them for the Society three years before (see *Later Years*, p. 127).

1911

Story: 'Blue Jimmy: the Horse-Stealer' by F. E. Dugdale
The Cornhill Magazine, February 1911, pp. 225–31.

A proof of this story by Hardy's future wife, in the possession of Mr. Frederick B. Adams, Jr., shows a number of additions in Hardy's own hand, particularly the note on p. 231. Two lines from 'A Tramp-woman's Tragedy' referring to Blue Jimmy serve as epigraph.

Poem: 'On the Doorstep'
The Fortnightly Review, April 1911, pp. 582–3.

A poem of 12 lines, printed here as the tenth of 12 'Satires of Circumstance' but well discarded when the others were collected in the volume of that name in 1914. The poem, though cancelled, appears in the MS. of *Satires of Circumstance* (see above, p. 171) where the group of 'Satires' is dated 1910. The title was afterwards given to an entirely different poem, published in *Moments of Vision*.

Poem: 'The Calf'
The Book of Baby Beasts, Pictures in Colour by E. J. Detmold, Descriptions by Florence E. Dugdale, London [October 1911], p. 105.

Four 5-line stanzas, unsigned. The poem is ascribed to Hardy by Mrs. Hardy's sisters (cf. below, 'The Yellow-Hammer', p. 316, and 'The Lizard', p. 317). It is probable that he had a hand in the revision of other poems in the book.

Note: A Correction of Misstatements
The Athenaeum, 28 October 1911, pp. 523–4.

Unsigned. A paragraph correcting 'a curious enlargement and embellishment of fact . . . in some newspapers this week [*The Daily News*, 23 October]' relating to Hardy's 'writing and collaborating for the theatre' and the disposition of his MSS.

Note: 'Mr. Hardy's Note on the Story'
The Three Wayfarers, The Distracted Preacher (Programme, Dorchester Debating and Dramatic Society), Dorchester, 15–16 November 1911, p. [4].

A note on the factual background of 'The Distracted Preacher' written for an amateur performance of two 'Hardy' plays (see Appendix, pp. 351 ff.). There were later issues of the programme for performances in London (27 November) and Weymouth (15 December).

1912

Symposium: 'Charles Dickens: Some Personal Recollections and Opinions'
The Bookman, February 1912, p. 247.

In a brief reply to several questions in this Dickens Centenary Number Hardy writes, 'I did not know Dickens, though when a young man in London I heard him read from his books in the Hanover Square Rooms. But as I was thinking more of verse than of prose at that time, I do not know that my literary efforts owed much to his influence.'

Symposium: 'How Shall We Solve the Divorce Problem?'
Nash's Magazine, March 1912, p. 683.

Hardy's contribution, under the title 'Laws the Cause of Misery', is in reply to a question raised by a proposed revision of the divorce laws of England and Wales. Reprinted in *Hearst's Magazine* (New York), June 1912, and *Life and Art* (New York, 1925), p. 120.

Letter: William Dean Howells
Harper's Weekly (New York), 9 March 1912, Part II, p. 33.

A letter of greetings and tribute to Howells, written 16 February 1912, for the celebration of his seventy-fifth birthday. The whole of this supplement to *Harper's Weekly* is a souvenir of the dinner on that occasion.

Speech: A Plea for Pure English
The Times, 4 June 1912, p. 7.

Hardy's speech of acceptance on being awarded the Gold Medal of the Royal Society of Literature at Max Gate, 2 June, his seventy-second birthday. For accounts of the occasion, see *Later Years*, p. 152, and *The Later Life and Letters of Sir Henry Newbolt*, ed. Margaret Newbolt (London, 1942), pp. 166–8.

Poem: 'A.H., 1855–1912'
Arthur Henniker, A Little Book for His Friends, London, 1912, p. 58.
A poem of 3 quatrains in memory of Major-General the Hon. Arthur Henry Henniker-Major, who died 6 February 1912. It was

written for his widow Florence Henniker, Hardy's good friend since 1893, who arranged this volume of obituaries, reminiscences, and letters of condolence. The poem was left uncollected because of its personal nature and also because the last quatrain was simply a recasting of an old epitaph Hardy had suggested for Alfred Pretor in 1907 (see *Later Years*, p. 126). The volume was published in October 1912. For further details of Hardy's friendship with Mrs. Henniker, see Appendix, pp. 342 ff.

Poem: 'The Yellow-Hammer'

The Book of Baby Birds, Illustrations by E. J. Detmold, Descriptions by Florence E. Dugdale, London [October 1912], p. 75.

Four quatrains, unsigned. The MS., written in pencil on the verso of a Macmillan presentation slip measuring $5'' \times 8''$, is now in the possession of Miss Constance Dugdale. Hardy has added as note: '[Have seen them flitting thus, but do they eat corn? They may not have been there for that—If so, will write a different verse.]' It is probable that he had a hand in the revision of other poems in the book.

1913

Letter: Sudermann's *The Song of Songs*

Hermann Sudermann, *The Song of Songs*, trans. Beatrice Marshall, London, 1913, pp. ix–x.

Written from Max Gate, 15 December 1910, in reply to a circular letter sent by John Lane to a number of well-known novelists, seeking their opinion of Sudermann's *The Song of Songs* on the threatened suppression of the book. Hardy's letter was not written for publication, but when Lane reissued *The Song of Songs* in June 1913 in a new translation, he added an Introduction with a full account of the controversy, printing Hardy's letter (largely adverse in its comments) among others. This was done with Hardy's consent, and he corrected a proof of the letter, amplifying it at several points. George Moore's letter to the President of the Society of Authors, quoted on p. xx, was in reality addressed to Hardy.

Letter: 'Performing Animals'

The Times, 19 December 1913, p. 9.

Written from Max Gate, 18 December, in retort to a special article,

'Performing Animals, The Psychology of Pain in Man and Beast', published in *The Times*, 17 December.

1914

Symposium: 'What is the Best Short Poem in English?'
> *The New York Times*, 5 July 1914, Section 5, p. [1].

Hardy's letter, undated, is in answer to the above question, put to twenty-five poets. Making no choice, he writes, 'I fail to see how there can be a "best" poem, long or short . . . This attempt to appraise by comparison is, if you will allow me to say so, one of the literary vices of the time . . .'

1915

Poem: 'A Hundred Years Since'
> *The North American Review* (New York), February 1915, pp. [173]–174.

A poem of 13 tercets, written for the centenary of the *North American Review*. Why Hardy left it uncollected is not clear, beyond the fact that the poem is to some extent topical and slightly reminiscent (especially in form) of 'The Jubilee of a Magazine' (written on a similar occasion for the *Cornhill* in 1910). The MS., a fair copy with several alterations, written on 2 leaves of fine paper measuring 8″× 10″ and marked by Hardy in red ink '[original MS.]', is now in the Bliss collection. It was the *North American Review* which consented to print in November 1903 'A Trampwoman's Tragedy', considered by Hardy 'upon the whole, his most successful poem.'

Poem: ['The Lizard']
> *The Book of Baby Pets*, Illustrations by E. J. Detmold, Descriptions by Florence E. Dugdale, London [March 1915], p. 75.

A single quatrain, unsigned, heading a chapter 'About Lizards'. The MS., written in pencil on a half-sheet of note-paper measuring $4\frac{3}{8}″ \times 7″$, was given to me by Mrs. Hardy. It is probable that Hardy had a hand in the revision of other poems in the book.

Symposium: 'The War and Literature'
> *The Book Monthly*, April 1915, p. 434.

> Reply in briefest form to the question, 'What effects, so far as they can be estimated ahead, is the *Great War* likely to exercise on English literature?' Reprinted in *Life and Art* (New York, 1925), p. 122.

Translations: 'Great Britain', 'Invasion'
> *The Book of France*, ed. Winifred Stephens, London and Paris, 1915, pp. 12–15, 61–62.

> Two prose translations, 'Great Britain' from the French of J. H. Rosny aîné (pp. 12–15) and 'Invasion' from the French of Remy de Gourmont (pp. 61–62). Published in July 1915 under the auspices of an honorary committee (of which Hardy was a member) in aid of the French Parliamentary Committee's Fund for the Relief of the Invaded Departments. The contributors to the volume were leading French writers, their work accompanied by translations made by well-known English men of letters.

Note: *Far from the Madding Crowd*
> *Far from the Madding Crowd* (Programme, Turner Films, Ltd.), London, 16 November 1915, pp. [2–11].

> A synopsis of the novel written for the souvenir programme of the private trade and press exhibition of a film version at the West End Cinema, London, 16 November 1915. Hardy's synopsis is accompanied on each page by 'still' photographs from the film, made by Turner Films, Ltd. (adapted and produced by Larry Trimble, to be released 28 February 1916).

Obituary: Mary Hardy
> *The Dorset County Chronicle* (Dorchester), 2 December 1915, pp. 8–9.

> An unsigned obituary notice of Hardy's favourite sister, who died at Talbothays 24 November (see *Later Years*, p. 170). Of all his family she was nearest him in age (b. 23 December 1841) and temperament. Hardy enclosed the obituary as his work in a letter to Sydney Cockerell.

Symposium: 'Which is the Finest View in Dorset?'
> *The Society of Dorset Men in London* (Year-book, 1915–16), London, 1915, pp. 31–32.

> Hardy offers a list of 8, with only the briefest comment.

1916

Speech: *Wessex Scenes from The Dynasts*
　　The Dorset County Chronicle (Dorchester), 14 December 1916, p. 6.
The 'Hardy Players' of the Dorchester Debating and Dramatic Society
gave three performances of *Wessex Scenes from The Dynasts* in Dorchester 6–7 December for Red Cross charities. Hardy prepared two
brief speeches on the scope of the play to be delivered from the stage
before the rise of the curtain, one for Mrs. Hanbury at the evening
performances and the other for the Countess of Ilchester at the matinée.
Mrs. Hanbury's speech is only 'reported' here, but Lady Ilchester's
(recited by her daughter, Lady Mary Fox-Strangways) is printed
verbatim as 'penned by Mr. Hardy himself'. The speech is a contrast
of Napoleonic and modern warfare. A portion had already appeared
in *The Times*, 9 December, and elsewhere. There are rough drafts in
pencil of both speeches among the Max Gate papers.

1917

Letter: The Harper Centennial
　　The Harper Centennial 1817–1917, New York, December 1917, p. 12.
A brief letter in the third person, written 29 May 1917 as Hardy's
contribution to this volume of centenary congratulations, printed for
private distribution.

1918

Preface: 'William Barnes'
　　The English Poets, ed. Thomas Humphry Ward, Vol. V (Browning
　　to Rupert Brooke), London, 1918, pp. [174]–176.
A biographical summary and critical introduction, followed by 10
selections from Barnes's poetry. Hardy was asked to undertake the
work by Humphry Ward in October 1916 and dispatched his MS.
on 24 November. The volume was delayed by the First World War,
and it was June 1917 when Hardy received his proof and November
1918 before the book was published. This is the fourth and last of
Hardy's notes on Barnes and his poetry (see above, pp. 135 ff., 295,
297), and he warned Ward at the outset, 'I fear that what I would
have to say would not be much more than a paraphrase of what I
have said about him elsewhere in past years. This is almost inevitable.'

The critical introduction repeats a few lines and phrases from the Preface to *Select Poems of William Barnes* (1908), and pages from that text were used as printer's copy. Hardy omitted, however, the final stanza of 'The Widow's House' and translated into 'common English' (without comment) the last two selections, 'White and Blue' and 'The Wind at the Door'.

Note: American Editors
The Times, 13 November 1918, p. 5.

A brief message (chiefly a quotation from *3 Henry VI*) read at Cecil Harmsworth's dinner to American editors at Dr. Johnson's House, 11 November.

1919

Preface: *A Book of Remembrance*
A Book of Remembrance, Being a short Summary of the Service and Sacrifice rendered to the Empire during the Great War by one of the many Patriotic Families of Wessex, The Popes of Wrackleford, co. Dorset. London, Privately Printed (For Use of the Family), 1919, pp. 5–6.

The remarkable record of the eleven sons and four daughters of Alfred Pope of Dorchester, described by Hardy as 'a household which has been for many years among my nearest neighbours.' Hardy not only contributed a 'Foreword', dated September 1918, but read and revised the proofs of the whole volume. It was handsomely printed at the Chiswick Press in an edition of 250 copies and issued in June 1919. Hardy's MS. is in the possession of the Pope family.

Note: Trade Unionism
The Shop Assistant, 21 June 1919, p. 405.

A word in favour of 'social re-adjustments rather than social subversions'.

1921

Preface: *Wessex Worthies*
J. J. Foster, *Wessex Worthies*, London, 1920 [1921], p. [ix].

Besides his 'Introductory Note', signed in facsimile, Hardy contributed 'valued suggestions' to this volume and permitted the reprinting of 'A Call to National Service'. Though dated 1920, it was published in

February 1921, with an *édition de luxe* of 50 copies and an 'Author's edition' of 325 copies. Foster, son of a Dorchester bookseller, was a boyhood acquaintance of Hardy's.

Symposium: 'A League of Thinkers'
 The New World, July 1921, p. [109].
Brief comment on proposals for 'A League of Thinkers' put forward by Léon Tolstoy, Jr., in the May issue.

Symposium: 'World Peace'
 The Times, 24 December 1921, p. 11.
A Christmas message (a single sentence) on the outlook for world peace.

1922

Letter: 'Tolstoy's Works'
 The Times, 29 April 1922, p. 17.
A letter appended to an appeal by Shaw for support of the forthcoming Oxford Press edition of Tolstoy, translated by Aylmer Maude.

Note: Horace Moule
 The London Mercury, October 1922, p. 631.
A brief biographical note on Horace M. Moule (1832–73) to accompany a reprinting (in a series of such forgotten poems) of Moule's 'Ave Caesar'. The poem was first published in *Once a Week*, 6 September 1862, and had been suggested by a painting of Gérôme's which Moule and Hardy both saw in the International Exhibition of that year. Hardy had a touching concern for the reputation of this early friend and patron and wrote at the end of his transcript of the poem (omitted in the *London Mercury*), 'It is hoped that this may be printed in any new edition of the Oxford Book of English Verse. T.H.'

Sketch: 'Robert Louis Stevenson'
 I Can Remember Robert Louis Stevenson, ed. Rosaline Masson, Edinburgh and London, 1922, pp. 214–16.
Hardy's contribution to this collection of personal reminiscences of Stevenson is, as he confesses, 'very meagre'. Much the same material, in briefer form, appears in the *Early Life*, pp. 229, 235, 237. There is a first draft among the Max Gate papers. Hardy's presentation copy of the volume is dated 4 November 1922.

1925

Note: *Tess of the d'Urbervilles*
John o' London's Weekly, 24 October 1925, p. [125].

A prefatory note, dated October 1925, to accompany the first instalment of a reprinting of *Tess*, 'now published serially for the first time complete in all its details as primarily written, a fragment of a chapter here embodied having been discovered but a short while ago.' (See above, p. 70.) The note is reproduced in facsimile.

Letter: *The Saturday Review*
The Saturday Review, 7 November 1925, Supplement, p. xiv.

A brief note of congratulation for the *Saturday Review*'s seventieth anniversary, in which Hardy describes himself as 'probably among its earliest readers still living, as I began to buy it when it was less than two years old.'

1926

Note: 'An Appeal from Dorset'
The New York Herald, European Edition (Paris), 25 April 1926, p. 4.

Endorsement, in briefest form, added to a letter of appeal (dated 18 April) from the Rev. H. G. B. Cowley for the restoration of Stinsford Church bells. Hardy's own draft of the appeal, made 27 February and in the third person 'as I cannot very well draw attention to my own writings personally', was not used.

Letter: Hopkins's 'Thomas Hardy and His Folk'
The Westminster Gazette, 4 June 1926, p. 6.

A letter of protest at erroneous statements about Hardy's family in an article by R. Thurston Hopkins, 'Thomas Hardy and His Folk', published 2 June. Hopkins printed two letters of apology and retraction, 8 and 11 June.

Letter: 'The dram of eale'
The Times, 17 June 1926, p. 15.

Written from Max Gate, 15 June, and suggested by a leader of that date on this crux in *Hamlet*, I. iv. It 'reminds me that in the eighteen-

sixties I worked at elucidating it, and marked in the margin of a copy
I used my own conjectural reading. . . .

> The dram of ill
> Doth all the noble substance leaven down
> To his own scandal.'

Note: Weymouth
> *The Times*, 6 July 1926, p. 13.

'A message of congratulation and friendship' presented by a civic dele-
gation from Weymouth, England, at Independence Day celebrations
in Weymouth, Massachusetts. See *Later Years*, p. 248.

Letter: Country-dances and 'The College Hornpipe' (as formerly danced in
Wessex)
> *E.F.D.S.* [*English Folk Dance Society*] *News*, September 1926, pp.
> 384–5.

A letter about country-dances, especially in *Under the Greenwood Tree*,
and 'The College Hornpipe', the figure of which is set down 'as nearly
as I can recall it sixty years after I last danced in it.' A similar figure
was printed in *The Three Wayfarers* (New York and London, 1930),
p. [vii].

1927

Letter: English Country-dances
> *The Journal of the English Folk Dance Society*, 1927, pp. 53–54.

Written in response to comments on Hardy's letter in *E.F.D.S. News*
(September 1926).

Note: ['The Ancient Cottages of England']
> *The Preservation of Ancient Cottages* [London, 1927], pp. 13–[16].

A pamphlet published by the Royal Society of Arts in March 1927 as
an appeal for contributions to a Fund for the Preservation of Ancient
Cottages inaugurated at a conference 26 January. Hardy's note, with
childhood memories of old-fashioned 'mud-wall' building, supplements
a more extended appeal by the Prime Minister, Stanley Baldwin. The
MS., now in the Dorset County Museum, bears the title 'The Ancient
Cottages of England' and is a signed fair copy, written on 2 leaves of
fine paper, measuring 8″ × 10″, and inserted by Hardy in a wrapper
of brown paper.

Note: Cruel Sports
  The Times, 5 March 1927, p. 7.

A brief message of support for a meeting at Taunton, 4 March, organized by the League for the Prohibition of Cruel Sports.

Note: South African Farmers
  The Dorset County Chronicle (Dorchester), 14 July 1927, p. 8.

A word of greeting to a group of South African farmers, touring south-western England and about to visit Dorchester.

1928

Hardy died 11 January 1928.

Preface: A French Translation of *The Dynasts*
  La Revue Nouvelle (Paris), January–February 1928, pp. [40]–41.

Written for Yvonne Salmon's unpublished French translation of *The Dynasts* (two specimens of which, the Preface of 1903 and the Fore Scene, are printed here). The Preface is dated December 1927 and has been translated into French. This is a special number of the *Revue Nouvelle*, entirely devoted to Hardy and planned before his death.

Poem: ['At a Rehearsal of One of J.M.B.'s Plays']
  The Plays of J. M. Barrie, London, 1928, frontispiece.

Two quatrains written during Hardy's last visit to London, 20–22 April 1920, when he stayed with Sir James Barrie and attended one of the final rehearsals of *Mary Rose* (produced 22 April). The poem was copied into Hardy's diary, and the portion of the page containing it (with entries for April and May 1921 on the recto) was given to Barrie by Mrs. Hardy when the diary itself was destroyed. It is written in pencil on a leaf measuring $3\frac{3}{4}'' \times 4\frac{1}{2}''$ and is identified only by the note '(At a rehearsal of one of J.M.B.'s plays.)', though Barrie has added as title 'On J.M.B.' The MS., now in the Houghton Library at Harvard, is reproduced in facsimile in the Barrie *et al.* Sale Catalogue (Sotheby & Co., 20–22 December 1937, facing p. 7). *The Plays of J. M. Barrie*, with the poem engraved below the frontispiece portrait of Barrie, was published in November 1928 (Mrs. Hardy's presentation copy was dated 23 November). In line 7 'mummery' is a misreading of Hardy's MS. for 'mumming'. The verses are reprinted in Denis Mackail, *The Story of J.M.B.* (London, 1941), p. 334.

[1947

Poem: 'Oh the old old clock'

The Times Literary Supplement, 23 August 1947, p. 432.

This poem of three 12-line stanzas, with Hardy's signature and the date 19 December 1855, was copied in pencil on the inside of the door of a grandfather's clock which formerly stood in his boyhood home at Higher Bockhampton and more recently came into the possession of Dr. E. W. Mann from the estate of Miss Katharine Hardy. Published here as 'Hardy's Earliest Verses' with a partial facsimile, the poem was almost immediately identified as 'The Old Cottage Clock' by Charles Swain, the Manchester poet (see *The Times Literary Supplement,* 30 August 1947, p. 439). The poem had also been privately printed as 'Thomas Hardy's first poem', under the title 'The Old Clock', by Carl J. Weber (Portland, Maine, December 1946).]

APPENDIXES

APPENDIX I

A CALENDAR OF HARDY–TINSLEY LETTERS 1869–75

Hardy's correspondence with his first publisher, William Tinsley (1831–1902) of Tinsley Brothers, 18 (later 8) Catherine Street, Strand, relating particularly to *Desperate Remedies, Under the Greenwood Tree,* and *A Pair of Blue Eyes.*[1] Covering as they do a fairly obscure period of Hardy's life, these letters have some biographical as well as bibliographical value. The publishing records of Tinsley Brothers have long been dispersed and destroyed. Tinsley's recollections of his dealings with Hardy, set down years after in his *Random Recollections of an Old Publisher* (2 vols., London and Bournemouth, 1900) and also in Edmund Downey's *Twenty Years Ago* (London, 1905), are inaccurate and of little value.

1869

Hardy: Bockhampton, Dorchester, 8 June 1869

Calling attention to the MS. of *The Poor Man and the Lady* already submitted and offering to obtain a personal introduction should it be necessary. ('Return' scrawled by Tinsley across the letter.)

Hardy: 3 Wooperton Street, Weymouth, 14 September 1869

Asking for the return of the MS. of *The Poor Man and the Lady* since the terms on which it might be published, as mentioned to his friend, are rather beyond him just now.

1870

Tinsley: 7 April 1870

Acknowledging receipt of the MS. of *Desperate Remedies* (except 3 or 4 final chapters).

Tinsley: 3 May 1870

Sending reader's opinion, indicating the novel should not be published without some alteration.

Tinsley: 5 May 1870

Terms on which Tinsley would publish the novel, Hardy paying in advance a part (£75) of the expense.

---

[1] Tinsley's letters are now in the Bliss collection; Hardy's are widely scattered in public and private hands.

Tinsley: 9 May 1870

An edition means 500 copies.

Tinsley: 9 December 1870

Acknowledging receipt of the MS. of *Desperate Remedies*, revised and completed.

Tinsley: 19 December 1870

Agreeing to publish the novel on the terms mentioned previously, Tinsley's reader believing that with the alterations Hardy has made the book ought to sell. (See above, pp. 4–5.)

Hardy: Bockhampton, Dorchester, 20 December 1870

Recapitulating Tinsley's terms for clarification. (See above, p. 263.)

Tinsley: 21 December 1870

Further explanation of terms, which Hardy has misunderstood. If acceptable to publisher and author, the book is to be published within *four* months from the date of agreement.

1871

Tinsley: 10 January 1871

Receipt for £75, 'the whole of Mr. Hardy's risk in the expense of printing and publishing' *Desperate Remedies*.

Tinsley: 19 January 1871

Printers sending proof in a day or two.

[*Desperate Remedies* published, 25 March 1871.]

Hardy: 3 Wooperton Street, Weymouth, 7 June 1871

Sending extracts from reviews of *Desperate Remedies* and suggesting they be used in advertisements of the novel.

Hardy: St. Juliot Rectory, Boscastle, Cornwall, 3 October 1871,

Suggesting an extract from 'the very favourable review' of *Desperate Remedies* in the *Saturday Review*[1] be advertised and offering to make a money payment if customary.

---

[1] Published 30 September and almost certainly the work of Hardy's friend, H. M. Moule, who later reviewed *Under the Greenwood Tree* and *A Pair of Blue Eyes* in the same place.

Tinsley: 5 October 1871

Agreeing to use an extract from the *Saturday Review*'s notice in advertising *Desperate Remedies*, but fearing it has come too late to do the book any good because it is already offered in Smith & Sons' and Mudie's lists very cheap.

Hardy: St. Juliot Rectory, Boscastle, Cornwall, 20 October 1871

Inquiring 'as to the probable issue of the account between us in "Desperate Remedies"'. 'Early in the summer I began, and nearly finished, a little rural story, but owing to the representation of critic-friends who were taken with D.R., I relinquished that and have proceeded a little way with another, the essence of which is plot, *without crime*—but on the plan of D.R.'

Tinsley: 23 October 1871

A summary of the sales of *Desperate Remedies*—not quite 300 copies before the notice in the *Saturday Review*, some 76 at reduced rates since then. 'I am almost afraid you will not get all the money back you paid . . .'

1872

Hardy: 1 West Parade, Weymouth, 3 January 1872

Asking for an accounting in the publication of *Desperate Remedies*, 'as I have rather delayed the completion of my new MS. till the result of the other is clear.'

Tinsley: 5 January 1872

Only 80 copies of *Desperate Remedies* on hand and these likely to be disposed of in about a month.

Tinsley: 22 February 1872

Sending the publishing account of *Desperate Remedies*. 'There is little doubt that had the "Saturday Review" notice come earlier the book would have done much better.' (For the account, see above, facing p. 5.)

Hardy: Bockhampton, Dorchester, 13 March 1872

Acknowledging the account but reminding Tinsley that no payment had been received on the 10th as promised.

Tinsley: 19 March 1872

Sending money due on *Desperate Remedies* and inquiring about Hardy's next book. 'I hardly think you *should* be disheartened because the first book has not done well, but this you know best about.'

Hardy: 4 Celbridge Place, Westbourne Park, W., 20 March 1872

Acknowledging a cheque and promising to call in a few days.

Tinsley: 15 April 1872

'If you are my way any day I will tell you what I think of "Under the Greenwood Tree".'

Tinsley: 22 April 1872

Offering £30 for the copyright of *Under the Greenwood Tree*.

Hardy: 22 April 1872

Agreement for the sale of *Under the Greenwood Tree* 'for the sum of thirty pounds to be paid one month after publication.'

Hardy: Bockhampton, Dorchester, Thursday [? May 1872]

Directing that H. M. Moule be notified when copies of the book are sent to reviewers. 'I am promised that it will be at once asked for—before another member of the staff gets it.'[1]

[*Under the Greenwood Tree* published, early June 1872.]

Tinsley: 8 July 1872

Looking for a serial to commence in the September *Tinsleys' Magazine* and asking to read any portion of Hardy's new story that is ready.

Hardy: 4 Celbridge Place, London, 9 July 1872

Nothing ready 'for I understood when I last called that you were not so likely to require a story from me for the magazine as I had previously imagined. On looking over the MS. I find it must have a great deal of re-consideration.'

Hardy: 21 July 1872

Receipt for £30 for Tinsley's purchase of the copyright of *Under the Greenwood Tree*.

---

[1] Moule's review of *Under the Greenwood Tree* appeared in the *Saturday Review*, 28 September.

Hardy: 4 Celbridge Place, London, 27 July 1872

Recapitulating terms (£200) for the publication of *A Winning Tongue Had He* [*A Pair of Blue Eyes*] in *Tinsleys' Magazine* and in a three-volume edition and enclosing a sketch for the first plate.

[Serial publication of *A Pair of Blue Eyes* commenced in the September *Tinsleys' Magazine*, 15 August 1872.]

Hardy: St. Juliot Rectory, Boscastle, Cornwall, 30 August [1872]

Sending a sketch for the October illustration and the names and addresses of six friends who have promised to order the magazine if presented with the first number. The October instalment is ready and will be sent in another week.

W. Croft[1]: 3 September 1872

Asking for copy for the next number at once.

Hardy: St. Juliot Rectory, Boscastle, 7 September 1872

'MS. for October is in Robson's [the printer's] hands by this post. . . . I will do my best to let you have future MSS. by the first of each month.'

Hardy: Bockhampton, Dorchester, 2 October 1872

Suggesting some sentences from the *Saturday Review*'s notice of *Under the Greenwood Tree* might be used in advertising *Tinsleys' Magazine* while *A Pair of Blue Eyes* is appearing.

Tinsley: 4 October 1872

Agreeing to advertise *Under the Greenwood Tree* again, though he fears it is no use. £10 owing Hardy for half the continental reprint right just sold. 'I am longing to read the 3rd portion of "Blue Eyes" for I *shall* lose my reputation as a judge of good fiction if you don't do great things.' (See above, p. 8.)

1873

Hardy: Bockhampton, Dorchester, 12 March 1873

Sending the conclusion of *A Pair of Blue Eyes* and referring to payments.

---

[1] Accountant for Tinsley Brothers and virtual editor of their magazine.

APPENDIX I

Hardy: Bockhampton, 31 March [1873]

> Asking for proofs of the volumes, since 'I am going from this place early in May (according to present arrangements)', and inquiring as to the advisability of changing Knight's name to Knighton on account of the Knight case.

Tinsley: 17 April 1873

> Business details, bills in settlement, &c.

Hardy: Bockhampton, Dorchester, 19 April 1873

> Acknowledging acceptances. 'I will call when I come to London, though it will not be so early in the season as usual. I have an idea of going abroad for a short time. Shall I receive proofs in the book form of the portions of the story which have appeared in the Magazine? I hope so, for there are several amendments to be made in the early part of the tale. I want to give it the benefit of my latest judgment. I mention this because the printers are only as yet sending the part which has not appeared in the serial form.'

[*A Pair of Blue Eyes* published, late May 1873.]

Hardy: 4 Celbridge Place, Westbourne Park, 18 June [1873]

> Inquiring if a copy of *A Pair of Blue Eyes* has been sent to the *Spectator*. One of the editors implies it would be favourably considered. (Tinsley's reply scrawled across the letter—most copies just being sent out.)

Hardy: Bockhampton, Dorchester, 22 November 1873

> Would have written a story for *Tinsleys' Magazine* with pleasure, but his next [*Far from the Madding Crowd*] was promised to a friend who asked for it more than a year ago and is to appear (this in confidence) in the *Cornhill*.

Hardy: Bockhampton, Dorchester, 30 November 1873

> Expressing regret that Tinsley should consider it a breach of courtesy that he had not been informed sooner of Hardy's arrangements with the *Cornhill* (for the publication of *Far from the Madding Crowd*).

1874

Hardy: St. David's, Hook Road, Surbiton, 24 November 1874

Asking if Tinsley is willing to part with the copyright of *Under the Greenwood Tree*, 'the only one of my novels of which I did not retain the copyright, and . . . also my favorite one'.

1875

Hardy: St. David's, Surbiton, 3 January 1875

Inquiring if there is any sum Tinsley would take for the copyright of *Under the Greenwood Tree*. A collected edition of Hardy's stories is likely to be published.

Tinsley: 5 January 1875

Offering the copyright, stocks, and stereotype plates of *Under the Greenwood Tree* for £300. 'I don't think up to this time I have made a shilling out of the book, but that you will ("if you please") make a great name as a writer of fiction I am as sure of, as if you had made it.—I hope you will not think me impertinent but how you could have made such mistakes *in art* in a work so brim full of genius as "*The Madding Crowd*" is one of the things I cannot understand. I think your genius truer than Dickenses [*sic*] ever was, but you want a monitor more than the great Novelist ever did. Apologising for being so plain spoken I am . . .'

Hardy: St. David's, Hook Road, Surbiton, 20 January 1875

Expressing surprise at the sum named for the copyright, twice what Hardy was prepared to pay, and assuming it is an intimation Tinsley does not wish to part with it.

Tinsley: 22 October 1875

Announcing a plan to print 'a nice little illustrated edition of *Greenwood Tree*' and offering to correct bad printers' errors.

Hardy: West End Cottage, Swanage, 24 October 1875

'I have been looking into "Under the Greenwood Tree"—the 2 vol. Edition, which is the only one I have—and I find no serious misprints there, or anything that could be set right by slight changes such as you mention. But I do see many sentences that I should rewrite or revise . . .'

APPENDIX II

SIX LETTERS OF LESLIE STEPHEN AS EDITOR OF THE *CORNHILL* RELATING TO *FAR FROM THE MADDING CROWD*

Twenty-six letters of Leslie Stephen (1832–1904) remain among the Max Gate papers. Some of these (and several no longer extant) Hardy contributed to F. W. Maitland's *The Life and Letters of Leslie Stephen* (London, 1906). Others are quoted in the *Early Life* and the *Later Years*. Though the letters run from 1872 to 1899, it is apparent that the correspondence is very far from intact, and none of Hardy's letters (with a trifling exception or two) are known to survive. Stephen was much the finest critic Hardy encountered in his career as novelist and 'the man whose philosophy was to influence his own for many years, indeed, more than that of any other contemporary'. The following letters (largely unpublished) suggest a little of his role as editor and critic in the writing of *Far from the Madding Crowd*. They are printed here by kind permission of Mrs. Clive Bell and Mr. Adrian Stephen.

I

Smith, Elder & Co
15 Waterloo Place
London S.W.
30 November 1872

Dear Sir,

I hear from Mr Moule that I may address you as the author of "Under the Greenwood Tree".

I have lately read that story with very great pleasure indeed. I think the descriptions of country life admirable and indeed it is long since I have received more pleasure from a new writer.

It also occurred to me, and it is for this reason that I take the liberty of addressing you, that such writing would probably please the readers of the Cornhill Magazine as much as it has pleased me. "Under the Greenwood Tree" is of course not a magazine story. There is too little incident for such purposes; for, though I do not want a murder in every number, it is necessary to catch the attention of readers by some distinct and well arranged plot.

If you are, as I hope, writing anything more, I should be very glad to have the offer of it for our pages. I of course cannot say anything more definite at present; but I should be very glad to hear from you whether there is any probability of my receiving such an offer. If I can give you any further information on the subject, of course I shall be very happy to do so. I will only say now

336

that if any agreement could be made between us I have no doubt it would be satisfactory in a pecuniary point of view. Meanwhile

Believe me to be,

> Your's truly
> Leslie Stephen
> (Editor of the Cornhill Mag.)

I have not seen "Desperate Remedies" though I have heard it highly praised.

2

> 8. Southwell Gardens,
> South Kensington.
> 8 January 1874

My dear Mr Hardy

I am glad to congratulate you on the reception of your first number. Besides the gentle Spectator wh. thinks that you must be George Eliot because you know the names of the stars, several good judges have spoken to me very warmly of the Madding Crowd. Moreover the Spectator, though flighty in its head, has really a good deal of critical feeling—I always like to be praised by it—and indeed by other people!

I write, however, on another matter. As printed the February number takes 29 pages. This is rather long and I propose to end with chapter 8 i.e. on page 26; where I think there is a better break.

The March number will then have 4 pages added to it, and would have to end either with Chap XV, wh. would make 23 pages or with Chap XVI wh. would make 32 pages. I think, as at present advised, that the first break would be the best; but I might have to go on to the other. Now Chap XVI is rather a long one; and it would be convenient to me if there were some possible halting-place between the two extremes. Would it be possible to divide Chap XVI into two and if so would you make the necessary alteration? Or, if you please, put a mark where the division may come, if necessary.

The story comes out very well, I think, and I have no criticisms to make. In Chap X the paying scene is judiciously reduced and I think it is now satisfactory.

I hope you approved of the illustration.

> Your's very truly
> L. Stephen

Let me know when you are coming to town, according to promise.

3

> 8 Southwell Gardens
> 17 February 1874

My dear Mr Hardy,

I have read through your MS with very great pleasure; though I had seen most of it before. As you ask me for my opinion I will say frankly that I think the sheepshearing rather long for the present purpose. When the novel appears as a whole, it may very well come in in its present form. For periodical purposes, I think it rather delays the action unnecessarily. What I should be inclined to do would be simply to omit the chapter headed the "shearing supper" and to add a few paragraphs to the succeeding or preceding, just explaining that there has been a supper. The chapter on the "Great Barn" and that called "A merry Mist" seem to me to be excellent and I would not omit them or shorten them. The other seems to me the least good of the three—and therefore the best to abridge. I don't know whether anything turns on the bailiff's story; but I don't think it necessary.

I shall take the MS to Smith and Elder's today and will tell them that they will hear from you. Please write to them (to S.E & Co 15 Waterloo Place S.W.) and say whether the whole is to be printed as it stands; or whether the chapter I mention is to be omitted; or whether you would like to have the MS again to alter previously to printing. Do whichever your judgement commends.

I have heard of the story from many people and have only heard one opinion of its merits, wh. coincides with my own. As it goes on and gets more into the action, I am sure that the opinion will be higher still. In short, I think you have every reason to be satisfied and encouraged.

The Spectator's instincts are better than its reasons. It generally recognizes a good thing; but almost always talks nonsense about the causes of its admiration. As for the supposed affinity to George Eliot, it consists, I think, simply in this that you have both treated rustics of the farming class in a humorous manner—Mrs Poyser would be at home I think, in Weatherbury—but you need not be afraid of such criticisms. You are original and can stand on your own legs.

Your's very truly
Leslie Stephen.

I have said frankly what I thought; but I hope you will not attach too much importance to my criticisms—Do exactly what you think right—I shall be content. Very likely, it will be best for you to see the whole in print before acting; if so, let it go to the press as it stands.

4

8. Southwell Gardens,
South Kensington.
12 March 1874

My dear Mr Hardy

I have read your proofs as corrected and I think that everything now runs very smoothly.

The story improves as it goes on and I hear nothing but good of it.

I have ventured to leave out a line or two in the last batch of proofs from an excessive prudery of wh. I am ashamed; but one is forced to be absurdly particular. May I suggest that Troy's seduction of the young woman will require to be treated in a gingerly fashion, when, as I suppose must be the case, he comes to be exposed to his wife? I mean that the thing must be stated but that the words must be careful—excuse this wretched shred of concession to popular stupidity; but I am a slave.

I hope to see you soon.

Yours in haste
L. Stephen

5

The Cornhill Magazine
13 April 1874

My dear Mr Hardy,

I have read the new instalment of the Madding Crowd with great pleasure—I think the story grows in interest and is equally vigorous in description. You need not be afraid of [   ] criticism [*half page torn away*] part of the story; wh., however, must be prefaced by the general remark that I object as editor, not as critic, i.e. in the interest of a stupid public, not from my own taste.

I think that the reference to the cause of Fanny's death is unnecessarily emphasized. I should, I think, omit all reference to it except just enough to indicate the true state of the case; and especially a conversation between your heroine and her maid, wh. is a little unpleasant. I have some doubts whether the baby is necessary at all and whether it would not be sufficient for Bathsheba to open the coffin in order to identify the dead woman with the person she met on the road. This is a point wh. you can consider. It certainly rather injures the story, and perhaps if the omission were made it might be restored on republication. But I am rather necessarily anxious to be on the safe side; and should somehow be glad to omit the baby.

However, these changes can be easily made when the story is in type and I shall send it to the printers now; and ask you to do what is necessary to the proofs.

We can talk about it when we meet. Meanwhile I am more than satisfied in all other respects.

I shall be very glad to see you when you come to town. Can you dine with us on Friday the 24th at ¼ to 8? If so, my wife bids me say that she will be delighted to see you. You will find me at home any morning.

Your's very truly
L. Stephen

6

Englefield Green, Staines.
25 August 1874[1]

My dear Mr Hardy,

I will speak about the November proof tomorrow. I saw nothing to alter, unless that it seemed to me in one or two cases that your rustics—specially Oak—speak rather too good English towards the end. They seem to drop the dialect a little. But of this you are the best judge.

You have, I am sure, no cause to be nervous about the book in any way.

Yours in haste—
L. Stephen

[1] The heading has been added by Hardy, a portion of the letter having been cut away.

A NOTE ON TILLOTSON & SON AND
THEIR NEWSPAPER FICTION BUREAU[1]

Messrs. Tillotson & Son of Bolton, during Hardy's years as a writer of fiction, were the proprietors of a series of Lancashire weekly newspapers, chief of which was the *Bolton Weekly Journal*. With these newspapers in mind the head of the firm, W. F. Tillotson (1844–89), founded in 1873 a syndicated fiction business. This Newspaper Fiction Bureau, as it came to be called, quickly outgrew the little group of Lancashire papers, and in the 80's and 90's Tillotson's were buying serial rights from the most popular authors of the day and selling their stories to provincial newspapers, and occasionally magazines, throughout England and abroad. By the turn of the century they were publishing annually in this fashion 'about thirty new Serial Stories and over 300 Short Stories of various lengths.'[2] While the larger English, Scottish, and Irish weekly newspapers took the stories in proof form, smaller papers that could hardly afford hand setting of such material and were often satisfied with the reissue rights were supplied with it in stereotype, and this was one basis of Tillotson's success. Further, these provincial papers 'though not individually able to pay so high a price as a national paper, had circulations which did not conflict with one another. Syndication in a number of such papers might thus yield an aggregate sum considerably higher than any magazine could afford to pay.'[3] The business was an original and significant development in the publication of fiction, creating and supplying a vast new group of readers. It suffered in the end by the appearance of literary agents like A. P. Watt and the growth of monthly magazines, the better authors caring less and less to write for the newspaper market, but in the 80's Tillotson's offered profitable opportunities and dominated a considerable field. Their list was a good one and included Wilkie Collins, Charles Reade, and Miss Braddon, and later Kipling, Barrie, Conan Doyle, and Wells.

Tillotson's had already approached Hardy several times, when in July

[1] I am indebted for material in this note to the kindness of Mr. Fred L. Tillotson, a son of W. F. Tillotson and a Director of the present firm.

[2] *The Progress of Newspapers in the Nineteenth Century* [1901], quoted by Graham Pollard, 'Serial Fiction', in *New Paths in Book Collecting* (London, 1934), p. 267.

[3] Graham Pollard, 'Novels in Newspapers', *The Review of English Studies*, January 1942, p. 73.

1881 he agreed to provide them with a Christmas story. He sold them in all the serial rights to four short stories and one novel:[1]

'Benighted Travellers' ('The Honourable Laura'): 1881
'A Mere Interlude': 1885
'Alicia's Diary': 1887
[*Too Late Beloved* (*Tess of the d'Urbervilles*): 1889
 The contract for this was subsequently cancelled, see above, pp. 71–73.]
'The Melancholy Hussar': 1890
The Pursuit of the Well-Beloved: 1892

Most of these titles were widely printed and reprinted for some years, 'Benighted Travellers' even after Hardy had collected the story in *A Group of Noble Dames*. Every printing was carefully entered with dates in Tillotson's ledger, and for the purposes of this bibliography the original ledger has been examined and the first printing of each story ascertained. In the case of simultaneous publication in a number of papers, the most important has been chosen.[2]

Hardy's relations with Tillotson's were of no very intimate nature, but he had met W. F. Tillotson in London and wrote at his death in 1889 that he had been 'much struck with the straightforward sincerity of his character.' He could hardly have failed to appreciate, too, the generosity of the firm later in that same year in the vexed business of *Too Late Beloved*.

---

[1] 'A Changed Man' in the *Sphere*, 21 and 28 April 1900, is described as 'Copyrighted by Tillotson & Son in the U.S.A.' but is not listed in Tillotson's ledger.

[2] This ledger is now in the possession of Newspaper Features Ltd., which bought Tillotson's Newspaper Fiction Bureau in 1935. In studying it I was much assisted by Mr. H. A. Taylor, one of the Directors.

A NOTE ON THE HON. MRS. ARTHUR HENNIKER

I. HER FRIENDSHIP WITH HARDY

The carefully inconspicuous place given the Hon. Mrs. Arthur Henniker in *The Later Years of Thomas Hardy* seems to warrant some account of her life and more particularly her friendship with Hardy. It was a friendship that meant much to him at a dark and embittered time and lends meaning to his last novel and a number of his poems. Her own novels are quite forgotten today, but in Hardy's biography she deserves to be remembered.

Mrs. Henniker was the Hon. Florence Ellen Hungerford Milnes. She was born in 1855, second of the three children of Richard Monckton Milnes, first Lord Houghton, the friend of Tennyson and the editor of Keats. In 1882 she was married to the Hon. Arthur Henry Henniker-Major, youngest son of the fourth Lord Henniker, almost on the eve of his departure in the Egyptian Expedition. He was exactly her own age, a Lieutenant in the Coldstream Guards, the ideal guardsman, an able and popular soldier before whom lay a successful career, notable service in the Boer War, and the rewards of a Major-Generalcy and the C.B.

It was nine years after her marriage that Mrs. Henniker began her career as novelist with the publication of *Sir George* (1891). She had obviously inherited something of her father's literary tastes, and the atmosphere of his houses, Fryston and Upper Brook Street, and the great circle of his friends entertained there did much to make her a writer. At the age of seven she had been busy with poetry, and her father wrote to a friend, 'The second little girl has developed into a verse-writer of a very curious ability. She began theologically and wrote hymns, which I soon checked on observing that she put together words and sentences out of the sacred verse she knew; and set her to write about things she saw and observed. What she now produces is very like the verse of William Blake, and containing many images that she could never have read of. She cannot write, but she dictates them to her elder sister, who is astonished at the phenomenon. We, of course, do not let her see that it is anything surprising; and the chances are that it goes off as she gets older and knows more. The lyrical faculty in men and nations seems to belong to a childish condition of mind, and to disappear with experience and knowledge.'[1] Thirty years later, with 'experience and knowledge', Mrs. Henniker turned novelist. *Sir George* was followed by five other novels, *Bid Me Good-bye* (1892), *Foiled* (1893), *Sowing the Sand* (1898), *Our Fatal Shadows* (1907), and *Second Fiddle* (1912); three collections of short stories, *Outlines* (1894), *In Scarlet and Grey* (1896), and *Contrasts* (1903); and at least one play, a 4-act comedy, *The Courage of Silence*, produced with little success in 1905. Mrs. Henniker was, not unlike her father, a gifted amateur.[2] She wrote fluently and with some skill of the world she knew, the aristocratic world of officers and statesmen in which she lived, and a strain of humour and irony saved her work from the sentimentality of the society novelist. Her earlier books were indulgently reviewed, the later ones ignored. Two at least, *Sir George* and *In Scarlet and Grey*, seem to have achieved a second edition. Gladstone (who had known her father) wrote to her that he recognized 'the proofs of real power' in her first novel, and the *Pall Mall Gazette*, in a phrase that may fairly stand, called her stories, 'the work of a keen and sympathetic observer of life, endowed with a simple and graphic literary style.'

It does not appear that Hardy really knew Mrs. Henniker until 1893. He had met her father in London in the early 80's and had been invited to Fryston, though he could not go. Indeed, Lord Houghton had sought him out. He had once remarked to his biographer, 'I think I know every man of letters now whom I want to know, except one', and the exception was Hardy, 'for whom he felt a great admiration.'[3] That admiration his daughter shared and, having some slight acquaintance with Mrs. Hardy (and possibly Hardy himself), she asked the two to Dublin for Whitsuntide in 1893, an invitation that the death of Hardy's father had postponed from the year before. She was then staying at the Viceregal Lodge as hostess for her younger brother, the second Lord Houghton, Lord Lieutenant of Ireland (later Marquess of Crewe). The details of that Whitsun visit, 19–25 May, are given from Hardy's diary in the *Later Years* (pp. 18–20), but there is little suggestion in the commonplace entries of the deep and immediate impression Mrs. Henniker made on him. She

[1] Milnes to C. J. MacCarthy, 24 October 1862. T. Wemyss Reid, *The Life, Letters, and Friendships of Richard Monckton Milnes, First Lord Houghton* (2 vols., London, 1890), ii. 85–86.
[2] This in spite of the fact that she was elected President of the Society of Women Journalists in 1896.
[3] Reid, op. cit. ii. 368.

was thirty-eight at the time, a woman of warm sympathies and unfailing charm, with something of those 'bland-smiling, semi-quizzical, affectionate, high-bred' qualities Carlyle had seen in her father. She had published three novels with some success; her interests were literary and humanitarian;[1] save for delicate health she might already have formed the salon for which she was so surely fitted. Hardy was at work on *Jude the Obscure*, and his own career as novelist was drawing to a close. His married life no longer held the happiness of the 'Sturminster Newton idyll' of fifteen years before, and Mrs. Hardy's growing eccentricities were painfully manifest in this very visit. One memorable word sufficed for Hardy's first impression of Mrs. Henniker. 'A charming, *intuitive* woman apparently', he wrote in his diary.

Their friendship ripened quickly. Back in London, a fortnight after the Dublin visit, Hardy records they met again and made a theatre party at *The Master Builder* with Sir Gerald and Lady Fitzgerald, Mrs. Henniker's older sister. But the further references to Mrs. Henniker in the *Later Years* are very few, for the most part perfunctory glimpses of her on Dorset visits a quarter of a century later, and we are left to piece out the story for ourselves. The two began a vigorous correspondence,[2] and there were frequent meetings in London or the country, Mrs. Henniker coming from Southsea where she was living for a day at Winchester or Salisbury, 'That journey of one day a week'. In the first months of their friendship Hardy inscribed copies of his books to her, *Tess* on 7 June, *A Laodicean* in July, *Desperate Remedies* in September. Mrs. Henniker in turn gave him many of the little pocket texts he liked to carry on his walks. In October they collaborated

---

[1] Her friend Lady Ilchester described her to me as having 'a wonderful tenderness for frail and delicate persons. She had almost a passion for the "under dog" in every sense of the word and she deeply resented the cruelties practised on animals in the cause of vivisection, and was morbidly conscious of any ill treatment of dumb creatures.' The sentence might describe Hardy himself.

[2] Hardy's letters to Mrs. Henniker were returned at her death in 1923 and are now with his papers in the Dorset County Museum. She had destroyed some of the earlier letters, and we can hardly assume that the correspondence, even as it was returned to Max Gate, is intact today. The letters range from 3 June 1893 to 29 May 1922 and are particularly frequent in the year 1893. Some bear the unusual signature 'Tom H.' Three of them have been published in part (see *Later Years*, pp. 21–22, 191–2, and W. R. Rutland, *Thomas Hardy*, London and Glasgow, 1938, pp. 107–8). A few of Mrs. Henniker's letters, 1910–22, are also among the Max Gate papers. Barrie read a portion of the correspondence when Mrs. Hardy was considering its publication and made some illuminating comments on it. He very shrewdly remarked, 'I rather grudge her being a writer at all, and indeed I believe he did also.' Barrie to Mrs. Hardy, 18 March 1928 (*Letters of J. M. Barrie*, ed. Viola Meynell, London, 1942, pp. 153–4).

in the writing of 'The Spectre of the Real' (see below), and in December Mrs. Henniker dedicated her first collection of short stories, *Outlines* (1894), 'To my friend Thomas Hardy'.[1] The collaboration and the dedication led critics to suppose Mrs. Henniker a disciple of Hardy's, which in some respects she was. He helped her tirelessly with her literary work, reading and criticizing what she wrote. In this same December Hardy urged Mrs. Henniker's work on Clement Shorter, then editor of the *English Illustrated Magazine* (he printed her story 'Bad and Worthless' in April 1894), and the next year wrote for Shorter an anonymous sketch of her in the *Illustrated London News*. Here, in impersonal terms, he suggested that 'her note of individuality, her own personal and peculiar way of looking at life, without which neither aristocrat nor democrat, fair woman nor foul, has any right to take a stand before the public as author, may be called that of emotional imaginativeness, lightened by a quick sense of the odd, and by touches of observation lying midway between wit and humour.'[2]

The friendship had its artificial side, it was in some ways another case of 'The Poor Man and the Lady', but these details give almost no idea of the impression Mrs. Henniker had made on Hardy. There are evidences of that impression, however, in *Jude the Obscure*, which he was writing in August 1893 and well on through the next year. Mrs. Hardy is my authority for the statement that Sue Bridehead was in part drawn from Mrs. Henniker. Hardy wrote to Gosse of Sue that she was 'a type of woman which has always had an attraction for me, but the difficulty of drawing the type has kept me from attempting it till now.'[3] There are more personal evidences in the poetry. Here the marks of a moving experience are discernible. The gravings, in his phrase, were deep, 'tragic, gruesome, gray.' No poem bears Mrs. Henniker's name, but a date in the 90's, particularly 1893, is often a key. 'A Broken Appointment' (the scene of which was the British Museum) and 'A Thunderstorm in Town' are both to be associated with Mrs. Henniker on Mrs. Hardy's express statement. Beyond these the following are significant: 'At an Inn' (in Winchester), 'In Death Divided', 'He Wonders about Himself', 'The Coming of the End' (stanza 4), 'The Month's Calendar', 'Last Love-Word', 'Alike and Unlike', and possibly

---

[1] The frontispiece, a photogravure portrait, shows Mrs. Henniker as she was at this time.

[2] *The Illustrated London News*, 18 August 1894, p. 195.

[3] *Later Years*, p. 42.

'The Recalcitrants' and 'Come not; yet Come!'[1] Most poignant of all is 'The Division', and it is interesting that Mrs. Henniker quotes (with no identification) two stanzas of this poem in her novel *Second Fiddle* (1912). These verses—and I think there are others—suggest 'a time-torn man' and the sympathy of a 'rare fair woman', an impossible love which she may hardly have guessed, the realization of a division 'more than distance, Dear, or rain, And longer than the years', and then 'it came to an end.' It had come to an end by December 1896 when Hardy wrote in 'Wessex Heights',

> As for one rare fair woman, I am now but a thought of hers,
> I enter her mind and another thought succeeds me that she prefers;
> Yet my love for her in its fulness she herself even did not know;
> Well, time cures hearts of tenderness, and now I can let her go.

Hardy's warm friendship for Mrs. Henniker continued to the end of her life. They exchanged occasional visits and sent each other their new books. In 1904 Mrs. Henniker brought with her to Max Gate her young friend Florence Emily Dugdale, who ten years later became the second Mrs. Hardy. At General Henniker's death in 1912 Hardy wrote some memorial verses on the 'laurelled soldier' for a little volume of tributes Mrs. Henniker collected (see above, pp. 315–16). When she died, 4 April 1923, he wrote in his diary, 'After a friendship of 30 years!' It was thirty years, almost to the month, since they had met in the Viceregal Lodge at Dublin, 'When that first look and touch, Love, doomed us two!'

2. THE WRITING OF 'THE SPECTRE OF THE REAL'

It is not without irony that such a friendship should have for sole monument, 'The Spectre of the Real'. Hardy and Mrs. Henniker undertook to collaborate in the writing of a short story in the autumn of 1893, not six months after their Dublin meeting. Quite properly the two agreed to keep their respective shares in it a secret to themselves, and no MS. is known to have survived. From Hardy's letters, however, and from the story itself, it is not difficult to reconstruct their procedure. The work was largely Hardy's. The story has familiar features, the clandestine romance and marriage of a 'noble lady' and a poor officer, the return of the vanished husband on the eve of his wife's remarriage, the removal of a troublesome character by drowning in a water-meadow. The style is Hardy's, and the

---

[1] MS. and other evidence for some of these ascriptions is presented above, under individual titles.

repellent details are reminiscent of *A Group of Noble Dames*. Indeed, one could easily imagine the story as discarded from that collection. Mrs. Henniker had a hand in constructing the plot and in revising the text. Beyond that her contribution was limited to a few descriptive passages. In short the collaboration consisted in Hardy's discussing the outlines of his story with Mrs. Henniker and incorporating in the finished work some brief paragraphs she had written.

Several of Hardy's letters to her at this time throw a good deal of light on the work. It had been laid aside while he finished collecting the stories for *Life's Little Ironies*, and he wrote, 22 October 1893, 'I could not take the "Desire" in hand till today, having been hunting up the tales I told you of ("Two Ambitions" being one of them).[1] They are now fastened together to be dispatched to the publisher, and I turn to the "Desire"— which by the bye, is the "Desire" no longer.—For I have planned to carry out Ending II—since you like it so much better: I feel I ought not to force the other upon you—wh. is too uncompromising for one of the pretty sex to have a hand in. The question now is, what shall we call it?—"The ressurection [*sic*] of a Love"?' Again, three days later, 'A word as to our story: in working it out I find it may possibly be necessary to effect a compromise between the two endings: for on no account must it end weakly.' And finally he wrote, 28 October:

I must let you know that the story is finished virtually, and that the MS. was sent early this morning to Miss Tigan. I have told her to return me the original (in case I should want to insert a little more detail from it) and to send to you direct the type-written copy. Will you please read it from the beginning (*without* glancing first at the end!) so as to get the intended effect, and judge of its strength or weakness. It is, as you wished, very tragic; a modified form of Ending II—which I think better than any we have thought of before. If anything in it is what you don't like please tell me quite freely—and it shall be modified. As I said last time, all the wickedness (if it has any) will be laid on my unfortunate head, while all the tender and proper parts will be attributed to you. Without wishing to make you promise, I suggest that we keep it a secret to our two selves which is my work and which yours. We may be amusingly bothered by friends and others to confess.

In reading it over, particularly the bride's doings in the morning from dawn till the wedding-hour, please insert in pencil any details that I have omitted, and that would only be known to a woman. I may not be quite correct in what

---

[1] The drowning in the water-meadow in 'The Spectre of the Real' is highly reminiscent of a similar episode in 'A Tragedy of Two Ambitions'.

I have hastily written, never having had the pleasure of being a bride-elect myself. If you will then send me the copy I will go through it for final corrections, and send it off.

The ending, good or bad, has the merit of being in exact keeping with Lord P.'s character. . . . I will send you back the pages of detail omitted, if you wd. like to have them, as they may be useful. You will *quite* understand that they were not omitted because they weren't good; but because the scale of the story was too small to admit them without injury to the proportions of the whole. I refer particularly to the description of the pool, and the bird tracks; which I *much* wished to retain.[1]

I did not mean to flow over into another sheet with literary affairs, but there are one or two things more to say under that head. One is the title. Our old title was in itself rather good, but as it does not quite apply, I have provisionally substituted "The Spectre of the Real".—"The Looming of the Real" is perhaps almost better. I have also thought of "A passion and after": "To-day's kiss and yesterday's".—"Husband's Corpse and husband's kiss", "A shattering of Ideals". When you have read the modifications you will be able to choose; or suggest.

The finishing touches were given the 'weird story' in London in December, but it was almost a year before it was printed. Then it appeared, as the leading contribution and with five illustrations by H. R. Millar, in the special Winter Number of Jerome K. Jerome's weekly, *To-Day*, 17 November 1894. Mrs. Henniker collected it two years later in her volume *In Scarlet and Grey* (London, 1896). This final text shows a number of verbal alterations and a considerable improvement in the taste of several passages (notably at the end of Chap. VI and the beginning of Chap. VII). The story, nevertheless, was not well received. Mrs. Henniker's own work, which made up the bulk of the volume, was considered decidedly superior, and she was not commended for the collaborator she had chosen. The *Academy* found the story 'marred by those deflections from good taste which seem to have become characteristic of Mr. Hardy's later art.'[2] The *Athenaeum* thought it 'might well have been omitted',[3] and the *Spectator* called it 'undoubtedly very effective and indeed gruesome, but also superfluously repulsive' and concluded, 'Mr. Thomas Hardy, in his later phases, is hardly a judicious literary counsellor.'[4] All this was three years after the story had been written. Poor as it was, it was being read, it must be recalled, in the shadow of *Jude the Obscure* and all the obloquy that attended that novel.[5]

[1] This passage was apparently retained after all. See *In Scarlet and Grey*, p. 191.
[2] *The Academy*, 24 October 1896, p. 305.
[3] *The Athenaeum*, 26 September 1896, p. 417.
[4] *The Spectator*, 31 October 1896, p. 593.
[5] See *Jude the Obscure*, Preface, p. ix.

APPENDIX V

A NOTE ON THE PRIVATELY PRINTED PAMPHLETS OF CLEMENT SHORTER AND MRS. HARDY

Clement King Shorter (1857–1926) was a journalist, critic, and industrious collector of books and MSS. As editor of the *Illustrated London News* and the *English Illustrated Magazine* in the 90's and later of the *Sphere* and the *Tatler*, he printed a good deal of Hardy's work in prose and verse and claimed his acquaintance. There was no intimacy, however, between the two men, and at no time did Shorter enjoy Hardy's confidence. On a visit to Max Gate in 1908 he had asked to see Hardy's MSS. and, finding them unbound and unprotected, insisted on carrying them off to a binder and supervising the work for Hardy. When they were returned, Shorter would accept no reimbursement (and the MSS. though indifferently bound were numerous) but asked only to be allowed to choose one for his own—and chose, with some acumen, *The Return of the Native*. Importunate and acquisitive as he was, he showered Hardy with requests for MSS. and inscriptions. It was inevitable that he should wish to include Hardy's work in the series of privately printed pamphlets, 'A Bookman's Hobby', he issued from time to time in the manner of his friend and fellow-collector, T. J. Wise. These pamphlets were printed by Eyre & Spottiswoode, printers of the *Sphere*. They were undistinguished, even ugly, in format, and the limitation of issue was by no means rigidly adhered to. The colophon was so designed that copies could be numbered and signed or not as Shorter chose and an edition thus easily be doubled. The printers inform me that their records covering these years have been destroyed, and the actual size of each edition cannot be discovered. That there were generous over-printings is certain. Between 1914 and 1916 Shorter printed six such pamphlets of Hardy material.

In 1916 Sydney Cockerell, who had already assisted Hardy in the distributing of his MSS. among various public collections and had consented to act as his literary executor, pointed out that Shorter had very evidently found his ventures profitable and suggested that if material was to be printed in this way at all it might better be done by Hardy himself or his wife.[1] When, therefore, Shorter wrote for permission to reprint 'To

---

[1] The first proof of Mrs. Hardy's first pamphlet, 'To Shakespeare after Three Hundred Years', shows 'printed for the Author' in the colophon altered in Hardy's hand to '. . . Florence Emily Hardy'.

Shakespeare after Three Hundred Years' (his fourth such request in less than six months), Hardy replied, 6 May 1916, 'When I see you I will tell you why I cannot very well agree to a reprint of the Shakespeare poem. Apart from that, I fancy you are getting off the track in these private printings. Surely they are meant to be curiosities which for some reason have been or can be printed in no other form—not productions that the authors issue to the public in the ordinary way, as I shall probably do with this one if I bring out another volume of verses.' The poem was printed instead by Mrs. Hardy, and with it she began the private printing, particularly of poetry, which continued at irregular intervals virtually to the end of her life.

Except for a few in later years, hastily done for convenience in Dorchester by the local printer, Henry Ling, Mrs. Hardy's pamphlets were largely printed at the Chiswick Press in a handsome format, the details overseen by Sydney Cockerell.[1] The proofs were corrected, during his lifetime, by Hardy himself, and the pamphlets must be regarded in every way as authoritative. The limitations of issue were scrupulously observed, the form of the colophon requiring a numeral (and Mrs. Hardy's initials) for completion. Copies (of the earlier pamphlets, at least) were sent to the British Museum, the Bodleian, and the University Library, Cambridge; a small number were marketed through a London bookseller; the rest were sent as gifts to friends, though many copies of several of the later pamphlets remained undistributed at Mrs. Hardy's death. It was Hardy's custom, though not an invariable one, to sign and date the first and last copies of each issue.

There is a complete file of both Shorter's and Mrs. Hardy's pamphlets, copies formerly at Max Gate, in the Dorset County Museum.

[1] There are many proofs in his possession. The more important have been referred to under individual titles.

APPENDIX VI

A NOTE ON THE HARDY PLAYERS, WITH
A LIST OF THEIR PRODUCTIONS

From 1908 onwards the Dorchester Debating and Dramatic Society, later (1916) 'The Hardy Players', produced a series of dramatizations of the Wessex novels. These were amateur performances, intended primarily for local audiences. With a few notable exceptions, such as *The Famous Tragedy of the Queen of Cornwall* and *Tess of the d'Urbervilles*, the plays were not the work of Hardy himself. He did assist A. H. Evans and later T. H. Tilley with scenarios, snatches of dialogue, and suggestions, however, and followed rehearsals with considerable interest.[1] The programmes for the Dorchester, Weymouth, and London performances, the latter sponsored by the Society of Dorset Men in London, were frequently illustrated with Dorset views, scenes from the plays, music, &c., and Hardy occasionally read the proofs. The chief productions were:

1908

The Trumpet-Major by A. H. Evans
Dorchester, 18–19 November 1908

This dramatization followed on the success of a single scene, the party at Overcombe Mill, introduced as a dramatic and musical finale to a lecture by A. M. Broadley, 'Napoleon and the Invasion of England', at Dorchester, 4 February 1908. Hardy himself, as he wrote to Harold Child at the time, provided 'a rough idea of how the three remaining acts should be arranged'. Notices of the production were reprinted in pamphlet form as a 'Souvenir'. In a revised version the play was repeated at Dorchester, 27–28 November 1912, and in London, 5 December 1912. See *Later Years*, p. 154.

1909

Far from the Madding Crowd by A. H. Evans
Dorchester, 17–18 November 1909

[1]From unused notes among the Max Gate papers, detailed suggestions written out for Tilley, it appears that Hardy had studied the possibilities of 'The Romantic Adventures of a Milkmaid' and *The Mayor of Casterbridge* as well. See also *Later Years*, pp. 248–9.

London, 24 November 1909
Weymouth, 7–8 February 1910
See *Later Years*, p. 140.

1910

The Mellstock Quire (adapted from *Under the Greenwood Tree*) by A. H. Evans
Dorchester, 16–17 November 1910
London, 1 December 1910
Weymouth, 9 February 1911
See *Later Years*, p. 147. There were subsequent performances at Dorchester, 31 January 1918, and Sturminster Newton, 9 June 1921 (see *Later Years*, pp. 184–5, 222).

1911

The Three Wayfarers and *The Distracted Preacher* by A. H. Evans
Dorchester, 15–16 November 1911
London, 27 November 1911
Weymouth, 15 December 1911
See above, pp. 78 ff., and *Later Years*, p. 150. 'The Distracted Preacher' was a good deal altered and passages from *The Dynasts* introduced at Hardy's suggestion. There is a special 'Note on the Story' by Hardy in the programme (see above, pp. 314–15).

1913

The Woodlanders by A. H. Evans
Dorchester, 19–20 November 1913
London, 8 December 1913
Weymouth, 22 January 1914
See *Later Years*, p. 159. An earlier attempt by J. T. Grein to adapt this novel for the stage much interested Hardy (see *Early Life*, p. 289).

1916

Wessex Scenes from The Dynasts
Weymouth, 22 June 1916
Dorchester, 6–7 December 1916
See above, p. 319, and *Later Years*, pp. 171–2, 174. Hardy himself made up this 'patchwork' as he called it. The Prologue and Epilogue

written for Granville-Barker's production in 1914 are reprinted in the programme, of which there was a special (Dorchester) issue of 12 copies signed by Hardy. Some country scenes from *The Dynasts* had been acted by the Society as early as April 1908 (see *Later Years*, p. 131).

1920

The Return of the Native by T. H. Tilley
  Dorchester, 17–18 November 1920
  London, 27 January 1921
  See *Later Years*, p. 215. Hardy provided no assistance beyond the words of the mumming play (see above, pp. 212 f.).

1922

A Desperate Remedy by T. H. Tilley
  Dorchester, 15–17 November 1922
  London, 21 November 1922

1923

The Famous Tragedy of the Queen of Cornwall, O Jan! O Jan! O Jan!, and *The Play of St. George* (in a version by T. H. Tilley)
  Dorchester, 28–30 November 1923
  London, 21 February 1924 (with *An Old-time Rustic Wedding* by T. H. Tilley, from *Under the Greenwood Tree*, substituted for *The Play of St. George*)
  See above, pp. 227 ff., and *Later Years*, pp. 236–7. *O Jan! O Jan! O Jan!* was described as 'A Recension of a Wessex Folk-Piece by Thomas Hardy From memories of the Piece as played in his childhood, at his father's house, about 1844.' This was never printed. See *Friends of a Lifetime*, pp. 291–2. The *Dorset County Chronicle* notice (29 November) of the production was reprinted in a separate pamphlet.

1924

Tess of the d'Urbervilles
  Dorchester, 26–29 November 1924
  Weymouth, 11 December 1924
  See above, pp. 77–78, and *Later Years*, p. 240. There was a special 'First Edition' of the programme limited to 25 numbered copies.

INDEX

Principal page references are printed in italic type.

INDEX

'In Childbed', 145.
'In Church', 164.
'In Death Divided', *162*, 186, 345.
'In Front of the Landscape', *160*, 184.
'In Her Precincts', 197, *198*.
'In St. Paul's a While Ago' ('In St. Paul's: 1869'), 236.
In Scarlet and Grey. See under Henniker, Florence.
'In Sherborne Abbey', 239.
'In Tenebris' I, 116.
'In Tenebris' II, *116*, 186.
'In Tenebris' III, 116.
'In the British Museum', 168.
'In the Cemetery', 164.
'In the Crypted Way.' *See* 'In the Vaulted Way'.
'In the Days of Crinoline', 169.
'In the Evening', 245–6.
'In the Garden', 204.
'In the Marquee', 256.
'In the Matter of an Intent.' *See* 'Philosophical Fantasy, A'.
'In the Mind's Eye', *142*, 149, 182.
'In the Moonlight', *165*, 184.
'In the Night she Came', 142.
'In the Nuptial Chamber', 164.
'In the Old Theatre, Fiesole', 110.
'In the Restaurant', 165.
'In the Room of the Bride-Elect', 164.
'In the Servants' Quarters', 168.
'In the Seventies', 196.
'In the Small Hours', 222.
'In the Street', 238.
'In the Study', 164.
'In the Time of War and Tumults.' *See* 'In Time of Wars and Tumults'.
'In the Vaulted Way', *142*, 149.
'In Time of Slaughter.' *See* 'Quid Hic Agis ?'
'In Time of "the Breaking of Nations" ', *176*, 186, 206.
'In Time of Wars and Tumults', 205–6.
'In Vision I Roamed', 97.
'In Weatherbury Stocks', 258.
'Inconsistent, The', 113.
Independent, The, 63, 299–300.
Indiscretion in the Life of an Heiress, An, 274–6.

'Inquiry, An', 239; *see also* 'Dream Question, A'.
'Inquiry, The', 144.
'Inscription, The', 225.
'Inscriptions for a Peal of Eight Bells', 243.
'Interloper, The', *200*, 202, 204.
'Interlopers at the Knap', 58, *59*.
International Disarmament (note), 272.
'Intra Sepulchrum', 225.
'Intruder, The.' *See* 'Waiting Supper, The'.
'Invasion', 318.
Isbister, W., 32–34.
'It Never Looks like Summer', 202.
'Ivy-Wife, The', 101.

James, Henry, 54 n. 2, 111, 192.
'January Night. 1879, A', 197.
Jerome, Jerome K., 348.
Jeune, Sir Francis, 85.
Jeune, Mrs. Francis (later Lady Jeune and Lady St. Helier), 59, 71, 73, 104, 123, 209.
'Jezreel', *209–10*, 216.
'Jingle on the Times, A', 192–3.
'Jog-trot Pair, A', 216.
'John and Jane', 140.
John Keats Memorial Volume, The, 216.
John o' London's Weekly, 70, 322.
John Rylands Library, 83.
Johnson, E. Borough, 69–70.
Johnson, Lionel, *The Art of Thomas Hardy*, vii, 11 n., 103, 103 n. 2, 295, 297.
Jonson, Ben, 153.
Jordon Hill, 113.
Journal of the English Folk Dance Society, 323.
'Joys of Memory', 195.
'Jubilate', 203.
'Jubilee of a Magazine, The', *170*, 317.
Jude the Obscure, 77, *86–91*, 95, 122, 168, 266, 304, 344–5, 348; collected editions, 279, 282, 287; letters defending, 269–70, 305; poems reminiscent of, 203, 205, 254, 255.
Jude the Obscure, A Letter and a Foreword, 269.

370

'Louie', 240.
Louis Napoleon and the Genesis of the Second Empire, 312.
'Louis Napoleon, and the Poet Barnes', 312.
'Love-letters, The', 253.
'Love the Monopolist', 199.
'Love Watches a Window', 253.
Lovell's Library, 47, 49.
'Lover to Mistress', 235.
Lowe, E. A., *English Handwriting*, 246.
Lowell, Amy, 68 n. 1.
Lucretius, 20.
Lyceum Theatre, 104.
'Lying Awake', 255.
Lytton, Earl of, 57.

Macbeth-Raeburn, H., 86, 92, 96, 281.
McCall's Magazine, 245.
MacCarthy, C. J., 343 n. 1.
McClure, S. S., 152.
McClure's Magazine, 153.
McCutcheon, George Barr, 71 n., 79, 140, 151.
Macdonald, F. C., *Handley Carr Glyn Moule*, 264, 272.
Macdonald, J. F., 173 n.
McIlvaine, Clarence, 48, 77, 85, 118–19, 170.
Mackail, Denis, *The Story of J. M. B.*, 324.
Mackail, J. W., ed. *Select Epigrams from the Greek Anthology*, 244, 253, 258.
McKerrow, R. B., viii.
Macleod, Donald, 32.
Macleod, Norman, 72 n. 3.
Macmillan, Alexander, 4, 7, 275.
Macmillan, Frederick, 57, 122, 285, 286.
Macmillan, George A., 228.
Macmillan & Co., Ltd., 11, 122, 123 n., 125 n. 2, 172, 187, 207, 226–7, 255, 265, 267; correspondence with, 7, 78, 126, 131, 149, 188, 229, 247–8; Mellstock Edition, 12–13, 60, 286, 287–8; prose published by, 54–57, 58, 60, 151–2, 156, 262–3, 268–9; verse published by, 119–20, 123, 124–5, 129, 134–5, 138, 150–1, 160, 178–9, 187, 193, 214, 227, 234, 252; Wessex Edition, ix, 5, 8, 12, 23, 27, 40, 47, 54, 57, 60, 67, 77, 85, 91, 96, 106, 112–15, 119, 134, 140, 146, 150, 157, 172, 208, 227, 231, 248, 261, 262, 280, *282–6*, 288; other collected editions, 20, 91, 281–2, 287–8.
Macmillan Company (New York), 119, 124–6, 230, 248, 262, 267, 273.
Macmillan's Magazine, 34, 55–57, 73.
'Mad Judy', 115.
Maeterlinck, Maurice, 271.
Magdalene College, Cambridge, 178 n., 191, 207, 251–2.
Maggs Bros., 139.
'Maid of Keinton Mandeville, The', 215.
Maiden Castle, 101, 152, 157, 284.
'Maiden's Pledge, A', 219.
Maitland, F. W., *The Life and Letters of Leslie Stephen*, 16 n., 22 n., 23 n., 27 n., 106 n. 2, 162, 264, 336.
'Making of "The Dynasts", The', 272.
Malory, Sir Thomas, 229 n. 2.
'Man, A', 115.
'Man he Killed, The', *147*, 186.
'Man was Drawing Near to Me, A', 217.
'Man who Forgot, The', 205.
'Man with a Past, The', 202.
Manchester Central Public Library, 84.
Manchester Guardian, 159–60.
Manchester Literary Club, 295.
Manchester University Library, 83.
Manchester Weekly Times, 152.
Mandeville Place (London), 300.
Mann, Dr. E. W., ix, 325.
'Marble Monument, The.' *See* 'Marble Tablet, The'.
'Marble-streeted Town, The', 225.
'Marble Tablet, The', *223*, 235.
'Marchioness of Stonehenge, The', 61, *63–65*.
'Market-Girl, The', 144.
Marsh, Miss, 215.
Marshall, Beatrice, trans. *The Song of Songs*, 316.
Marston, R. B., 45.

INDEX

PRINTED IN GREAT BRITAIN
AT THE UNIVERSITY PRESS, OXFORD
BY CHARLES BATEY, PRINTER TO THE UNIVERSITY

DEC 21 1964